TAXING THE DIGITAL ECONOMY

The question of how to tax multinational companies that operate highly digitalised business models is one of the most contested areas of international taxation. The tax paid in the jurisdictions in which these companies operate has not kept pace with their immense growth and the OECD has proposed a new international tax compromise that will allocate taxing rights to market jurisdictions and remove the need to have a physical presence in the taxing jurisdictions in order to sustain taxability. In this work, Craig Elliffe explains the problems with the existing international tax system and its inability to respond to challenges posed by digitalised companies. In addition to looking at how the new international tax rules will work, Elliffe assesses their likely effectiveness and highlights features that are likely to endure in the next waves of international tax reform.

CRAIG ELLIFFE is a Professor of Taxation Law at the University of Auckland. Prior to becoming an academic, he spent twenty-three years as a tax partner for major international legal and accounting partnerships. He was the first New Zealander to be appointed to the Permanent Scientific Committee of the International Fiscal Association and a member of the New Zealand government's 2018/2019 Tax Working Group. His book *International and Cross-Border Taxation in New Zealand* won international plaudits and the JF Northey prize for the best legal book published in New Zealand in 2015.

CAMBRIDGE TAX LAW

Tax law is a growing area of interest. It is included as a subdivision in many areas of study and is a key consideration in business needs throughout the world. Books in this series expose the theoretical underpinning behind the law to shed light on taxation systems, so that the questions to be asked when addressing an issue become clear. These academic books, written by leading scholars, are a central port of call for information on tax law, with content illustrated by case law and legislation. The books will be of interest to those studying law, business, economics, accounting and finance courses.

Series Editor
Professor Peter Harris, Law Faculty, University of Cambridge,
Director of the Centre for Tax Law.
Professor Harris brings a wealth of experience to the series. He has taught and presented tax courses at more than a dozen different universities in as many countries and has acted as an external tax consultant for the International Monetary Fund for over twenty years.

TAXING THE DIGITAL ECONOMY

Theory, Policy and Practice

CRAIG ELLIFFE
University of Auckland Faculty of Law

CAMBRIDGE
UNIVERSITY PRESS

University Printing House, Cambridge CB2 8BS, United Kingdom

One Liberty Plaza, 20th Floor, New York, NY 10006, USA

477 Williamstown Road, Port Melbourne, VIC 3207, Australia

314–321, 3rd Floor, Plot 3, Splendor Forum, Jasola District Centre, New Delhi – 110025, India

79 Anson Road, #06-04/06, Singapore 079906

Cambridge University Press is part of the University of Cambridge.

It furthers the University's mission by disseminating knowledge in the pursuit of education, learning, and research at the highest international levels of excellence.

www.cambridge.org
Information on this title: www.cambridge.org/9781108485241
DOI: 10.1017/9781108750691

© Craig Elliffe 2021

This publication is in copyright. Subject to statutory exception and to the provisions of relevant collective licensing agreements, no reproduction of any part may take place without the written permission of Cambridge University Press.

First published 2021

A catalogue record for this publication is available from the British Library.

Library of Congress Cataloging-in-Publication Data
Names: Elliffe, Craig, 1961– author.
Title: Taxing the digital economy : theory, policy and practice / Craig Elliffe, University of Auckland Faculty of Law.
Description: Cambridge, United Kingdom ; New York, NY : Cambridge University Press, 2021. | Series: Cambridge tax law series | Includes bibliographical references and index.
Identifiers: LCCN 2020043494 (print) | LCCN 2020043495 (ebook) | ISBN 9781108485241 (hardback) | ISBN 9781108719339 (paperback) | ISBN 9781108750691 (epub)
Subjects: LCSH: Corporations–Taxation–European Union countries–Data processing. | Electronic commerce–Taxation–Law and legislation–European Union countries. | Corporations–Taxation–Law and legislation–European Union countries. | Information technology–Economic aspects–European Union countries.
Classification: LCC KJE7198 .E45 2021 (print) | LCC KJE7198 (ebook) | DDC 343.2406/7–dc23
LC record available at https://lccn.loc.gov/2020043494
LC ebook record available at https://lccn.loc.gov/2020043495

ISBN 978-1-108-48524-1 Hardback

Cambridge University Press has no responsibility for the persistence or accuracy of URLs for external or third-party internet websites referred to in this publication and does not guarantee that any content on such websites is, or will remain, accurate or appropriate.

This book is dedicated to my wife Sharyn and our children, Timothy, Nicholas and Alexia. Thank you for your love and support.

CONTENTS

List of Figures x
Preface xi
Acknowledgements xiv

Part I

1 **Taxing Cross-Border Business Income**   3
   1.1 What Is Cross-Border Taxation?   3
   1.2 Fundamental Concepts of International Taxation: Residence and Source   5
   1.3 The History of International Double Taxation: The "1920s Compromise"   9
   1.4 Justifying Source and Residence Taxation   16
   1.5 The Benefit Theory and Its Relationship to Value Creation   34
   1.6 Observations about Source and Residence Taxation in the Context of Cross-Border Business   41
   1.7 Exploring the Limits of Domestic Source-Based Taxation   46
   1.8 Base Erosion and Profit Shifting and the Emerging Threat of Digitalisation in Business   55

2 **The Development of Digital Business**   57
   2.1 The Dynamic Information Age   57
   2.2 The Defining Characteristics of Digital Markets   63
   2.3 Doing Business Using a Multi-sided Platform   68
   2.4 Using the Reseller Model   76
   2.5 Using Vertically Integrated Firms   77
   2.6 Using Firms That Are Input Suppliers   77
   2.7 Observations about the Key Characteristics of Digitalised Business Models   77

3 **Challenges to the Tax System Posed by the Digitalisation of Business**   84
   3.1 Introduction to the Challenges   84

3.2 The Vanishing Ability to Tax Business Profits   89
3.3 The Use of Data, the Contribution of Users and the Measurement of Their Value   97
3.4 The Reliance on, and Mobility of, Intellectual Property   102
3.5 The Characterisation of Transactions and Income   104
3.6 The Failure of Transfer Pricing with Certain Multinational Enterprises and Their Transactions   106
3.7 The Inadequacy of Residence-Based Taxation   108
3.8 Competition by States   110

4 **Responding to the Challenges: Legal Constraints on Any Changes to the Current Framework**   112
4.1 Introduction   112
4.2 International Tax at the Crossroads   113
4.3 Interim Measures   119
4.4 Constraints Imposed by the Scope of Double Tax Agreements (DTAs)   121
4.6 Constraints Imposed by the Membership of the WTO   146

Part II

5 **The OECD Secretariat's and Inclusive Framework's Proposals for Multilateral Reforms**   167
5.1 Introduction   167
5.2 Pillar One: Allocation of Taxing Rights and Nexus   167
5.3 Pillar One: What Is Proposed in the Unified Approach Proposal? Three Components of Income: Amount A   176
5.4 Amount B: Fixed Remuneration for Marketing and Distribution   193
5.5 Amount C: The "Top-Up"   198
5.6 Dispute Prevention and Resolution   200
5.7 Pillar Two: Global Anti-base Erosion Proposal   204
5.8 Conclusion   211

6 **Examining the Proposals for Multilateral Reforms**   213
6.1 Does the 2020s Compromise Address the Challenges of the Digital Economy to the International Tax Framework?   213
6.2 Dealing with the Vanishing Ability to Tax Business Profits   216
6.3 The Use of Data, the Contribution of Users and the Measurement of Their Value   223
6.4 The Reliance on, and Mobility of, Intellectual Property   226
6.5 The Characterisation of Transactions and Income   227

	6.6	The Failure of Transfer Pricing with Certain Multinational Enterprises and Their Transactions 228
	6.7	Tackling the Inadequacy of Residence-Based Taxation 232
	6.8	Competition by States 233
	6.9	Conclusion 235
7	**Implementing the Proposals for Multilateral Reforms** 237	
	7.1	Issues with the Implementation of the 2020s Compromise? 237
	7.2	Implementing the Changes Proposed by Amount B 251
	7.3	Issues with Implementing Amounts A, B and C 253
	7.4	Issues with Implementing Key Elements of Pillar Two 254
	7.5	Common Pillar One and Two Implementation Issues 260
8	**The Influence of Alternative Policy Strategies on the 2020s Compromise** 263	
	8.1	Where Do the Strategies of the 2020s Compromise Originate? 263
	8.2	Destination-Based Cash Flow Taxation 265
	8.3	Residual Profit Allocation by Income 272
	8.4	Formulary Apportionment 280
	8.5	Expanding the Concept of Permanent Establishment 285
9	**Interim Solutions and Long-Term Reforms** 305	
	9.1	Crossroads: Responding in a Unilateral or a Unified Way? 305
	9.2	Key Generic Design Issues with DSTs 306
	9.3	Significant Areas of Change in the 2020s Compromise 313

Index   322

FIGURES

2.1 The conceptual view of the layers in information and communication technology   60
2.2 Multi-sided marketplace business models   72
2.3 Multi-sided business platform using social media or search engines   75
2.4 The basic structure of resellers   76
2.5 The basic structure of vertically integrated firms   77
7.1 Establishing a new nexus and taxing rights   238
7.2 Determining the profits attributable to marketing and distribution taxable presence   252

PREFACE

Background to This Book

In 2018, the total global e-commerce market was worth roughly US$7.7 trillion. Despite the size of this economy and its extraordinary growth rate, many multinational companies paid little tax in the countries in which they did business. This is not a problem that can be ignored. Digital companies grow much faster than other firms. In 2006, technology companies accounted for 7 per cent of the top twenty market capitalisation of EU companies; by 2017, this had grown to 54 per cent. Digital companies rely less on physical presence, utilising intellectual property that enables companies to set up a business far away from their consumers, where some of the actual economic activity takes place. Most concerning is the fact that, on average, digitalised businesses face an effective tax rate of only 9.5 per cent compared to 23.2 per cent for traditional business models.[1] Consequently, there is widespread concern from governments and the public about the low level of income tax paid by companies operating in the digital economy.

The appropriate taxation of multinational enterprises is one of the most challenging problems facing the international tax system. The OECD/G20 Base Erosion and Profit Shifting (BEPS) project, developed to address this issue, has operated for the last seven years or so. BEPS has made a significant difference in a variety of areas and influenced many aspects of international tax systems. It has encouraged a greater exchange of information and corporate transparency, introduced anti-avoidance and anti-treaty abuse rules, and suggested changes to the OECD Model Treaty and domestic law recommendations. While the earlier BEPS project has already had a discernible effect on multinational groups' behaviour, policymakers are struggling to find solutions to ensure fair

---

[1] European Commission-Fact Sheet, *Questions and Answers on a Fair and Efficient Tax System in the EU for the Digital Single Market*, Brussels, 21 March 2018.

and effective taxation of the digital economy and hence the need for the BEPS 2.0 project.

The framework and its underpinning principles developed by the League of Nations in the 1920s need modernisation. The BEPS 2.0 project focuses on weaknesses in the international tax framework and together the Inclusive Framework and the OECD are seeking consensus on significant reforms which, if implemented, will revise the allocation of taxing rights, override the limitation of physical presence or nexus, and challenge the arm's-length principle.

This book analyses seven challenges to the international tax system posed by highly digitalised businesses and examines the BEPS 2.0 response to these challenges. One conclusion is that the response proposed largely addresses different problems that emerge in international tax. For example, of the two pillars in BEPS 2.0, Pillar One addresses the vexed problem of nexus for the taxation of the state of source and allocates new taxing rights to that market jurisdiction. Pillar Two assists in addressing other significant problems concerned with the inadequacy of residence taxation, the mobility and misuse of intellectual property, and competition between states. The new taxing rights proposed under Pillar One are based on taxation which occurs on a destination basis and hence they constitute the most radical reform to international taxation for a hundred years.

As a consequence of this, international tax is at a crossroads. There are broadly two options to respond to the challenges posed to the international tax system by the digitalised economy. Either the world develops and finalises a consensus-driven multilateral solution to establish a new international tax framework or it endures a plethora of rather "ugly" unilateral domestic taxes, undertaken without that consensus.

Structure of the Book

This book is divided into two parts. Part I examines the digital tax landscape and commences with an examination of residence and source taxation in the context of cross-border transactions.

To understand our existing settings in international tax, Chapter 1 examines the basis for the historical 1920s compromise (the negotiated international tax framework utilised for the last 100 years). It searches for the theoretical justification for source taxation and explores the legal limits of jurisdictions' ability to impose domestic source-based taxation.

Chapter 2 explains the development of digital business and the most common methods employed to observe the key characteristics of digitalised business models. Chapter 3 discusses seven challenges to the international tax system posed by the digitalisation of business. These are the problem areas that the OECD/Inclusive Framework must address in their proposed solution. Chapter 4 examines alternative responses to these challenges in the form of digital services taxes (DSTs) and in particular any legal constraints imposed on such interim measures.

Part II deals with the OECD/Inclusive Framework response to these challenges, describing in Chapter 5 the broad outline of the proposals (described as the "2020s compromise"). In Chapter 6, these proposals are critiqued against the challenges identified to assess whether they address the problems. Chapter 7 deals with issues arising on implementation of BEPS 2.0. In Chapter 8, the book looks at the influence of important alternative policy strategies which have shaped the design of the proposed 2020s compromise. This enables the identification of key policy contributions to the new international tax framework.

Finally, Chapter 9 discusses the desirability of pursuing a unilateral reform (with an analysis of generic design issues arising with digital services taxes) versus pursuing a unified multilateral consensus. In conclusion, Chapter 9 highlights five significant areas of change in the 2020s compromise which are likely to form part of international tax changes in the future.

ACKNOWLEDGEMENTS

Many people have helped me hugely in the writing of this book. First, the New Zealand Law Foundation (NZLF), which funded me as their 2018 International Research Fellow, Te Karahipi Rangahau ā Taiao. This enabled me to participate in discussions at the OECD in Paris, and talk with other key people around the world. I am hugely grateful for the support and guidance of the NZLF director, Lynda Hagan, and its manager, Dianne Gallagher.

Second, although they are too numerous to individually identify, a group of people generously gave their time to me in discussions which formed part of the research for this book. You know who you are, and thank you. They include PwC in Italy and the United Kingdom, Philip Baker QC and Tsilly Dagan. In particular, I would like to thank those people involved in the Centre for Business Taxation at the University of Oxford, who were so kind and generous with their time and made me feel very welcome during my study leave at that wonderful university.

Third, my own University of Auckland, and in particular the Faculty of Law, who gave me research and study leave and otherwise provided support in many different ways. Research is a product of many different factors and the support of colleagues and senior management makes a huge difference.

Fourth, I would like to thank my research assistants who were involved in the editing and indexing of this publication. Thank you to Jakob Gibson, Peter Muzariri, Barny Poulter and Yvonne Rothwell for their diligent help and conscientiousness.

Last but not least, the team at Cambridge University Press. Thank you to Matt Gallaway, Cameron Daddis and Joan Dale Lace for your excellent guidance and help.

Part I

1

Taxing Cross-Border Business Income

1.1 What Is Cross-Border Taxation?

1.1.1 Introduction

Cross-border trade is the flow of goods and services across the international borders of different jurisdictions. Taxation is the levy, which may be either direct taxation (income taxes, estate taxes, gift taxes and social security contributions) or indirect taxation (consumption taxes such as value-added or goods and services taxes, sales taxes and customs duties), imposed by sovereign countries to fund their public goods and services in the areas of, amongst other things, law and order, health care, infrastructure, education and security. In most countries revenue raised from taxation is redistributed to support various members of society such as the elderly, those with young families, the sick and the poor.

Cross-border business income taxation is, therefore, that form of taxation:

1. Where the resident of a jurisdiction is doing business overseas and the jurisdiction concerned decides to impose taxation on the resident. The taxation of this overseas income is sometimes complicated because another country's tax laws may apply to this income (see point 2) and this will have consequential implications in the resident's jurisdiction (*outbound investment*). The key concept applicable to this outbound investment income is the concept of residence because it is upon this concept that the jurisdiction imposing taxation bases its claim.
2. Where the government of one country taxes the business being carried out in its jurisdiction by a non-resident (*inbound investment*). The key concept applicable to this type of income is whether the income of the non-resident is sourced in the jurisdiction that wants to tax it.

Cross-border taxation can be distinguished from purely domestic taxation (i.e. a sovereign government taxing its residents on business carried out within its own jurisdiction).

There has been enormous growth in international transactions due to the liberalisation of trade, the abolition of currency controls and, more recently, technological advancement. Academic studies indicate that in 2007, the year before the Great Financial Crisis, world trade was about two times greater than in 1997, six times greater than in 1972 and thirty-two times greater than in 1950. These same studies suggest that global exports are more than 4,000 times larger than in 1913.[1]

Over the decades this has led to a dramatic increase in the flow of capital investments among countries so that national economies have become interconnected. The features of globalisation include the free movement of capital and labour, developments in technology and telecommunications, the growth of the service component in the economy, the increased importance of intellectual property, and the use of integrated supply chains. These features have enabled businesses, through sophisticated transfer pricing techniques (involving, for example, the pricing of goods and services, location of indebtedness and intellectual property), fragmentation of business activity and the ability to transact without a physical presence in a jurisdiction, to locate productive activities, risks and, most importantly, profits to jurisdictions with little or no taxation.

1.1.2 Income Tax and Cross-Border Trade: A Relatively Recent Phenomenon

While it is reasonable to surmise that cross-border trade significantly predates direct (income) taxation, there has likely always been some link between international trade and some form of taxation. Originally this taxation may have simply taken the form of a rudimentary toll or levy (for example, a payment made to allow a ship to pass a chain blockading passage along a river). More sophisticated means of taxation such as income tax (late eighteenth century in a country such as the United Kingdom to fund the Napoleonic wars) are associated with the development of nation-states emerging, after the Peace of Westphalia in 1648, from the religious wars.[2] Although the Silk Roads (the ancient trade route

---

[1] Giovanni Federico and Antonio Tena-Junguito *A Tale of Two Globalizations: Gains from Trade and Openness 1800–2010* (Centre for Economic Policy Research, Working Paper 16-02, February 2016) at 1.

[2] See M Shaw *International Law* (8th ed, Cambridge University Press, 2017) at 19–21; L Gross "The Peace of Westphalia, 1648–1948" (1948) 42 AJIL at 40.

network of the Chang'an–Tianshan corridor) are much older than income tax, it is conventional to view cross-border taxation as simply a nineteenth- and twentieth-century phenomenon. Due to the comparatively recent nature of cross-border taxation, it may be helpful to see whether the past can help to provide any potential solutions to some of the issues described in this book. In that sense, it may be possible to regard the partial move to destination taxation as a step consistent with older historical concepts of taxation where taxes were imposed when goods were brought to the market or physically transferred from one jurisdiction to another.[3]

1.2 Fundamental Concepts of International Taxation: Residence and Source

The majority of countries tax both consumption and income.[4] The taxation of consumption occurs when a transaction results in the exchange of goods and services for consideration. This will often be to a final end-user (value-added taxes, goods and services taxes and retail sales taxes), but it might also occur on transactions between businesses before the final sale. Excise taxes and import duties are levied on particular goods or services. The common feature is that consumption taxes are normally levied where the consumer is located, which is the importing country (described as the place of destination).[5]

The taxation of income normally takes place in respect of net income earned over a period of time and is usually on an annual basis. The right of an international jurisdiction to taxation is said to be founded either on the relationship to a person (described in the OECD Commentary as the taxpayers' personal attachment to the state)[6] or on the relationship to a territory.[7]

---

[3] See Section 9.3.1 "A Move to Destination Taxation".
[4] OECD *Addressing the Tax Challenges of the Digital Economy, Action 1-2015 Final Report* (OECD Publishing, 2015) at 19–33.
[5] The destination principle is also an important possibility for income tax reform. This is discussed in further detail at Chapter 8, as the principle is utilised in many of the alternative policy strategies which have influenced the 2020s compromise.
[6] OECD *Model Tax Convention on Income and on Capital: Condensed Version 2017* (OECD Publishing, November 2017) at 105.
[7] W Schon "Persons and Territories: on the International Allocation of Taxing Rights" (2010) 6 BTR 554 at 554. In this article, Schon successfully sets out to show the fragility of the concepts of personal and territorial attachment which purportedly underpin the power to tax.

1.2.1 Residence Taxation

When considering the relationship between a right to tax and the taxpayer's personal attachment to the state, the question of where the taxpayer's residence is located (for tax purposes) is the critical issue in most jurisdictions.

It seems clear that international law accepts that a state may levy taxes against a taxpayer not within the territory of the state, so long as there is a real link between the state and the taxpayer, such as nationality or domicile.[8] So it is even clearer that a state can levy taxes for a taxpayer resident in its own jurisdiction even when the profits it wishes to tax are earned abroad.

With respect to cross-border business income, residence-based taxation applies to *outbound investment*, as discussed above.

If a country operates a *worldwide tax system*, it subjects the residents of that country to tax in respect of income sourced both in and outside their country. In contrast, if the country operates a *territorial system* then it subjects its residents to tax only on income derived from sources in its own jurisdiction. Particularly when dealing with corporate income tax most countries operate hybrid systems adopting features from both the worldwide and territorial regimes. The OECD points to the difficulty for the tax administration in collecting information with respect to the foreign-sourced income of their residents as the reason why these hybrid systems proliferate.[9]

1.2.2 Source Taxation

Source taxation is imposed because of the connection between the territory in which the income is earned and the taxpayer.

Concerning *inbound investment* (a state imposing tax on non-residents doing business in their jurisdiction),[10] tax is imposed on income sourced in their jurisdiction. Determining whether income is sourced in a jurisdiction is usually a matter of domestic law for the jurisdiction concerned.[11] Accordingly, the source rules vary from country to country but they follow a broad pattern. While active business income

---

[8] See Shaw, above n 2 at 486.
[9] OECD, above n 4 at 23.
[10] See Section 1.1.1 "Introduction".
[11] See Section 1.7 "Exploring the Limits of Domestic Source-Based Taxation".

is normally taxed on a net income basis at the marginal tax rate of the non-resident taxpayer, other forms of passive income such as interest, royalties and dividends are taxed on a gross basis. The OECD suggests that this is due to the difficulty in establishing the expenses a non-resident incurred in earning such passive income.[12] As this source-based taxation takes place on the gross income, the tax rate is normally low.

1.2.3 The International Tax Dilemma Arising from the Competing Demands of Residence and Source Taxation

In theory, countries could operate exclusively on residence-based taxation or source-based taxation. The problem with operating on a worldwide residence-based system is that for it to be effective you need all the other countries to be doing the same. That is, there is an agreement that all countries in the world would tax their residents on worldwide income and no country would tax non-residents on income sourced in their jurisdiction.

Operating a territorial source-based system does not require the same degree of international cooperation and, historically, many countries did just that and operated their tax systems based on income earned in their own jurisdiction. It is now rare to find examples,[13] and given the global mobility of capital it would be hard for many of us to contemplate such a regime whereby residents diverted all their capital overseas and escaped local tax.

In an increasingly global economy, countries will have both exports and imports (with the resultant offset of the two being the balance of payments) and they will also operate a capital account which reflects the net change in ownership of national assets (in other words, it records the change in foreign ownership of domestic assets together with the change in domestic ownership of foreign assets).

Source taxation is generally unpopular among economists writing on international taxation.[14] They acknowledge that it is consistent with capital import neutrality (CIN), which is the principle requiring all

---

[12] OECD, above n 4 at 24.

[13] The taxation of business profits in Hong Kong is one such example. Profits Tax is only charged on profits which arise in or are derived from Hong Kong. In simple terms this means that a person who carries on a business in Hong Kong but derives profits from another place is not required to pay tax in Hong Kong on those profits.

[14] Described by L Kaplow "Taxation" in M Polinsky and S Shavell (eds) *Handbook of Law and Economics* (Volume 1, Elsevier, 2007) at [5.5] (chapter 10).

investors to pay the same marginal tax rate notwithstanding whether they are residents or non-residents. Under CIN, all savers (regardless of where they are resident) face the same after-tax returns resulting in the efficient allocation of savings.[15] These economists say that taxes on investment in the home jurisdiction lead to a reduction in investment because investors will seek the highest after-tax return and that the home jurisdiction, through high taxation, diverts investments away from itself to other, more tax-friendly jurisdictions. This can distort investment and production and they believe the incidence of the tax falls on domestic labour and other fixed factors. They acknowledge, however, that developed countries typically employ source taxation.[16]

On the other hand, residence-based taxation adheres to the principle of capital export neutrality (CEN) because an investor is neutral about whether they invest domestically or overseas. This is because both provide the same marginal rate of income tax regardless of where capital is invested. Economists generally like CEN because of its apparent worldwide economic efficiency, recognising that the location of investments is unaffected by taxation.[17]

Michael Graetz argues that despite the repeated reference to the CEN and CIN principles by international tax policymakers it is impossible to achieve the outcome of simultaneous adherence to them unless we have a worldwide government or identical income tax bases and rates in all nations.[18] Graetz supports this by highlighting an "irreconcilable conflict" between three simple principles:

1 People should pay equal taxes on their income regardless of the country that is the source of that income.
2 All investments in a country should face the same tax burden regardless of whether a foreigner or a local made their investment.
3 Sovereign countries should be free to set their own tax rates and vary them.

He then points out that the first two principles can only hold simultaneously when capital income is taxed at the same rate in all countries, requiring identical tax systems, not just rates but also tax bases and

---

[15] M Graetz "Taxing International Capital Income: Inadequate Principles, Outdated Concepts, and Unsatisfactory Policies" (2001) 54 Tax L Rev 261 at 271.
[16] Kaplow, above n 14 at 689.
[17] Ibid at 689.
[18] Graetz, above n 15 at 272.

sourcing rules. This can never happen unless the third principle is breached.

It is said that capital-exporting and capital-importing nations have "conflicting financial interests: capital importers have the most to gain from taxation at source, capital exporters from the taxation of residents".[19] Another way to look at this is the way Louis Kaplow summarises it: "that a large net capital importer will wish to tax the inflow and a large net exporter benefits by taxing the outflow".[20] Developed countries tend to be net capital exporters, developing countries net capital importers. From these generalities, one can see that there is a geopolitical dimension to international tax as well as the theoretical economic and legal construct.

When countries decide that they will continue to operate on worldwide residence-based taxation and to tax non-residents on income sourced in their jurisdiction then double taxation must arise. A resident of one country earning income in another jurisdiction will be legitimately subject to tax twice: first by the source jurisdiction where the income is earned, and secondly by the country in which they are resident.

This international tax dilemma led to the system of international taxation that we currently have. How have the competing demands of capital-importing and capital-exporting countries been dealt with in terms of the framework that we currently have in our international tax regimes?

1.3 The History of International Double Taxation: The "1920s Compromise"

This part of the chapter deals with a brief history of international double taxation and describes the formation of the "1920s compromise".[21] This was a problem arising out of industrialisation and was due to the implementation of income tax regimes around the world and increasing

---

[19] M Graetz and M O'Hear "The 'Original Intent' of US International Taxation" (1997) 46 Duke LJ 1021 at 1033–4.
[20] Kaplow, above n 14 at 689.
[21] This is the terminology employed by Michael Graetz and Michael O'Hear in their outstanding article on the history of the US tax policy and in particular the impact of Thomas Adams, a professor of economics at Yale and tax advisor to the Treasury Department and Treasury's principal advisor on issues of tax policy and administration. See Graetz and O'Hear, above n 19 at 1026.

cross-border trade.²² Commentators trace the current international tax regime to the model originally developed as a result of the unification of Germany and applied in double tax treaties entered into by the predecessor states of the German Empire.²³ The first international double tax agreement was concluded on 21 June 1899 between the Kingdom of Prussia and the Austro-Hungarian Empire and it dealt with the double tax issue in a way that is very familiar to us all, by allocating taxing rights to the state of domicile (which of course we now think of as residence) concerning personal taxes, and the state of source in relation to business and property taxes.²⁴

In the years following the First World War the world was increasingly moving from a territorial system to a worldwide residence system and at the same time increasing rates of tax. This was necessary because of the enormous expenditure incurred by many economies around the globe. The resultant combination of juridical double tax and high tax rates led the International Chamber of Commerce conference held in Brussels in 1920 to initiate a request to the League of Nations to address the problem of double taxation. In turn, the Financial Committee of the League of Nations asked four economists to consider the economic consequences of double taxation (from the perspective of the equitable distribution of burdens and interfering with the free flow of capital), to propose any general principles to remove the "evil consequences of double taxation" and to ascertain whether such principles were capable of application to a new international convention.²⁵

These four economists were not randomly chosen but were somewhat representative of the post-war economies.²⁶ Two were from capital-importing (source-taxation-favouring) countries, Professor Bruins from the Netherlands and Professor Einaudi from Italy. Sir Josiah Stamp was from the United Kingdom, which was historically a major capital-

---

[22] S Jogarajan "Prelude to the International Tax Treaty Network: 1815–1914 Early Tax Treaties and the Conditions for Action" (2011) 31(4) OJLS 679.

[23] J Hattingh "On the Origins of Model Tax Conventions: 19th-Century German Tax Treaties and Laws Concerned with the Avoidance of Double Tax" in John Tiley (ed) *Studies in the History of Tax Law* (Volume 6, Hart Publishing, 2013); Maikel Evers "Tracing the Origins of the Netherlands' Tax Treaty Network" (2013) 41(6/7) Intertax 375.

[24] Jogarajan, above n 22 at 679.

[25] G Bruins, M Einaudi, E Seligman and J Stamp *Report on Double Taxation* (League of Nations Economic and Financial Commission, Document E.F.S.73. F.19, April 1923).

[26] Reuven Avi Yonah *Advanced Introduction to International Tax Law* (Edward Elgar, 2015) at 3–4.

exporting country (residence-taxation-favouring) and Professor Seligman was from the United States (a country that had been capital importing but was now the largest exporter of capital). These economists met and thrashed out a way forward and delivered a report in April 1923 (the 1923 Report) which has been seen by some as the foundation stone of the international tax regime.[27] Others suggest that the 1923 Report, whilst influential, was not quite as fundamental as many people think it was.[28]

Two key observations emerge from an examination of the original reports of the League of Nations.[29]

1.3.1 Observation One: The Recommendation Was to Allocate Taxing Rights for Different Categories of Income between Residence and Source Countries

The 1923 Report proposed that an ideal solution would be that the individual's "whole faculty" (the taxpayer's capacity or ability to pay) should be taxed, but only once, and that the "liability should be divided among the tax districts according to his relative interests in each".[30] This division of taxation should occur after ascertaining where the "true economic interests of the individual are found". This required an analysis of the "economic allegiance" that exists between the taxpayer and the state and involved an evaluation of four factors: (i) the production of wealth (also described as the origin of the wealth or acquisition); (ii) the position of wealth (also described as the situs and location of the wealth);

---

[27] Ibid. See also Hugh Ault "Corporate Integration, Tax Treaties and the Division of the International Tax Base: Principles and Practice" 47 Tax L Rev 565 at 567.

[28] Graetz and O'Hear, above n 19 at 1078. They suggest that while the 1923 Report in its organisational structure and rejection of source-based taxation of interest and dividends represents the basic blueprint of modern tax treaties, the really important concepts could be found in the existence of the recognition of the validity of source-based taxation and the importance of the foreign tax credit found in US legislation in 1919 and 1921 and the work of the International Chamber of Commerce (i.e. the work of Thomas Adams).

[29] Bruins, Einaudi, Seligman and Stamp, above n 25; League of Nations (Technical Experts from Belgium, Czechoslovakia, France, Great Britain, Italy, the Netherlands and Switzerland) *Double Taxation and Tax Evasion* (F 212, Geneva, February 1925); League of Nations (Technical Experts from Argentina, Belgium, Czechoslovakia, France, Germany, Great Britain, Italy, Japan, the Netherlands, Poland, Switzerland, USA, Venezuela) *Double Taxation and Tax Evasion* (C. 216. M. 85, Geneva, April 1927); League of Nations (General Meeting of Government Experts) *Double Taxation and Tax Evasion* (C. 562. M. 178. Geneva, October 1928).

[30] Bruins, Einaudi, Seligman and Stamp, above n 25.

(iii) the enforcement of the rights to wealth (legally enforceable rights); and (iv) the disposition of wealth (the consumption or sale in a market).[31]

Even after carefully working through these four "fundamental considerations"[32] and trying to apply the various contributions made by different states to the production and enjoyment of income, the economists concluded "that it is almost impossible in economic theory to get a direct assignment of a quantitative character of finally resultant income amongst all the national agents who may be said to have had a finger in the pie".[33] Given this theoretical difficulty, they concluded that in practice it was going to be necessary to have "a compromise or arbitrary assignment" of taxing rights.[34]

In essence, the 1923 Report concluded that there were four alternatives to prevent/reduce double taxation:[35]

1 the use of the credit method, whereby the residence state would give a foreign tax credit for any tax paid in the source state;
2 the use of the exemption method, whereby the source state exempted all non-residents from tax on income within their jurisdiction;
3 a proportional tax (so that a portion of the tax is paid in both the source and the resident state);
4 an allocation method, whereby certain categories of income would be subject to source state taxation (such as rents of land) whilst others would not be subject to source taxation (such as interest). The country of residence would allow a foreign tax credit where the country of source had required the payment of tax, but in circumstances where the country of source exempted it, they would get a full amount of taxation.

The four economists suggested a split between land, business enterprises directly dependent upon the land (like mines and oil wells), industrial establishments consisting chiefly of factories and commercial establishments with a fixed location, and that these should all be subject to tax in the source country. In contrast, income arising from shares (dividends)

---

[31] Ibid at 20–4.
[32] Ibid at 22.
[33] Ibid at 45.
[34] Ibid.
[35] Ibid at 41–2.

1.3 HISTORY OF INTERNATIONAL DOUBLE TAXATION 13

and debt instruments (interest) together with professional earnings would be taxed exclusively in the country of residence.[36]

The final conclusion in the 1923 Report[37] was that the exemption method (in point 2 above), which is a pure residence-based form of taxation, was their preferred method. This was notwithstanding the comment about the need for a compromise or arbitrary assignment of taxing rights which would reflect a balance between source-based and residence-based taxation.[38]

In reality, the economists' second choice of the fourth method listed above reflected this compromise, and the history of the development of the early double taxation treaty models shows that the allocation method became the most important one.

1.3.2 Observation Two: The Recommendation Recognises the Competing Claims of Source and Residence Taxation, Acknowledging That Source Countries Have the First Opportunity and Right to Tax, While the 1923 Report Suggested a Theoretical Preference for Residence Taxation, Later Discussions Were Far More Pragmatic

Michael Graetz and Michael O'Hear suggest that the approach of using the principle of economic allegiance taken in the 1923 Report was generous to the residence-based taxation viewpoint.[39] The 1923 Report, albeit reluctantly, clearly acknowledged that source taxation was the dominant and "instinctive" principle behind many countries' approach to taxation.[40] The economists were strongly critical of this instinctive principle of source taxation. This strength of feeling comes through when they say "But if we recognised *facts* and were not prevented by historical accidents and administrative cowardice or frailty from taxing every man in one sum upon his total resources instead of getting it from him piecemeal, the 'origin' idea would be far less instinctive".[41]

The major reasons why source taxation was not seen by the economists as appropriate were twofold: (i) it led to the consequence that the cost of double taxation was borne by the residence country (because if the source

---

[36] Ibid at 39.
[37] Ibid at 51.
[38] Noted by Graetz and O'Hear as having virtually no importance outside of Great Britain. See Graetz and O'Hear, above n 19 at 1078.
[39] Ibid at 1077.
[40] Bruins, Einaudi, Seligman and Stamp, above n 25 at 40.
[41] Ibid.

country has already taxed the income it falls to the residence country to provide a foreign tax credit) and (ii) it was seen as somewhat selfish ("it is only the urgency of their own claims that they are prepared to recognise"),[42] and expedient (the government when attempting to attract foreign capital is willing to forgo the tax on the foreigner whereas it will apply taxation "when the foreigner has made investments already and is helpless".[43]

Consistent with this attack on source taxation, when the 1923 Report compares and contrasts the general justifying principles of taxation, it concludes that the theoretical basis for residence-based taxation is preferable. It does this by comparing the so-called exchange theory with the faculty theory. We know these theories by slightly different names nowadays. The exchange theory could be subdivided into the cost theory and the well-known benefit theory. The cost theory says the taxes ought to be paid in accordance with the cost of services performed by the government, while the benefit theory justifies taxation upon the particular benefits conferred upon an individual. The faculty theory, also known as the ability to pay theory, was seen as more comprehensive "because it includes what there is of value in the benefit theory".[44] Despite clearly having a preference for residence-based taxation, the 1923 Report does not clearly spell out the benefits of residence taxation, only the above-mentioned disadvantages of source-based taxation.

The 1923 Report was not the end of the story. In 1925 a Committee of Technical Experts, having been appointed by the Fiscal Committee of the League of Nations, delivered their report with suggestions for alleviating double taxation (the 1925 Report). According to Graetz and O'Hear, the 1925 Report "was an effort to transform the pro-residence 1923 Report into a more balanced product".[45] The Technical Experts allocated personal taxes to residence, and impersonal schedular taxes to the source jurisdiction broadening the role and scope of source taxation. In doing so, they reflected that the majority of their group came from debtor rather than creditor nations. The decision on the division was made based on "purely practical purposes" and "no inference in regard to economic theory or doctrine should be drawn from this fact".[46]

---

[42] Ibid at 41.
[43] Ibid at 40.
[44] Ibid at 18.
[45] Graetz and O'Hear, above n 19 at 1080.
[46] League of Nations (Technical Experts from Belgium, Czechoslovakia, France, Great Britain, Italy, the Netherlands and Switzerland), above n 29 at 15.

An expanded group of countries was added to the group of Technical Experts[47] and developments of great significance took place, including the introduction of the concept of a "permanent establishment". Thus business profits in the draft bilateral convention contained in the report of the Committee of Technical Experts in 1927 (the 1927 Report) would be taxable only in the source state where they possess permanent establishments.[48]

The draft bilateral convention contained in the report of Government Experts of 1928 (the 1928 Report) was starting to look relatively familiar to modern eyes. It had a rule to tax industrial, commercial or agricultural undertakings in the state in which the permanent establishment was situated and this included "centres of management, branches, mining and oil fields, factories, workshops, agencies, warehouses, offices, depots" but a "*bona fide* agent of independent status (broker, commission agent, etc.)" was expressly excluded from being a permanent establishment.[49]

1.3.3 Reflections on the 1920s Compromise

This brief history of the foundation of the original double tax agreements discloses a series of important reflections on the role of any general principles in formulating a justification for taxation. These include:

(a) It is very difficult to justify the allocation of taxing rights on a coherent theoretical basis. Thomas Adams, who was involved in the 1927 Report and the 1928 Report, criticised Edwin Seligman's (and by implication the 1923 Report's) theory of "economic allegiance" which was the touchstone for the conclusions reached by the four economists. Writing about this theory he said:[50]

> I find this theory, I regret to say, little more than a generalised label covering a number of separate judgements which the authors of the theory have reached about the expedient place to tax certain persons or transactions, conclusions based upon diverse considerations which unfortunately vary with the business habits and stages of

---

[47] Expanding the group from seven to thirteen members.
[48] League of Nations (Technical Experts from Argentina, Belgium, Czechoslovakia, France, Germany, Great Britain, Italy, Japan, Netherlands, Poland, Switzerland, USA, Venezuela), above n 29 at 10.
[49] League of Nations (General Meeting of Government Experts), above n 29 at 8.
[50] Thomas Adams "Interstate and International Double Taxation" in Roswell Magill (ed) *Lectures on Taxation* (Commercial Clearing House, 1932) 101 at 125.

development of the various countries of the world. ... The theory leads many of its advocates to endorse exaggerated claims concerning the rights of the jurisdiction of domicile (residence). These exaggerated claims rest partly on the fact that their advocates are citizens of creditor states.

As previously discussed (Section 1.3.2), in the 1925 Report the Technical Experts did not try to justify the allocation of taxing rights on theoretical grounds, instead saying "the division which we have established ... has been made for purely practical purposes and no inference in regard to economic theory or doctrine should be drawn from this fact".[51]

(b) The position taken by countries (or their experts) may sometimes reflect their self-interest and in the terminology of the 1923 Report, a creditor or debtor state worldview. However, a broader approach might be taken and a good example of this was the conflicting approach taken by the two US economists heavily involved in the 1923–28 Reports. As a creditor nation, one could expect that the United States might have taken an exclusively residence-based approach, but the evidence overwhelmingly shows that the "original intent" of US international tax was that of source taxation with a foreign tax credit being permitted.[52]

(c) There was universal recognition in the 1923 Report, 1925 Report and the subsequent reports that source-based taxation could occur in an unfettered way, absent any international agreement to the contrary.

The 1923 Report discussed the benefit theory and the ability to pay theory before using the theory of economic allegiance to assess and justify the allocation of taxing rights. It will be necessary to revisit this concept of economic allegiance as we examine the case justifying source and residence taxation.

1.4 Justifying Source and Residence Taxation

As we have seen, the allocation of taxing rights originally determined in the 1920s and adopted as the framework for the international tax system can best be viewed as "an arbitrary compromise, albeit one that has come

---

[51] League of Nations (Technical Experts from Belgium, Czechoslovakia, France, Great Britain, Italy, Netherlands and Switzerland), above n 29 at 15.
[52] Graetz and O'Hear, above n 19 at 1021.

1.4 JUSTIFYING SOURCE AND RESIDENCE TAXATION

to be accepted by large parts of the international community".[53] This could be viewed as "where" we have landed in the field of international taxation, but it does not explain "why" we are here. To do that we should at least try to "justify" the principles of taxation, particularly as they relate to cross-border business. There are numerous different meanings given to the word "justify" in theology and law but the most relevant for our purposes is "to show or maintain the justice or reasonableness of (an action, claim, etc.); to give a justification for; to defend as right or proper".[54]

When the great Klaus Vogel tackled the issue of justification for taxation he described it as "a forgotten question".[55] His article focused on the broader question of justifying taxation from a jurisprudential perspective rather than specifically focusing on cross-border business but many of the principles are, of course, relevant to this international dimension.

In the Middle Ages taxation was permitted only as an emergency measure.[56] This was documented by theological scholars such as Francisco Suarez attributing the origin to the moral philosophy of Thomas Aquinas.[57] The permissible purposes for taxation included funding warfare and armament, living expenses of the sovereign (including any ransom from imprisonment) and the dowry for his daughters.[58] Given the emergency nature of taxation, it was levied and used for a specific purpose and if this purpose went away, then Suarez documented that it needed to be refunded or applied to another legitimate purpose.

There have been a succession of philosophers, economists and political theorists who have written on this important topic,[59] as Richard Musgrave says,

---

[53] M Devereux and J Vella "Are We Heading towards a Corporate Tax System Fit for the 21st Century?" (2014) 35(4) Fiscal Studies 449 <https://ssrn.com/abstract=2532933>.
[54] Oxford English Dictionary, definition of "justify" at 6.a (3rd ed, 2013), Oxford University Press.
[55] Klaus Vogel "The Justification for Taxation: A Forgotten Question" (1988) 33(1) Am J Juris 19.
[56] Ibid at 24.
[57] Ibid at 24 and 25 where Vogel refers to the work of Suarez in the work "Tractatus de legibus ac deo legislatore", Lib. V Cap. 13, 15 (1612).
[58] Ibid at 55.
[59] For a summary, see Edwin Seligman *Progressive Taxation in Theory and Practice* (2nd ed, American Economic Association, Princeton University Press, 1908).

for good reason: the duty to pay taxes, or the power to tax, is among the most tangible of all links between subject and sovereign, or citizen and society. The struggle to overcome arbitrariness in taxation was one of the early objectives of constitutional government, and the setting of tax maxims provided a means of defining the status of the individual in the social compact.[60]

Most traditional, and indeed current, theories[61] for the justification of tax fall loosely into two major categories.[62] These are the benefit theory and the ability to pay theory. The conventional view is that the benefit theory is used to support source taxation, whilst the ability to pay theory supports residence taxation, but this viewpoint's validity is questioned.[63]

1.4.1 What Are the Benefit and the Ability to Pay Theories?

The difference between the two theories is based upon the fundamentally different worldview of public finance (that is, the relationship between revenue and expenditure). In the benefit theory, the taxpayer and government are seen as economic actors exchanging consideration with each other. In other words, an exchange of goods and services – something of value (taxation) in return for something of value (public goods and services).

In contrast, in the ability to pay theory there is no connection between the benefits received and the payment of tax. Tax is therefore viewed as compulsory, without any relationship to the market.

Musgrave notes that both approaches have advantages and drawbacks. The benefit theory does not intuitively work in the area of distribution (or redistribution from the wealthy to those at risk or in need of support

---

[60] R Musgrave *The Theory of Public Finance: A Study in Public Economy* (McGraw-Hill, 1959) at 61.

[61] There are at least two other distinct theories – the sovereignty doctrine and the realistic doctrine. These are referred to in N Tadmore "Source Taxation of Cross-Border Intellectual Supplies – Concepts, History and Evolution into the Digital Age" (2007) BFIT at 2. In some respects these theories seem to be statements of attributes rather than theories in their own right. The sovereignty doctrine observes that the jurisdiction to make tax law exists only as far as sovereignty exists. The realistic doctrine has an inverse relationship to the sovereignty doctrine. It argues that since no rules of international law exist to limit a country's taxing jurisdiction and therefore the restriction is only one of practical enforcement.

[62] Ibid at 61. Vogel (above n 55) also makes the point that these are best expressed as two fundamental directions or groups of theories, but he also describes the distinction as too narrow because of the multiplicity of theories and their historical development.

[63] Devereux and Vella, above n 53 at 2.

in society), although in his view does have "the great merit of tying the choice of public services to the preferences of the individual members of the community".[64] There is also a very important disadvantage in that it is hard to establish how benefits are to be determined. Musgrave references John Stuart Mill, who described it as a relationship which was quid pro quo.[65] Indeed, John Stuart Mill sharply rejected the benefit approach because of the regressive nature of the taxation if there was an equivalence between need and taxation.[66] He could not accept that the poor would be taxed proportionately more because of their greater need. What seems clear to some nowadays is that it is very much not quid pro quo in the sense that the exchange between the parties (state and the individual) is on a very general level (not an exact supply of benefits to any one taxpayer in any particular period). Furthermore, the value of the exchange is not in any way necessarily equivalent in the sense that we understand the colloquial use of the term quid pro quo.

The advantage of the ability to pay theory is that it simplifies the relationship to one of compulsion which then enables the state to determine how payments can be made to allocate expenditure, distribute and secure price-level stability and full employment.[67] Of course, the ability to pay theory does not tell us how to distribute the tax burden or how to allocate the expenditure.

1.4.2 A Brief History of the Development of the Theories

Studies on the development of tax theory [68] illustrate some of the social, philosophical and historical changes through the centuries. As described earlier in this part of the book, taxation originally began as an emergency measure. Later in the seventeenth century taxation began to evolve from being on an extraordinary basis to a continuous levy. The general requirement of public necessity or utility began to replace taxation on a specific-purpose basis.[69] German jurisprudence on public finance

---

[64] Musgrave, above n 60 at 62.
[65] Ibid at 61; see Musgrave's reference to the publication by John Stuart Mill *Principles of Political Economy* (WJ Ashley ed, Longmans, 1921) at 804.
[66] Musgrave, above n 60 at 804.
[67] Ibid at 63.
[68] For a detailed analysis of the very many economists, philosophers and tax academics see Musgrave, above n 60 at 61; Vogel, above n 55; K Vogel "Worldwide vs Source Taxation of Income – A Review and Re-evaluation of Arguments (Part I)" (1988) 8–9 Intertax 216.
[69] Vogel, above n 68; Vogel, above n 55.

documented an early form of the benefit theory based on the social contract. The social contract theory was based on the benefit the state provided to an individual, not on the general "public benefit" of the tax.[70]

Adam Smith encapsulated both the benefit and the ability to pay theories in his first maximum of taxation:[71]

> The subjects of every state ought to contribute towards the support of the government, as nearly as possible, in proportion to their respective abilities: that is, in proportion to the revenue which they respectively enjoy under the protection of the state. The expense of the government to the individuals of a great nation is like the expense of management to the joint tenants of a great estate, or all obliged to contribute in proportion to their respective interests in the estate.

In this statement, Smith identifies that everyone benefits from general public services and everyone should contribute to the cost of sustaining them (consistent with the benefit theory). In the absence of a practical assessment of what the individual benefit is, or what cost contribution is required, Adam Smith introduces the concept that taxation should be "in proportion to their respective abilities" (consistent with the ability to pay theory).

In the nineteenth century, the ability to pay theory had taken a slightly more extreme form in the view of mostly German philosophers and economists.[72] Described as the "sacrifice theory", it can be summarised in the words of Vocke as follows:[73] "There is no choice of the individual to determine a certain consideration for the sum of services rendered to the individual by the community. In contrast, every individual with everything he is and owns belongs to the community." By the twentieth century, the extreme nature of the sacrifice theory seemed to have morphed back into the more reasonable ability to pay concepts.[74] Vogel attributes this to the development of the modern state and the

---

[70] F Mann *Steuerpolitische Ideale* (1937). Described in footnotes 21 and 35 of Vogel, above n 55.

[71] Adam Smith *The Wealth of Nations* (E Cannan ed, Vol 2, GP Putnam's Sons, 1904) at 310.

[72] Such as Rau, Schmoller, Schaffle, Vocke, and Wagner, all of whom are discussed in Vogel, above n 55 at 28–30.

[73] W Vocke *Die Abgaben, Auflagen und die Stuer vom Standpunkt der Geschichte und der Sittlichkeit* (Cotta, 1887) at 174.

[74] Vogel in his review notes that the literature following this period nearly always lead in terms of ability to pay instead of using the sacrifice concept. Vogel, above n 55 at 31.

1.4 JUSTIFYING SOURCE AND RESIDENCE TAXATION

fact that the sacrifice theory was no longer needed to accomplish the political goal of implementing a general income tax.[75]

Of course, one of the most important features of the ability to pay theory is that it can be linked to the residence of the taxpayer without any reference to benefits provided to them. This lack of connection between residence-based taxation and benefits is a double-edged sword. Some analysts see the administrative advantages of collecting tax from residents as well as allowing the full assessment of a person's ability to pay as superior and therefore recommend "a worldwide system of residence principle taxation".[76] It leads some theorists, however, to the conclusion that residence-based taxation is inappropriate (as you can end up taxing people who get no benefit or only a small benefit from their state).

1.4.3 The Ability to Pay Theory and Taxing Non-Residents

The residence-based tax also enables a full determination of the taxpayer's true worldwide income position, thus accurately permitting progressive tax. The ability to pay theory is therefore directly linked to worldwide income (however that is measured) earned by the taxpayer. Elkins expresses it as follows: "the role played by residence in international tax is a function of the normative underpinnings of *home-country* income taxation" (emphasis added). He distinguishes home country taxation (the tax imposed by a country on its own residents) from host country taxation (the tax imposed by a country on foreign residents who engage in economic activity, including passive investment, within its territory).[77] Justifying income tax by reference to the ability to pay tax can take a variety of different forms and doctrines. These include:[78]

(a) the utilitarian doctrine as discussed in the works of Jeremy Bentham and John Stuart Mill: taking a dollar from a wealthy individual causes less disutility than taking a dollar from a poor individual, and taking a dollar from a wealthy individual and using it for public services enhances the total happiness;

---

[75] Ibid at 36.
[76] David Bradford US Treasury Tax Policy Staff *Blueprints for Basic Tax Reform* (2nd ed, Tax Analysts, 1984) at 89–90.
[77] D Elkins "The Myth of Corporate Tax Residence" (2017) 9 Col J of Tax Law 5 at 12.
[78] See the excellent description of the various theories together with the footnotes in ibid.

(b) Rawlsian principles: Rawls suggests that everyone has an equal moral claim to material resources and that justice permits deviation from an equal distribution of wealth only to the extent that such inequality works to the benefit of the least well-off stratum of society – so if the market distribution is unequal, then justice requires a redistribution of resources;

(c) the sacrifice theory: each person should experience the same degree of pain from paying taxes and because of the declining marginal utility of money a wealthy individual would need to pay more to have the same sacrificial experience.

The ability to measure who is in a position to contribute to the fisc is one of the major desirable characteristics of the ability to pay theory and it influences important government policy such as that developed in the US Treasury.[79] Applying the ability to pay theory to corporate income tax is not as sound as it might be to the taxation of individuals since it is unclear if the tax is borne by the company or the company's shareholders. If these shareholders are resident in another jurisdiction the theory fails.[80]

While the ability to pay theory has proven an important justification for residence taxation (at least in many commentators' eyes), it has little or no relevance to most forms of source taxation. Expressed another way, the ability to pay theory has not been used, at least conventionally, to justify host country taxation. Other commentators have simply recognised that "the source of net income is simply irrelevant to ability-to-pay".[81]

Reuven Avi-Yonah playfully says that "source rules are a wonderful thing for lawyers and something that causes economists to despair".[82] He goes on to explain that economists would prefer a world without any source-based taxation. Instead, a country simply taxes its residents. From time to time, Avi-Yonah suggests that economists have influenced the US Treasury and zealously discussed the creation of a residence-based tax

---

[79] Bradford US Treasury Tax Policy Staff, above n 76.
[80] Devereux and Vella, above n 53 at 3.
[81] C Fleming, R Peroni and S Shay "Fairness in International Taxation: The Ability-to-Pay Case for Taxing Worldwide Income" (2001) 5 Fla Tax Rev 299 at 311. It is recognised that the authors were talking about the actual source of net income (i.e. from one source rather than another) and so the quota is not quite contextual, but the principle is valid nonetheless.
[82] R Avi-Yonah *International Tax as International Law* (Cambridge University Press, 2007) at 38.

1.4 JUSTIFYING SOURCE AND RESIDENCE TAXATION

system. One such example is found in the Report on Global Electronic Commerce prepared by the US Treasury in 1996, which discussed "source-based taxation losing its rationale and being rendered obsolete by electronic commerce. By contrast, almost all taxpayers are resident somewhere".[83] Accordingly, the Report concluded:[84]

> Therefore, United States tax policy has already recognised that as traditional source principles lose their significance, residence-based taxation can step in and take their place. This trend will be accelerated by developments in electronic commerce where principles of residence-based taxation will also play a major role.

It seems very unlikely that the world will embrace purely residence-based taxation, a viewpoint that Avi-Yonah reinforces for two reasons: (1) it would lead to an overwhelming shift of revenue from the developing to the developed world and (2) many countries, including the United States, would be reluctant to give up their right to tax foreigners on a source basis. This second reason is highlighted by more recent US Treasury commentary:[85]

> The US system was developed to the time when the United States was the primary source of capital investment and dominated world markets. The global landscape has shifted considerably over the past decades, with other countries challenging the US position of economic pre-eminence. The United States is now a net recipient of foreign investment rather than the largest source.

All this leads to the conclusion that the ability to pay theory is important to worldwide taxation and so is a critical part of cross-border taxation. Nevertheless, when dealing with inbound or host country taxation it is to the benefit theory that we must look.

In addition to developments that took place in the ability to pay theory, there were further developments in the benefit theory. These have been described by Musgrave as "the Renaissance of the benefit approach".[86] These developments focus on the idea of interpreting tax

---

[83] United States Department of the Treasury Office of Tax Policy *Selected Tax Policy Implications of Global Electronic Commerce* (November 1996) at 23.
[84] Ibid at 23.
[85] Office of Tax Policy, United States Department of the Treasury *Approaches to Improve the Competitiveness of the US Business Tax System for the 21st Century* (December 2007) at 54.
[86] Musgrave, above n 60 at 68.

as consideration for state services, moving away from the idea of individuals receiving benefits into a more community-based approach.[87]

1.4.4 The Renaissance of the Benefit Theory

Vogel chooses to single out two compatriots who in his eyes have made significant advancements in the theory of justification for taxes, with a particular focus on the benefits theory.[88] The first is Lorenz von Stein, a lawyer and philosopher writing at the end of the nineteenth century.[89] Stein argues that it is only through taxation that the community is placed in the position to provide individuals with the "economic conditions required for their development".[90] This is a concept of mutual benefit or relationship, with individuals returning to the community a portion of the economic progress they have derived from the community. In other words, a state has provided the environment to allow the creation of economic value. In turn, taxation of this income returns to the state part of the increase in economic value.

The other key nineteenth-century author, according to Klaus Vogel, was Georg von Schanz. For students of tax, it is worthwhile pointing out that Schanz was the original author of the comprehensive concept of income. Henry Simons, when writing his famous text on *Personal Income Taxation*,[91] acknowledged two writers whose income concepts coincided with his own, Schanz and Robert Haig.[92]

Schanz was one of those people who thought residence-based taxation was unfair because of the lack of connection between residence and benefits provided by the state. On the other hand, he was also opposed to double taxation, which would occur if both the residence and source states imposed a tax on the same income. In his article, he proposed a fair and equitable distribution of tax burdens between the residence and source state based upon a principle of taxation known as "economic allegiance".[93] This is the term adopted by the four economists in the 1923 Report but, it will be remembered from the previous section, the

---

[87] Ibid at 68–89. See Musgrave's discussion of the work of Wicksell and Lindahl.
[88] Vogel, above n 55 at 33–46.
[89] L von Stein *Lehrbuch der Finanzwissenschaft* (5th ed, 2 vols, Leipzig, 1885).
[90] Ibid at 348.
[91] H Simons *Personal Income Taxation: The Definition of Income as a Problem of Fiscal Policy* (6th ed, University of Chicago Press, 1938).
[92] Ibid at 60.
[93] G von Schanz "Zur Frage der Steuerpflicht" (1982) 9(11) Finanzarchiv 1, 4.

1.4 JUSTIFYING SOURCE AND RESIDENCE TAXATION

first choice and principal recommendation of the economics professors was to exempt source taxation and leave taxation at the residence level. This led to the 1920s compromise resulting from the 1923 Report, but the point is that the term originally used by Schanz was subsequently misapplied by the four economists. As Vogel says about the use of the economic allegiance principle in the 1923 Report: "neither were the reasons for this conclusion convincing nor was it politically acceptable ... Consequently, the further development of tax treaty policy was taken out of the hands of economics professors and transferred to technical experts."[94]

What Schanz meant by economic allegiance was fundamentally different from the residence-based taxation originally proposed as the best option in the 1923 Report. Schanz proposed that both the state of residence and the state of source (where investment was made) can legitimately claim taxation. In the case of the state of source, this is on the grounds of services provided to the taxpayer. In Schanz's view, the share of taxation based on the services provided by the source state would be higher than that provided by the state of residence.

This means that where a person has business activities, or income arising in another state, then the allegiance to this source state is more important than to the state of residence. Although the state of residence should get its fair share, Schanz proposed that three-quarters of the income in question should be taxed by the state of source, with the residual one quarter taxed in the state of residence. Vogel clearly supports this proposition and goes further, arguing that if indirect taxes already compensate the residence state for its services, then full taxation by the source state is justified.[95]

Consistent with the views of Schanz and Stein that the right to tax is linked in some way to the economic environment provided by the source state, is the American professor Arthur Harding's work on overcoming double taxation in the US state tax environment.[96] Similar to Stein, he observes that economic production is an outcome of an interactive

---

[94] Vogel, above n 68 at 220.
[95] K Vogel "Worldwide vs Source Taxation of Income – A Review and Re-evaluation of Arguments (Part III)" (1988) 11 Intertax 393 at 395.
[96] A Harding *Double Taxation of Property and Income, a Study in the Judicial Delimitation of the Conflicting Claims of Taxing Jurisdiction Advanced by the American States* (Harvard University Press, 1933).

community rather than individual contributions and that the state is important in that interaction.[97]

> We see that the economic existence, nature and function of the State is to be found in this economic mechanism functioning within its territorial limits and contributing to the life, progress and happiness of the individual members of the group and, of necessity, of the group as a whole.

Harding then ties the state's right to tax into the benefits it provides to enable the group to undertake its coordinated task of producing utility or wealth.[98]

> It appears that the State may tax all property, goods, labour, services and the like, which had become identified with the economic structure of the State, by incorporation into or integration with the business mechanism so defined ... the right to tax then depends upon the fact that the economic wealth is being used in the coordinated economic task of the social group: that it is producing utility or wealth or service in connection with, as a part of, and because of the economic solidarity of the social group.

Although Vogel, writing in 1988, expressed great admiration for Harding's work, he gave it less emphasis because it referred to interstate taxation and not cross-border taxation, and because it had been superseded by subsequent judicial decisions.[99] This position requires reassessment in the light of the US Supreme Court's decision on 21 June 2018, in *South Dakota v Wayfair, Inc.*[100] This decision is discussed in the next section.

The line of thinking that links the justification for taxation and source taxation with the benefit theory has been present at the League of Nations and the OECD for some considerable time. In the previous section of this book, we discussed the so-called 1920s compromise.[101] This compromise of allocating taxing rights between source and residence countries was an integral part of the history of the rules which form the basis of the modern international tax system and the OECD double tax model. Arising out of the 1923 Report was the concept of economic allegiance.[102]

---

[97] Ibid at 42, cited in Vogel, above n 68 at 221.
[98] Ibid.
[99] Vogel, above n 68 at 221.
[100] *South Dakota v Wayfair, Inc, et al, Certiorari to the Supreme Court of South Dakota*, No. 17-494. Argued April 17, 2018 – Decided June 21, 2018, 585 US-(2018).
[101] See Section 1.3 "The History of International Double Taxation: The '1920s Compromise'".
[102] Bruins, Einaudi, Seligman and Stamp, above n 25 at 20.

1.4 JUSTIFYING SOURCE AND RESIDENCE TAXATION

This concept of economic allegiance recognises various contributions made by the source and residence state to the production and enjoyment of income. In other words, the 1920s compromise was comfortable with the concept of allocating taxing rights to the source jurisdiction on the basis that foreign-owned entities enjoyed the benefits provided by the source state (such as public services and the protection of property rights).

The four economists involved in preparing the 1923 Report discussed the four elements of economic allegiance, describing them as follows:[103]

1. The production of wealth; which means all the stages involved up until the wealth comes to fruition, by which they mean "the oranges upon the trees in California are not acquired wealth until they are picked, and not even at this stage until they are packed, *and not even at that stage until they are transported to the place where demand exists and until they are put with a consumer who can use them*".[104]

    Under this heading, it can be seen that the production of wealth involves both the supply/residence side (manufacturing and production) and the demand/source side (transportation to the market where they are purchased and consumed). This is a more relevant category for business income.

2. The location of the wealth; where the wealth is situated.

    Often this will be the location of the property. Relevant for passive investment income, the location of the investment capital could be in the state of source or the state of residence.

3. The possession of wealth; which means, substantially, the legal framework of society and the place where property rights are enforceable.

    Under this heading, the right to enforce property rights can be in both the supply/residence side and the demand/source side, such as enforcing intellectual property rights or creditor/debtor obligations.

4. The disposition of wealth; which means the stage where the wealth has reached its final owner who can consume it, or reinvest it, but in the exercise of the will to do any of these things it resides with the owner, and their ability to pay taxes is apparent.

    Under this heading, residence tax is mostly relevant as the owner consumes or disposes of the property. It could be noted that the property could well be situated in another state.

---

[103] Ibid at 22–3.
[104] Ibid at 23 (emphasis added).

After analysing these four principles the 1923 Report concludes that the stages of production "up to the point where wealth reaches fruition, may be shared in by different territorial authorities".[105] It is acknowledged by the OECD that "this 'origin of wealth' principle has remained a primary basis for source taxation through the many committees and draft conventions prepared under the auspices of the League of Nations".[106]

In a 1991 Report, the OECD recognised the right for source countries to tax income originating within their borders, including income accruing to foreigners:[107]

> One justification for this entitlement is that the foreign-owned factors of production usually benefit from the public services and the protection of property rights provided by the government of the host country. A source-based tax like the corporation tax may also serve to prevent foreign investors from capturing all of the "economic rent" which may arise when foreign capital moves in to exploit the host country's production opportunities, e.g. its natural resources.

1.4.5 The Benefit Theory in the Digital Age: Does the Absence of Physical Presence in a Jurisdiction Nullify the Source Jurisdiction's Taxing Rights?

(a) The Wayfair Decision

South Dakota has a retail sales tax. The problem was that it was unenforceable for remote sales made by an out-of-state vendor when they had no physical presence in South Dakota. Two previous US Supreme Court decisions had held that South Dakota (or any other US state) did not have the jurisdiction to require a business that had no physical presence in the state to collect its sales tax.[108] In order to try and prop up its sales tax base and raise essential revenue for state and local services, South Dakota passed legislation requiring out-of-state vendors to collect and remit sales tax "as if the seller had a physical presence in the State". The

---

[105] Ibid at 23.
[106] *Taxing Profits in a Global Economy – Domestic and International Issues* (OECD, 1991) at 32, discussing the numerous committee reports and founding double tax agreements that form the basis of the OECD Model Convention.
[107] Ibid at 36–7.
[108] *National Bellas Hess, Inc v Cap department of Revenue of Ill.*, 386 U.S. 753; *Quill Corp. v Cap North Dakota*, 504 U.S. 298.

court in the *Wayfair* decision decided (by a narrow five to four majority) to override the previous decisions requiring retailers to account for sales tax when they trade remotely but deliver goods to people within the state, even when they lack a physical presence in the taxing state.

South Dakota v Wayfair, Inc is, therefore, an important decision which upheld the right of the South Dakota Legislature (or other US states) to enact a law requiring out-of-state sellers to collect and remit sales tax when they deliver items to in-state purchases. From now on, states can require remote sellers to collect tax if the seller has a "substantial nexus" with the taxing state. There is not a great deal of clarity about what constitutes a substantial nexus and Reuven Avi Yonah has predicted that this will lead to more litigation.[109] Justice Kennedy, delivering the majority judgment, cited a previous Supreme Court decision that "such a nexus is established when the taxpayer [or collector] avails itself of the substantial privilege of carrying on business in that jurisdiction".[110] In this case, the majority considered that the "nexus is clearly sufficient based on both the economic and virtual contacts respondents have with the State".[111]

The South Dakota Act applied only to sellers that deliver more than $100,000 of goods or services into South Dakota or engage in 200 or more separate transactions for the delivery of goods and services into the state annually. Justice Kennedy concluded: "This quantity of business could not have occurred unless the seller availed itself of the substantial privilege of carrying on business in South Dakota. And respondents are large, national companies that undoubtedly maintain an extensive virtual presence."[112]

Avi Yonah considers that the *Wayfair* decision has broad implications for both the European Union and international tax.[113] He highlights the "eloquent" statement of rationale which allows states to require remote sellers to collect tax by reflecting that "the market jurisdiction provides the benefits that are indispensable for the generation of profits by the remote sellers".[114] What he was referring to was the remarkably clear

---

[109] R Avi-Yonah "The International Implications of Wayfair" (2018) 160 Tax Notes 215.
[110] *South Dakota v Wayfair, Inc, et al, Certiorari to the Supreme Court of South Dakota*, No. 17-494. Argued April 17, 2018 – Decided June 21, 2018, 585 US-(2018) at 22, citing *Polar Tankers, Inc v City of Valdez*, 557 U.S. 1, 11 (2009).
[111] Ibid at 22.
[112] Ibid at 23.
[113] Avi-Yonah, above n 109.
[114] Ibid.

statement by the Supreme Court of the benefits theory expressed by Justice Kennedy as follows:[115]

> Wayfair offers to sell a vast selection of furnishings. Its advertising seeks to create an image of beautiful, peaceful homes, but also says that "one of the best things about buying through Wayfair is that we do not have to charge sales tax." What Wayfair ignores in its subtle offer to assist in tax evasion is that creating a dream home assumes solvent state and local governments. State taxes fund the police and fire departments that protect the homes containing their customers' furniture and ensure goods are safely delivered; maintain the public roads and municipal services that allow communications with and access to customers; support the "sound local banking institutions to support credit transactions [and] courts to ensure collection of the purchase price," and help create the "climate of consumer confidence" that facilitates sales. According to respondents, it is unfair to stymie their tax free solicitation of customers. But there is nothing unfair about requiring companies that avail themselves of the States' benefits to bear an equal share of the burden of tax collection.

The US Supreme Court in *Wayfair* reversed the two previous Supreme Court judgments which had required a physical presence in order to constitute a substantial nexus. The majority made the following points about the physical presence test:[116]

- It was not clear to the court why a single employee or a single warehouse should create a substantial nexus while physical aspects of pervasive modern technology do not.
- A company with a website accessible in South Dakota may be said to have a physical presence in the state via the customers' computers. A website may leave cookies saved to the customers' hard drives, or customers may download the company's app onto their phones.
- A company may lease data storage that is permanently, or even occasionally, located in South Dakota.
- "Between targeted advertising and instant access to most consumers via any internet-enabled device, a business may be present in a State in a meaningful way without" that presence "being physical in the traditional sense of the term".
- "[A] virtual showroom can show far more inventory, in far more detail, and with greater opportunities for consumers and seller interaction that might be possible for local stores".

---

[115] *South Dakota v Wayfair, Inc, et al, Certiorari to the Supreme Court of South Dakota*, No. 17-494. Argued April 17, 2018 – Decided June 21, 2018, 585 US (2018) at 16.
[116] Ibid at 15.

The absence of physical presence, therefore, did not in any way constrain the US Supreme Court from asserting that the substantial virtual connections to the state were sufficient to constitute a substantial nexus. The Supreme Court applied the benefit theory to recognise substantial virtual connections. While the context is one of state taxation, it is difficult to see any theoretical difference between interstate arrangements and cross-border taxation.

(b) Is There a Requirement That You Can Only Recognise the Benefits Provided to Non-Resident Businesses Where They Have a Physical Presence in the Country of Source?

In 2003, a Technical Advisory Group (TAG) of the OECD produced a report examining the settings of the treaty rules and the taxation of business profits in the context of e-commerce.[117] The TAG could not reach agreement, but clearly some members felt that, even with the absence of any physical presence in the country of source, that country still had the right to tax business profits. This is important, because as Michael Lennard points out in his article, there was a lack of consensus in 2003, "even among a body composed almost entirely of representatives of developed countries, corporates or advisors":[118]

> 43. The members of the TAG disagreed, however, on an important related issue: i.e. whether a supplier which is not physically present in a country may be considered to be using that country's legal and economic infrastructure and, if that is the case, whether and to what extent, such use of a country's legal and economic infrastructure should be considered to be one factor which, under the supply-based view, would allow that country to claim source taxing rights on a share of the enterprise's profits.
>
> 44. For some members, source taxation is justified in such a case because the business profits of the foreign enterprise derive partly from the enterprise's use of important locational advantages provided by that country's infrastructure which make the business operations profitable. These may include, but are not limited to means of transportation (such as roads), public safety, a legal system that ensure the protection of property rights and a financial infrastructure.[119]

---

[117] OECD Technical Advisory Group on Monitoring the Application of Existing Treaty Norms for Taxing Business Profits *Are the Current Treaty Rules for Taxing Business Profits Appropriate for E-Commerce? Final Report* (Centre for Tax Policy and Administration, 2003).

[118] M Lennard "Act of Creation: The OECD/G20 Test of 'Value Creation' as a Basis for Taxing Rights and Its Relevance to Developing Countries" (2018) 25(3) Transnat'l Corp 55 at 67.

[119] Footnote 20 reads: "Thus the benefit principle, which provides a justification for rejecting exclusive residence taxation (see above) can also be put forward as a principle

45. Other members, however, disagreed. For them, business profits derive from the carrying on, by the enterprise, of business activities and a country is only justified to consider that profits originate from its territory if the enterprise carries on activities thereon. They do not regard an enterprise which may have access to a country's market as necessarily "using" that country's infrastructure and, even if that were the case, they consider that such mere use of a country's general infrastructure would be too incidental to the business profit-making process to consider that a significant part of the profits are attributable to that country.

Around about the same time as the release of this report in 2003, Professor Dale Pinto considered the same question and concluded that it wasn't necessary for a foreign enterprise to maintain a physical presence in the country for the country of source to justify its taxing rights. He argues that benefits provided to non-resident vendors, even when they lack a physical presence and source countries, can still be considered as part of the justification for the right for the source country to tax the resultant income.[120]

Pinto considers an argument raised by Charles McLure that the benefit principle suggests that a physical presence is *probably* necessary to establish tax nexus.[121] The reason for this is that, according to McLure, many of the services (such as police and fire protection) are relevantly provided only where a non-resident business maintains a physical presence in the source country. Pinto cites Arvid Skaar's book, which concludes that even if a business does not have a physical presence in the source country it can still benefit substantially from its infrastructure and should make a contribution by way of taxation. In Skaar's view:[122]

> A [permanent establishment] is merely a piece of *evidence* of economic allegiance, not the reason for source-state taxation ... It seems an enterprise which does not need to invest in immovable facilities, or other fixed places of business, may still derive considerable advantages from the community in which its income sources are located. Today, the performance of a business activity in another country, the duration of the activity

for determining the source of the business profits. The same reasoning has also been articulated in terms of the 'principle of economic allegiance'" (referred to in footnote 12).

[120] D Pinto *E-Commerce and Source-Based Income Taxation* (IBFD Publications BV, Netherlands, 2003) at 22–3.

[121] C McLure "Source-Based Taxation and Alternatives to the Concept of Permanent Establishment" in Canadian Tax Foundation (ed) *2000 World Tax Conference Report* (2000) at [6.5].

[122] A Skaar *Permanent Establishment: Erosion of a Tax Treaty Principle* (Kluwer Law and Taxation Publishers, 1991) at 559–60.

and the profits arising from it, are *per se* significant arguments ... [that] requires all enterprises which obtain such benefits from country to render a corresponding contribution to the society, whether or not they have a permanent establishment.

(c) The Source Country Contribution to Digital Businesses

It is possible to point to at least five major areas where the source country makes a contribution to the carrying on of digitalised business in their jurisdiction:[123]

1 the contribution to the business environment and economy: this includes the general business confidence, corruption and law and order, affluence and ability to consume. Often goods and services purchased by a resident in the source country are then consumed either in the production of further business activities (requiring a viable environment) or in private consumption (requiring a consumer with spending power);
2 the contribution to the technological infrastructure: this includes suitable telecommunications infrastructure, Wi-Fi and broadband, and a population with appropriate devices (computers and smartphones);
3 the contribution to the legal system: this includes providing reliance to enforce payment for transactions, uphold intellectual property rights (such as trademarks), and maintain a competitive and conducive business environment. The protection of intellectual property rights (for example, in the case of computer software) is critical to vendors of intangible products and digitalised services. The ability to deal with fraudulent and criminal behaviour is also important, as are consumer protection laws;
4 the contribution to infrastructure: modern infrastructure to allow physical delivery of goods in a timely and protected way, provision for waste disposal for packaging materials;
5 the contribution of users to the digital business: this may take many forms, which will be discussed in Chapter 3 but include the role of users and social media (designing or providing content), the contribution individuals make to the network effect (family, followers and friends), the provision of assets and services as part of the sharing economy (either physically located or physically performed in the

---

[123] This list was compiled with the assistance of the list of benefits discussed in Pinto, above n 120 at 22–3.

source jurisdiction), the process of review, validation and assessment (on services or goods), etc.

It seems clear that the benefit theory retains its credibility as a justification to tax non-residents in circumstances where the non-resident enterprise is enjoying or utilising the type of contribution made by the source state (or by economic actors – for example, users – in the source state). This is not a modern idea but appears to have been present right from the original theoretical construct in the 1920s compromise. The concept of economic allegiance, while it is admittedly indistinct, clearly encompasses an apportionment of taxing rights between states when the activities carried on by a non-resident enterprise utilise and benefit from the public services, legal and technological infrastructure provided in the source state.

While this theoretical argument might justify taxation by a source state in the context of dealing with digital business, this clearly is only a question of justification. It does not suggest that the current international tax framework permits the taxation of digital business when there is no physical presence.

An important recent development in the OECD is the concept of value creation. What is this concept, where has it come from and how does it relate to the benefit theory?

1.5 The Benefit Theory and Its Relationship to Value Creation

The European Commission states that "it is an internationally agreed principle that profit should be taxed where value is created".[124] The Commission's statement is referenced to the OECD/G20 Base Erosion and Profit Shifting Project (BEPS). Indeed, the OECD BEPS Project has had its focus on ensuring that "profits are taxed where economic activities take place and value is created".[125] A strong case can be put forward to support the proposition that value creation is internationally agreed but it seems rather unclear what countries are agreeing to. The most recent pronouncements of the OECD/G20 Inclusive Framework represents over 125 countries and repeats the concept that the BEPS Project is

---

[124] European Commission *Communication from the Commission to the European Parliament and the Council* (COM, Brussels, 21 March 2018) at 4.
[125] OECD *Explanatory Statement: 2015 Final Reports* (OECD/G20 Base Erosion and Profit Shifting Project, 2015) <www.oecd.org/ctp/beps-explanatory-statement-2015.pdf>.

"restoring taxation to the place where economic activities and value creation occur".[126] In addition, Actions 8 to 10 of the BEPS Action Plan profess to ensure that transfer pricing outcomes are aligned with "value creation".[127]

Value creation is also referred to in publications outside of the OECD/G20 programme by the European Commission,[128] as well as individual countries discussing reforms on taxing the digitalisation of the economy, such as the United Kingdom,[129] Australia[130] and New Zealand.[131]

1.5.1 The Origin and Purpose of the Concept of Value Creation

Several observations might be made about the concept of value creation. The first is to do with its origin and purpose. It seems that the concept of value creation "emerged (out) of the blue"[132] and as "a messy, political idea"[133] rather than a thoroughly analysed guiding principle. As Professor Johanna Hey explains: "Nowhere in all of the publications regarding the OECD/G20 BEPS initiative, is it possible to find any explanation why this should be the underlying principle of the inter-

---

[126] *Inclusive Framework on BEPS, Progress Report July 2018–May 2019* (9 June 2019) at 1; OECD/G20 Base Erosion and Profit Shifting Project *Addressing the Tax Challenges of the Digitalisation of the Economy* (Public Consultation Document, 2019) at [11]; OECD/G20 Inclusive Framework on BEPS *Programme of Work to Develop a Consensus Solution to the Tax Challenges Arising from the Digitalisation of the Economy* (2019) at [23] and [53].

[127] OECD *Aligning Transfer Pricing Outcomes with Value Creation, Actions 8–10 Reports* (OECD/G20 Base Erosion and Profit Shifting Project, 2015) at 3.

[128] As referred to above, n 124, in the statement by the European Commission *Communication from the Commission to the European Parliament and the Council* at 4.

[129] HM Treasury *Corporate Tax and the Digital Economy: Position Paper* (November 2017) at [1.1], which states that the "government believes in the principle that a multinational group's profits should be taxed in the countries in which it generates value".

[130] Australian Treasury Discussion Paper *The Digital Economy and Australia's Corporate Tax System* (October 2018) at 13. See the discussion at [4.1] on the current tax framework and its failure to properly capture the value to digitalised business of certain transactions.

[131] New Zealand Inland Revenue Policy and Strategy *Options for Taxing the Digital Economy – a Government Discussion Document* (June 2019) at 4. See the discussion at paragraph 2.5 on attribution of income by reference to the value generated in New Zealand compared to overseas.

[132] J Hey "Taxation Where Value Is Created" and the OECD/G20 Base Erosion and Profit Shifting Initiative (2018) BIT 203 at 205.

[133] S Morse "Value Creation: A Standard in Search of a Process" (2018) BIT 196 at 197.

national allocation in respect of taxing rights".[134] The idea of value creation is an integral part of the BEPS programme, having its origin in preventing harmful tax competition, protecting corporate tax levels and upholding "the populist concept of taxing corporations in order to regulate their wealth and power".[135]

As Michael Devereux and John Vella have pointed out, what began as "the guiding principle of the BEPS project ... quickly became widely accepted as the guiding principle for taxing corporate profit in an international setting more generally".[136]

The principle of value creation seems to have captured the imagination of important policymakers and has morphed from the BEPS initiative designed to deal with aggressive tax planning and tax avoidance into one far more fundamental in dealing with the actual allocation of taxing rights.

1.5.2 As a Concept of Principle It Is Vague and Indistinct

The second observation is that because value creation is a concept or principle it is quite vague. Value creation could be attributed to employee location, sales location, location of production capacity, location of management or the location where capital is raised.[137] These numerous factors are necessary components of the generation of profit but may be spread over a number of countries, "making it impossible – even conceptually – to pinpoint the contribution of each specific location to the overall profit earned".[138] The only thing that seems clear, because of its BEPS and anti-avoidance background, is that no value is created where there is no real economic activity or business. Academic commentators have pointed out that this imprecision is somewhat misleading and that value creation's real problem is that "the new guiding principle stems from the fact that it pretends to give better answers to the questions of allocation, while eventually turning out to be only a new variant of the

---

[134] Hey, above n 132 at 203.
[135] Morse, above n 133 at 197.
[136] M Devereux and J Vella "Value Creation as the Fundamental Principle of the International Corporate Tax System" (2018) Oxford University Centre for Business Taxation.
[137] Morse, above n 133 at 197.
[138] M Devereux and J Vella "Implications of Digitalisation for International Corporate Tax Reform" (2017) Oxford University Centre for Business Taxation at 9.

source principle".[139] This lack of clarity has led to a suggestion from Professor Susan Morse that there is a need for a value creation dispute resolution forum, which could disclose both its procedural rules and its decisions and therefore make "hard" case law which would have precedential value and be both transparent and influential in determining allocations of income and deductions to different jurisdictions.[140]

1.5.3 Alignment with the Benefit Theory

The third observation, relevant to this part of the book on the justification for taxation, is that there is a strong argument that the concept of value creation is simply a new version or name for the benefit theory. When a country makes a contribution through public services and the legal and economic environment which enable the creation of value for an enterprise, then the benefit theory justifies taxation.[141]

Value creation, as indicated above, might be attributed to the activities undertaken by employees, the impact of the market, the legal, physical and technological infrastructure, and these and other activities could permit market countries to claim a share of the tax base.[142]

The OECD recognises in the commentary on Actions 8–10 that value creation can even include "location savings", which are those cost savings attributable to operating in a particular market.[143] Of course, the value will also be created in the location of production (wherever that might be for highly digitalised businesses). It is equally likely to justify the corporate taxing rights for a company's head office, based on the value created from capital raising or the use of intellectual property, amongst many other factors.

All of this suggests that value creation is a sufficiently broad and diverse principle to justify the allocation of taxing rights to both the country of source and of residence.

The advance that the concept of value creation brings to international taxation in highly digitalised businesses is the possibility of nexus being

---

[139] Hey, above n 132 at 205.
[140] Morse, above n 133 at 198–9.
[141] The articles in the Bulletin for International Taxation by Professors Johanna Hey and Susan Morse conclude similarly.
[142] Hey, above n 132 at 204.
[143] *Aligning Transfer Pricing Outcomes with Value Creation, Actions 8–10* – 2015 Final Reports (OECD/G20 Base Erosion and Profit Shifting Project, 2015) at 43–4.

established without physical presence. In that sense, value creation is focused on the justification of tax and not the attribution of income.

The next stage of attributing profits to value creation is far more difficult than the principle of justification for tax. As various commentators have pointed out, attributing profits to value creation is a very difficult task,[144] in fact as difficult a task as trying to establish the correlation of profits to the benefits provided by a state.[145]

1.5.4 Is Value Creation Different from the Existing International Tax Principles? Can It Be Constrained by the Pragmatism of the 1920s Compromise?

As discussed in Section 1.3, the existing international tax system is based on a pragmatic compromise. This framework allocates certain kinds of income (predominantly passive income such as interest, royalties and dividends) primarily to the residence state, whilst enabling the source state to tax business income (subject to the permanent establishment threshold).

1.5.5 The Relationship between Value Creation and the Existing International Tax Framework

It is not possible to reconcile value creation to the existing international tax framework, despite the best attempts of the OECD to do so.[146] The

---

[144] Hey, above n 132 at 205: "Some of these problems arise from the incoherence between the theoretical foundation and the tax base to which it is applied ... Consequently, the use of public goods is neither a good justification for taxing income nor does it provide any guidance for measuring and attributing the income of an MNE to different jurisdictions. Some MNE's could make intense use of public goods but ultimately realise significant losses, such as in the shipbuilding industry."

[145] Devereux and Vella, above n 136 at 6: "First, profit is likely to be a poor proxy for the benefit received. Highly profitable companies may make limited use of public services and resources, while loss making companies may place a very heavy burden on them." These two authors also make the same point in their excellent article, M Devereux and J Vella "Taxing the Digitalised Economy: Targeted or System-Wide Reform?" (2018) 4 BTR 387 at 393.

[146] As previously discussed, the OECD put forward the proposition that the focus of the BEPS project was to ensure that "the profits are taxed where economic activities take place and value is created". See *Explanatory Statement* (OECD/G20 Base Erosion and Profit Shifting Project, 2015) <www.oecd.org/ctp/beps-explanatory-statement-2015.pdf>.

1.5 THE BENEFIT THEORY

principle of value creation is a change from the 1920s compromise and therefore a replacement for that hybrid mix of residence and source taxation.

For a start, the value creation concept has nothing to do with residence taxation. Many jurisdictions impose worldwide taxation on their resident corporations (although quite a few exempt active business income). The taxation of a resident corporation on its foreign-sourced income cannot be justified under the concept of value creation.[147]

Secondly, value creation, as discussed above, can be attributed at least in part to the marketplace, giving a source country taxing rights purely on the grounds of its customers. According to the OECD, in the view of many countries that justifies taxation of highly digitalised business models because of a misalignment between the existing nexus and profit allocation rules between the location in which profits are taxed and the location in which value is created:[148]

> most of the countries in this group reject the idea that a country that provides the market where foreign enterprise's goods and services are supplied on its own provides a sufficient link to create a nexus for tax purposes, regardless of the scale of these supplies. Instead, they consider that profits should continue to be taxed exclusively where the factors that produce the income are located, in accordance with the long-standing principles of the existing tax system (e.g., aligning profit with value creation).

These countries are deeming value to be created only by activities on the supply side (research and development, production and marketing) and not on the demand side (purchasing the goods or services). Maartin de Wilde asks the question: "if the demand side is relevant for creating income, why then does international tax law currently take no account of this when apportioning companies' international profits? The answer would seem to be that this is simply how things have evolved as ... a 'product of history'".[149]

Devereux and Vella carefully (and correctly) point out that ignoring value creation on the demand side "flies in the face of basic economic

---

[147] Devereux and Vella, above n 136 at 3.
[148] *Tax Challenges Arising from Digitalisation – Interim Report* (OECD Publishing, 2018) at 172 (emphasis added).
[149] Maartin de Wilde "Tax Jurisdiction in a Digitalizing Economy: Why 'Online Profits' Are So Hard to Pin Down" (2015) 43(12) Intertax 796 at 798.

logic".¹⁵⁰ They then go on to illustrate how value is created on the market (demand) side:¹⁵¹

> The income being allocated among countries owes as much to the market as it owes to the various parts of the supply chain. Income depends on the price charged at the point where supply and demand meet: it simply would not have arisen in the absence of a market. It is not entirely clear why the international corporate tax system should depart from a simple and uncontroversial economic understanding of value creation.

In the 1923 Report, the economists discussed the production of wealth and gave an example which supports the same point – taxing rights can be shared between the supply and demand sides of the market:¹⁵²

> The oranges upon the trees in California are not acquired wealth until they are packed, and not even at this stage until they are packed, and not even at that stage until they are transported to the place where demand exists and until they are put with a consumer can use them. These stages, up to the point where wealth reaches fruition, may be shared in by different territorial authorities.

The current international tax system does not allocate taxing rights in respect of business profits unless the Permanent Establishment (PE) threshold is established and, furthermore, the business of the foreign entity is being carried on through the PE. The 1920s compromise prevents the source state from fully taxing active business income and allocates some taxing rights to the residence state where the PE threshold is not met.

Non-resident enterprises can "do" business in a jurisdiction in many different ways, some requiring a physical presence in the jurisdiction and some not (contracts might be concluded or partly performed in the source country, which may not require actual physical presence). Most countries' domestic sourcing rules require certain activities to be carried on in the country in order to constitute business income. Sometimes this threshold under domestic law is quite low and quite vague.¹⁵³

Value creation, arguably, is another reiteration of the benefit theory which is challenging the 1920s compromise. Seen in this light, the OECD

---

[150] Devereux and Vella, above n 145 at 394.
[151] Ibid.
[152] Bruins, Einaudi, Seligman and Stamp, above n 25 at 23.
[153] See Section 1.7 "Exploring the Limits of Source-Based Taxation".

is correct, in its more recent documents,[154] to describe the use of value creation as a "new taxing right".[155]

The OECD/G20 Inclusive Framework on BEPS has described, under the heading of "revised nexus and profit allocation rules",[156] three new proposals to allocate more taxing rights to the jurisdiction of the consumer and/or user which they refer to as the "market jurisdictions" in situations where they say: "value is created by business activity through (possibly remote) participation in that jurisdiction that is not recognised in the current framework for allocating profits".

As you can see from this, the OECD/G20 are seeing the value creation principle as justifying the right to consider the taxation of entities deriving income from cross-border activities in the digital age (establishing a nexus) in the absence of physical presence, and at the same time recognising that the existing rules do not permit this due to the consequences of constraint arising from the 1920s compromise. Hence the need to describe the current proposals, using value creation as a "new" taxing right. This new compromise, the 2020s compromise, is self-evidently possible and can be theoretically based on the concept of value creation viewed as a development in the benefit theory.

1.5.6 Conclusion

The proposition put forward from this discussion is that the concept of value creation is a further development of the benefit theory, justifying (as in showing the reason for, or fairness of) source taxation but doing no more.

The hard questions relating to attributing profits to activities carried on in a jurisdiction or any of the other questions relating to quantification and apportionment are not answered by such a concept.

1.6 Observations about Source and Residence Taxation in the Context of Cross-Border Business

1.6.1 Residence-Based Corporate Tax Is Contestable but It Acts as a Backstop

Although source taxation can be justified on a theoretical basis, the grounds for residence-based corporate taxation are somewhat less robust.

---

[154] Which appears not to have been previously acknowledged.
[155] OECD/G20 Inclusive Framework on BEPS *Programme of Work to Develop a Consensus Solution to the Tax Challenges Arising from the Digitalisation of the Economy* (2019) at 11.
[156] Ibid at 11. Also known as Pillar One and referred to in the document.

There are problems with residence-based corporate taxation which have implications for the overall international tax framework.

The first is that, as a practical matter, corporate tax residence is often not that straightforward but usually involves an assessment of a complex matrix of factual matters. This leads to a lack of certainty, creating a situation of aggressive tax planning or less deliberate actions leading to potential exposures if the residency of the company is asserted elsewhere.

Corporate tax residency is likely to be highly contested because it is one way to overcome the perceived deficiencies of the current international tax system, which we will go on to discuss in more detail[157] – namely, the failure of source taxation to successfully tax digital and other businesses that can operate in an economy without creating a taxable presence or permanent establishment.

Countries do not necessarily use the same basis to determine the residence of their companies under domestic law. Some countries, like the United States, rely on the test of formation or incorporation so that a company formed in the United States is a resident even though it may do no business and hold no property there. Other jurisdictions look to less legal or formal tests and examine the activities of directors and senior management in order to determine the place of effective management or central management and control. Lastly, some jurisdictions use a mixture of both concepts of formal and factual elements in their residency tests. The position under DTAs, while mostly being more consistent in selecting the effective place of management as the most usual dual resident tie-breaker under the OECD Model Art 4 (3), has also been criticised for a lack of precision.[158]

As a number of recent cases indicate, clearly determining residence as a practical matter is a difficult issue in respect of individuals,[159] and it is even more problematic in respect of companies, as pointed out by John Avery Jones.[160] These somewhat arbitrary domestic law tests of residency (for example, the location of directors' meetings and even the formal test of incorporation) have given rise to the opportunity for significant

---

[157] See Section 3.7 "The Inadequacy of Residence-Based Taxation".

[158] J Avery-Jones "2008 OECD Model: Place of Effective Management – What One Can Learn from the History" (2009) 63 BIT 183.

[159] *Harding v Commissioner of Taxation* [2018] FCA 837; *Van Uden v Commissioner of Inland Revenue* [2018] NZCA 487.

[160] *Bywater Investments Ltd v Commissioner of Taxation and Hua Wang Bank Berhad v Commissioner of Taxation* [2016] HCA 45; *HMRC v Smallwood and Another* [2010] STC 2045; *Development Securities (No 9) Ltd & Others v HMRC* [2017] UKFTT 0565.

1.6 SOURCE AND RESIDENCE TAXATION

multinational tax planning as corporations have been structured to be resident in a tax jurisdiction more favourable than the most obvious natural choice. This phenomenon has led Reuven Avi-Yonah to observe that "the residence of corporations is difficult to establish and relatively meaningless".[161]

This gives a significant multinational enterprise which operates a digital business the possibility of residence in a low-tax jurisdiction while conducting business around the world without attracting source taxation. Such a multinational will only pay a limited amount of tax in the low-tax jurisdiction. The multinational's worldwide earnings, earned outside the low-tax jurisdiction, either do not technically have a source in the foreign jurisdictions, or there exists no permanent establishment of the company in that foreign jurisdiction.

When you consider the consequences of worldwide taxation (and the potential tax on foreign earnings) then it is easy to see why there might be assertions of residence made by tax administrations. If these assertions are successful so that the corporation is found to be resident in the more highly taxed jurisdiction, this will result in tax not only on the profits earned on worldwide operations but also any profits earned in the low-tax residence jurisdiction – this is why it is termed a backstop tax.[162]

1.6.2 Problems in the Justification of Residence-Based Taxation of Corporations: Because It Does Not Necessarily Represent Taxation of Shareholders and Therefore Has a Tenuous Theoretical Basis

The second point is rather an obvious one. Profits earned by a company are usually regarded as separate income from the distributions made to the shareholders/owners of the company. As the profits of the company are the same economic income when distributed as dividends to share-

---

[161] Avi-Yonah, above n 82 at 11.
[162] The term "backstop" has both a more general usage and one peculiar to the American sport of baseball (the wall or netting behind home plate that keeps the ball on the field). It is used to describe the views of TS Adams, who was the US Treasury's spokesperson before the House Ways and Means Committee and the Senate Finance Committee. In their article Michael Graetz and Michael O'Hear describe Adams's view of residence taxation as an important backstop. See Graetz and O'Hear, above n 19 at 1038. This is, of course, an oversimplification as other issues such as dual residency and the tie-breaker provisions of any applicable double tax agreement would need to be considered as well as the question of foreign tax credits.

holders this creates a major double tax problem. If the company's income was to be taxed in the hands of shareholders this problem would not arise but this does not happen in practice because the common view is that if tax was not imposed at the corporate level then there would be indefinite deferral because corporate profits would be retained and not distributed as taxable income to shareholders. Although most jurisdictions around the world offer some form of integration between taxation at the corporate level and at the shareholder level, this integration (through, for example, imputation, or reduced rates of tax) still results in significant tax at the corporate level. Professor Richard Vann suggests that little income tax is collected from the shareholders and the "main" tax on the income occurs at the corporate level.[163]

As previously discussed,[164] there is a complex relationship between the principle of personal attachment justifying worldwide income taxation and tax being levied principally on companies rather than shareholders. The grounds for taxing individuals because of residence are much stronger than in the case of companies. As previously indicated, corporate residence can be manipulated and is dependent upon relatively arbitrary tests. Avi-Yonah asserts that "moreover, multinationals are not part of a single society and their income does not belong to any particular society for distributive purposes".[165] Vann agrees, saying "to put it another way, the traditional residence source analysis only makes sense in the case of individual taxpayers".[166]

This leads Vann to conclude that "the theoretical arguments for residence-only taxation, whatever their validity for individual investment income, do not apply to the income of firms".[167] This conclusion is consistent with that of Professor Wolfgang Schon, who says that the "worldwide corporate income taxation of companies is not legitimised by lofty principles but by the simple fact that some tax authority has to pick up the residual responsibility to tax all income not claimed by other countries (in particular as non-distributed profits are, for the time being, not taxed at the level of the shareholder as well)".[168]

---

[163] R Vann "Taxing International Business Income: Hard-Boiled Wonderland and the End of the World" (2010) 2(3) WTJ 291 at 295. See also part I of the appendix.
[164] See Section 1.2.1 "Residence Taxation".
[165] Avi-Yonah, above n 82 at 11.
[166] Vann, above n 163 at 304–5.
[167] Ibid at 305.
[168] Schon, above n 7 at 559.

1.6.3 This Leads to the Conclusion That Source-Based Taxation of Active Business Profits Is Likely to Continue to Be Preferred by Most Countries

The 1920s compromise resulted, broadly, in the residence jurisdiction having the primary right to tax passive (investment) income, while the source jurisdiction has the primary right to tax active business income.[169] It is highly likely that this hybrid compromise will be continued in some way for the following reasons:

(a) countries on some pragmatic and practical level are committed to source taxation on non-residents doing business in their country. The four economists in the 1923 Report rather wistfully recorded that "if the origin and source of income are within a country's borders, it is assumed that that country has the *prime* right of taxation on that income, although it goes to some person abroad. There are a few modifications, but this is the *main* instinctive principle".[170] Countries that exercise their right to tax income sourced in their jurisdiction will have the first opportunity for taxation, so it is extremely difficult to stop the source-based jurisdictions that wish to impose tax. Obviously, the most significant mechanism to prevent source-based taxation is by bilateral and other tax treaties.

(b) source taxation is justified by the benefit principle as explained at some length in the previous section (Section 1.4). In contrast, residence-based taxation is criticised for concerns about its potential for abuse and lack of connection (in a practical sense) with the true owners, the shareholders. This is so notwithstanding the preference for many economists to move to an exclusively residence-based tax regime.

(c) the process of achieving political consensus has expanded greatly, with the current OECD/G20 Inclusive Framework on BEPS having more than 125 countries involved. Amongst these, many countries are developing countries and net capital importers. They are likely to have more of a say in the development of an international tax framework than has previously been the case and they would be keen to tax the demand side, rather than the supply side, of the market. It has been pointed out that it is important to distinguish between the market country as a source country (that is, where the

---

[169] Avi-Yonah, above n 82 at 11.
[170] Bruins, Einaudi, Seligman and Stamp, above n 25 at 40.

taxpayer has established a presence which goes beyond the supply of goods and services) as opposed to simply a market country as a destination country (where consumers purchasing goods and services give rise to taxing rights).[171]

(d) the role of NGOs and the general awareness of the public suggests that the amount of tax paid by multinational enterprises is a matter of significant political importance. It is politically acceptable to encourage multinational enterprises (MNEs) to pay their fair share and at the same time difficult to defend when such powerful and influential businesses pay little in local taxes. This is not just a matter of who bears the tax burden for the jurisdiction; it is a matter of competition. This is particularly true if the MNE operates in such a way as to pay little tax in the country of source and organise in order to pay little tax in the country of residence. Political pressure does not necessarily make for good tax policy but it would be naive to think that politicians will not consider public perception in working out their taxation settings.

1.7 Exploring the Limits of Domestic Source-Based Taxation

Several propositions have emerged from the earlier parts of this chapter. The first is that the fundamental position taken by countries in the historical allocation of taxing rights was simply an international compromise (the 1920s compromise) on the allocation of taxing rights.[172] This preserved the right of source countries to tax active business income but limited this right to circumstances where the non-resident entity had a permanent establishment threshold in the source country.

Secondly, the theoretical justification for tax, being based on the benefit theory, suggests that the source state:[173] (1) can substantiate its right to tax a non-resident entity where that entity is utilising and benefiting from public services, legal and technical infrastructure provided to the entity in the source state and (2) that this right to tax is not dependent upon the non-resident entity having a physical presence in the source state; there being no obvious reason for this physical requirement

---

[171] W Schon "10 Questions about Why and How to Tax the Digitalised Economy" (2018) 72 (4/5) BIT 278.

[172] See Section 1.3 "The History of International Double Taxation: The '1920s Compromise'".

[173] See Section 1.4 "Justifying Source and Residence Taxation".

other than the 1920s compromise and the way in which business was performed at the time of reaching that agreement and for a substantial period of perhaps ninety years afterwards.

The question now posed is whether, in a general way, domestic source-based taxation limits the right of states to exercise taxation. In other words, are there any conventions in law (international law, principles in either common law jurisdictions or civil law jurisdictions) which would suggest that a source state ought to be constrained in taxing non-residents?

1.7.1 The Purpose of Source Rules

As previously discussed (Section 1.2.2), source taxation is an integral part of the international tax framework. Non-resident entities are only subject to tax on income sourced from the source state. The definition of what is income sourced in a country therefore controls that country's taxation in respect of inbound investment. Source rules, whilst defining taxation for non-residents, are also important in the context of residence taxation. This is because most jurisdictions give a credit to the resident taxpayers for foreign taxes imposed on foreign sourced income. Usually these jurisdictions will not give a foreign tax credit in circumstances where foreign taxation has been imposed on locally sourced income. In other words, generally the foreign tax credit is available to offset against residence tax only when the foreign tax credit is attributed to foreign sourced income.[174]

1.7.2 Different Types of Source Rules: Specific or Formal Rules

(a) Formal Source Rules

There are fundamentally two different types of source rules in common law countries. The first type of rule is specific or sometimes described as "formal".[175] An example is the sourcing rule in some jurisdictions for determining the source of dividends. Many jurisdictions look simply to the residence of the paying company.[176] Wherever the payor is resident, that is the country of source for the dividend. This type of rule provides

---

[174] Avi-Yonah, above n 82 at 38–40.
[175] Ibid at 42.
[176] The United States and New Zealand are examples of this type of test. The New Zealand rule contained in section YD 4 (10) of the Income Tax Act 2007 (NZ) provides that

certainty and is relatively easy to administer because the country of source is also the same country in which the company paying the dividend is a resident. It should also be added that some countries do not follow this formal sourcing rule approach in respect of dividends but instead look to see where the company actually earned the income. In such circumstances, irrespective of the residence of the company, the dividend is deemed to have a source in the country in which the profits were derived. For example, an Atlantis resident company paying the dividend to shareholders when it had derived all its profits in Australia would be deemed to be paying an Australian sourced dividend.[177] The use of Atlantis as a fictional country to which no double tax treaty has been concluded is deliberate because, under the OECD Model tax convention, there is no sourcing rule for dividend income, but there is a prohibition contained in Article 10(5). This paragraph prohibits the state in which business is carried on from taxing dividends belonging to a resident of another state.[178]

There are numerous examples of these specific or formal sourcing rules found in different jurisdictions, and of course there are variations in different countries. In addition to dividends, interest is often sourced in the residence of the payor.[179] An alternative is a rule that looks to where the money has been lent.[180] Even if the money has been lent outside the jurisdiction, the source of the interest is linked to where the business activity of the borrower occurs.[181]

(b) Substantive Source Rules

The second type of rule attempts to trace the economic source of the income. Avi-Yonah refers to this type of rule as a substantive rule.[182]

"income derived from shares in, or membership of, a company resident in New Zealand has a source in New Zealand".

[177] Income Tax Assessment Act 1936 (Cth), s 44(1). This provides, inter alia, that dividends are assessable in Australia if a non-resident shareholder derives dividends paid to the shareholder by the company to the extent to which they are paid out of profits derived by it from sources in Australia.

[178] See the discussion on the section entitled D. Australia, in P Kaka "Source Taxation: Do We Really Know What We Mean?" (2017) Tax Notes Int'l 1221 at 1224.

[179] Avi-Yonah, above n 82 at 43. This is in reference to the US rule but the same is also true for the New Zealand sourcing rule.

[180] An example of this is the New Zealand interest income sourcing rule in section YD 4 (11) of the Income Tax Act 2007 (NZ).

[181] Ibid.

[182] Avi-Yonah, above n 82 at 44.

Active forms of income, such as business income or employment income, try to source income at the place where the activity which produces it occurs. This is often problematic because in contrast to the formal sourcing rules, the test seems to be resolved, first, on a case-by-case factual analysis and, secondly, in a very pragmatic way. Either way, the substantive rules are much less certain and require more judgement to be exercised by the taxpayer and the tax authority. The possibility for dispute is therefore much higher.

1.7.3 The Development of the Law in Common Law Countries

Consider how to determine the source of employment income. The critical matters to evaluate are the particular employment relationship and where the performance of duties actually occur. A state may have a test that says that employment income has a source in a country if it is "earned" in that country.[183] So what exactly does earned mean? Is it where the employment contract is concluded, the services performed or the payment made? Any of these factors could be more important than the others in any particular case. The decision of Barwick CJ in the High Court of Australia in *Federal Commissioner of Taxation v Mitchum*[184] explains the common law approach to such a substantive test:[185]

> The conclusion as to the source of income for the purposes of the Act is a conclusion of fact. There is no statutory definition of "source" to be applied, the matter being judged as one of practical reality. In each case, the relative weight to be given to the various factors which can be taken into consideration is to be determined by the tribunal entitled to draw the ultimate conclusion as to source. In my opinion, there are no presumptions and no rules of law which require that the question be resolved in any particular sense.

The two general principles emerging from this decision are: first, the test is a conclusion of fact to be determined by the appropriate tribunal; and secondly, the approach taken by the tribunal should be one where a practical person looks to determine the real source of income.

This second proposition, that the test is focused on where a practical person would look to determine the real source of income, suggests that in common law countries, source is not so much a legal concept but a

---

[183] For example, see Income Tax Act (NZ) 2007, Section YD 4(4).
[184] *Federal Commissioner of Taxation v Mitchum* (1965) 113 CLR 401 (HCA).
[185] Ibid at 407.

practical one (or at least the concepts are merged).[186] Porus Kaka, in an article based on his David R Tillinghast lecture on international taxation in 2016, traces the common law approach and examines the judicial origins of source in the United Kingdom, Australia, South Africa and pre-independence India and Pakistan.[187] The approach of these different jurisdictions bears a remarkable similarity, which is probably not surprising given the nature of the various courts and the similarity of the legal systems.

From the perspective of taxing cross-border business, the common law countries have returned time and again to the test of "something which a practical man would regard as a real source of income".[188] This test appears to have first emerged in the High Court of Australia's decision in *Nathan v Federal Commissioner of Taxation*.[189] In this decision an English company, which had its incorporation in England together with its central management and control, paid a dividend to Mr Nathan (an Australian resident). The question before the Court was whether these dividends were subject to tax in Australia on the basis of the Australian source rules (which as pointed out above, in referring to s 44(1) of the Income Tax Assessment Act 1936, under Australian law included dividends paid out of profits of that part of the business carried on by the UK company in Australia). At that point in time, Mr Nathan was not subject to tax in respect of these dividends on the basis of his Australian residency – if these were not Australian-sourced dividends, then they would not be subject to tax at all in Australia. Isaacs J delivered the unanimous judgment of the Court that these English company's dividends did have an Australian source. His famous dictum was as follows:[190]

> The Legislature in using the word "source" meant, not a legal concept, but something which a practical man would regard as a real source of income. Legal concepts must, of course, enter into the question when we have to consider to whom a given source belongs. But the ascertainment of the actual source of a given income as a practical, hard matter of fact.

---

[186] Kaka, above n 178 at 1223.
[187] Ibid at 1222–4. If he had included New Zealand as well, the result would have been consistent because the New Zealand Court of Appeal adopted the reasoning in the Privy Council decision of the Australian case *Nathan v Commissioner of Taxation* (1918) 25 CLR 183.
[188] Readers will find it strange to have the test phrased in this sexist way.
[189] *Nathan v Federal Commissioner of Taxation* (1918) 25 CLR 183 (HCA).
[190] Ibid at 189.

1.7 EXPLORING THE LIMITS OF TAXATION

In 1940 the Privy Council in *The Liquidator, Rhodesia Metals Limited v Commissioner of Taxes*[191] considered whether an English company which had purchased immovable property in Southern Rhodesia and subsequently sold the company's mining rights for a profit could be said to have derived that profit from Rhodesia. The question was whether this was a taxable amount "received by any person from any source within the Territory". The liquidator argued that the only source of the business's profit was in England because that was where the management and control of the company took place, where the contracts of purchase and sale were made, and where the sale proceeds were received. The Judicial Committee's judgment delivered by Lord Atkin rejected these submissions and held that the source of the income was in Rhodesia. They were influenced by two factors: (1) an earlier English case, *Sao Paulo (Brazilian) Railway Co Ltd v Carter*,[192] which had concluded that an English company could be taxed on the profits of its business earned from running a railway in Brazil and even more clearly that such sums were received from a source in Brazil and (2) the view expressed in the dissenting judgment of De Villiers JA in the Appellate Division of the South African Supreme Court (from which court the appeal was made to the Privy Council), who had effectively adopted exactly the same test of Isaacs J in the *Nathan* decision.[193] Given these two factors, Lord Atkin concluded:[194]

> The company never adventured any part of its capital except on that or those immovables. As a hard matter of fact the only proper conclusion appears to be that the company received the sum in question from a source within the Territory, viz, the mining claims which they had acquired and developed there for the very purpose of obtaining the particular receipt.

There are other appellate decisions which have adopted and applied this approach, leading to very similar conclusions. The appellate division of the Supreme Court of South Africa in *Commissioner for Inland Revenue v Lever Bros and Another*[195] and the New Zealand Court of

---

[191] *The Liquidator, Rhodesia Metals Limited (in Liquidation) v Commissioner of Taxes* 1940 AD 432 (PC) at 436.
[192] *Sao Paulo (Brazilian) Railway Co Ltd v Carter* [1896] AC 31.
[193] Using exactly the same words as Isaacs J, *The Liquidator, Rhodesia Metals Limited (in Liquidation) v Commissioner of Taxes* 1940 AD 432 (PC) at 436 at 441.
[194] Ibid.
[195] *Commissioner for Inland Revenue v Lever Bros and Another* (1946) AD 441.

Appeal in *Commissioner of Inland Revenue v NV Philips' Gloeilampenfabrieken*[196] are but two examples. In both cases the non-resident companies (English in the case of the *Lever Bros*, and Dutch in the case of *Philips'*) were successful in arguing that interest paid by a debtor located in South Africa and New Zealand, respectively, did not have a source (and so was not interest income sourced) in either of those two countries. Looking at the real substance of the facts with the eyes of a practical man apparently led to the conclusion that the source of interest income was from the provision of monies made by the English and Dutch companies.[197]

The "common thread running through all those judgments", as Kaka describes it,[198] is the concept of what a practical man would conclude is the source of the income irrespective of the legal analysis. This overarching principle was one of enormous pragmatism and suggests that there really is no limitation on the concept of source from the perspective of the common law.

1.7.4 Is There a Consistent View between Countries on the Concept of Source?

According to Vogel, many of the Germanic countries (i.e. Germany and Austria, with Switzerland following a similar approach, but through case law) allocated the source of business profits according to a single, comprehensive source rule.[199] As early as the end of the nineteenth century these countries used the permanent establishment concept to allocate business profits in both statutory and treaty law. Many other European countries followed the same general rule. The income attributable to the permanent establishment gives rise to a source of business income in the country where the permanent establishment is located on the deemed basis of it being an independent enterprise. Dividends, interest and royalties are considered business income in Central Europe, if connected to business activities, whereas in common law countries they usually have their own particular sourcing rules.[200]

---

[196] *Commissioner of Inland Revenue v NV Philips' Gloeilampenfabrieken* [1955] NZLR 868 (CA).

[197] As Porus Kaka notes in his article, the OECD now takes a contrary view with respect to sourcing so that interest is deemed to arise in a contracting state when the payer is a resident of that state. See Kaka, above n 178 at 1224.

[198] Ibid at 1224.

[199] Vogel, above n 68 at 226.

[200] Ibid at 227.

As can be seen, the Central European approach to the sourcing of business income suggests there is a greater alignment between domestic law and the approach taken in the OECD Model. The permanent establishment concept is therefore more significant in Europe with the connection between domestic source and DTAs. In contrast, the domestic law in common law countries is likely to have a broader scope in defining the source of income. Accordingly, in such jurisdictions the DTAs may provide more of a limitation on the ability of common law jurisdictions to tax business income.

Academic opinions are divided on whether there is a common view on what constitutes the source of business income. The fundamental nature of the question has led some commentators to doubt whether it is possible at all to determine the source of income. Klaus Vogel, for instance, suggested that it is "far from truth" to suggest that source is a "natural, self-defining concept",[201] and that a discussion on the preference of sourced-based taxation over residence-based taxation could "by no means ... be based on a common understanding of what is meant by "source"".[202] De Wilde agrees, saying that while "with some effort" we can determine who has derived or earned profit, it is much more difficult, "or perhaps even impossible", to answer the question of "where that profit is earned".[203] While it is true that "there are no universally accepted definitions of source",[204] it is relatively apparent that countries have not deviated much from an international norm. The absence of an ability to determine the source of income would advocate that countries would not have a common view of source, but largely they do.

Reuven Avi-Yonah argues that most source rules are part of customary international law, that they are similar and follow a relatively common global practice.[205] In other words, "they are rules that countries feel they have to follow because most other countries do so".[206] Yariv Brauner explains that in contrast to many rules in the international tax system, source rules apply only to cross-border transactions and that therefore "the result is that the international tax system of any country 'shares'

---

[201] Ibid at 223.
[202] Ibid at 229.
[203] de Wilde, above n 149 at 798.
[204] J Avery Jones and others "Tax Treaty Problems Relating to Source" (1998) 38 Eur Tax 78 at 79.
[205] Avi-Yonah, above n 82 at 63.
[206] Ibid.

some of its components with the purely domestic tax system".[207] After analysing source rules and different domestic jurisdictions, Brauner concludes:[208] "In conclusion, the source rules are close to being de facto harmonised already. Certain differences could be solved in a world tax regime, but most of them would not be relevant since they arise from the bilateral nature of the current regime." Even if the sourcing rules are de facto harmonised, which is contestable, this doesn't deal with the real problem – which is trying to quantify and identify the answer to the question "what is the income attributable to any source?"

Simply put, it seems very difficult to draw a clear connection between economic activities being carried on by an entity and the notion of the source of income. Hugh Ault has described it as follows:[209] "The idea that income has a locatable source seems to be taken for granted, but the source of income is not a well-defined economic idea." In the real world of taxation there is a need to focus on the transactions and activities of people and to allocate income accordingly. The problem, as Ault points out, is that there is little theoretical guidance on what the appropriate economic outcome should be in terms of the appropriate allocation of income. He suggests that the existing international rules might be more influenced by factors involving administration and enforceability than any economic principles. Vogel describes the connection as vague or ambiguous, linking the source of income "in some way or other" to the production of income, or to the creation of value for goods.[210] He believes that the type of connection that establishes the source of income cannot be defined in a general sense.

All of this is not very helpful, as not only does it appear difficult, if not impossible, to establish a common understanding of what is meant by source, then allocating appropriate amounts of income becomes a second and equally difficult hurdle to overcome.

1.7.5 Conclusion

From the foregoing, it is possible to postulate that there is little practical limitation on the concept of source for business income. It is true that

---

[207] Y Brauner "An International Tax Regime in Crystallisation" (2003) 56 Tax L Rev 259 at 266.
[208] Ibid at 282.
[209] H Ault "Some Reflections on the OECD and the Sources of International Tax Principles" (2013) 70(12) Tax Notes Int'l 1195 at 1200.
[210] Vogel, above n 68 at 223.

there are common conventions which might prevent overreach and which in the eyes of some analysts support the view that there are customary international law limitations on the concept of source. Older case law supports a pragmatic approach, particularly in common law countries, which says that the source of income is that which an ordinary person would regard as a real source of income. Therefore, it is also true that "a state's only real limitation on another state's tax reach is its enforcement competence".[211]

For many countries, this latter principle, that domestic taxing rights are sovereign unless constrained by international agreements, may be the dominant feature in the international tax landscape. This is particularly concerning unless a sensible, long-term multilateral solution can be found in terms of an international allocation of taxation rights which would enable a new framework to be established.

1.8 Base Erosion and Profit Shifting and the Emerging Threat of Digitalisation in Business

As described in the introductory section of this book, international taxation has been in a maelstrom of change in the last decade. Originally this was driven by a variety of aggressive tax planning techniques and countries entering into, or permitting, tax competition between themselves. The Action Plan on Base Erosion and Profit Shifting (BEPS), and the BEPS package itself consisting of fifteen action points was agreed to by all OECD and G20 countries in November 2015. The BEPS package is designed to achieve certain fundamental changes in behaviour from both countries and multinational enterprises, including:

- competition on the basis of a lack of transparency;
- the artificial location of profit where there is little or no economic activity;
- the exploitation of loopholes or differences in countries' tax systems (cross-border arbitration).

A multilateral forum, the OECD/G20 Inclusive Framework, has been established, with more than 130 countries representing over 95 per cent of global GDP. There has been much progress made in a remarkably short period of time.

---

[211] Kaka, above n 178 at 1234.

Notwithstanding all these cooperative and multilateral actions, the tax challenges of the digitalisation of the economy have been identified as one of the key foci of the BEPS Action Plan.[212] The Action 1 Report includes two key conclusions:

- that the whole world economy is digitalising, and it is difficult, if not impossible, to ring-fence the digital economy; and
- beyond BEPS (and aggressive tax planning), the digitalisation of the economy raises a number of challenges relating to the question of the allocation between countries of taxing rights.

This chapter began by describing the key characteristics of cross-border taxation. The majority of countries around the world operate hybrid systems involving the taxation of their residents (sometimes on worldwide income but sometimes not) and non-residents on income which has a source in their jurisdiction. In order to lay some foundational groundwork for the later examination of the taxation of digitalised business, the history of the original 1920s compromise was discussed in order to establish the arbitrary nature of the framework and, in part, to try and understand why it has been so outstandingly successful for such a long period of time.

The next part of the chapter looked at the fundamental question of how we justify taxation. The particular focus, in the context of cross-border taxation and trade, was on the taxation of non-residents doing business in a country. The benefit theory suggests that a modification to the 1920s compromise can be justified to expand the taxing rights of multinational enterprises in the digital age. This is also supported by the absence of any constraints in domestic source taxation.

We next examine the key characteristics of digital businesses in order to establish how they work and why they pose such a challenge to the international tax system.

---

[212] *Addressing the Tax Challenges of the Digital Economy, Action 1-2015 Final Report* (OECD/G20 Base Erosion and Profit Shifting Project, 2015).

2

The Development of Digital Business

2.1 The Dynamic Information Age

2.1.1 A Background of Constant Change

Prior to analysing the key features and new business models of the digital economy, it is important to briefly reflect on the enormous changes that are occurring in the information age. Rapid technological progress in the area of information and communication technology have dominated a cycle of innovation, market growth, competition and, in turn, reduced costs to consumers. Products become successful, are copied by competitors and then compete on cost unless the original producer can somehow differentiate its product through special features or bundling with other components.[213] Digitalisation is an important source of entrepreneurship, has created new efficiencies and is constantly improving productivity.[214] Many observations can be made about the consequences of the digitalisation of the economy, but two key conclusions stand out:

- there are enormous welfare-enhancing benefits from these changes and
- it is not possible to ring-fence the digital economy from the rest of the economy.

(a) The Huge Benefits Arising from Digitalisation

It is an important point that digitalisation has been driving and will continue to drive welfare-enhancing changes in virtually every country's economy. These benefits can be listed as follows:[215]

---

[213] OECD *Addressing the Tax Challenges of the Digital Economy, Action 1 – 2015 Final Panel Report* (OECD Publishing, 2015) at 3.1.
[214] OECD *Tax Challenges Arising from Digitalisation – Interim Report 2018: Inclusive Framework on BEPS* (OECD Publishing, 2018) at 1.2.
[215] Australian Government *The Digital Economy and Australia's Corporate Tax System* (Treasury of Australia, October 2018) at 1.2.

- *Productivity:* Digitalisation has allowed consumers and businesses to do more with less.[216] Social media allows for instant communication. Digital books and music reduce the costs of goods and services. Evidence suggests that there are sizeable potential productivity gains, such as output and productivity increases, improving data quality and access to data, and lower costs.[217] The Digital Agenda for Europe estimated in 2014 that half of all productivity growth derives from investment in Information and Communications Technology (ICT).[218]
- *Competition:* Digital disruption has led to increased competition in certain markets, lowering barriers to entry and more broadly affecting the business environment by bringing down transaction costs and increasing price transparency,[219] benefiting consumers where incumbents had previously used market power to charge high prices or provide consumers with poor service.[220]
- *Choice and convenience:* Digitalisation and globalisation have expanded the range of goods and services that consumers and businesses can access.
- *Innovation:* The new ways of interacting and doing business have provided significant cost savings in communication but also in many other areas. For example, technology has enabled the use of the sharing economy to reduce the cost of short distance transportation and accommodation, whilst competition from digital means of payment have encouraged banks to improve the quality of their services, driving the introduction of virtually instantaneous transfers and contactless card payments.[221]
- *Profitability:* Entities operating in the area of technology, media and telecommunications (TMT) have taken advantage of advances in digital technology which open new markets, stimulate growth and provide opportunities for companies that seize leadership positions to capture enormous value. McKinsey & Company's research on 2,400 publicly traded companies around the world suggests that the

---

[216] International Monetary Fund *Measuring the Digital Economy* (International Monetary Fund, April 2018) at 32.
[217] OECD, above n 214 at 1.1, see box 1.1 which details selected productivity enhancements.
[218] European Commission *Expert Group on Taxation of the Digital Economy Working Paper: Digital Economy – Facts and Figures* (European Commission, March 2014) at 1.2.
[219] OECD, above n 214 at 1.2.
[220] Australian Government, above n 215 at 1.2.
[221] Ibid at 1.2.

economic growth generated by TMT companies grew a hundredfold, or by US$200 billion, from 2000 to 2014.[222]

Change is not always positive. Rapid growth and the dramatic change in business models has led to significant disruption for existing or traditional businesses. The digital transformation is also raising issues beyond commerce, changing the way we interact with each other and highlighting a number of concerning issues in privacy, security, education, health, jobs and skills as well as taxation.[223]

(b) The Difficulty of Separating the Digital Economy from the Rest of the Economy

A key conclusion from the OECD's work is that "because the digital economy is increasingly becoming the economy itself, it would be difficult, if not impossible, to ring-fence the digital economy from the rest of the economy for tax purposes".[224] This conclusion is supported by the International Monetary Fund, which says:[225]

> The "digital economy" is sometimes defined narrowly as online platforms, and activities that owe their existence to such platforms, yet, in a broad sense, all activities that use digitalised data are part of the digital economy: in modern economies, the entire economy. If defined by use of digital data, the digital economy could encompass an enormous, diffuse part of most economies, ranging from agriculture to R&D.

The OECD's 2015 and 2018 reports identify a number of important features of digitalisation which are potentially relevant from a tax perspective.[226] These include mobility, reliance on data, network effects, the spread of multi-sided business models, a tendency towards monopoly or oligopoly and volatility. The use of business models involving varieties of e-commerce, app stores, online advertising, cloud computing, participative network platforms, high-speed trading and online payment services are now commonplace, while the OECD has observed that some

---

[222] Tushar Bhatia, Mohsin Imtiaz, Eric Kutcher and Dilip Wagle "How Tech Giants Deliver Outsize Returns – and What It Means for the Rest of Us" (September 2017) McKinsey & Company, <www.mckinsey.com/industries/technology-media-and-telecommunications/our-insights/how-tech-giants-deliver-outsized-returns-and-what-it-means-for-the-rest-of-us>.
[223] OECD, above n 214 at 1.2.
[224] OECD, above n 213 at 11.
[225] International Monetary Fund, above n 216 at 6.
[226] Ibid at 7, and OECD, above n 214 at 1.3.2.

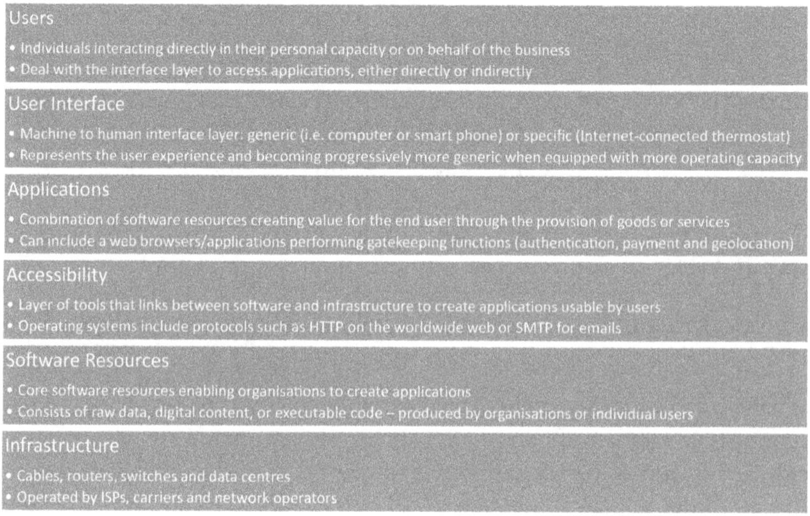

Users
- Individuals interacting directly in their personal capacity or on behalf of the business
- Deal with the interface layer to access applications, either directly or indirectly

User Interface
- Machine to human interface layer: generic (i.e. computer or smart phone) or specific (Internet-connected thermostat)
- Represents the user experience and becoming progressively more generic when equipped with more operating capacity

Applications
- Combination of software resources creating value for the end user through the provision of goods or services
- Can include a web browsers/applications performing gatekeeping functions (authentication, payment and geolocation)

Accessibility
- Layer of tools that links between software and infrastructure to create applications usable by users
- Operating systems include protocols such as HTTP on the worldwide web or SMTP for emails

Software Resources
- Core software resources enabling organisations to create applications
- Consists of raw data, digital content, or executable code – produced by organisations or individual users

Infrastructure
- Cables, routers, switches and data centres
- Operated by ISPs, carriers and network operators

Figure 2.1 The conceptual view of the layers in information and communication technology

phenomena such as the collection and exploitation of data, network effects and the emergence of new business models such as multi-sided platforms are exacerbating the challenges to the existing tax rules.

(c) The Relationship of Technology, Software and Users

In the OECD's 2015 Final Report on Action 1, *Addressing the Tax Challenges of the Digital Economy*, a conceptual diagram laid out how (at that time) different layers of integrated hardware and software worked together in order to provide the key components of information and communication technology at the heart of the digital economy.[227]

Figure 2.1 illustrates this relationship, which involves the transfer of information between the different levels or strata.[228] At the top sits the users (sometimes providing content or just transacting through the use of the Internet). The next conceptual level is that of the machine-to-human interface layer, known as the "user experience". Usually, this is through a device such as a computer, smartphone or tablet. The third level down is

---
[227] OECD, above n 214 at figure 3.1.
[228] OECD, above n 213 at [99–108].

that of the applications. An application is a combination of software resources creating value for the end-user through the provision of goods or services.

The application utilises accessibility, the structure necessary for software applications to take advantage of the underlying infrastructure and core software resources of the Internet. The next level down are these software resources, stored on servers that are located in data centres and organisations all around the world, enabling organisations to create applications and consisting of raw data, digital content or executable code. Finally, there exists a base infrastructure of the Internet. This consists of the cables, tubes, routers, switches and data centres that are designed and manufactured by firms specialised in network interconnection, operated by ISPs, carriers and network operators.

(d) The Conceptual View of the Layers in Information and Communication Technology

Even though this conceptual representation was produced in 2015 it already seems dated. The world has seen phenomenal growth in the use of personal computing devices – with a trend towards diversified and more specialist devices (from personal computers to smartphones, tablets and integrated devices in household appliances such as TVs, fridges and cars).

Significant changes have occurred in all areas of information and communication technology, such as telecommunication networks, software, the use of content (which includes copyrighted content produced by professionals, enterprise-generated content and non-copyrighted user-generated content, such as consumer reviews or comments on online forums). Businesses (and governments) have access to substantial amounts of data, much of which is personal and which is used for a variety of different purposes such as customising the experience of the user and generating productivity and efficiency. Personal data may be acquired voluntarily (for example, when a user registers for an online service and discloses hobbies, interests, preferences and expertise) or by observation (by recording Internet-browsing activities and location data showing shopping habits or interests), or by inference (by observing and analysing online activities to enable databases to be built such as credit ratings).[229] The capacity to collect useful data is increasing as the number

---

[229] OECD, above n 214 at 3.1.5.

of Internet-connected devices rises and increasingly sophisticated techniques are being developed to process and analyse this collected data. The consequence of standardising and commoditising resources, including hardware, network infrastructure and software, enables some businesses to combine these resources and make them available through the Internet as services. The Internet has accelerated a transition from traditional software business (goods) to XaaS ("X as a Service") models. Such models are based on the fact that a website is essentially a software application providing a service delivered over the Internet (rather than locally or on-site). Many business to consumer ("B2C") applications are delivered as software, as a service such as search engines and social networking applications provided through a web browser without the need to download any executable code beforehand. Integral to the ability to connect individuals, content and things in everyday lives are powerful software-powered processes whose resources are stored and executed in the cloud.

Cloud computing is a general term that is better divided into three categories: Infrastructure as a Service ("IaaS") – where big players like Amazon and Google rent out immense computing infrastructure to other companies; Platform as a Service ("PaaS") – online spaces where developers create online applications for specific sets of users; and Software as a Service ("SaaS") – where clients use software over the Internet.

At its heart, cloud computing involves using the power of the Internet to outsource tasks you might traditionally perform on a personal computer – anything from handling simple storage to complex development and processing – to a vast and powerful remote network of interconnected machines. This has the potential to disrupt entire business models because it permits new approaches that don't require significant hardware whilst encouraging mobility and flexibility. McKinsey Global Institute estimates that the total potential economic impact for Cloud technology could be US$1.7–US$6.2 trillion in the form of surpluses from the use of cloud-enabled Internet services and US$500–700 billion from productivity improvements for enterprise ICT.[230]

(e) Further Developments

The ability to use the Internet to connect any smart device or object to a network is enabling the "Internet of Things" ("IoT"). The term refers to a series of components of equal importance including machine-to-machine

---

[230] McKinsey Global Institute *Disruptive Technologies: Advances That Will Transform Life, Business, and the Global Economy* (McKinsey & Company, May 2013) at 51.

communication, cloud computing, big data analysis, sensors and actuators, combining to further developments in machine learning and remote control.[231] According to Ericsson, around 29 billion connected devices are forecast by 2022, of which around 18 billion will be related to IoT.[232] Mobile phones are already expected to be surpassed in numbers by IoT devices, which include connected cars, machines, meters, wearables and other consumer electronics.

While digitalisation has already dramatically reduced the cost of interacting with others from a distance, it is important to recognise that it is still at quite an early stage. Some sectors of the economy, such as advertising, retail, media and transport, have been disrupted but others, including asset-intensive industries, have generally been slower to adopt digital technologies.[233] Existing digital businesses rely on Internet, computers and smartphones but future technologies involving blockchain, cryptocurrencies, augmented virtual reality, 3D printing, artificial intelligence and machine learning mean change will continue at an even faster rate.[234]

From this rather broad conceptual description, it is now possible to move to discuss in greater detail the digitalisation of the economy with particular emphasis on its market dynamics, business models and key features. This understanding will assist us in identifying why the existing tax rules are proving problematic and what potential solutions might look like.

2.2 The Defining Characteristics of Digital Markets

2.2.1 Understanding the Features of Digital Markets

In the view of the OECD, certain characteristics have become increasingly important in the way in which firms do business and have led to a structural transformation of the economy. These characteristics are not unique to the digital economy and while they are also found in the conventional business world, it is the prevalence of these features in the digital economy which

---

[231] OECD, above n 214 at 3.2.1.
[232] Ericsson "Internet of Things Forecast", <www.ericsson.com/en/mobility-report/internet-of-things-forecast>.
[233] Simon Blackburn and others *Digital Australia: Seizing the Opportunity from the Fourth Industrial Revolution* (McKinsey & Company, March 2017) at 19.
[234] Australian Government, above n 215 at 1.2

defines them as being relevant. There is widespread consensus on some defining characteristics of digital markets, which are as follows:[235]

- *Direct network effects:* In digital markets, consumers benefit from the number of other participants in the market. The larger the network, the greater the benefit to the end-user. For example, social media and its associated messaging services. Any individual has greater utility when a larger number of family and friends are part of the network. Another example is an online marketplace. A vendor (or a purchaser) benefits from the largest number of potential people to transact with.
- *Indirect network effects:* Indirect network effects arise where a multi-sided market exists. Take an online platform and the group of users who interact with the social network. This specific group of end-users benefit, mostly socially, from interacting with each other. But another group of participants also benefit from interacting with this group of end-users, namely advertisers who provide advertisements (sometimes targeted depending on the end-users' preferences, which are analysed using data voluntarily provided or otherwise extracted). The utility to one group of users increases with the size of the other group of users. An increasing number of platform-based businesses exist which utilise the multi-sided nature of the platform to advertise goods and services or otherwise generate revenue.
- *Economies of scale and mobility:* Often the production of digital goods and services involve significant upfront costs and then lower variable costs. A good example of this is software development. Once the initial (often considerable) investment in human labour and infrastructure is made, the costs of maintenance, distribution and sales are quite low. The digital economy allows a digital product to be replicated at almost no cost.[236] In addition to reducing the costs of doing business, geographic mobility is dramatically enhanced in the digital economy, enabling companies to operate in markets anywhere in the world[237] and exposing local markets and firms to additional multinational competition.[238] Due to the ability to distribute globally using the Internet, the combination of low marginal cost and very large potential

---

[235] OECD, above n 214 at 2.2.
[236] European Commission, above n 218 at 1.1.1.
[237] Ibid at 1.1.1.
[238] International Monetary Fund, above n 216 at 6.

markets allow the possibility for a significant market position to be taken by a dominant firm with the potential for very high profitability.
- *Switching costs and lock-in effects:* Often end-user devices use different operating systems (android or iPhone for example) and a customer may be substantially locked into a particular system. Part of this is psychological as well as driven by the costs of change. In addition, membership of a social media or other platform may be viewed as "hard to change" because of the amount of information, number of contacts and other data stored with the provider.
- *The importance of data:* In addition to driving down the cost of collecting, storing and analysing data, many market transactions can be analysed to determine consumer behaviour. Web clicks, online purchases, search engine entries, peer reviews of products and services all contribute to the accumulation of huge amounts of data which can be analysed in order to target products and services to individual consumers.[239]
- *Complementarity:* Many of the goods and services are complementary to each other. A customer will find their utility from using their laptop or smartphone is enhanced with a number of useful applications.

The OECD notes that if single firms become large enough to influence market prices then they can become price makers as opposed to price takers.[240] On the other hand, it has been observed that it is possible for new entrants to replace an incumbent firm in a relatively short time by offering a qualitatively superior good or service. It is possible to think back in the past to search engines and web browsers which have become less popular or significant than other more recent rivals and this demonstrates the point (for example, Yahoo no longer holds the market position it once did).

The features of the digital economy that seem most significant are:

- a global marketplace (which can hugely expand the customer base while at the same time making the assignment of activities to jurisdictions more complex);
- low marginal costs for sales and distribution;
- the marketplace consequences and significant positive externalities of both direct and indirect networks (which can give almost monopolistic power to some platforms when they achieve critical mass);

---

[239] European Commission, above n 218 at 1.1.3.
[240] OECD, above n 214 at 2.2.

- multi-sided markets, where platforms are used to connect different groups of people and where pricing strategies on different sides of the platform are connected but can be adjusted and
- the cheap collection of data (uploaded by users and analysed and used as inputs to generate profit).

Together, in combination, these features have enabled some firms to gain a significant competitive advantage and, effectively, dominate markets.[241]

2.2.2 New Business Models

As a result of these features, transactions between end-users can be concluded in real time and information can be exchanged provided devices are connected to the Internet. This leads to faster dissemination, immediate settlement, faster circulation with greater information and more accurate targeting of customers. These structural changes have led to the development of new business models and the transformation of older ones.

The variety and types of digital business models operating are bewildering. For a start, they might operate on a variety of different payment models. Netflix uses a subscription model. Facebook, Instagram, Google and Twitter operate under a free model. Some businesses in the sharing economy allow a payment to access the benefit of use, such as Airbnb. As previously discussed (Section 2.2.1), it is common to find an interdependent suite of products and services that increase in value to the consumer depending on the number owned (Apple users stay with Apple products/services). Many businesses use the immediacy of digital technology to connect users who want a service and have money to those who have the need for money and the time to perform the service. Thus a company like Uber takes advantage of an on-demand model to generate value to themselves, their customers and their drivers. A popular business model is the "freemium pricing" model employed by companies like LinkedIn. Users get a basic version of the product/service and pay to upgrade.[242] The mechanism for payment (or monetising the digitalised business), however, does not tell us the

---

[241] Justus Haucap and Ulrich Heimeshoff *Google, Facebook, Amazon, eBay: Is the Internet Driving Competition or Market Monopolization?* (Heinrich-Heine-Universitat Dusseldorf, Dusseldorf Institute for Competition Economics, January 2013); they concluded that a more interventionist approach beyond the application of general competition rules appeared unwarranted at the time they were writing.

[242] Warren Knight "7 Business Models of Digital Disruption" (8 May 2018) <https://warren-knight.com/2018/05/08/7-business-models-digital-disruption/>.

2.2 CHARACTERISTICS OF DIGITAL MARKETS

type of business. The payment mechanism may be dependent on the type of business but it does not determine the form of the business.

A huge number of businesses around the world use websites, applications or similar interfaces to sell their products and services to customers but that is not the focus here. The platform for business can be organised in fundamentally different ways involving different groups of people. Most of these digitalised businesses have managed to create and scale successful platforms that had benefited from both direct (the advantage of having a large network cohort) and indirect (involving the creation of complementary products or services and usually on the other side of the multi-sided platform such as advertisers) network effects.[243] The OECD (in 2015) provided an illustrative list of these various business models, but it conceded that the list was both incomplete and overlapping.[244]

In the OECD's 2018 publication[245] it listed four *types* of new business models and the classification is very helpful in order to understand the basis of transactions and then to analyse the tax implications. The categories were drawn from a Harvard Business School working paper by A Hagiu and J Wright.[246]

The OECD notes that the categorisation is of a particular business model and not a company. Amazon Marketplace belongs to one category while Amazon e-commerce belongs to another.[247] The largest companies frequently have more than one business line and use more than one business model type. There are four types of significant business models in digital markets. They are:

(a) *multi-sided platforms:* These are the types of businesses described below, being platforms that allow end-users to transact with each other, leaving key control rights and obligations with the supplier end-user (rather than the platform).

---

[243] Tushar Bhatia and others "How Tech Giants Deliver Outsized Returns – and What It Means for the Rest of Us" (September 2017) <www.mckinsey.com/industries/technology-media-and-telecommunications/our-insights/how-tech-giants-deliver-outsized-returns-and-what-it-means-for-the-rest-of-us>.

[244] OECD, above n 213 at 4.2 at [116]. This includes electronic commerce, business-to-business models, business-to-consumer models, consumer-to-consumer models, payment services, app stores, online advertising, cloud computing, high-frequency trading and participative network platforms.

[245] OECD, above n 214 at 2.2.2.

[246] Andrei Hagiu and Julian Wright *Multi-Sided Platforms* (Harvard Business School, 16 March 2015).

[247] OECD, above n 214 at 2.2.2.

It is possible to segregate this category into two subcategories; namely:

- **a multi-sided marketplace platform for goods and services delivered both online and off-market.** Examples of businesses that use this type of multi-sided platform are Uber, Airbnb, Hotels.com, Bookings.com, eBay, and Amazon Marketplace, amongst many others.
- **a multi-sided platform where the end-users deal primarily with themselves**, but receive advertisements and other invitations which are sometimes targeted based on data that they have voluntarily supplied. Examples of these businesses are Google, Facebook and LinkedIn.

(b) *resellers:* These are businesses that acquire products and services from suppliers and resell them to buyers, controlling the price and assuming liability towards the customers. Examples of these businesses are Amazon Retail, Alibaba, Spotify and Netflix (where it purchases content).

(c) *vertically integrated firms:* These are businesses that have acquired ownership over their suppliers, and therefore have integrated the supply chain within their own companies. Examples of these firms are Netflix (where it produces its content), and Huawei (hardware and cloud computing).

(d) *input suppliers:* These are businesses that supply (as intermediaries) the inputs required for a production process of goods or services in another firm. They interact only with the other firm and not with the final customer. An example is Intel, the semiconductor chip manufacturer.

2.3 Doing Business Using a Multi-sided Platform

One of the most important changes brought about through digitalisation is the increase of importance of multi-sided markets.

2.3.1 What Are Multi-sided Markets?

All of us are very used to single-sided markets. A bakery sells bread, cakes and other baked products. It has a defined market and usually a defined location where it sells its product. The consumers go to the bakery to buy its products, not hardware or electronic goods.

2.3 BUSINESS USING A MULTI-SIDED PLATFORM 69

We are also very used to multi-sided markets. They are part of the old-economy industries as well as the new digital-economy businesses.[248] A newspaper is a good example, or television, whose firms provide their product to inform or entertain while at the same time displaying advertisements from another group of suppliers who wish to target the audience of readers or viewers. The structural changes referred to above (Section 2.2.1) have led to the emergence of new firms that utilise all of the features and benefits of multi-sided markets. In particular, as a result of digitalisation, businesses can quickly and cheaply communicate with the global base of suppliers, users and customers. They can also establish user networks across different jurisdictions through websites, online platforms and mobile applications.[249]

A multi-sided platform provides a way for two or more types of participants to get together. It is called a platform because it is a base which typically operates on a physical or virtual basis and each side of the platform consists of participants who can use the platform to connect. An example of a physical platform is a shopping mall. On the one side are the different stores, and on the other the shoppers. A ride-sharing app, such as Uber, is a virtual platform using cloud-based software and accessed through Internet-connected mobile phones. It matches up drivers and passengers who are the participants on the two sides.[250] Multi-sided platforms sell participants in each group access to the participants in the other group, and this means that the customers are very important to the platform service. Take the shopping mall example and consider what will make it successful. The mall will recruit a diverse and attractive range of shops in order to encourage shoppers to come and shop. On this platform (the mall) stores get access to shoppers and shoppers get access to stores.[251]

There is much debate about exactly what a multi-sided market is: the OECD defines it as the joint presence of two characteristics;

---

[248] David Evans and Richard Schmalensee *The Industrial Organization of Markets with Two-Sided Platforms* (National Bureau of Economic Research, Working Paper 11603, September 2005).
[249] OECD, above n 214 at 2.2.1.
[250] David Evans *Multisided Platforms, Dynamic Competition, and the Assessment of Market Power for Internet-Based Firms* (Coase-Sandor Institute for Law and Economics, No 753, March 2016).
[251] Ibid at 8.

(1) an indirect network externality and (2) a non-neutral pricing strategy.[252]

The indirect network externality occurs when a specific group of end-users benefit from interacting with another group of end-users on the same platform. The larger the group of end-users who are on Facebook enjoying social networking, the greater the utility of advertisers (the other group of end-users) as they have more people to advertise to. Both types of end-users indirectly benefit if there are more end-users on the other side of the market: more advertisers can supply relevant advertising to the social networking group (or a lesser number of advertisements for the same revenue stream because the distribution is greater). In this situation, the online platforms provide intermediation services across the different sides of a digital market and the success of the business model relies on reaching a critical mass of end-users on both sides of the market. A key feature is the ability of the platform to adapt its pricing structure by levying different membership and usage fees on each side of the market. In the case of the social networking group, this is free while the advertisers pay. The business operates simply by collecting revenue from the advertisers, while the social networkers enjoy their interaction on a seemingly costless basis.

The non-neutral pricing structure is the second characteristic of the multi-sided platform. Optimal prices can be set below the marginal cost of provision on one market side while the other side is subsidising. This enables end-users with lower-priced elasticities to be overcharged and those with high price elasticities not to be charged at all (or at a subsidised rate). Consequently, on one side of the market you see barter transactions arising whereby valuable inputs such as user data and user-generated content are traded for a free service on the social networking platform, email service or media providers. The platform operator (the social networking firm) will extract data from users (and their transactions) and then sell services (such as advertising) based on that data to the other side of the market. The best example of this transaction with the other side of the market is the sale of customer-targeted advertisements. The OECD suggests this feature, of indirect network externalities affecting the price structures across market sides, is part of the multi-sided definition.[253]

---

[252] OECD, above n 214 at 2.2.1.
[253] Ibid at 2.2.

Another definition of what constitutes a multi-sided platform is provided in a Harvard Business School working paper by A Hagiu and J Wright, as follows:[254]

- they enable direct interactions between two or more distinct sides; and
- each side is affiliated with the platform.

The nuance to the OECD definition that is provided by these academics is the use of the term "direct interaction". What they mean by that is that two or more distinct sides retain control over the key terms of the transaction. In the case of trading, this could be the pricing, bundling, marketing and delivery of the goods or services traded, the ability to determine the nature and quality of services offered, the terms and conditions etc., with the other side of the platform. A platform might facilitate those people who want to rent out their house and, at the same time, offer accommodation to those who want to rent. Under the Harvard Business School definition it is significant that the pricing of the rental is originally set and controlled by the homeowner and then negotiated with the renter. Direct interactions between the multiple sides therefore sets multi-sided platforms apart from resellers (where the platform purchases goods from the vendor on one side and then resells them to the purchaser on the other side). In the reseller situation, the two (or more) sides of the platform do not have a direct interaction or negotiation with each other.

By "affiliation", Hagiu and Wright mean that the users on each side consciously make platform-specific investments that are necessary in order for them to be able to deal directly with each other. This could include a fee, expenditure on resources (including spending time and money on learning how to transact on the platform) or an opportunity cost. Affiliation helps to distinguish multi-sided platforms from a supplier (the business model is better known as an "input supplier") of goods or services. Take, for example, a law firm, which gathers the input of its lawyers (whom it employs) and then delivers legal advice to its clients. Although clients deal directly with the lawyers, there is no affiliation between the employees or the clients with the firm of the kind contemplated above. For completeness, neither is there a direct interaction. Lawyers negotiating key terms of the service, such as fees, do so on behalf of the firm and not in their personal capacity.

---

[254] Andrei Hagiu and Julian Wright *Multi-Sided Platforms* (Harvard Business School, 16 March 2015).

Although multi-sided platforms have been a feature of different kinds of business in the past (such as advertisements in newspapers), digital market platforms have provided the infrastructure to enable an enormous, burgeoning use of the business structure in the information age.

2.3.2 Multi-sided Marketplace Business Models

In the simplified diagram shown in Figure 2.2 you can see some of the key features of the multi-sided marketplace business model. The two user groups, which might be vendors and purchasers for either goods or services (perhaps for second-hand goods on a peer-to-peer trading exchange) deal directly with each other. The vendors pay a commission to the trading platform. The direct interaction between the two user groups enables them to set the price and any other terms (such as timing, payment and delivery).

There are many different variations to this basic model but the key elements remain the same. The various platform business models were analysed and presented in a paper by Täuscher and Laudien.[255] This study analysed a sample of digital marketplace business models in a quantitative and qualitative way. It identified six main clusters or types of marketplace business models and concluded that the sample firms provided value through efficiency and cost savings while generating revenue mostly through commission fees, subscription fees, listing and advertising fees. The six main types of marketplace business models were as follows (grouped into four main categories):

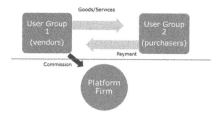

Figure 2.2 Multi-sided marketplace business models

[255] Karl Täuscher and Sven Laudien "Understanding Platform Business Models: A Mixed Methods Study of Marketplaces" (2016) Euro Mgmt Journal 319.

1 Platforms that are marketplaces for physical products
   - *Marketplaces for physical products involving mostly consumer-to-consumer transactions:* The majority (two-thirds of the group) were firms that facilitated transactions between individuals selling physical goods between each other. The platform firm (by a two-thirds majority) generated their income from commissions, the others by subscriptions (charged to the seller side for additional services, increased visibility or access to customer data).[256] Firms like eBay were originally founded on this business model. Together with eBay, Amazon and Alibaba are also examples of such business models which have moved into the second category (providing a marketplace for businesses to sell to consumers while making a commission charged to the vendor).
   - *Marketplaces for physical products involving mostly business-to-consumer transactions:* The majority of firms were targeting suppliers in a particular area or industry and customers who shared a passion for a certain product type – for example, collectibles or art products (firms like Artsy). The marketplace firms all charged the sellers, with the vast majority being on a commission basis and a small minority on a subscription model.
2 Platforms that are marketplaces for digital products
   - *This marketplace primarily caters to an active community of like-minded people described as a "digital product community".*[257] The majority of firms in this marketplace charge a commission fee. Examples of the firms in this cluster is the self-publishing firm Sellfy, which allows the creators of a variety of digital content to sell e-books, videos, audio and music. These platforms, which have the highest share of globally operating marketplaces, build a community of independent authors, musicians and designers that actively maintain a social network profile and interact directly with buyers.
3 Platforms that are marketplaces for digital services
   - *Marketplaces for online services:* The largest marketplace group, it tends to focus on one specific market segment (skills such as language tutoring or video-based courses, and professional services like divorce attorneys and financial advisers). The remuneration system

---

[256] Ibid at 324.
[257] Ibid at 324.

is different here in that the majority of marketplace firms set a fixed price, leading Täuscher and Laudien to the conclusion that these services are commodified to a certain extent.[258]

4 Platforms that are marketplaces for services delivered offline

- *Marketplaces that match service firms with consumers:* As opposed to the preceding group, the services are delivered offline. These are things like hairdressing, tourist activities which might require an appointment, or some other form of capacity management such as shipping or construction. The marketplace firm charges a commission fee from sellers, while buyers mostly use the marketplace for free. This cluster has the highest percentage of firms that provide reviews of sellers. Given the location dependence associated with the provision of offline service, the firms mostly focus on one geographic market and one market segment.

- *Marketplaces that match individual provision of service to consumers:* Described as a peer-to-peer exchange of services, this might involve individuals sharing their physical resources (such as accommodation like Airbnb) or their time and resources (a good example is Wag!, a platform that matches dog walkers to dog owners). These firms provide a novel source of income on the supply side, and create value to the buyer side through an increase in transaction efficiency. The firms often offer a review system to generate trust between the users. Revenue streams are predominantly generated by commission fees, including fixed fees. Although more than half the firms generate revenue from the seller, the firms that charge buyers are the highest number amongst all the clusters.

At the risk of generalising, in these six types of marketplace transactions, the firm is selling their services. They are providing the marketplace and introducing vendors to purchasers and primarily receiving commission for performing that role.

2.3.3 Using Multi-sided Business Platforms in Other Ways to Generate Revenue

There are, broadly, two other ways in which a digital firm generates revenues. They can sell information about consumers (for example, in

---

[258] Ibid at 326.

2.3 BUSINESS USING A MULTI-SIDED PLATFORM 75

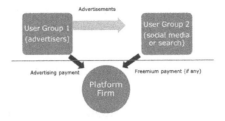

Figure 2.3 Multi-sided business platform using social media or search engines

the form of cookies) and they can sell space to advertisers.[259] With respect to the first way, personal data, typically consisting of consumers' identities, habits, needs and preferences, can be sold online in several ways, such as the supply of information about users' activities to direct marketing companies. Firms can partner with data management platforms – aggregators that place cookies on users' computers and collect online activity or data that can be sold indirectly, bundling information and services such as targeted advertising or matchmaking services such as crowdfunding.[260]

With respect to the second way, many of the most popular platforms in the world, such as Google, Facebook and YouTube, generate income from search advertisements (which are links shown alongside results from queries typed into search engines) or display advertisements (images or animations shown next to web content).[261]

The multi-sided platform is also used in circumstances where the relationship between the two user groups is more implied than expressly authorised. In the situation of social media and search engines the user group is a group that is provided (predominantly) free access to interact with other members of the group or search the Internet using key terms and words (Figure 2.3). In return, information and data is collected and this is used by the platform to attract a relevant group of advertisers who place ads with the first user group for a fee. Sometimes, the platform will also charge the first user group. This can be either a supplementary set fee for a "premium" service or require a payment termed a "freemium" (by

---

[259] Anja Lambrecht and others *How Do Firms Make Money Selling Digital Goods Online?* (Springer Science+Business Media, Mark Lett, 24 June 2014) 331–41 at 333.
[260] Ibid at 335.
[261] Ibid at 336.

which a payment is made to suspend the advertising service, and is usually based on the cost of the advertising).[262]

2.4 Using the Reseller Model

Not all digital business models (new or old) use a multi-sided platform. These are businesses that acquire products and services from suppliers and resell them to buyers, controlling the price and assuming liability towards the customers. Reselling is a traditional business model and its use by digitalised businesses is not, unlike multi-sided platforms, necessarily attributable to the numerous benefits of digitalisation (although it does benefit from the efficiency of the digital platform).

There are clear differences between resellers and the multi-sided platform operators referred to above. The resellers do not allow for the interaction of the two groups of end-users because the model involves contracting directly with the firm. Accordingly, resellers do not necessarily require their customers to affiliate to the online platform (apart from the contract of purchase). As a consequence, Figure 2.4 describing the business relationship is quite different from the two previous examples shown in Figures 2.2 and 2.3 involving participative multi-sided platforms (or networks).

There are quite a few major companies that operate using this form of digital model. The best examples are major companies like Amazon e-commerce, Alibaba, Spotify and Netflix (in circumstances where they purchase their content). The OECD notes that several of the larger digitalised companies started with a single line of business that was a multi-sided platform and developed integrated or hybrid structures with additional business lines that may take different business forms (such as reselling).[263]

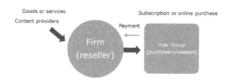

Figure 2.4 The basic structure of resellers

---

[262] Marcin Kotarba "Digital Transformation of Business Models" (2018) 10 Fndn of Mgmt 123 at 140.
[263] OECD, above n 214 at 2.2.2.

2.7 DIGITALISED BUSINESS MODELS

2.5 Using Vertically Integrated Firms

Vertically integrated firms have some similar characteristics to resellers as their transactions with the end-users (purchasers or subscribers) are controlled by the firm. Indeed, some online streaming companies started out as pure resellers and then expanded their operations to include film and media production. Vertically integrated firms therefore do not exhibit the same characteristics as those operating a multi-sided platform where there is direct interaction between the two user groups. Integrated firms are businesses that have acquired ownership over their suppliers and therefore have integrated the supply chain within their own companies, as indicated in Figure 2.5.

2.6 Using Firms That Are Input Suppliers

This is the fourth type of digital business model identified in the Harvard Business School working paper by A Hagiu and J Wright.[264] The focus of these businesses is to supply intermediary inputs as part of a production process of either goods or services to another firm, which in turn supplies the end-user. Input suppliers, therefore, do not interact with the final customer, only with the firm. Intel, for example, as an input supplier, provides microprocessors (and other parts) required to construct personal computers and does not interact directly with customers.[265]

2.7 Observations about the Key Characteristics of Digitalised Business Models

2.7.1 Common Features of Digital Business and the Most Likely Business Model to Exploit the Feature

This chapter has briefly discussed developments in the technological progress of the information age with a particular focus on digital business

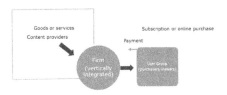

Figure 2.5 The basic structure of vertically integrated firms

---
[264] Hagiu and Wright, above n 254.
[265] OECD, above n 214 at box 2.1 at 2.2.2.

models. There are some key characteristics that have been identified in these digital business models which have significance and importance when we look at the challenges to the tax system posed by digitalisation.

In the OECD's 2018 report they suggested the following common features of digital businesses:[266]

- *Reliance upon intangible assets* (including intellectual property rights): Clearly, the use of intangibles is a feature of the carrying on of digitalised business. It is also a very significant part of all forms of modern business including that which does not have a focus on digitalisation. Accordingly, while it is true that reliance upon intangible assets represents one of the common characteristics leading to the extraordinary growth in digitalised business, concerns from a tax perspective have arisen relating to the valuation, location and licensing of intangible assets. These concerns are broader than those arising in respect of digitalised business models.

  Most likely digital business model to benefit from intangible assets: all.

- *Network effects and globalisation:* This includes both direct (the positive externality arising from the utility of having a larger network) and indirect (benefits arising on a multi-sided platform for one group of users, such as advertisers, from having a larger group of users on the other side of the platform, such as members of a social network) network effects.

- Through digitalisation and a global marketplace, the network effects for digital businesses are considerable. Businesses are able to operate with significant reach across borders and as described by the OECD, many digitalised businesses can "effectively be heavily involved in the economic life of different jurisdictions without any, or any significant physical presence, thus achieving operational scale without mass".[267]

- With respect to various marketplaces (physical products/digital products/digital services etc.) the network effects will differ in the way in which they are geographically constituted. For instance, generally speaking, digital products and digital services are more global marketplaces because of the ability to deliver the product immediately at a very low cost to the end-user. So in certain instances, the vendors and purchasers of certain products can literally be anywhere on the planet. On the other hand, a platform that provides a marketplace between

---

[266] Ibid at 2.5.2 at [135–8].
[267] Ibid at 2.5.1 at [131–4].

vendors and purchasers of used cars are more likely to be limited to a certain geographic area.
- With multi-sided platforms however, it is important to remember that even if the end-users are purchasers or consumers who are located in a particular geographical area, the platform firm itself may be doing its business activities without a physical presence in the jurisdiction, and so too may the other end-users who might be advertisers. In other words, it is important to focus on the business activity undertaken by the digitalised business firm. It may be deriving commission income or advertising income from locally-based business counterparties who might be claiming legitimate source deduction expenses without any locally based source income being returned by the digitalised firm.

Most likely digital business models to benefit from network effects: multi-sided platforms, resellers and vertically integrated firms.

- **Pricing and dealing between user groups:** There are two aspects to this characteristic. The first is that a digital platform provides the ability for participants on both sides of the platform to deal directly with each other and retain key elements of control (such as pricing). Thus, vendors can set the prices for goods and services to purchasers (an example of which is Airbnb or any of the hotel multi-sided platforms). The platform firm derives its commission without having to know any of the sophisticated complexities of the vendors' offerings or the purchasers' needs because the parties deal with that themselves. There is therefore an increased level of engagement or "affiliation" between the users on each side.
- This level of engagement or/and control may make the business more efficient and more personalised as it effectively allows the two groups of end-users to deal seamlessly with each other. Consider the difference between a passenger with a smartphone revising their pickup place directly with the driver, in contrast to using a centralised ordering system for taxis.
- The second aspect of pricing is the possibility of non-neutral pricing structures which permit one side of the end-users in the market to subsidise (sometimes completely) the end-users on the other side of the market. As previously discussed, social networking firms extract data from users in return for a "free" social networking experience, while being compensated through the advertisements provided (and paid for) by the advertising end-user group.

Most likely digital business model to benefit from non-neutral pricing and the aspect of end-user control on key terms: multi-sided platforms.

- *Efficiencies, economies of scale and low marginal costs:* The ability to negotiate low prices for purchased goods, or to leave the end-user vendors with the ability to set their own pricing means that volume-based selling can drive down costs. In some cases the cost of delivery (particularly for digital products and services) will be virtually zero. Digital products and services present a unique combination of traits: (1) they are non-rival (consumption of the good does not decrease its availability to others – supply is limitless); (2) they have near-zero marginal cost of production and distribution even over large distances; (3) they have lower marginal costs of search than products sold in physical stores and (4) they have lower transaction costs than non-digital products.[268]

- Furthermore, there are significant efficiency gains for purchasers, who can immediately see the best price and key features from a range of suppliers (think, for example, about the location and price of hotel accommodation on one of the hotel multi-sided platforms). Furthermore, end-users or purchasers can be rewarded with loyalty programmes (free nights after ten hotel stays) and have their preferences recorded through the registration process.

The most likely digital business models to benefit from efficiencies, economies of scale and low marginal costs: multi-sided platforms, resellers, vertically integrated firms and input suppliers.

- *Data capture, reviews and content creation (user participation):* A significant change with the introduction of digitalisation is the role that users play. The first aspect of this is the collection of the data provided by the users. This is primarily passive on behalf of the users. Data can be collected by the company through the use of cookies even after the user is no longer on the specific platform of the business but using other websites. Firms dealing with purchasers/vendors, social networks and search engine users have the ability to capture consumer preferences and private information (such as creditworthiness, spending and hobbies and interests) and to use this to monetise their platforms through the sale of advertising. The OECD described this phenomenon

---

[268] Lambrecht and others, above n 259 at 333.

as "the use, collection and analysis of data is becoming an integral part of the business models of most digitalised firms. As the process of digitalisation continues, these features can be expected to become an increasingly important part of the business models of an even wider range of firms".[269] In some cases the benefits of data analysis are linked to a specific customer giving information to enable targeted advertisements to specific users. In other businesses the data collected is used to improve operations, product design or marketing activities.

- The second aspect is where there is a broader and active contribution (in addition to data) made by the users. Many digital businesses have business models that use the time and expertise of end-users to generate value (it being a controversial and quite open question as to how much value). It would seem hard to argue that user participation is not valuable for a social network business. Users of a social network business contribute content in different forms (photos, videos and comments) and expand the network by inviting family and friends. Why would social network businesses operate free of charge to users unless they could monetise the other side of their user platform and attract advertisers?
- Not all digital businesses rely as heavily on user participation. As the OECD points out, vertically integrated businesses focus on a main interaction with the customer involving the sale and purchase of a product (or services). The OECD concluded that although there is "the possibility of data collection and user participation in the production process, but it is limited (although it will expand in the future) and less likely to contribute to the value creation process in a meaningful way".[270]
- The OECD has categorised active participation into three broad categories, which it assesses as low, medium or high depending on the participation and the value of the user action.[271]
- Activities such as bookmarking, tagging and rating are seen as different kinds of filtering actions requiring a low level of effort. Businesses categorised by low user participation include cloud computing and vertically integrated businesses. Data stored in the cloud is generally not available for detailed analysis by a cloud provider and usually not shared with other users (although some businesses involved in cloud

---

[269] OECD, above n 214 at 2.5.3 at [139].
[270] Ibid at 2.5.3 at [144].
[271] Ibid at [148].

storage like Dropbox do expand the user base by inviting others to share files).
- A medium level of participation is needed for activities such as writing comments or reviews (such as TripAdvisor). The user activity is designed to help other users to choose a product/service and to engender trust in the platform. Reviews enable other end-users to make decisions based on the experience of their peers and so they are influential in marketing, provided they are credible. They also can regulate behaviour by one or more of the groups of end-users. Good examples of this are the way reviews or ratings can be used to ensure good behaviour and quality control (particularly on multi-sided platforms where the firm does not have control over the transaction). A business that is an example of a medium level of user participation is a platform that is a marketplace for physical products (like eBay, or certain parts of Amazon). Reviews and ratings are employed to improve interaction between vendors and purchasers.
- The OECD suggests that a marketplace for digital or intangible goods and services is likely to have a higher user participation intensity (because users can increase the customer base by sharing their playlists or actively creating content for online games).[272] Businesses providing services which are contracted for online (even where the services are delivered offline) also have a slightly higher user participation. A good example of this is a hotel booking platform such as Booking.com. A user will disclose their preference for size of accommodation, room configurations, budget and neighbourhood in selecting their options. They are also invited (sometimes persistently) to write reviews and share product or service descriptions including photos. Likewise the ability of both the drivers and riders using Uber to rate each other serves as a mechanism to engender trust in the level of services provided and allows influential public monitoring of behaviour.
- The most intensive form of user engagement is that previously referred to in the context of social networking. Users perform actions which directly enlarge the platform by adding friends, creating communities and networking. In many instances the end-users will be spending significant time and energy recording their ratings and observations, creating videos and other content which entertain or inform other members of the network. Using their time, skills and connections,

---

[272] Ibid at [154].

users are directly responsible for a direct network effect (through the increase in numbers of end-users) and also the indirect network effect (the attractiveness of the platform to advertisers or the other group of end-users on the multi-sided platform). For example, more purchasers in the network will mean that the platform is more attractive to vendors. Even though the users contribute to the success of the platform, the platform itself, developed through investment in technology, intangibles and algorithms has an important role in attracting the users.

The most likely digital business models to benefit from these features (use of data in its various forms and user participation): multi-sided platforms and to a lesser extent resellers and vertically integrated firms.

3

Challenges to the Tax System Posed by the Digitalisation of Business

3.1 Introduction to the Challenges

In the previous chapter, the many benefits of digitalisation were discussed. These include increased efficiency, productivity and positive economic changes generally leading to a higher standard of living for people. The consequences of these changes are being felt in a range of different areas, having a huge social impact in its broadest sense (including such things as live streaming of terror attacks, alleged interference with the electoral process and selective exposure to self-justifying news sources), privacy law and data protection. In the area of taxation, the changes are just as dramatic. New ways of doing business, and better ways to do existing business practices, are currently challenging and will in the future dramatically challenge the existing tax system.

3.1.1 Allocating Taxing Rights

Corporate tax paid by non-resident companies *doing business* in a jurisdiction (with due acknowledgement of the difficulties in defining exactly what "doing business" is) is likely to be an important part of the overall tax take for most jurisdictions. Many jurisdictions take the view that the international tax framework currently does not allocate taxing rights to the source state in circumstances where the multinational is carrying on what can be described as "remote sales". In other words, source taxing rights only arise when a multinational is trading *in* rather than trading *with* a country. This principle is well expressed in the United Kingdom's document on Corporate Tax and the Digital Economy as follows:[273]

> The overall principle underpinning that framework is to tax a multinational group's profits in the countries in which it undertakes its

---

[273] HM Treasury *Corporate Tax and the Digital Economy: Position Paper* (HM Treasury, PU2117, November 2017) at 2.5.

3.1 INTRODUCTION TO THE CHALLENGES

value-generating activities, such as where major operating decisions are made and where important assets and risks are controlled.

That is a principle that the government continues to support. It does not, for example, believe that another country should have a general right to tax profits that a UK business generates from a product that is designed in the UK, manufactured in the UK, marketed in the UK and then sold remotely to that country's customers.

Equally it does not believe that the UK should have a general right to tax the profits that a foreign business generates for a product that is designed in another country, manufactured and marketed in that country and then sold remotely to a UK consumer.

As has been previously discussed,[274] one of the most important and significant international tax debates is the apparent adoption by the OECD and G20 of the mantra that "the profits are taxed where economic activities take place and value is created".[275] This value creation principle was originally the touchstone for the BEPS project which was focused on preventing harmful tax competition, protecting corporate tax and consequently reducing (if not eliminating) aggressive tax planning by multinationals. Moving from the BEPS project to becoming a guiding principle for taxing corporate profits more generally has been criticised on the grounds that value creation is a principle that has, in fact, not been widely agreed or properly considered.[276] As discussed in Section 1.5, commentators have criticised value creation for its vagueness and imprecision,[277] while at the same time pointing out that it could permit market or source countries to claim a share of the tax base if the impact of the market's consumer supply-based factors form part of the creation of value, together with other infrastructural aspects such as the legal, physical and technological framework for doing business, are considered. This is why Devereux and Vella argue, and they must be right, that it is not logical to, on the one hand say that taxation should take place where value is created, and on the other hand support the

---

[274] See Section 1.5 "The Benefit Theory and Its Relationship to Value Creation".
[275] OECD *OECD/G20 Base Erosion and Profit Shifting Project Explanatory Statement* (OECD, 2015) at 1.
[276] Michael Devereux and John Vella *Value Creation as the Fundamental Principle of the International Corporate Tax System* (Oxford University Centre for Business Taxation, WP 17/07, 31 July 2017).
[277] Johanna Hey "'Taxation Where Value Is Created' and the OECD/G20 Base Erosion and Profit Shifting Initiative" (2018) 4/5 Bull for Int' Tax 203, and Susan Morse "Value Creation: A Standard in Search of a Process" (2018) 4/5 Bull for Int' Tax 196 at 197.

proposition that remote sales can never result in value being created in the source state.[278]

Seen in this light, the majority consensus of countries conventionally see the existing rules on international tax leaving remote sales outside the framework of source-based taxation for foreign-owned entities making such sales to a customer in another jurisdiction. More current thinking from the OECD indicates that a new consensus may arise which would allocate more taxing rights to the jurisdiction of the consumer and/or the user "in situations where value is created by business activity through (possibly remote) participation in that jurisdiction that is not recognised in the current framework for allocating profits".[279] This consensus may emerge, but at the time of writing it does not currently exist. There are therefore two issues to discuss. The first, referred to above, is whether a new taxing right may emerge for market or source countries simply because of the presence of the customer and/or digital user. The second is whether the existing rules are adequate to deal with the proliferation of businesses using a digital business model.

3.1.2 The Importance of Corporate Tax

The OECD's analysis of corporate tax statistics shows that in 2016, corporate tax revenues (for resident and non-resident entities) accounted for 13.3 per cent of total tax revenues on average across the eighty-eight jurisdictions for which data is available. This figure increased from 12 per cent in 2000 despite the overall trend of falling corporate tax rates in that period. Corporate taxation is even more important in developing countries, comprising on average 15.3 per cent of all tax revenues in Africa and 15.4 per cent in Latin America and the Caribbean, compared to 9 per cent in the OECD.[280] In the traditional business models, in addition to corporate tax payments, non-resident companies employ local employees who pay employment taxes and social security contributions, while the companies themselves are responsible for property taxes (to both central and local governments), consumption taxes and environmental taxes.

---

[278] Devereux and Vella, above n 276.
[279] OECD *Programme of Work to Develop a Consensus Solution to the Tax Challenges Arising from the Digitalisation of the Economy* (OECD, May 2019) at 23.
[280] OECD "Corporate Tax Remains a Key Revenue Source, Despite Falling Rates Worldwide" (15 January 2019) OECD <www.oecd.org/tax/corporate-tax-remains-a-key-revenue-source-despite-falling-rates-worldwide.htm>.

3.1.3 Are the Rules "Fit for Purpose"?

The key characteristics of the digitalised business models discussed in Chapter 2 significantly change the picture painted by the statistics referred to above. The combination of businesses using direct and indirect network effects, together with the efficiencies of that marketplace and the low cost of operation, and a global marketplace made available through the Internet, means that there is a superior way to sell goods and services for many businesses. It is an obvious point, but much of this business does not require a physical presence in a jurisdiction. Many transactions involving consumer to consumer, business to consumer and business to business no longer need someone "on the ground" to organise the deal. The European Commission expressed its view as follows:[281]

> The application of the current corporate tax rules to the digital economy has led to a misalignment between the place where the profits are taxed and the place where value is created. In particular, the current rules no longer fit the present context where online trading across borders with no physical presence has been facilitated, where businesses largely rely on hard to value intangible assets, and where user generated content and data collection have become core activities for the value creation of digital businesses.

As discussed, there has been quite significant criticism of the idea that a fundamental principle of the international corporate tax system is "value creation".[282] The European Commission is articulating the commonly held view that the international tax rules are no longer "fit for purpose". These views are largely shared by many other countries, including the United Kingdom,[283] Australia[284] and New Zealand.[285]

---

[281] European Commission *Proposal for a Council Directive Laying Down Rules Relating to the Corporate Taxation of a Significant Digital Presence* (European Commission, COM (2018) 147 final 2018/0072 (CNS), March 2018) at 1.

[282] Devereux and Vella, above n 276.

[283] HM Treasury, above n 273 at 4.2, which states: "There needs to be broad international acceptance of the need to address the challenges that digital businesses create for the tax system and agreement on a process and timetable for achieving meaningful reform of the international tax framework."

[284] The Australian Government *The Digital Economy and Australia's Corporate Tax System* (Treasury of Australia, October 2018) at 2.2, where the discussion recognises that foreign businesses have for decades operated business models where a majority of profit-generating assets and labour have been located offshore but notes "increasing digitalisation an increasingly mobile intangible assets intensify this challenge, particularly in the sectors of the economy most affected by Digital disruption".

[285] New Zealand Inland Revenue Department *Options for Taxing the Digital Economy. A Government Discussion Document* (Policy and Strategy of Inland Revenue, June

Where multi-sided platforms are concerned, the firm usually makes its money from advertising, subscription or, most commonly, commission. Even where services must be performed in the geographic location (such as accommodation or transportation) the multi-sided platform allows the two end-users sufficient control to enable them to perform key tasks in the negotiation of the contract, provision of the goods or service, and receiving payment, quite often independently of the firm operating the platform. This means that the multi-sided platform firm can remain physically remote from the end-users on either side of the platform and any activities they perform. This issue of a lack of nexus (or physical connection in the source country) is the first broad category of three main policy changes in direct taxation posed by digitalisation identified by the OECD.[286]

Whether the tax rules relating to permanent establishments have kept pace with technological changes is possibly the most obvious and significant challenge, but it is neither the only challenge nor completely unrelated to the other two identified by the OECD. The issue of data being gathered and used to generate business value is integral to many of the digital models. It was also strongly connected to the lack of nexus challenge, as the participation by users (to a greater or lesser extent) arguably does not constitute a permanent establishment.[287]

Lastly is the issue of how certain transactions in digitalised business should be characterised. Payments made in respect of new business models, particularly in the area of cloud computing have created uncertainty as to the appropriate tax treatment.

The seven major areas of challenges posed to the tax system by the digitalisation of business are now analysed. The first relates to the question of nexus and the difficulty posed by the ability of digitalised businesses to do substantial business in a country whilst not meeting the permanent establishment threshold.

2019) at 1.4, which states: "the digital economy provides many benefits to New Zealanders, and it is an important source of future growth for the country. However, its under-taxation impacts the sustainability of Government revenues in the fairness of the tax system. It also distorts investment in favour of digital multinationals, which pay lower worldwide income tax compared with other industries."

[286] OECD *Tax Challenges Arising from Digitalisation – Interim Report 2018: Inclusive Framework on BEPS* (OECD Publishing, 2018) at [381].

[287] It should be noted that this is sometimes contested by various countries, discussed in Chapters 5 and 8.

3.2 The Vanishing Ability to Tax Business Profits

3.2.1 Business Profits and Permanent Establishments

As detailed previously,[288] the principles of taxation for non-resident entities deriving business profits sourced in a country other than their own are drawn from the so-called 1920s compromise. Designed in the early twentieth century, the context was one of industrialisation, increasing cross-border trade, increasing rates of tax and a movement from a territorial to worldwide system of tax. Hence the focus was very much on eliminating double taxation. The original 1923 Report, which was very supportive of residence-based taxation and somewhat less enthusiastic about source taxation, was amended by the 1925 and 1927 Technical Experts Reports. The 1925 Report acknowledged that "the division which we have established ... has been made for purely practical purposes and no inference in regard to economic theory or doctrine should be drawn from this fact".[289] These 1925 and 1927 Technical Expert groups introduced the concept of a "permanent establishment" so that business profits earned in the source country would only be subject to tax there if the foreign enterprise had sufficient connection. What is the necessary connection or nexus to constitute a permanent establishment?

3.2.2 The Permanent Establishment Threshold

According to Brian Arnold, the taxation of business profits of non-residents under a country's domestic laws and tax treaties can be divided into six basic stages.[290] These are:

1 What is the country's legal or constitutional right to tax non-residents? As discussed in Chapter 1, there is little practical limitation on the concept of the source of business income under domestic law.[291] Older case law, found in common law jurisdictions, supports a pragmatic approach which defines the source of income as that which an

---

[288] See Section 1.3 "The History of International Double Taxation: The '1920s Compromise'".
[289] Technical Experts from seven jurisdictions: Belgium, Czechoslovakia, France, Great Britain, Italy, Netherlands and Switzerland *Double Taxation and Tax Evasion* (League of Nations, F 212, 7 February 1925) at 15.
[290] Brian Arnold "Threshold Requirements for Taxing Business Profits under Tax Treaties" (2003) 57 Bull for Int' Tax 467 at 477.
[291] See Section 1.7 "Exploring the Limits of Domestic Source-Based Taxation".

ordinary person would regard as the real source of income. It would seem "clear that there must be some connection with the country, even if just as a practical matter, before the country can tax a non-resident".[292]

2 What constitutes a business being carried on in the jurisdiction? This involves determining what business income is, as opposed to investment income, under domestic law and tax treaties.
3 Once a country determines that a business exists within its jurisdiction, it must decide whether to tax all the profits, or whether it will impose tax only if the non-resident's business in the country meets or exceeds a minimum threshold. This threshold is traditionally one of having a "permanent establishment" – the concept introduced in the 1925 and 1927 Reports.
4 Once this minimum threshold has been met, rules (often referred to as geographic source rules) necessarily determine what business profits derived by the non-resident entity are attributable to, and taxable by, the source country.
5 It is then necessary, usually under domestic rules, to compute the business profits that are subject to tax.
6 A country has rules to determine the tax payable and methods of collection of tax. Sometimes the methods of collection for non-residents (such as various forms of withholding tax) differ from those residents are subject to (reflecting the difficulty of collecting tax from non-residents).

You can see from these six steps that there is a close connection between the various stages and also that there is close interaction between domestic law and the rules of double tax treaties.

The third stage above is the key one for the purposes of this discussion. As indicated, under Article 7 (1) of both the OECD and UN models, countries have agreed not to tax business profits earned in their jurisdiction by non-residents unless the foreign entity of the residence state has crossed the threshold of having a permanent establishment (PE) in the other contracting state, so that its activities could no longer be described "as small or not intimately connected to the economy" of the jurisdiction.[293] In the absence of a PE, the business profits derived in the source

---

[292] Arnold, above n 290 at 477.
[293] Ekkehart Reimer, Stefan Schmid and Marianne Orell *Permanent Establishments: A Domestic Taxation, Bilateral Tax Treaty and OECD Perspective* (4th ed, Wolters Kluwer Law & Business, 2015) at 35.

country by a non-resident are exempt from tax and accordingly are taxable only in the residence country.

Ekkehart Reimer describes three objectives behind the permanent establishment principle.[294] The first is that it is, as a matter of international justice, necessary to grant the right to tax in exchange for the efforts by the state to create, maintain and safeguard good economic conditions for foreign investors. This can be viewed as a benefit theory justification, discussed in Chapter 1. It is particularly significant, according to Reimer, in circumstances where a double tax agreement exists between developed and developing countries rather than a double tax agreement between two developed countries. This is because when dealing with two developed countries it is assumed that there is relatively equal investment flow; in a situation of reciprocity between the two countries the question of the amount of source taxation becomes somewhat irrelevant. In the situation of a developing country, however, the width of the PE definition (or the lowest threshold) becomes very important for the allocation of taxation rights to the source country. Accordingly, for developing countries the negotiation of service PEs, building and construction PEs, and the specific examples contained in Article 5 (2) of the OECD Model Convention take on great significance.[295]

The second objective is to place the PE on equal footing with the local resident business owner and thus provide neutrality between residents and non-residents. When foreign investors are taxed by the source state, they experience capital import neutrality and this removes an otherwise competitive advantage over resident businesses.

Lastly, there is a significant practical justification to use the PE principle as a threshold. Small operations, or infrequent and limited trading/involvement with a country, may cause a foreign business unnecessary compliance and administration costs. As Reimer puts it, "it is for this reason that loose economic bonds with a foreign country should leave exclusive taxation by the State of residence unaffected".[296]

Article 5 of the OECD[297] and UN models[298] define, respectively, the meaning of a PE. They fall into three broad categories:

---

[294] Ibid at 38.
[295] OECD *Model Tax Convention on Income and on Capital Condensed Version* (OECD, 21 November 2017) at Article 5.
[296] Reimer, Schmid and Orell, above n 293 at 40.
[297] OECD, above n 295.
[298] United Nations *United Nations Model Double Taxation Convention between Developed and Developing Countries* (United Nations, 2017) at Article 5.

- The first is the **physical "situs" tests** generally defined in paragraph (1) and specifically listed in paragraph (2) of Article 5 (including a place of management, a branch, an office etc). Also included in this category is a building site, construction or installation project where it lasts for a certain duration (twelve months in the case of the OECD Model and six months in the case of the UN Model).
- The second category is the **contractual or relationship "deemed" test**. Contained in Article 5 (5), the dependent agency rules require that the enterprise has a deemed PE if any person is acting as a dependent agent, and/or otherwise is acting so as to habitually conclude contracts, or plays a leading role in concluding the contracts.[299]

In the case of the UN Model, the actions of a "dependent agent" may constitute a permanent establishment, even without having and habitually exercising the authority to conclude contracts in the name of the enterprise, where that person habitually maintains a stock of goods or merchandise and regularly makes deliveries from the stock (paragraph 5 (b)).[300]

- The third category is a **temporal or physical presence test**. This requirement overlaps with the first requirement of physical situs in many circumstances but not all. For example, activities carried on in a building site, construction or installation project are a PE only provided the requisite amount of time (either six or twelve months) has elapsed. Furthermore, the OECD Commentary observes that a place of business, more generally, is required to have a certain degree of permanency and not be purely temporary in nature. Accordingly, it states:[301]

> Whilst the practices followed by member countries have not been consistent in so far as time requirements are concerned, experience has shown that permanent establishments normally have not been considered to exist in situations where a business had been carried on in a country through a place of business that was maintained for less than six months (conversely, practice shows that there were many cases where a permanent establishment has been considered to exist where the place of business was maintained for a period longer than six months).

---

[299] OECD, above n 295 at Article 5(5).
[300] United Nations, above n 298 at Article 5(5)(b).
[301] OECD, above n 295 at [28].

In some circumstances, particularly when dealing with the UN Model, countries have adopted a service PE. This operates on the basis of deeming a PE to exist where there is:[302]

> The furnishing of services, including consultancy services, by an enterprise through employees or other personnel engaged by the enterprise for such purpose, but only if activities of that nature continue within a Contracting State for a period or periods aggregating more than 183 days in any 12-month period commencing or ending in the fiscal year concerned.

It is observed that it is purely the furnishing of services for the requisite period of time within the source state by personnel engaged by the enterprise which triggers the PE threshold. In other words, there is no requirement for there to be a fixed place of business (such as that found in the first category above). Thus it is a test involving simply the performance of services in a country for a period of time.

With these observations about the requirements of the PE threshold, the question now posed is the extent to which the PE definition captures the types of activities carried on by firms using the digitalised business models referred to previously in this book.

3.2.3 Examining the Adequacy of the Current PE Definition

The conventional view is that the features of the PE developed in the nineteenth century are not adequate to deal with the business models of the twenty-first century.[303]

Arnold, however, makes the point that a blanket statement that the PE concept is inappropriate for the new economy of the twenty-first century is "misleading because it focuses on only part, albeit the basic aspect, of the definition of PE".[304] What Arnold means is that it is necessary to examine each part of the PE definition to understand whether it is adequate overall in the context of changing business models. Writing in 2003, Arnold was making the point that the drafters of the predecessors to the OECD Model always recognised that the fixed place of business threshold was too limited and therefore incorporated the dependent

---

[302] United Nations, above n 298 at Article 5(3)(b).
[303] Wolfgang Schön "10 Questions about Why and How to Tax the Digitalised Economy" (2018) 72 Bull for Int' Tax 278 at 278.
[304] Arnold, above n 290 at 479.

agent PE requirement, so that it has never been a test which focused exclusively on a fixed place of business threshold alone.

Although the fundamental issues remain similar, since 2003 the growth in the nature and scale of the digital economy has led many to rethink the adequacy of the current PE settings. The current position is largely reflected by the OECD's expressed view which recognises that business models in general, and the growth of the digital economy in particular, have resulted in non-resident companies operating in quite a fundamentally different way from the past. The OECD say:[305]

> For example, while a non-resident company has always been able to sell into a jurisdiction without a physical presence there, advances in information and communication technology (ICT) have dramatically expanded the scale at which such an activity is now possible ... The fact that less physical presence is required in market economies in typical business structures today – an effect that can be amplified on certain types of businesses in the ICT sector – therefore raises challenges for international tax.

Any business still needs to source and acquire inputs, create or add value and sell to customers. Digitalisation changes the way in which some of these activities are carried on, such as:[306]

- enhancing the ability to carry out activities remotely;
- increasing the speed at which information can be processed, analysed and utilised;
- expanding the number of potential customers (because distance forms significantly less of a barrier to trade);
- processes previously carried out by local personnel can now be performed across the border by either a centralised team or, more likely, automated equipment; and
- the changing roles performed by staff in the context of sophisticated software programs and algorithms.

As a consequence, a customer base in a country simply does not need the level of local infrastructure and personnel that a similar business ten or fifteen years ago would require. Multinational enterprises are much freer to choose where they locate their business operations, and whilst some may place core resources close to markets, others have increasingly

---
[305] OECD *Addressing the Tax Challenges of the Digital Economy, Action 1 – 2015 Final Panel Report* (OECD Publishing, 2015) at 3.1.
[306] Ibid, chapter 7 at [253].

located their personnel, information technology infrastructure and decision-making capabilities (much of which can be automated) away from the marketplace.

3.2.4 Examining the Component Parts of the Test

(a) A Fixed Place of Business through Which the Business of an Enterprise Is Wholly or Partly Carried On

The PE definition in Article 5 (1) requires "a fixed place of business through which the business of an enterprise is wholly or partly carried on". There are three requirements under this test. There needs to be, first, a "place of business"; secondly, this place of business must be "fixed"; and lastly, the carrying on of the business of the enterprise must be, wholly or partly, through this fixed place of business.

The use of the term "fixed" in the definition makes it clear that under this limb of the test there is a geographical requirement, while the use of the term "permanent" establishes a temporal quality. The ability to operate in and to be heavily involved in the economic life of another country, without having a fixed place of business, is readily available to digitalised firms.

It seems clear that many digitalised businesses will be able to operate successfully without having a fixed place of business.

(b) Operating Using a Dependent Agent

The failure to maintain a fixed place of business does not mean that a foreign enterprise does not have a PE. Under the current definition in Article 5 (5), where a person undertakes for the enterprise activities which involve:

- habitually concluding contracts;
- or habitually plays the principal role leading to the conclusion of contracts that are routinely concluded without material modification by the enterprise; and
- these contracts are

    (a) in the name of the enterprise; or
    (b) for the transfer of the ownership of, or for the granting of the right to use, property owned by that enterprise or that the enterprise has the right to use; or
    (c) for the provision of services by that enterprise

Once again, a digitalised business can carry on its activities without the need to either engage a dependent agent or have personnel with contract-concluding ability (or something short of that, like circumstances where they are negotiating all but the final contractual document).

(c) Operating in the Country of Source under Any of the Relevant Temporal Tests

As indicated, some of the PE tests, and in particular the service PE test, require the presence of (usually) personnel but sometimes construction or installation projects or substantial equipment in a jurisdiction for a period of time. Obviously, the ability of digital businesses to carry on without either people or assets in a jurisdiction renders these types of tests unfulfilled.

3.2.5 Sufficient Nexus for Digitalised Business with an Economic (but Not Physical) Presence in the Source State?

It is an obvious point that under a traditional analysis[307] many digitalised businesses will not meet the threshold and therefore fail to have a permanent establishment in the state in which they are doing business. This is because they will have neither a fixed place of business nor will they be acting through a dependent agent (as that term is known in Article 5 of the OECD and UN Model Tax conventions). What is actually missing is the physical presence of the business in the source state because, in general, digitalised businesses do not need this physical presence to carry out their commercial activities. This physical presence is manifested by the presence of premises (such as an office, factory or plant) or by the presence of human employees (who are carrying on activities which make it clear that they are a crucial part of the business, for example a dependent agent concluding contracts). The inability to establish a nexus (or a PE) in the source state where the business has an economic presence is the first significant challenge posed by the digitalisation of business.

This outcome (it would be pejorative to describe it as a deficiency) has led to the latest OECD/G20 Programme of Work in 2019 and 2020. In particular under Pillar One is the consideration of proposals which use the value creation principle to justify a right to tax entities deriving

---

[307] It should be noted that some states have applied, or are seeking to apply, a rather more aggressive view on what constitutes a permanent establishment to seek to include significant economic presence within the concept of permanent establishment. This is discussed further in Chapter 5.

income from cross-border activities in the absence of physical presence.[308] This will be described in further detail in Chapters 5 and 6.

3.3 The Use of Data, the Contribution of Users and the Measurement of Their Value

The second challenge to the tax system posed by the digitalisation of the economy is actually a series of three interconnected issues. The first of these is the use of data by some of the most successful multinationals utilising digital business models. Digital technologies have permitted the collection, storage and use of data, crossing borders and enabling remote collection directly from users, consumers or otherwise generated through analysis, or indirectly from third parties.[309] Data has been sometimes collected with the express knowledge of the users and sometimes through their implicit consent, although largely the quality and nature of the information is within the control of the users, as evidenced by the information provided by people involved in social networks and the uploading of information in cloud computing.

Although data collection is not a new phenomenon, the ability to collect and categorise it usefully is due to the increase in computer processing and the growth of the Internet. The use of data has historically been underestimated, and, in the view of Becker and Englisch, "activities such as local data collection or warehousing that were previously considered to be of a merely auxiliary nature, typically contributed only marginally to business profits and were therefore neglected for the purposes of profit allocation or justified only low profit attributions".[310]

With the use of Big Data Analytics, what was previously regarded as a simple routine function, namely tailoring a service or product to accommodate the specific needs of local customers, has become a key success factor enabling large multinationals to deliver superior customer value through the collection of data and mass customisation.[311] The OECD maintains that data gathered from various sources "is often a primary input into the process of value creation in the digital economy" by

---

[308] OECD/G20 *Inclusive Framework on BEPS Programme of Work to Develop a Consensus Solution to the Tax Challenges Arising from the Digitisation of the Economy* (OECD, 2019) at [22–5].
[309] OECD, above n 305 at 3.1 at [262].
[310] Johannes Becker and Joachim Englisch "Taxing Where Value Is Created: What's 'User Involvement' Got to Do with It?" (2019) 47 Intertax 161 at 162.
[311] Ibid at 162.

allowing businesses to segment populations in order to tailor offerings, improving the development of products and services, assessing variability in performance, and improving decision-making.[312] Perhaps the most obvious example of demonstrating the ability to monetise this data and information are those highly digitalised businesses which have developed the capability of collecting user data and instantly identifying user preferences in order to deliver highly targeted advertising.[313]

Integral to data collection is the second interconnected issue. This is the role that user participation makes in driving value for certain kinds of digital businesses. The approach taken by the OECD is to recognise that "digitalisation has reshaped the role of users, allowing the possibility for them to become increasingly involved in the value creation process".[314] In originally proposing an interim Digital Services Tax at the European Union, the European Commission focused on two main types of digital services, these being the placement of advertising on digital interfaces and intermediary digital interfaces or marketplaces whose main purpose is to facilitate the direct interaction between users, while stating: "The common feature of such services is that they are heavily reliant on the exploitation of user participation or data obtained about users as a way to generate revenues."[315] The UK Government, in particular, has focused on user participation by examining multi-sided business platforms such as social media networks and online marketplaces and concluded that the success of these businesses is "much more reliant on the activities, decisions and participation of users with whom the business forms a more sophisticated and sustained relationship".[316] HM Treasury identifies that the participation of the user is not under the control of the business and therefore independently:[317]

- contributes to the creation of the brand;
- generates valuable data; and
- contributes to the development of a critical mass of users, which helps to establish market power and allows businesses to take advantage of low marginal costs.

---

[312] OECD, above n 305 at [262].
[313] Australian Government, above n 284 at 1.2.
[314] OECD, above n 305 at [145].
[315] European Commission *Time to Establish a Modern, Fair and Efficient Taxation Standard for the Digital Economy* (European Commission, COM(2018) 146 final, 21 March 2018) at 9.
[316] HM Treasury *Corporate Tax and the Digital Economy: Position Paper* (HM Treasury, PU2117, November 2017) at 3.19.
[317] Ibid at 3.20.

In subsequent work,[318] HM Treasury spelled out that certain key aspects of user participation were driving value for certain digital businesses. These were, first, those online platforms which operated with substantially **user-generated content**. Examples of such businesses are social media companies that generate revenue from selling advertising on a platform which is populated by users' posts and photos. It is true that the users derive benefits from the platform (the free use of the platform software and the ability to communicate with friends and relatives). But the business which binds the network users together is that content generated by other users. The platform uses this content to attract members and then offers that audience to the advertisers (on the other side of the platform) in order to generate revenue.

A second key aspect of user participation, identified by HM Treasury, was the **depth of engagement** with the platform. This reflects the amount of time that users spend engaging with the platform, actively contributing to content and interacting with other users. This might include some of the actions referred to above in generating content, but it also includes building trust in the validation of experience through the posting of reviews and consumer experiences on goods and services provided to the users. These sustained engagements allow the platform to build up a detailed picture based on user behaviour, and allows intensive monitoring of users' interests and consumption habits.

The third aspect relating to the creation of value by users is the contribution to the **network effect**. The network effect, in its direct form, is established by the number of active users on any platform. The greater the network, the more powerful the business model as the increased number of users attracts more users on either side of the platform. In other words, on a marketplace platform the presence of more purchasers (such as people looking for short-term accommodation) attracts more vendors (people offering short-stay lets). The experience for the users (user utility) is greatly enhanced where there is a greater choice of offerings.

In its indirect form, the network effect extends across the platform to the other group of users on the other side of the platform. This is relevant to platforms such as social media or other user-generated content (such as video sharing) as it enables the advertisers on the other side of the platform greater access to more potential buyers.

---

[318] HM Treasury *Corporate Tax and the Digital Economy: Position Paper Update* (HM Treasury, March 2018) at chapter 2.

Lastly, the users make a **contribution to the brand**. This can be in association with the other contributions but is primarily found in reviewing and rating content or services provided by third parties and otherwise regulating what appears on the platform and establishing an important trust mechanism for other users. A very good example of this is the online marketplace – a vendor will want to establish (and maintain) their reputation in order to facilitate future sales. Consequently, they will ensure that they provide the very best goods or service (or service relating to the sale of either) in order to ensure their reputation is validated. This leads to enhanced confidence across the marketplace and enables it to function successfully.

The collection of data, and the various forms of user participation referred to above, give rise to the third, and most difficult, part of this challenge: trying to attribute and measure value arising from the data and the actions of the users. As the OECD has recognised:[319]

> While it is clear that many businesses have developed ways to collect, analyse, and ultimately monetise data, it may be challenging for purposes of an analysis of functions, assets, and risks, to assign an objective value to the raw data itself, as distinct from the processes used to collect, analyse and use that data.

Data has value which may be monetised when the business is sold, but the process of establishing its value may depend greatly on the capacity of the purchaser to analyse and make use of it. There is also the small matter of ownership, with most jurisdictions passing data protection and privacy legislation which conventionally recognises that this information is the property of the individual from which it is derived. The OECD simply recognises that it is extremely hard to value,[320] and acknowledges the difficulties in cross-border situations, where data may be collected from customers or devices in one country using technology developed in a second country, processed in that second country, and then used to target advertisements to customers in the first country. The data may be stored and processed using cloud computing, making the location of processing even more difficult to ascertain. There are huge practical difficulties, including in trying to ascertain the value of data collected under a multi-sided platform. This information may be of interest to advertisers on the other side of the platform, but the OECD recognises that the

---

[319] OECD, above n 305 at [263].
[320] Ibid at [264].

location of advertising customers and the location of users are frequently aligned in practice, so that the value of the user data is often reflected in the advertising revenue generated in a particular country.[321]

HM Treasury has asserted that the UK Government does not think that the mere collection of data from users/customers means that those people are participating in the creation of value. The focus is instead on user participation, which the Treasury asserts is creating value, whilst the sourcing of operational and personal data through passive or transactional relationships with customers does not result in value creation.[322]

Becker and Englisch[323] have analysed the degree to which users are involved in value creation, dividing them into two categories based on the OECD's analysis: active and passive.[324] They considered three different types of user contribution, starting with what they considered was the most passive, network effects and consumption externalities. They concluded that the network effect did give rise to an arguable case that a firm should have a nexus to a given country in circumstances where it actively creates a network that is exploited as a core resource for the generation of its business profits. In other words, that the user contribution in creating a network effect was a situation of real value creation for the business.

In the middle of the scale, the next most active user contribution was the use and sale of data, and the effect of feedback provided by users (reviews etc). This activity, they concluded, was very hard to value given the wide variety of different kinds of data. Data collection itself, however, would often be a merely routine task that should not justify the allocation of significant profits.[325] This conclusion accords with the approach taken by the UK Government referred to above. In contrast, they concluded that a sustained user relationship, built through the provision of online services or the supply of smart devices, could constitute a potentially valuable source of value creation in the production process. They recognised that the valuation of the sustained user relationship as an intangible asset would be very difficult and dependent on a variety of factors such as "the quality and strength of a typical relationship over time, the type of

---

[321] Ibid at [266].
[322] HM Treasury, above n 318 at 2.37–2.40.
[323] Becker and Englisch, above n 310 at 166.
[324] OECD *Tax Challenges Arising from Digitalisation – Interim Report 2018: Inclusive Framework on BEPS* (OECD Publishing, 2018) at 55 at [147].
[325] Becker and Englisch, above n 310 at 168.

data that can be collected, and its relevance as a resource for the information needs of certain business models".[326]

The most active user engagement, user content contribution and crowdsourcing was, in the view of Becker and Englisch, something that should be largely disregarded for the purposes of the allocation of taxing rights. This is somewhat of a surprising result, with the user activity being classified as consumption which creates positive externalities for the business – but the argument is that the users are entertaining themselves or socialising and that the value to the multi-sided platform is just the users' sustained engagement with the platform and (presumably) the network effect referred to previously. Overall, the authors conclude that a sustained user relationship is equivalent to a productive (and potentially marketable) intangible asset that can lend itself to creating a nexus for source-based taxation. As you can see from this discussion, this is one of the more difficult challenges posed to the tax system by the digitalisation of business but there seems to be a clear consensus that the engagement by users with the business results in the creation of value to that business. If one accepts that this creation of value gives rise to taxing rights, it will be a very difficult exercise to quantify how much value is created and therefore what proportion of the profits are attributable to the actions and engagement of the users.

3.4 The Reliance on, and Mobility of, Intellectual Property

Digitalised businesses often utilise intangible assets including intellectual property rights.[327] As Wolfgang Schön highlighted as one of two fundamental assumptions concerning the digitalisation of the economy:[328]

> The business models behind the success of firms and digitalised markets are built on intangible assets (patterns, algorithms etc) and economies of scale (network effects in particular). Multinational firms are therefore able to choose at will the location of central functions and value drivers, including jurisdictions which are neither the country where the ultimate consumer resides nor the country where the parent company is resident.

---

[326] Ibid at 169.
[327] OECD, above n 324 at 46 at [108], where the OECD discusses the use and ownership of intellectual property by social network companies as follows: "Social network companies generally protect their intellectual property rights for the combination of trademarks, trade dress, domain names, copyrights, trade secrets and patents."
[328] Schön, above n 303 at 278.

3.4 THE RELIANCE ON INTELLECTUAL PROPERTY

The two components in Schön's statement are key challenges to the tax system posed by the digitalised economy, although it is fair to recognise that the exploitation of intangible assets are an increasingly important driver of value creation in all businesses and not just digitalised business.[329]

The first part is the phenomenal growth in intellectual property rights utilised by business. All the evidence points to the growth and importance of intellectual property as a key component in business growth but also selected case studies show how it is being used in digitalised businesses. Statistics from the World Intellectual Property Organization, referred to by the OECD, cite an annual average increase in total intellectual property rights applications of 7.1 per cent per annum from 2004 to 2016 (an increase of 125 per cent over the thirteen-year period).[330] In a more detailed examination of business structures, the OECD compared the activities of a traditional taxi company to that of a digital ride-for-hire company and concluded that in the traditional entity structure there were no examples of the use of intellectual property whilst in the digital model the following three components had substantial reliance on intellectual property: network promotion and contract management (development of rating algorithms); service provisioning (running of algorithms to match users and set fares); and network infrastructure operation (development of app and platform, and algorithms to match users and set fares).[331]

The second aspect referred to by Schön is the mobility of location for intellectual property. This makes this type of asset class easy to transfer from one jurisdiction to another and, at the same time, very hard to value for transfer pricing purposes. This transfer pricing problem arises because of a lack of comparable transactions, in part because of the network effects inherent in digitalised businesses creating monopolistic or oligopolistic characteristics.[332] The ability to locate intellectual property assets feeds into the "vanishing ability" to tax business profits referred to at the beginning of this chapter – the ease with which people in different countries can be connected through an online platform gives businesses great flexibility to locate their business activities where they wish and access different geographic markets from a limited

---
[329] OECD, above n 324 at [138].
[330] Ibid at chapter 2 at [136].
[331] Ibid at annexure figure 2.A.4.
[332] Becker and Englisch, above n 310 at 162.

number of remote locations, without the need for a material local presence.³³³

3.5 The Characterisation of Transactions and Income

It is clearly recognised by all, including the OECD, that there is quite considerable work necessary to make clear the correct tax classification for various types of new digital products and services.³³⁴ Essentially, transactions might be classified as business profits (if they are regarded as the provision of goods or services), technical services (in which case some treaties may regard them in a special category as royalties, or in the alternative as ordinary services and so business profits) or royalties (this is particularly the case where the treaties define royalties to include payments for the rental of commercial, industrial or scientific equipment). Thus, many new digital products and services have a question mark over their classification and this characterisation is frequently both a matter of domestic law and the definition of various categories contained in the relevant treaty. This uncertainty is particularly true in respect of cloud computing, as Lee and Yoon note in their International Fiscal Association General Report:³³⁵

> According to the branch reports, no National tax administration has yet established or issued any clear and concrete interpretive guideline on taxation of income arising from cloud computing. As a result, the traditional rules and theories on international taxation of services still regulate the taxation of cloud computing. Because cloud computing is a very recent phenomenon and no jurisdiction has domestic law that caters for this new type of transactions yet, application of the "old" law, currently in force, may potentially lead to a number of difficult problems in determining the character and source of the relevant income. In particular when it comes to treaty application, it boils down, for the most part, to the familiar issue of taxation of service, and withholding is seldom considered as relevant.

It appears as though the classification of some transactions is relatively straightforward. The purchase of "shrink-wrap" or the download of

---

[333] HM Treasury above n 316 at 3.10.
[334] OECD above n 324 at 5 at [381].
[335] Chang Hee Lee and Ji-Hyon Yoon "Withholding Tax in the Era of BEPS, CIVs and the Digital Economy" (2018) 103b IFA Cahiers de Droit Fiscal International 219 at 253.

"click-wrap" software is generally recognised by most countries as income in the nature of business profits. Accordingly, unless the enterprise selling such software has a permanent establishment in the jurisdiction in which it is sold there is unlikely to be source state taxation. Under the traditional OECD view, this analysis of the transaction as business profits remains unless the buyer/user acquires a legal right to modify or reproduce the software for their own use or for resale to third parties. If such a right to modify or reproduce the software exists then most countries regard this as a royalty.[336]

The more complex characterisation arises in the area of cloud computing, as already indicated. Because the customer has continual access, cloud computing does not involve a singular purchase or downloading of the software or digital contents. The category "X as a service" (XaaS) or "Platform as a Service" (PaaS) involve cloud operators giving their customers access to the servers so customers can make use of computer software or applications or computing platforms or programming tools. In most countries around the world, these transactions are largely understood as the provision of services and hence unless there is a specific treaty or domestic law definition (such as a technical service fee) they will default into business income. Some countries regard a third category of software services, "Infrastructure as a Service" (IaaS), as falling more within the category of the lease of the property and so within the definition of royalties, particularly if there is a definition of royalty including rentals of commercial, industrial or scientific equipment found in the treaty.

As the OECD discussed in the 2015 Final Report on addressing the tax challenges of the digital economy,[337] there is a need for a careful examination of the rationale behind existing rules in order to ensure that there is not an arbitrary tax outcome for transactions which are substantially similar in nature. Withholding taxes on certain categories of income (perhaps expanding the definition of royalty to include certain digital business-type transactions) can be another solution[338] to the challenges posed by the digitalisation of business.

---

[336] Ibid at 252.
[337] OECD, above n 305 at 3.1 at [272].
[338] In place of, or in addition to, expanding the definition of permanent establishment, which is the obvious response to the problem of lack of nexus identified at Section 3.1.

3.6 The Failure of Transfer Pricing with Certain Multinational Enterprises and Their Transactions

The suitability of the transfer pricing regimes around the world was a key part of the BEPS project. The final report on BEPS Actions 8–10[339] contained nearly 200 pages of revisions to the OECD Transfer Pricing Guidelines.[340] Despite these substantial revisions the overriding impression is that the changes to the transfer pricing rules post-BEPS still leave much to be desired. Paul Oosterhuis and Amanda Parsons describe the application of the arm's-length standard as "plagued with difficulties and weaknesses".[341] The complexity and sustainability of the changes have been questioned,[342] and their susceptibility to controversy,[343] as indeed has the fundamental nature of separate entity accounting (inherent in the arm's-length standard) for its inability to "attribute the effects of integration and synergies".[344]

This last problem, as Johanna Hey succinctly points out, is this: "Treating the members of an MNE as if they were independent is a fiction, which inherently ignores the economic facts and outcome of an integrated business and, therefore, the real nature of MNE's."[345] The reason for MNEs is that it is the combination of different production factors that can be spread across the world and involve input from all parts of the integrated business. The Oxford International Tax Group, chaired by Michael Devereux, summarises this aspect:[346]

---

[339] OECD *Aligning Transfer Pricing Outcomes with Value Creation, Actions 8-10-2015 Final Reports* (OECD Publishing, 2015).
[340] OECD *OECD Transfer Pricing Guidelines for Multinational Enterprises and Tax Administrations* (OECD Publishing, 2017).
[341] Paul Oosterhuis and Amanda Parsons "Destination-Based Income Taxation: Neither Principled Nor Practical?" (2018) 71 Tax L Rev 515 at 529 where they state: "For example, the challenge of accurately pricing intangibles, the fact that the arm's-length standard does not account for efficiencies that are achieved when transactions occur on an intercompany rather than third-party basis (as described by Coase), as well as the overall complexity of applying the arm's-length standard, have each week in the application of the standard."
[342] Richard Collier and Joseph L Andrus *Transfer Pricing and the Arm's Length Principle after BEPS* (Oxford University Press, 2017). See Chapters 7 and 8 for greater detail.
[343] Joe Andrus and Paul Oosterhuis *Transfer Pricing after BEPS: Where Are We and Where Should We Be Going* (TAXES The Tax Magazine, March 2017) at 104.
[344] Hey, above n 277 at 206.
[345] Ibid at 206.
[346] Michael Devereux and others *Residual Profit Allocation by Income. A Paper of the Oxford International Tax Group chaired by Michael Devereux* (Oxford International Tax Group, WP 19/01, March 2019).

3.6 THE FAILURE OF TRANSFER PRICING

More precisely, the hierarchical organisation of a worldwide value chain generates profits that go beyond the sum of the profits that would be derived by the individual group entities in an open-market situation. These synergies (and the economic rents generated by them) are not only hard to capture and in practice they are not even allocable to specific corporate units or geographic locations in theory.

These issues are of course not isolated to digitalised businesses but extend across the whole ambit of business activity. In addition to the concerns raised by commentators that there needs to be an urgent focus on clear definitions regarding the returns to funding activities and capital, clearer descriptions of how the normal cases where function and risks are spread throughout the group can be dealt with and how one can determine which entities bear the risks of actual returns, there are additional questions relating to the digital economy.[347] These include questions such as:

- How does one address issues in the transfer pricing methodologies relating to quantification of value associated with direct and indirect network effects?
- Is there value attributable to efficiencies relating to economies of scale and mobility?
- How does one assess the value of data?
- What about the role of user-sustained engagement, content creation and their previously discussed connection?
- What about multi-sided markets? In particular, where there are opportunities to non-neutrally price (prices on one side set below the marginal cost, while the other side subsidises the platform).

These issues, together with the costs and complexity of trying to address them, have led some practitioner commentators to suggest that the demise of the arm's length principle is imminent.[348] Other commentators like Jefferson VanderWolk have taken a different view:[349]

> As the arm's-length standard enters its second century, it appears (to this writer, at least) that the standard is likely to be with us as long as we are

---

[347] Andrus and Oosterhuis, above n 343 at 104.
[348] Grant Thornton "Say Goodbye to the Arm's Length Principle" (24 July 2019) <www.grant-thornton.ch/globalassets/1.-member-firms/switzerland/insights/pdf/2019/201907/say-goodbye-to-the-arms-length-principle.pdf>.
[349] Jefferson VanderWolk "The Arm's Length Standard Enters Its Second Century" (2019) Tax Notes Int' 961.

living in a world in which different sovereign jurisdictions impose income tax on business income. The standard may evolve to deal with new fact patterns, as it has over the past 30 years, and it will undoubtedly be interpreted in new ways by judges applying local-law versions.

Overall it is probably fair to suggest that the tide is going out on the universal acceptance that transfer pricing can provide the right answer in all circumstances. The OECD Secretariat's Proposal on Pillar One makes these observations:[350]

> While there seems to be adherence among Inclusive Framework members to the principle that routine transactions can normally be priced at arm's length, there are increasing doubts that the arm's length principle can be relied on to give an appropriate result in all cases (such as, for example, cases involving non-routine profits from intangibles). Moreover, there seems to be agreement that the arm's length principle is becoming an increasing source of complexity and that simplification would be desirable to contain the increasing administration and compliance costs of trying to apply it. Thus, an "administrable" solution is essential, especially for emerging and developing countries. And a simple system will lower the risks of disputes, which currently endanger the cohesion of the international tax system.

In short the OECD has concerns about the accuracy, cost and administrability of the current transfer pricing regime and its reliance on the arm's-length standard.

3.7 The Inadequacy of Residence-Based Taxation

This issue has previously been discussed in the section in this book that examined the justification for various forms of tax, such as source and residence-based taxation, in the context of cross-border business.[351] The failure of source taxation to adequately deal with the carrying on/out of digitalised businesses in a jurisdiction without establishing a nexus and hence a taxable presence,[352] can be compounded by the inadequacy of residence-based taxation. Challenges created by problems in residence taxation include the following.

---

[350] OECD *Public Consultation Document Secretariat Proposal for a "Unified Approach" Under Pillar One* (OECD, October–November 2019) at 6 at [17].
[351] See Section 1.6 "Observations about Source and Residence Taxation in the Context of Cross-Border Taxation".
[352] See Section 3.2 "The Vanishing Ability to Tax Business Profits".

3.7.1 The Mobility and Ease of Establishing Corporate Residence

International tax planning has relied, in part, on the ability to create subsidiary companies located in favourable tax jurisdictions. There is no doubt that with careful attention to detail it has been possible to establish such tax residence for both domestic and tax treaty purposes. Tests such as incorporation, central management and directorial control are a mixture of formal and factual elements which are often somewhat arbitrary and certainly capable of manipulation. Such residency requirements are sometimes curiously difficult to administer in practice, especially when there is a breakdown in communication between the tax director of a company and other management, resulting in unexpected outcomes and unanticipated tax risks. The usual dual residence tie-breaker test, namely the effective place of management, has also been the subject of criticism for its ambiguity and lack of precision.[353] Coupled with the challenges of taxing digitalised businesses in source countries due to a lack of nexus, it is easy to see why the OECD's Action 1 was such a controversial and political touchstone. Multinationals operating a digital business can organise themselves so that they have historically been able to pay tax in a low-tax jurisdiction through the use of subsidiaries resident in that jurisdiction.

3.7.2 The Ability to Separate Shareholder Taxation from Corporate Taxation

Nearly all jurisdictions impose tax on a company's income separately from the tax on distributions made to the shareholders. The reason for this is that if tax was not imposed at the corporate level there would be very limited tax paid. Although most jurisdictions provide for some form of integration or relief, corporate tax remains a very significant contribution to total tax in the business area.[354] The challenge arising from this separation of taxation is linked to the first bullet point above. If shareholders are not subject to tax on the profits made by the company, it is possible to ensure that there is substantial deferral. Prior to the recent changes in international taxation in the United States, it was possible for

---

[353] John Avery Jones "2008 OECD Model: Place of Effective Management What One Can Learn from the History" (2008) 63 Bull for Int' Tax 183.

[354] Richard Vann "Taxing International Business Income: Hard Boiled Wonderland and the End of the World" (2010) 2 WTJ 291 at 295 and Part I of the Appendix.

US-based multinationals to aggregate their foreign subsidiaries earnings in relatively low-tax jurisdictions without further US taxation. In many respects, much of the BEPS project was focused on multinationals doing just such activities. One important mechanism to overcome this challenge is the use of controlled foreign companies (or CFC) regimes which can attribute profits from a company to shareholders.[355]

3.8 Competition by States

Upon reflection, this should perhaps be the first and most difficult challenge of the current international tax framework and the digitalisation of business. It is easy, however, to lose sight of an important problem with our existing international tax framework. Countries can, and do, compete with one another to attract economic activity and, sometimes, to favour domestic businesses. The problem that the BEPS Project sought to address was in part due to the active competition of countries to attract or retain investment, and in some cases tolerance towards legitimate, if aggressive, tax planning. For example, listed amongst a category of major BEPS risks in the area of direct taxation in the analysis by the Directorate General for Internal Policies which was requested by the European, Parliament's Special Committee on Tax Rulings, are the preferential tax regimes including patent boxes and tax rulings.[356] The study notes:[357]

> The fact that governments create incentives and mismatching opportunities in their fiscal policies is seen by some as "healthy" tax competition by MNEs and they believe that only tax harmonisation would bring an end to it. As investors expect MNEs to maximise their post-tax earnings (and not pre-tax earnings), they find it natural that MNEs are responding to government's incentives.

The BEPS Project has seen greater cooperation from a huge number of countries that are members of the Inclusive Framework, but consistent with the above observation and the advice to the European Parliament are the 2014 comments by Devereux and Vella:[358]

---

[355] OECD *Designing Effective Controlled Foreign Company Rules, Action 3 – 2015 Final Report* (OECD Publishing, 2015).
[356] Directorate General for Internal Policies *Tax Challenges in the Digital Economy* (European Parliament, IP/A/TAXE2/2016-04 PE 579.002, June 2016) at 3.4.1.
[357] Ibid at 3.4.5.
[358] Michael P Devereux and John Vella "Are We Heading towards a Corporate Tax System Fit for the 21st Century?" (20 November 2014) SSRN <https://papers.ssrn.com/sol3/papers.cfm?abstract_id=2532933>.

3.8 COMPETITION BY STATES 111

If countries acting in their own interests believe that they have an incentive to undermine the international consensus, then that international consensus cannot provide a stable long-run system. There is ample evidence that countries have been doing precisely that. Furthermore, quite beyond the current uncertainty surrounding the outcome of the OECD BEPS initiative, even if it is successful in its own terms the BEPS initiative will not eliminate these competitive forces.

It seems obvious and clear that these issues of competition and the possibility of undermining international consensus remain relevant in the current project to reform potential changes to the nexus and profit allocation rules. The OECD/G20 are leading this project and attempting to manage members of the Inclusive Framework to undertake a coherent and concurrent review of "the profit allocation and nexus rules that would consider the impacts of digitalisation on the economy, relating to the principle of aligning profits with underlying economic activities and value creation".[359]

It does seem as though there has been some evidence of greater cooperation amongst the approximately 130 members of the Inclusive Framework but the challenges are numerous. In addition to the important technical work carried out by the OECD, there is a level of political engagement and endorsement which go beyond these technical issues and "will have an impact on revenues and the overall balance of taxing rights".[360] Any proposals and developments are made by the OECD on a "without prejudice" basis,[361] meaning that there is a great deal of "wait and see" by members of the OECD/G20 and the Inclusive Framework.

---

[359] OECD *Tax Challenges Arising from Digitalisation - Interim Report 2018* (OECD Publishing, 2018) at 5 at [397].
[360] OECD, above n 279 at 23.
[361] OECD *Addressing the Tax Challenges of the Digitalisation of the Economy - Policy Note* (OECD, 23 January 2019).

4

Responding to the Challenges

Legal Constraints on Any Changes to the Current Framework

4.1 Introduction

Part I of this book is designed to set out the landscape and framework for the international tax regime, with a particular focus on the challenges posed by the rapid growth of digitalised businesses. We began by looking at the current international tax settings arising from the historical compromise reached in the 1920s. The justification for source and residence taxation was examined next, in order to understand the theoretical basis for the source country imposing a tax on non-resident entities or taxpayers. Having concluded that there was a theoretical basis for imposing a tax, namely the contribution that the source country makes to the carrying on of digitalised business in its jurisdiction, it was observed that there is little constraint to the imposition of source-based taxation under domestic law in many jurisdictions.[362]

The development of highly digitalised businesses[363] has led to numerous challenges to the international tax system discussed in the previous chapter. One key challenge is whether there will be sufficient international consensus to undertake a successful review of the profit allocation and nexus rules discussed in Section 3.2, or whether states will default to competition and self-interest. There is concern that tax competition will continue, with the reduction in the United States federal corporate income tax rate possibly stimulating rate cuts elsewhere.[364]

---

[362] See Chapter 1, and in particular Section 1.7 "Exploring the Limits of Domestic Source-Based Taxation".
[363] Described in Chapter 2.
[364] See Section 3.8 "Competition by States", and the conclusions reached by International Monetary Fund *IMF Policy Paper: Corporate Taxation in the Global Economy* (IMF Publications, Policy Paper No. 19/007, March 2019), [13]–[14] at 11–12.

112

This chapter continues the examination of the international tax landscape and sets out the two broad options available for reform to the international tax framework with a particular focus on legal constraints that are present in existing international tax and trade obligations.

In responding to the challenges posed by the digitalised economy, the world is faced with the possibility of either a consensus-driven multilateral solution or, alternatively, an increasing number of countries entering into unilateral domestic taxes. International tax, and countries individually and collectively, are at a crossroads. There is widespread agreement, through the Inclusive Framework, that there is a need to respond to the challenges of digitalised business. In examining the options, one path of the crossroads can only be traversed if there is consensus amongst a significant number of countries. The other path, using unilateral domestic taxes, can be undertaken by countries independent of this consensus.

In examining the design of such unilateral taxes, it is important to analyse how existing international legal arrangements (such as international treaties in the area of taxation and trade) may apply to constrain or influence key factors. After outlining the two broad options available, the remainder of this chapter focuses on the legal landscape for the design of unilateral taxes.

4.2 International Tax at the Crossroads

4.2.1 Digitalised Businesses and BEPS

Right from the beginning, the tax challenges that emerged from the digitalisation of business were identified as a major part of the OECD/G20 Base Erosion and Profit Shifting (BEPS) Project. The big problems, identified in the 2015 Action 1 Report,[365] were that, first, the increasing digitalisation of the economy meant that it may be impossible to have a different set of rules for the high-tech digital economy from those that applied to more traditional business models. Secondly, although progress was made on indirect tax, it was clear that there was not a straightforward solution in the area of direct tax. Accordingly, it would not be unfair to describe the 2015 Final Report as being anything but "final", with the OECD/G20 recognising that this was a stream of work which would have the potential to continue for some considerable period of time.

---

[365] *OECD/G20 Base Erosion and Profit Shifting Project: Addressing the Tax Challenges of the Digital Economy, Action 1 – 2015 Final Report* (OECD Publishing, October 2015).

The digitalisation of business has facilitated BEPS issues. As discussed in Chapter 3, many digital businesses do not have permanent establishments in the jurisdiction in which they have a lot of economic activity. Furthermore, they have located their intellectual property and other intangibles in low-tax jurisdictions and used transfer pricing and treaties to divert their profits. There is some evidence that the opportunity for profit shifting remains a significant problem, particularly for developing countries, and furthermore that this problem continues in the post-BEPS environment.[366]

4.2.2 More than BEPS

The Action 1 Report, although not as conclusive as the other fourteen Reports, was dealing with a much bigger problem than aggressive tax planning or the weakness of treaty or domestic tax rules. Beyond BEPS was a systemic issue that highly digitalised businesses were using business models (such as multi-sided platforms) which enabled these businesses to generate income on a scale and with such speed and disruption to more traditional competitors not previously seen – all without paying a great deal of (if any) tax. The question emerging was not so much the aggressive tax planning that the BEPS Project was aimed at but a more fundamental issue – namely, was the allocation of taxing rights under the current rules appropriate given the change in the way in which business is currently being conducted? As the OECD described in its Public Consultation Document:[367]

> Action 1 Report observed that ... digitalisation raised a series of broader direct tax challenges, which it identified as data, nexus and characterisation. These challenges chiefly relate to the question of how taxing rights on income generated from cross-border activities in the digital age should be allocated among countries.

Following on, perversely, from the Action 1 (Final) Report was the interim report (Interim Report)[368] of the Task Force on the Digital

---

[366] International Monetary Fund *IMF Policy Paper: Corporate Taxation in the Global Economy* (IMF Publications, Policy Paper No. 19/007, March 2019), [11]–[12] at 10.

[367] OECD/G20 *Base Erosion and Profit Shifting Project: Addressing the Tax Challenges of the Digitalisation of the Economy* (OECD Publishing, February 2019) at [5].

[368] OECD/G20 *Base Erosion and Profit Shifting Project, Tax Challenges Arising from Digitalisation: Tax Challenges Arising from Digitalisation – Interim Report 2018* (OECD Publishing, March 2018).

4.2 INTERNATIONAL TAX AT THE CROSSROADS 115

Economy (TFDE), a group mandated by the G20 and made up of members of the Inclusive Framework. The Interim Report discussed many of the challenges referred to in Chapter 3 of this book, namely scale without mass, reliance on intangible assets and the importance of data, user participation and their synergies with intangible assets. The Interim Report also noted that the various BEPS measures proposed in the other fourteen Actions were "already having an impact".[369] These were detailed by the OECD as follows:[370]

- Actions 8–10, multinational groups had realigned their tax arrangements with real economic activity by adjusting their transfer pricing positions and moving intangible assets back into the residence jurisdiction;
- Action 7, several highly digitalised multinational groups had changed the distribution models which had previously been based on remote sales, and instead now employed a local "buy–sell" distribution model; and
- Action 13, there was a more holistic approach to the review of cross-border transactions.

Even after such a restructuring as referred to in the second bullet point above (from remote sales to a "buy–sell" distribution model), the OECD noted that there was concern expressed by some countries about a risk that these highly digitalised multinationals would use limited risk distributors to justify only minimal tax being paid in market jurisdictions. They were still able to "shift a disproportionately high amount of the profit to a small number of affiliates in remote locations".[371] This is based upon a certain level of physical activity involving business carried on in those remote areas that control risks and functions relating to the development, enhancement, maintenance, protection and exploitation of intangibles (DEMPE).

The three major characteristics observed in highly digitalised business models have the following implications for the existing profit allocation and nexus rules:[372]

---

[369] OECD *Base Erosion and Profit Shifting Project, Public Consultation Document: Addressing the Tax Challenges of the Digitalisation of the Economy* (OECD Publishing, February 2019) at [5].
[370] Ibid at 5–6.
[371] Ibid at 6.
[372] Ibid at 6.

- Scale without mass – results in a reduction in the number of jurisdictions where a taxing right can be asserted over a business's profits. The absence of source-based taxation in the market country is viewed as a significant erosion to the corporate tax base over time.
- Reliance upon intangible assets – allows for income to be allocated to different parts of the multinational group and, in particular, creating opportunities for locating income in low- or no-tax entities.
- Data and user participation – poses similar problems to the scale without mass issue, namely that the existing nexus and profit allocation rules are unlikely to mean that there will be any taxation in the jurisdiction where the users are located notwithstanding their active participation in the business in various forms.

The Interim Report indicated that countries had different views on these challenges – broadly falling into three groups. Two of these groups considered that there was a need to change the existing profit allocation and nexus rules (the first of these two groups were particularly focused on data and user participation and so were more interested in targeted changes to the existing tax rules), while the third group of countries thought that there was "nothing to see here – move along" and that no action was needed beyond addressing the BEPS issues.[373] From around mid-2017 the OECD seemed to coalesce into a group that was prepared to explore a longer-term solution to the international tax problems exposed by the digitalising economy through the development of new rules involving profit allocation and nexus.

4.2.3 The Brave New World

Members of the Inclusive Framework have, therefore, moved on from the position set out in the Interim Report and are attempting to work together to provide a consensus-based long-term solution in their final report of 2020. The Inclusive Framework approved a Policy Note on 23 January 2019 which advanced two proposals (termed "pillars"), both on a "without prejudice" basis:[374]

- **Pillar One** addresses the broader challenges of the digitalised economy and focuses on the allocation of taxing rights. To do this, there is a

---

[373] OECD, above n 368 at 171–2.
[374] OECD/G20 *Base Erosion and Profit Shifting Project: Addressing the Tax Challenges of the Digitalisation of the Economy – Policy Note* (OECD Publishing, January 2019).

need to review the profit allocation and nexus rules, whilst raising questions of where tax should be paid (and how much) in a world where enterprises can be heavily involved in the economic life of a jurisdiction without significant physical presence.
- **Pillar Two** looks at the remaining BEPS issues and seeks to develop rules that would provide jurisdictions with the ability to tax when income has been allocated (or diverted) to a jurisdiction which has a lower rate of tax.

The various proposals in Pillar One are the most far-reaching international tax reforms for a hundred years. They are discussed in detail in Chapters 5–8. Why are they seen as being so radical? There are three major reasons (at least) why this is so:

- **They revise the allocation of taxing rights.** Some of the proposals allocate more taxing rights to the market or user jurisdictions. The Inclusive Framework suggests that this reallocation of taxing rights reflects situations where value is created by business activity through participation in the user or market jurisdiction that is currently not recognised in the existing rules.[375] This is controversial because the market has not traditionally been seen as a sufficient link to create a nexus for taxation.[376] The factors involved in the production of income associated with supply, rather than demand (obviously linked to the market) have historically been the factors where income has been located.
- **They override the limitation on taxing rights determined by reference to a physical presence (of a person or situs).** This has generally been accepted as a cornerstone of the current rules, with the definition of a permanent establishment having a long-standing history dating back to the 1920s compromise. An increasing number of countries have voiced their dissatisfaction because of the failure of "the existing profit allocation and nexus rules [to] take into account the increasing ability of businesses, in certain situations, to participate in the economic life of a jurisdiction without an associated or meaningful physical presence".[377]

---

[375] Ibid at 2.
[376] OECD, above n 369 at [8].
[377] OECD/G20 *Inclusive Framework on BEPS: Programme of Work to Develop a Consensus Solution to the Tax Challenges Arising from the Digitalisation of the Economy* (OECD Publishing, May 2019) [11] at 7.

- **They challenge the arm's length principle.** The vulnerability of the international corporate tax system is in part ascribed to the "limitations of the arm's length principle" in a report to the Executive Board of the International Monetary Fund (the IMF Report).[378] Some of the proposals require a reconsideration of the current transfer pricing rules as they relate to non-routine returns, and other proposals would require modifications going beyond non-routine returns. These suggestions, "in all cases, ... would lead to solutions that go beyond the arm's length principle".[379]

No one is underestimating the difficulty of this task. This is because, first, as discussed, the Inclusive Framework is trying to revisit some long-standing and fundamental tenets of the international tax system. The existing system, for all its faults, has had a remarkably long tenure. The new solution has to reflect a balance between precision and practicality (remembering the wide gulf of capabilities between the largest and most developed countries and the smallest and developing countries) with a sound conceptual and logical economic basis. The rules should neither result in taxation where there is no economic profit nor result in double taxation.[380] In short, dealing with the corporate tax implications of digitalisation and new business models is potentially such a fundamental change in the tax system that it has been described as "highly contentious, politically and intellectually".[381]

The second reason is the lack of a common starting point and the competitive pressures between different nations, such as the developed and developing world. The IMF Report records that the only consensus in the initial OECD/G20 report on digitalisation and taxation[382] "was that attempts to isolate for special treatment a 'digital economy' (or 'digital activities') are misplaced, given how pervasive these technologies are, and so unpredictable as their future development".[383] Countries have widely differing perspectives pending a longer-term solution: some see targeted unilateral action as a political imperative given domestic views on under-taxation, while others see any unilateral measures as merely a

---

[378] IMF, above n 366.
[379] OECD/G20, above n 374 at 2.
[380] Ibid at 3.
[381] IMF, above n 366 [20] at 14.
[382] OECD/G20, above n 365.
[383] IMF, above n 366 [20] at 14.

grab for revenue from a few prominent and largely US-owned companies.[384]

Thirdly, not only is the task somewhat Herculean, but so is the timeframe. The plan is to deliver a long-term consensus-based solution in 2020. This is described by the OECD/G20 Inclusive Framework as "extremely ambitious".[385] The first 1920s compromise took approximately five years to gestate.

4.3 Interim Measures

If the Inclusive Framework does not deliver a solution that achieves consensus within the agreed G20 timeline, then the risk of widespread unilateral action is high. As the OECD recognises:[386]

> A growing number of jurisdictions are not content with the taxation outcomes produced by the current international tax system, and have or are seeking to impose various measures or interpretations of the current rules that risk significantly increasing compliance burdens, double taxation and uncertainty.

In any event, many countries were concerned about what happens to the taxation of highly digitalised businesses in the immediate future. These countries were, and are, facing domestic political pressure to take action. Recognising that agreeing and implementing a global solution would take some time, these countries considered what to do in the interim whilst waiting for the process to be put in place by the Inclusive Framework.

There was a lack of consensus back in 2018 on the merit or need for interim taxes. The divergence of views can be simplified into two groups: those opposed to unilateral taxes because of the risks and adverse consequences of them; and those who recognise the concerns of the first group, but on balance consider that the need to ensure taxation is paid on certain transactions outweigh these risks. The second group considered it was helpful to set out guidance on design considerations, partly to mitigate some of the adverse consequences, and partly to standardise the response by any country proposing interim measures.[387]

Those countries contemplating an interim tax had in their sights digitalised businesses with a significant market but little physical

---

[384] Ibid at [21] at 14.
[385] OECD/G20, above n 377 [12] at 7.
[386] Ibid at [11] at 7.
[387] OECD/G20, above n 368 [403–4] at 178.

presence in their jurisdiction. They employed business models that relied heavily on intangible property, data, user participation and network effects.[388] These are the types of businesses discussed in Chapters 2 and 3 of this book.

4.3.1 Concerns about Interim Taxes

All countries, including those in favour of the introduction of interim taxes,[389] were concerned about the following "risks and adverse consequences that would arise in respect of such a tax".[390] These can be categorised into three major headings.[391]

(a) Economic Concerns about Investment, Innovation, Adverse Growth and Economic Incidence

The problem with imposing a tax on the supply of services is that it increases the cost of capital, reducing the return and the incentive to invest, resulting in the potential for a negative effect on growth. The sector that has been the most innovative and growth-orientated is the digitalised business sector and a tax could well stifle such innovation and reduce competition to existing dominant businesses. If growth is not inhibited, then more resources would be used to achieve the same level of production, resulting in a negative impact on the overall welfare of an economy.

There is also the potential for the incidence of tax (the true cost of payment) to fall on local customers, rather than on the non-resident supplier upon whom it is imposed. In circumstances where there is little competition and the customers have little choice but to purchase, regardless of the price, then the supplier is likely to on-charge the tax cost so that the burden falls upon the local consumer.

(b) Taxation Concerns

As will be discussed in Section 4.4.2(b)–(d), there are certain constraints arising from international treaties and obligations that mean the tax must take a particular form. In general terms, this means that the tax must be imposed as an excise tax (on gross income rather than net income), apply

---

[388] Ibid, [406] at 178.
[389] Ibid, [408] at 179.
[390] Ibid, [407] at 178.
[391] Ibid at 178.

to both residents and non-residents alike, and not be creditable against other direct income taxes. This is likely to make the tax "ugly" in the sense that it can over-tax payments where there is no actual income (for example, a loss-making entity) and is most likely to cause double taxation.

(c) Implementation, Compliance and Administration Costs

Introducing a tax for a short period of time (at least it is hoped for a short period time) involves both the tax administration and taxpayers (and their advisors) gearing up to comply with new sets of rules and obligations. The costs of this when measured against the revenue collected may make the tax relatively expensive as a percentage of revenue gained. Being cross-border, the costs of auditing and verifying tax returns and any associated information will be high and there may be substantial non-compliance.

These important drawbacks have to be measured against what many countries perceive as the mismatch between taxable profit and value creation in their jurisdiction. For them, ignoring this mismatch can create an environment where the fairness, sustainability and public acceptability of the system is called into doubt.[392] Key limitations on the imposition by any country of any new interim tax include compliance with their international tax agreements, trade agreements, including membership of the World Trade Organization (WTO) and any obligations arising from regional political and economic openings such as those in the European Union (EU) and the European Economic Area (EEA).

4.4 Constraints Imposed by the Scope of Double Tax Agreements (DTAs)

4.4.1 Do DTAs Prevent the Imposition of Interim Taxes?

The Problem: DTAs generally provide that business profits are taxed only in the residence state unless the enterprise has a permanent establishment (PE) in the source state. Therefore, DTAs will prevent countries from imposing a tax on income derived by a non-resident which takes the form of business profits, assuming the non-resident does not have a PE in the source state.

---

[392] Ibid, [408] at 180.

Starting from the beginning: a country is free to determine its mode and method of taxation. A sovereign state uses domestic law to establish its taxation laws. A bilateral double tax treaty is an instrument of public international law and is usually, of course, negotiated between two sovereign states. When the double tax treaty becomes part of the domestic tax law of a country it is special legislation and is, generally speaking, presumed to override the general domestic tax law of a country. In some countries the overriding nature of the double tax treaty is implicit, based on the *lex specialis* principle of interpretation, while in others it is made express.[393] A double tax treaty is made with the purpose, amongst other things, of relieving double taxation. To achieve this purpose the double tax treaty relieves domestic taxing rights or provides a credit. Relief from double taxation is often achieved by the treaty reducing, and sometimes eliminating, domestic taxation on various types of income. This is the point of Article 7 of the OECD and the UN Model Treaties concerning business profits.

Both the OECD and the UN Model Treaties provide that business profits earned by an enterprise resident in one state are taxed in that state, unless the enterprise carries on business in the other state through a permanent establishment.[394] An interim tax will therefore be constrained by the existence of a DTA unless either one of the two following circumstances are present:

1 The DTA does not apply because the interim tax is not covered by the provisions of the DTA (discussed in Sections 4.4.2–4.4.4); or
2 The DTA applies, but does not restrict the imposition of the interim tax (discussed in Sections 4.4.5–4.4.6). This may occur, potentially, in one of two ways: first, the interim tax is within the scope of the DTA, but the business profits article does not prevent the interim tax from having effect. Secondly, the question is whether the non-discrimination article in the DTA has application.

4.4.2 *The DTA Does Not Apply*

This is one of the more controversial questions in the debate about interim taxes. As will be discussed, the OECD has given a somewhat

---

[393] For a description of this process see C Elliffe "The Lesser of Two Evils: Double Tax Treaty Override or Treaty Abuse?" (2016) 1 BTR at 62–88.

[394] OECD *Model Tax Convention on Income and on Capital: Condensed Version 2017* (OECD Publishing, November 2017). The first sentence of Article 7 of the OECD Model states as follows: "Profits of an enterprise of a Contracting State shall be taxable only in that State unless the enterprise carries on business in the other Contracting State through a permanent establishment situated therein."

qualified view that certain types of interim taxes would fall outside the scope of most DTAs.[395] This would mean that the problem set out above, namely that the DTA would prevent the imposition of an interim tax, does not occur. At the risk of stating the obvious, if the interim tax is within the scope of the DTA, then there is the prospect that it cannot be validly enforced since, generally speaking, the DTA overrides the domestic law.

(a) What Type of Taxes Are within the Scope of the DTA?

A starting point for this enquiry is to acknowledge that this is a question for a specific type of tax and a specific DTA. It is therefore conceptually difficult to answer the question as part of a general analysis – the detailed analysis will depend on the particular terms of the DTA and the particular tax (and the context in which it is enacted: such as the purpose, rate and ability to credit against other forms of taxation).

It seems generally accepted by most states that a tax is (a) a compulsory levy, which is (b) imposed by an organ of government, (c) for public purposes, and (d) without regard to the particular benefits received by the taxpayer.[396] This is a very broad definition and it is necessary to narrow it down through a careful interpretation and analysis of Article 2 of the OECD Model.

It is also generally accepted that not all taxes are within Article 2. The OECD Commentary eschews the term "direct taxes", saying that it is "far too imprecise"[397] to be helpful in defining the taxes referred to as within the scope of the DTA. Everyone in the tax world, however, seems to agree with Philip Baker when he states: "it is clear that it [Article 2] is not intended to apply to indirect taxes".[398]

Article 2 of the OECD Model deals with what taxes are covered in the DTA. It has four paragraphs which have been characterised as falling into two groups.[399]

---

[395] OECD/G20, above n 368, [413]–[424] at 181–3.
[396] HM Helminen-Kossila "The Notion of Tax and the Elimination of Double Taxation or Double Non-Taxation: General Report" (2016) 101a and 101b Cahiers de Droit Fiscal International at 161.
[397] OECD, above n 394, Commentary on Article 2(1) at [2].
[398] Philip Baker *Double Taxation Conventions* (3rd ed, Sweet and Maxwell, 2019) at 2B.10.
[399] M Lang "'Taxes Covered' – What Is a 'Tax' According to Article 2 of the OECD Model?" (2005) 59 Bull For Int' Tax at [216].

(b) Article 2(1) and (2)

The first two paragraphs are general and broadly describe the scope of the OECD Model in a general way in their definition of the term "taxes on income and on capital". Key aspects of the first two paragraphs include:

1. the fact that the taxes can be imposed by a Contracting State, one of its political subdivisions or local authorities;
2. it does not matter how the taxes are levied;
3. they include all taxes "on total income, on total capital, or on elements of income or of capital";
4. they include taxes on gains from the alienation of property;
5. they include taxes on the total amounts of wages or salaries paid by enterprises and
6. they include taxes on capital appreciation.

The OECD Commentary notes that there are three types of taxes discussed in Article 2(2). They are, first, taxes on income (total or elements thereof) and taxes on capital (total or elements thereof); secondly, taxes on capital gains from the alienation of property as well as capital appreciation; and lastly, taxes on the total amounts of wages or salaries paid by undertakings (payroll taxes).[400]

At a general level, therefore, it is the first category of the three above that is the focus of this enquiry. An interim tax is unlikely to take the form of a tax on a capital gain from the alienation of property, nor is it similar to payroll or salary and wage taxes.

(c) Article 2(3) and (4)

If the first two paragraphs are general and broad, the next two paragraphs have a different type of focus. They are specific and they are domestic. Paragraph (3) contains the list of existing domestic taxes to which, as agreed between the two Contracting States, the DTA applies. Paragraph (4) goes on to provide that the DTA will also apply to "any identical or substantially similar taxes that are imposed after the date of signature of the Convention in addition to, or in place of, the existing taxes".[401]

---

[400] OECD, above n 397, Commentary on Article 2(2) at 3.
[401] Ibid at Article 2(4).

(d) Tax Is an Undefined Term: What Rule of Interpretation Should We Apply?

Neither the OECD Model nor the UN Model defines the term "tax". Article 2 defines the types of taxes covered by the Models, but does not define the term "tax" itself. This means that we should apply the rule of interpretation required under Article 3(2).[402] Essentially, Article 3(2) provides that any term which is not defined shall have the meaning that it has under the law of the state for the purposes of the taxes to which the Convention applies (the domestic meaning) unless the context otherwise requires (an autonomous international meaning).

The difference between these two groups of paragraphs noted above has led Lang to assert that they should be considered in quite a fundamentally different way from the perspective of interpretation. He suggests that paragraphs (1) and (2) do not refer to domestic law at all and they should be seen as having only an "autonomous" or international meaning, whereas paragraphs (3) and (4) must be interpreted in the light of the substantive domestic law (and the taxes in place) at the time the treaty was signed.[403] Helminen argues that it is a contextual treaty meaning that should be searched for.[404] She concludes that there is no general agreement on whether one should use domestic law meanings or an autonomous treaty meaning.[405]

Several key points can be made, supporting a broader contextual approach to interpretation. As Lang and Helminen suggest:[406]

- Using Article 3(2) to interpret the meaning of "taxes" in these circumstances is a circular definition (a circular definition is defining a term by using the term in the definition). Which domestic tax laws are covered by the treaty if the meaning of the term tax is unknown?
- There should be an autonomous interpretation approach to the generic paragraphs of Article 2 (paragraphs (1) and (2)) which do not refer to domestic law at all, but must have a context that includes domestic law since there would be no taxes without domestic law. As previously noted, there are various categories or types of taxes that paragraph (2) focuses on.

---

[402] Ibid at Article 3(2).
[403] Lang, above n 399 at 216.
[404] Helminen-Kossila, above n 396 at 168.
[405] Ibid at 168.
[406] Lang above n 399 at 216; see also Helminen-Kossila, above n 396 at 168.

- There will need to be a much greater domestic law focus with respect to the interpretation of Article 2(3) as it has a specific list of certain domestic law taxes. However, it is clear that it is not an exclusive list. The use of the words "in particular" in paragraph (3) highlight that other taxes may be included and of course paragraph (4) is about the addition of "identical or substantially similar taxes" imposed after the Convention is signed.

(e) Conclusion

The practical outcome of this is that, first, there will be certain times when the domestic law takes a larger role in the process of interpreting whether a tax is included within the scope of the DTA. If a particular tax is listed in paragraph (3), but would not fall within the generic definitions in paragraphs (1) and (2), then the question arises as to whether the role of paragraph (3) is to extend the autonomous and general definition of "taxes". The answer to that seems to be "yes". In 1969, Working Party Number 30 suggested:[407]

> Paragraph 3 has quite obviously the power (although being principally an illustration to paragraphs 1 and 2) to amplify the scope of the Convention so the taxes and charges might be included in the Convention even if they were not considered to be "taxes on income (capital)" within the meaning of paragraphs 1 and 2.

Secondly, and as highlighted by Lang,[408] excluding a particular tax from paragraph (3) does not necessarily mean it is excluded from the scope of the treaty. In this case it will be an example of where the autonomous international meaning overrides or adds to the domestic meaning. Even if a tax is not specifically outlined in paragraph (3) it can be included under the general provisions of paragraphs (1) and (2). In order to exclude taxes "which are or might probably be "taxes on income (capital)" within the meaning of paragraphs 1 and 2, then it is, in the opinion of the Working Party, "not sufficient to exclude such taxes or charges solely from the list of taxes in paragraph (3), but it is necessary to make express reference in the Article that those taxes and charges are excluded from the scope of the Convention".[409]

---

[407] Working Party Number 30 of the OECD Fiscal Committee (Austria-Switzerland), received on 12 June 1969, FC/WP 30 (69), marginal number 40; see also Lang, above n 399 at 221.

[408] Lang, above n 399 at 220.

[409] Working Party Number 30, above n 407, marginal number 41; see also Lang, above n 399 at 220.

Perhaps as a consequence of this second point of the implications arising from this contextual interpretation, it is quite common to find that Contracting States exclude paragraphs (1) and (2) from their bilateral treaties and instead simply list the taxes dealt with in the format of paragraph (3). Paragraph 6.1 of the OECD Commentary provides the text which makes paragraph (3) the new paragraph (1) and omits the words "in particular".[410]

4.4.3 What Are "Taxes on Income and on Capital"?

(a) Text to Be Given a Broad Interpretation

From the above analysis on the approach to interpretation, the logical approach is to analyse, from primarily an autonomous international meaning perspective, whether the interim tax will fall within the term in paragraph (2), which refers to "all taxes imposed on total income, on total capital, or on elements of income or of capital". As previously highlighted (Section 4.4.2), because of the circularity of this definition (that is, there is no international articulated meaning for "tax" in the OECD Model text or Commentary), one must have recourse back to domestic law examples of taxes on income and on capital in order to see whether the interim tax is in substance of a kind which has similar characteristics or features of such domestic taxes. Before embarking on the exercise of looking for characteristics of these taxes in domestic law, it is important to see what parameters are framed by paragraphs (1) and (2). There are only a few areas of guidance. The first point to note is that these paragraphs are broadly drafted. The Convention applies to taxes "irrespective of the manner in which they are levied". The Commentary repeats this directive by saying that the method of taxation levy is immaterial "by direct assessment or by deduction of the source, in the form of surtaxes or surcharges, or as additional taxes".[411]

Not only is the method of collection immaterial, but the use of terminology is also discouraged by the OECD. The Commentary tells us: the term "direct taxes" is "far too imprecise" to be used.[412] This approach has been considered "wise" given how difficult it is to distinguish between indirect taxes and withholding taxes.[413] Commentators

---
[410] OECD, above n 397, Commentary on Article 2 at [6.1].
[411] Ibid, Commentary on Article 2 at [1].
[412] Ibid at [2].
[413] Lang, above n 399 at 217.

often point to the fact that withholding taxes are imposed on gross amounts of passive income (dividends, interest and royalties) and the obvious application of the DTA to them, establishing clearly that gross withholding taxes can in some circumstances be within the scope of the DTA.[414]

It is obvious that paragraphs (1) and (2) are designed to paint the concept of taxes on income and on capital with a broad brush, particularly when one considers that paragraph 1 of the OECD Commentary on Article 2 reads as follows:[415]

> to widen as much as possible the field of application of the Convention by including, as far as possible, and in harmony with the domestic laws of the Contracting States, the taxes imposed by their political subdivisions or local authorities, to avoid the necessity of concluding a new convention whenever the Contracting States' domestic laws are modified, and to ensure for each Contracting State notification of significant changes in the taxation laws of the other State.

Article 2 is one of the very few articles of the Model Convention "that have not been substantially modified since their first adoption by the OECD in 1963".[416] Furthermore, the wording of Article 2 in the 1963 OECD Model was very similar to the draft article recommended by the Organisation for European Economic Co-operation (OEEC) in 1959, with the result that many of the historical materials still remain relevant.[417] Paragraph 1 of the OECD Commentary owes its origin to the original 1957 Working Party notes, so the position has remained unchanged for more than sixty years.[418]

It is possible to assert from this review of the text of the OECD Model and Commentary that it was intended that any tax on "total income, on total capital, or on elements of income or of capital" should be broadly interpreted.

---

[414] Helminen-Kossila, above n 396 at 177.
[415] OECD, above n 394, Commentary on Article 2 at [1].
[416] T Dubut "Article 2 from an Historical Perspective: How Old Materials Can Cast New Light on Taxes Covered by Double Tax Conventions" in T Ecker and G Ressler (eds) *History of Tax Treaties – The Relevance of the OECD Documents for the Interpretation of Tax Treaties* (Linde, 2011) 115 at 117.
[417] Ibid at 117.
[418] Working Party No. 3 of the Fiscal Committee (1957), "F.C./W.P.3 (57)", referred to in OECD/G20, above n 368, [417] at 181.

(b) Taxes That Are "In Substance" Income Taxes or Taxes on Capital: Case Law

As indicated in the previous section, trying to interpret the meaning of the term "all taxes imposed on total income, on total capital, or on elements of income or of capital" may begin as an attempt to ascertain an international autonomous meaning, but sooner or later there will be a need to make an assessment as to whether the particular tax in question (for example, the interim tax) has characteristics which make it in substance an income tax or a tax on capital. In order to do this, it is submitted that it will be necessary to make some comparison with domestic law taxes on income and capital. There are some helpful decisions in this area but they mostly concern whether the deduction of foreign tax is available as credit under domestic tax credit provisions. These cases are therefore illustrative of a type of approach or reasoning rather than any direct precedential value.

The first decision is an English case, *Yates v GCA International*,[419] in the Chancery Division in 1991. The taxpayer company had claimed a credit against its UK corporation tax for Venezuelan tax deducted on a contract for services partially performed in the United Kingdom and partially performed in Venezuela. The Venezuelan tax was deducted at a fixed rate from 90 per cent of the gross remuneration paid under the contract. The percentage of gross receipts liable to be taxed varied between different trades and professions (it was 90 per cent in the particular case involving *GCA International*) but the intention behind the tax was that it was designed to tax net profits. Under the UK provisions, the foreign tax had to "correspond" to income tax or corporation tax in the United Kingdom. The UK Revenue claimed that this was not the case; a tax on 90 per cent of gross receipts was a turnover tax. It was held by Scott J that the tax did correspond to income tax or corporation tax within the relevant provision. The difficulty of collecting tax from foreign individuals or companies was dealt with in the Venezuelan tax code by allowing an automatic deduction for 10 per cent of the gross receipts in order to produce taxable income or net profits. Although this was a gross underestimate of the cost to the taxpayer of carrying on its business, the intention was to charge tax on net profits and accordingly

---

[419] *Yates (HMIT) v GCA International Ltd (formerly Gaffney Cline & Associates Ltd)* [1991] BTC 107 (Ch).

the Venezuelan tax corresponded to the UK income tax or corporation tax.

The second decision was *de Romero v Read*[420] in the High Court of Australia in 1932. Upon their separation, a husband had entered into a separation agreement, and promised to pay to his wife the clear sum of £10,000 "free from State income tax". The dissenting judgment of Evatt J was the only one to consider the meaning of the phrase "all State income tax" as the majority judgment did not have to consider that point. Evatt J held that unemployment relief tax was an income tax, given the subject matter and essence of the charge, not the label it was given. He concluded:[421]

> It is true that the tax in question is not called "income" tax but "unemployment relief" tax. But in essence, it is an additional income tax assessed in accordance with the Income Tax (Management) Act itself. The subject matter of the tax, so far as it affects the present case, is "net assessable income", which means the gross income after excluding all income exempt from tax and after making the allowed deductions.

The third decision, *Kempe v The Queen*,[422] is from the Tax Court of Canada and concerned whether a German church tax was eligible as a tax credit. The tax, payable by all members of the church and levied on the basis of German federal law, was charged at 8 per cent on income tax or wage tax. The Court held that the church tax was a tax, enforceable by law, imposed under the authority of a legislature and of a similar nature to an income tax because it was based on the income or wages tax.

There are of course many other decisions that look at the eligibility for a foreign tax credit under domestic law. Of course, the tests are all specific to the jurisdiction concerned but there is a certain amount of commonality in approach. In part, this is due to the fact that by the very nature of a foreign tax credit the domestic legislation is looking for something that is similar in substance and that the nomenclature or even the process of collection can be quite different. What can be observed from these decisions is the need to assess the nature of the tax holistically with due consideration of the purpose and structure of the tax (including its legal authority).

---

[420] *De Romero v Read* (1932) 48 CLR 649 (HCA).
[421] Ibid at 675.
[422] *Kempe v The Queen* [2001] 1 CTC 2060 (TCC).

Turning from these general observations about how to interpret Article 2, the focus now turns to what type of interim tax would be outside the definition of "taxes on income or capital".

(c) Guidance from the OECD

As indicated previously,[423] the guidance provided by the OECD in 2018 treads a narrow line and indicates that certain interim taxes will not fall within the scope of the ordinary DTA.[424] There are several important points made by the OECD:

- From a conceptual level, "taxes on income" focus on the recipient rather than on the consumer of a supply of specific goods or services.[425]
- This is a very important and fundamental difference. An income tax usually is, well, a tax on income. In order to ascertain a company or a person's income, one usually needs to look at what has come in to that person, their economic circumstances, the expenditure they incurred in deriving that income and, in a progressive tax system, the overall level of their income. The OECD makes the point that where the interim tax is imposed on the *supply itself*, rather than the supplier, and is calculated by focusing exclusively on the expenditure side of the payment (the nature and value of the supply) then it is less likely to be a tax on income and so fall outside Article 2.[426]

Another way to look at this conceptual basis is to consider whether the interim tax inherently causes double taxation. Hohenwarter, Kofler, Mayr and Sinnig suggest that this is not the case and that an interim tax (in this case they were critiquing the European Commission's proposed digital services tax), like a VAT or other turnover/sales tax, is levied on a "destination basis".[427] They say that, on this basis, within a coherent interim tax system (i.e. where every country only taxed using the interim tax basis), double taxation is theoretically impossible because it is always imposed where the consumption takes place.[428]

---

[423] Chapter 4.2, and 4.3.
[424] OECD/G20, above n 368, [413–24] at 181–3.
[425] Ibid, [417] at 181.
[426] Ibid, [420] at 182.
[427] D Hohenwarter and others "Qualification of the Digital Services Tax Under Tax Treaties" (2019) 47(2) Intertax at 143.
[428] This is the theoretical basis for the destination-based tax reforms proposed in the article: MP Devereux and J Vella "Are We Heading towards a Corporate Tax System Fit for the 21st Century?" (2014) 88/2014 Fiscal Studies.

What actually happens when the interim tax is imposed in conjunction with a corporate income tax is that the double taxation that arises comes from the combination of the interim tax and ordinary income tax. This can also occur in purely domestic situations where residents are caught with both the interim tax and their own corporation income tax. This is based on the assumption that the interim tax is not creditable.

- Indicia of tax based on the supply, rather than the supplier.[429]

The OECD provides three elements which would indicate a stronger argument that the tax is not a "tax on income". These are:

1. it is levied on the supply of a category of services and imposed on the supply without reference to the particular economic or tax position of the supplier; or
2. it is charged at a fixed rate and without reference to the net income of the supplier (or the income from the supply); or
3. it is not creditable or eligible for any other type of relief against income tax imposed on the same payment.

- It makes no difference whether the taxes are levied by way of withholding at source or whether the tax is on a net or gross amount.[430]

The most difficult part of this is that sometimes income taxes are imposed on a gross amount of income and so they look as though they are being imposed on the supply. As a result, it is easy to confuse turnover taxes and such income taxes. One only needs to think back to the *Yates* case referred to above where a Venezuelan tax on 90 per cent of gross revenue was in dispute as to whether it would be creditable because it corresponded to income and corporation tax. As commentators have pointed out, "even though a tax levied on (almost fully) gross revenues may be considered an 'income' tax, in order to determine whether a tax is an income tax in such cases, the assessment must take into account the nature of the tax as a whole".[431] The Venezuelan tax was in substance an income tax even though it was imposed (almost fully) on gross income.

Another example is where withholding tax is imposed on the gross payment of royalties. The OECD alerts us to the fact that whilst generally an income tax is imposed on the net income of a taxpayer, sometimes the

---

[429] OECD/G20, above n 368, [421] at 182.
[430] Ibid at [419].
[431] Hohenwarter et al, above n 427 at 143.

collection mechanism operates on the gross payment (usually at a low rate) as an administrative convenience for the source country. In such circumstances, the withholding tax is creditable against the recipient's full income tax liability in their own home country.[432] Hohenwarter, Kofler, Mayr and Sinnig describe this gross basis of taxation as "a historic compromise and not the inevitable conclusion derived from a clearly defined notion of 'income', which is commonly understood to be a net (flow) amount after the deduction of current expenses".[433] The inclusion of withholding taxes within the concept of "income" can, therefore, be seen as "the historical compromise of balancing taxing rights of source and residence states".[434] They also note that Articles 10(2) and 11(2) of the OECD Model do not prevent the source state from calculating a tax on dividends and interest in a different way (or a different rate) but simply provide a maximum amount of source taxation permissible. The primary reason for such an approach is administrative – ease of collection, enforcement and prevention of avoidance and evasion.

The point of this is that withholding tax can be imposed on turnover, both where the underlying tax is an income tax, and where it is not an income tax (rather it is an excise or turnover tax). As in the *Yates* case, it is necessary to analyse the underlying form of taxation to determine, in substance, which type of tax it is.

- It is essential to consider the wording of the particular bilateral treaty.[435]

This point must not be overlooked and it is very significant for a couple of reasons. Many bilateral treaties deviate from the OECD Model and so it is necessary to construe the particular text. This may lead to the possibility of more interim taxes falling within the scope of Article 2, but the likelihood is actually the converse, namely that the actual text of the bilateral treaty will make it more obvious that an interim tax is excluded from the scope of the DTA. As previously discussed (Section 4.4.2(e)), the most common amendment from the OECD Model is to omit paragraphs (1) and (2). The implication of this omission is that the scope of Article 2 is defined exclusively by the taxes listed in paragraph (3) as extended by paragraph (4), namely new taxes which are "identical or

---

[432] OECD/G20, above n 368, [418]–[419] at 182.
[433] Hohenwarter et al, above n 427 at 144.
[434] Ibid at 144.
[435] OECD/G20, above n 368, [422] at 182.

substantially similar" to those in (2). This will increase the focus on domestic taxes which are actually in force at the time of entering into the Convention and eliminate (or at least significantly reduce) the focus on a generic autonomous definition of income taxes which could be broader than the listed taxes.[436]

(d) The Approach from Jurisdictions Contemplating (or Implementing) Interim Taxes

The above guidance from the OECD is helpful in determining whether the nature of an interim tax will fall within the scope of Article 2 of the OECD Model. In a period of rapid change and dynamic decision-making, it is worthwhile reflecting that, largely, jurisdictions that are contemplating (or indeed have already implemented) interim taxes are clearly confident that they are not in breach of their international obligations under their DTA network. Even private-sector firms seem to have come to this conclusion.[437] Clearly these jurisdictions will have sought and obtained assurance on the legal question of whether their proposed interim taxes will be effective. As you would expect given the possibility of challenge, these are not public documents, and so what is not clear is the level of risk highlighted in these legal opinions.

Nevertheless, it is possible from some of the publicly made comments, to draw some inference on the legal advice, and assuming that the advice is not too far different from the analysis above (including the OECD's articulated framework), that the inference drawn is that the states contemplating an interim tax do not believe they are in breach of their international DTAs.

The European Union was quite well progressed in its development of a Digital Services Tax (DST) until it was dropped in March 2019. The logic behind the European Commission's package of measures was to act in a harmonised way on an interim solution to tackle the "misalignment between the place where the profits are taxed and the place where value is created, notably in the case of business models heavily reliant on user participation".[438]

---

[436] See the discussion at Section 4.4.2(d) "Tax Is an Undefined Term: What Rule of Interpretation Should We Apply?".

[437] CFE Fiscal Committee *Opinion Statement FC 1/2018 on the European Commission proposal of 21 March 2018 for a Council Directive on the Common System of a Digital Services Tax on Revenues Resulting from the Provision of Certain Digital Services* (CFE Tax Advisors Europe, Opinion statement FC 1/2018, May 2018) at 6.1.

[438] European Commission *Proposal for a Council Directive on the Common System of a Digital Services Tax on Revenues Resulting from the Provision of Certain Digital Services* (European Commission, COM (2018) 148 final 2018/0073 (CNS), March 2018) at [2].

The legal advice to the Council of the European Union seemed to studiously avoid being definitive on the question of whether the proposed EU DST would be in breach of obligations under double tax agreements, concluding that "this determination does not, as such, provide the answer to the question whether DST falls within the scope of double tax treaties concluded by Member States".[439]

The legal advice made it clear that whether the proposed DST "falls within the scope of existing international double tax treaties concluded by the Member States" was a question that "ought to be addressed on a case-by-case basis, regarding the specific characteristics of each double tax treaty and of the applicable rules of international law".[440]

Notwithstanding this absolutely correct statement that each treaty must be considered individually, the overwhelming opinion seems to be that the proposed DST did not fall under Article 2 of the OECD Model. For example, Hohenwarter, Kofler, Mayr and Sinnig, after reviewing official and academic commentary, suggest "with regard to the DST ... nearly all commentators have explicitly or implicitly concluded that it would not [fall under Article 2 of the OECD Model]".[441]

Broadly speaking, the DST proposed by the EU has been largely adopted by those European countries that have enacted, or are planning to enact, their own interim taxes, including France, Spain, Austria, Czech Republic, Poland and Italy. These countries all seem to be proceeding, no doubt with legal opinions confirming their approach (and highlighting risk), on the basis that they are not in breach of their DTA networks.

Some jurisdictions, such as the United Kingdom, have spelt out in a little more detail the reasons why they believe their version of an interim tax is not in breach of their DTAs.[442] The analysis is as follows:[443]

- The definition in Article 2 of the OECD Model covers income taxes listed by the Contracting States, taxes that are identical or substantially

---

[439] Ibid at [46]. It can be noted that the Opinion of the Legal Service when examining whether the DST is a tax within the meaning of Article 113 of the Treaty on the Functioning of the European Union concluded that the proposed DST was neither an excise tax nor a turnover tax. They also considered that it did not easily fall within the scope of "other forms of indirect tax".
[440] Council of the European Union *Opinion of the Legal Service* (European Parliament, SJ-0601/18, November 2018) at [6].
[441] Hohenwarter et al, above n 427 at 141.
[442] HM Treasury *Digital Services Tax Consultation* (November 2018).
[443] Ibid, [10.12]–[10.25] at 32-3.

similar to those listed taxes, and more generally taxes on income or capital.
- The UK DST is not a listed tax, nor is it identically or substantially similar to any listed taxes, and so the question is whether the DST meets the general definition of a tax on income.
- The OECD Commentary does not include a definition of an "income tax" or a definition of the term "income". Income is commonly understood to be a measure of the net accretion to the taxpayer's economic wealth between two points in time. This is generally calculated by measuring the taxpayer's gross receipts and then deducting relevant costs and expenses incurred in generating this income.
- The DST is different, and as a tax on the gross receipts from certain digital business activities it only takes account of the costs incurred in generating those revenues in the application of the UK safe harbour provision (which applies only in exceptional cases where the tax would otherwise have a disproportionate effect).[444]
- The UK Government distinguishes the DST from income tax imposed on gross receipts (as the OECD discusses above in respect of withholding taxes on royalties).

  1 The DST is not like the withholding tax because the latter is designed to "approximate and substitute for the taxation of income i.e. the tax on gross receipts is a tax in lieu of income".[445] They give examples of such a tax which would be still an income tax, where a country for administrative reasons "allows certain taxpayers to pay a lower rate of tax on a simplified measure of income under which only limited costs are deductible".[446]

  2 Another example is withholding tax on royalties and fees for technical services, "which clearly form part of a country's approach to taxing income, as evidenced by the fact that: (a) they are not applied to payments to local residents that are taxed directly on income from said sources: and (b) they are typically creditable against a tax

---

[444] Ibid, chapter 7 at 24. This safe harbour reference is a feature of the United Kingdom's proposed DSTs as described in the document. It is a mechanism to allow businesses to elect to make an alternative calculation of their tax liability under the DST when they are in situations of very low profit margins or making losses. The DST, under this argument, still has a primary character of a tax on gross revenues, but the safe harbour exists to ensure that it does not place a disproportionate burden on those taxpayers who are making a low or no profit margin on their transactions.
[445] Ibid [10.22] at 32.
[446] Ibid [10.23] at 32.

4.4 CONSTRAINTS IMPOSED BY THE SCOPE OF DTAS

liability of the recipient that has been calculated on the basis of net income."

On this basis, the UK Government does not believe the DST can be classified as a tax in lieu of corporate tax given that it will be applied separately to, and not in place of, corporate tax.

This conclusion is consistent with the view reached by Australia, even though that country is not progressing with a version of a DST but is awaiting the OECD consensus-driven plan.[447] Whilst acknowledging that "the scope of each of Australia's tax treaties would need to be separately considered, but as an excise, an interim measure would not be expected to be covered by Australia's tax treaties."[448]

New Zealand has not committed to introducing a DST but supports the OECD's attempts to find an international solution. In the event that the OECD cannot make sufficient progress, New Zealand will "seriously consider adopting a DST" and has provided a draft of it in the government's discussion document.[449] The New Zealand Government, after analysing its proposed DST in the light of the OECD's guidance, reached a similar conclusion to the UK and Australia as follows:[450]

> we consider that our proposed DST would not be an income tax. It would be levied on the supply of narrowly defined services (in those provided by in-scope business activities), it would be charged at a fixed rate by reference to the consideration paid (that is, the gross turnover attributable to the in-scope business activities) and not the net profit of the recipient, and it would not be creditable against New Zealand income tax. In particular, the DST would be paid in addition to our income tax, so it is not in any way in lieu of income tax.

While the majority of opinion seems to support targeted DST being able to override DTA obligations, other academic commentators, such as Adolfo Martín Jiménez, disagrees with this assessment. Taking a more holistic approach with respect to the proposed EU DST, he concludes:[451]

---

[447] Australian Treasury *The Digital Economy and Australia's Corporate Tax System* (The Australian Government, Treasury Discussion Paper, October 2018).
[448] Ibid at 28–9.
[449] New Zealand Inland Revenue *Options for Taxing the Digital Economy – A Government Discussion Document* (Policy and Strategy of Inland Revenue, June 2019) [5.3] at 48.
[450] Ibid [3.61] at 21.
[451] Adolfo Martín Jiménez *BEPS, the Digital(ized) Economy and the Taxation of Services and Royalties* (UCA Tax Working Papers 2018/1, August 2018) at 43.

Second, the interim tax (digital sales tax) – regardless of what the Commission asserts and its flaws in defining its objective scope (its arbitrary, not well-targeted design) – has the substance of an income tax or a tax on elements of income (it targets revenue, seeks to reach a person, i.e. mainly US high-tech companies, and not only a specific service, is directly connected with the SEDP PE Directive) and, therefore, if adopted, will lead to uncertainty and litigation, as it can be regarded as falling within the scope of income tax treaties (Article 2 of the OECD Model, even in cases where Article 2 (1) and (2) of the OECD Model are not included, the 'substantially similar taxes' clause equivalent to Article 2 (4) of the OECD Model may be able to capture this new tax).

Outside of the EU proposals and the subsequent adoption of broadly the same approach by individual EU countries, not all academic commentary supports the conclusions reached by the OECD. For example, India's equalisation levy, introduced as early as 2016, has been critiqued as being in conflict with its DTAs.[452] Despite these concerns, there does not appear to have been litigation which contends that the Indian equalisation levy is ineffective because of the international obligations under India's DTAs.

Should the multilateral consensus fall away, and DSTs start to proliferate and raise taxes in Europe, the United Kingdom and elsewhere, then Jiménez's prediction that their implementation will lead to uncertainty and litigation is most likely to be fulfilled.

4.4.4 Conclusion on the Ability of DTAs to Constrain Interim Taxes

The above analysis considers the following:

- the basis of interpretation of Article 2;
- case law concerning domestic provisions;
- the guidance of the OECD;
- the stated reasoning of governments proposing, or implementing their interim taxes; and
- academic commentary.

Based on this reasoning it is possible to conclude that the characteristics of some (or indeed most, if not all) of the planned DSTs would not fall

---

[452] S Wagh "India – The Taxation of Digital Transactions in India: The New Equalisation Levy" (2016) 70(9) Bulletin for International Taxation at 538; and more recently, Dhruv Sanghavi "Ruminating over Equalisation Levies" (23 May 2019) Kluwer International Tax Blog <www.kluwertaxblog.com>.

within the definition of taxes on income in Article 2. Of course, individual DSTs need to be analysed in the light of individual DTAs.

4.4.5 Restrictions within the DTA: The Interim Tax Is within the Scope of the DTA, But the Business Profits Article Does Not Prevent the Interim Tax from Having Effect

(a) What Are Business Profits?

If the DTA applies, then the key question becomes whether the income subject to the interim tax is made up of business profits earned by the enterprise in the other state. As indicated, if it is business profits and there is no permanent establishment of the non-resident enterprise in the source state, then the DTA will prevent the imposition of the tax. This statement, of course, begs the question "what are business profits?" The OECD Commentary makes it clear that this is a broad term.[453]

> 71. Although it has not been found necessary in the Convention to define the term "profits", it should nevertheless be understood that the term, when used in this Article and elsewhere in the Convention, has a broad meaning including all income derived in carrying on an enterprise. Such a broad meaning corresponds to the use of the term made in the tax laws of most OECD member countries.

Generally speaking, courts have followed this guidance and taken business profits to be an all-encompassing definition. For example, various cases have expanded on the issue of whether profits from isolated or one-off investment activities are included within Article 7 of the OECD Model.[454] The conclusions reached by both the Canadian Supreme Court[455] and the High Court of Australia[456] confirm that transactions in the nature of one-off profits were within the business profits article and support the broad and liberal interpretive approach taken in the OECD Commentary.

In practice, the most effective limitation on the application of the business profits article is paragraph (4) of Article 7.[457] This makes it

---

[453] OECD, above n 394, Commentary on Article 7 at [71]; see also, OECD, Annex: Previous Version of Article 7 and its Commentary at [59].
[454] For an explanation of these authorities see C Elliffe *International and Cross-Border Taxation in New Zealand* (2nd ed, Thomson Reuters Ltd, 2018) 17.4.2 at 376–82.
[455] *Minister of National Revenue v Tara Exploration & Development Co* [1972] CTC 328 (SCC).
[456] *Thiel v Commissioner of Taxation* (1990) 171 CLR 338.
[457] For those countries that rely on the previous version of Article 7, the relevant paragraph is (7).

clear that where profits include items of income which are dealt with separately in other articles (such as interest or royalty articles) then those specific income articles will apply and Article 7 does not override the specific treatment that they describe. The role of Article 7(4) is discussed in the Commentary as follows:[458]

> 74. The question, however, could arise with respect to other types of income and it has therefore been decided to include a rule of interpretation that ensures that Articles applicable to specific categories of income will have priority over Article 7. It follows from this rule that Article 7 will be applicable to business profits which do not belong to categories of income covered by these other Articles, and, in addition, to income which under paragraph 4 of Articles 10 and 11, paragraph 3 of Article 12 and paragraph 2 of Article 21, fall within Article 7.

The implication of paragraph (4) is that if the supply of services (of the various kinds described in Chapters 2 and 3) fall, for example, within the definition and scope of a royalty, then they would be dealt with under Article 12 rather than Article 7. Depending on the treaty policy of the country concerned, this may, if Article 12 provides for source taxation (or may not if it does not so provide) give the source country greater taxing rights. The OECD Commentary goes on to discuss the relationship between domestic law and the rule of interpretation that specific articles override the business profits article provided in Article 7(4). The Commentary makes it clear that it is to the domestic law that one should look in determining how the income is characterised:[459]

> This rule does not, however, govern the manner in which the income will be classified for the purposes of domestic law; thus, if a Contracting State may tax an item of income pursuant to other Articles of this Convention, that State may, for its own domestic tax purposes, characterise such income as it wishes (i.e. as business profits or as a specific category of income) provided that the tax treatment of that item of income is in accordance with the provisions of the Convention.

As previously discussed in Section 3.5 "The Characterisation of Transactions and Income", many new digital products and services have a question mark over their classification. Whilst some software is clearly recognised as business profits if the purchaser acquires a legal right to

---

[458] OECD, above n 394, Commentary on Article 7 at [74]; see also OECD, Annex: Previous Version of Article 7 and its Commentary at [62].
[459] OECD, above n 394, Commentary on Article 7 at [7]; see also OECD, Annex: Previous Version of Article 7 and its Commentary at [62].

modify or reproduce the software for their own use or resale to third parties, most countries will regard a payment for such a purchase as a royalty. It appears as though the income characterisation for cloud computing is particularly problematic in this respect, although the authors of the International Fiscal Association General Report for 2018 suggest that cloud computing income is mostly characterised as service income and so falls within the business profits article.[460]

In another context, but illustrative of the type of dispute that can emerge in this area, the Supreme Court of Brazil in 2012 had to grapple with the question of whether a withholding tax on foreign contractors' service income fell within the scope of "business profits" in Article 7 of the Brazil–Canada DTA and the Brazil–Germany DTA.[461] In COPESUL,[462] the Brazilian-based company obtained supplies of services from foreign contractors based in Canada and Germany. Neither of these service providers had a permanent establishment in Brazil. COPESUL paid the contractors gross without deducting the 25 per cent withholding tax normally imposed under domestic law and they did so on the basis that the DTA provided that the business profits of the foreign enterprise were not subject to Brazilian tax under Article 7. The Brazilian tax authorities challenged this treatment, claiming that the payments were not business profits but were rather "other income", which fell within Article 21 of the respective treaties. Article 21 in both DTAs gave the taxing rights to the country of source, Brazil.

The Supreme Court held that these payments fell within the scope of the "business profits" article. Business profits were not limited only to the net profits of the foreign enterprise (as had been argued) but included all gross payments, which, after taking account of deductions, constituted an element in the computation of business profits. The Supreme Court held that the payments were not "other income" under Article 21 and domestic law could not deem them to be such.

---

[460] CH Lee and JH Yoon *Withholding Tax in the Era of BEPS, CIVs and the Digital Economy* (Volume 103(B), IFA Cahiers de Droit Fiscal International, Seoul, 2018) at 253.

[461] Convention Between the Government of Canada and the Government of the Federative Republic of Brazil for the Avoidance of Double Taxation with Respect to Taxes on Income, Canada-Brazil CTS 1985 11 (opened for signature 4 June 1984); Agreement Between the Federative Republic of Brazil and the Federal Republic of Germany for the Avoidance of Double Taxation with Respect to Taxes on Income and Capital, Brazil–Germany (Agreement not in force since 1 December 2006).

[462] *National Treasury v COPESUL – Companhia Petroquímica do Sul*, 15 ITLR 18.

The decision was consistent with the generally accepted international practice that even though such payments of foreign contractors' income constitutes gross payments and will only become an item of net business profits when expenses and other deductions are taken into account, they should nonetheless fall within the "business profits" article of double taxation conventions.

This leaves us in the general position that it is likely that most income generated by highly digitalised businesses will constitute business profits under the ordinary construction of the term. It does leave open the possibility that a state could, obviously, bilaterally agree to include the income within the definition of royalties or some other category of income. Furthermore, it is possible that a state could seek under domestic law to unilaterally redefine income for its own domestic tax purposes in compliance with the observation of the OECD Model Commentary. As illustrated in the Brazilian Supreme Court, such a unilateral domestic measure may not necessarily be successful.

4.4.6 Restrictions within the DTA: Application of the Non-Discrimination Article in the DTA

As indicated earlier, any interim tax introduced ought not to be in breach of the international obligations entered into by the jurisdiction proposing the new DST. One of the matters that the jurisdiction will need to consider is whether the interim tax breaches the non-discrimination article of the OECD Model (Article 24). It is noted at the outset that the countries implementing or considering interim taxes have assumed that they apply to resident and non-resident taxpayers alike.[463] This design feature assists with the analysis under the WTO and other trade agreements as well as the obligations under Article 24 of any relevant DTA.

(a) Scope of Article 24

Article 24 is unusual in the OECD Model for quite a few different reasons. These include its scope (the taxes to which it applies), which arises, mostly, because of its history. The policy of preventing discrimination in carrying on business in another jurisdiction significantly pre-dates the appearance, at the end of the nineteenth century, of DTAs. In

---

[463] For example, all the European countries currently borrowing from the EU proposed DST, including the United Kingdom and New Zealand.

order to extend and strengthen the diplomatic protection of their nationals, Contracting States entered into arrangements to accord nationals of another state equality of treatment with their own nationals. These arrangements took a great many forms, such as consular or establishment conventions, and treaties of friendship or commerce. While provisions prohibiting tax discrimination by other countries have a long history, Article 24 of the OECD Model is a more recent development, appearing first in the OECD Draft Model (1963), where it has remained largely unchanged. Due to the retention of the original purpose of the non-discrimination article in the OECD Model, it has also commonly retained a broader scope, applying to "any taxation or any requirement connected therewith",[464] as opposed to the normal limitation on the types of taxes customarily defined in Article 2, which are "taxes on income" (or taxes on elements of income).[465] For this reason, even if the substantive articles of the DTA which affect the allocation of income tax rights do not apply to an interim tax, there is still scope for the non-discrimination article to apply in a theoretical sense given that the article applies to any "taxation or any requirement connected therewith". This makes Article 24 broadly applicable to other forms of taxes not dealt with by the substantive articles of the DTA.[466]

Another feature of Article 24 is its somewhat eclectic selection of rules. Owing to its historical origins, many of the concepts incorporated into the non-discrimination article seem somewhat haphazard and ill-defined. Article 24 contains five substantive paragraphs, each of which has a significantly different focus. The Committee on Fiscal Affairs, which one could have assumed would have considered the possibility of rationalising and giving a common theme to the Article, clearly does not wish the various non-discrimination paragraphs to be read too broadly or collectively. It instead suggests: "The various provisions of Article 24 prevent differences in tax treatment that are solely based on certain specific grounds (e.g. nationality in the case of paragraph 1). Thus, for these provisions to apply, other relevant aspects must be the same."[467] In other

---

[464] OECD, above n 394, Article 24(1).
[465] See the discussion at Section 4.4.2(a) "What Type of Taxes Are Within the Scope of the DTA?", suggesting that a DST can be structured so that it does not constitute a "tax on income".
[466] OECD, above n 394, Article 24(6) reads as follows: "The provisions of this Article shall, notwithstanding the provisions of Article 2, apply to taxes of every kind and description."
[467] Ibid, Commentary on Article 24 at [3].

words, the various "heads" contained in the different paragraphs of Article 24 are to be considered independently. Article 24 usually prevents states, on a reciprocal basis, from discriminating on the grounds of nationality (paragraph 1), or from discriminating against PEs (paragraph 3), deductibility (paragraph 4), and foreign control (paragraph 5).

The concern is that Article 24 (1), which prohibits discrimination on the grounds of nationality (for example, citizenship or incorporation), might have application when dealing with the introduction of an interim tax. The other paragraphs of Article 24 do not seem relevant (i.e. an interim tax does not focus on deductions of interest or royalties nor does it apply particularly to permanent establishments, or foreign-controlled entities).

(b) Article 24(1)

Article 24(1) of the OECD Model establishes the principle that taxation discrimination on the grounds of nationality is prohibited. The nationals of one state may not be less favourably treated in the other state than the nationals of that other state *in the same circumstances* and vice versa. The paragraph declares:[468]

> Nationals of a Contracting State shall not be subjected in the other Contracting State to any taxation or any requirement connected therewith, which is other or more burdensome than the taxation and connected requirements to which nationals of that other State *in the same circumstances*, in particular with respect to residence, are or may be subjected. This provision shall, notwithstanding the provisions of Article 1, also apply to persons who are not residents of one or both of the Contracting States.

When comparing the treatment of nationals, the comparison must be of taxpayers "in the same circumstances". As the OECD Model Commentary records: "The expression 'in particular with respect to residence' makes clear that the residence of the taxpayer is one of the factors that is relevant in determining whether taxpayers are placed in similar circumstances."[469] The changes made to the above article in the OECD Model in 1992 were designed to reinforce the difference between nationals and residents, but arguably they were clarifying something already well understood in most jurisdictions. An example of this,

---

[468] Ibid, Article 24(1) (Emphasis added).
[469] Ibid, Commentary on Article 24 at [7].

namely that the Commentary was simply clarifying the existing legal position, was the decision of the New Zealand Court of Appeal reached in the early 1970s. The decision in *Commissioner of Inland Revenue v United Dominions Trust Ltd*,[470] had held that discrimination on the basis of residence was not in breach of the non-discrimination provision in the New Zealand–United Kingdom DTA (1966).

United Dominions Trust Ltd, a United Kingdom banking and finance company carrying on business in England, had to pay income tax at a higher rate on interest income from its New Zealand subsidiary than it would have had to pay had it been a resident of New Zealand. The court was asked to consider whether the difference in residence was a valid basis for applying a different tax rate and whether it was nationality upon which the distinction was made. In the view of the President of the New Zealand Court of Appeal (McCarthy P): "In my judgement the better view is that the discrimination against the respondent of which it complains is based on a difference of residence and not on nationality, and that this discrimination is not in breach of the Agreement."[471] This analysis supports the position reached in the Interim Report of the OECD and suggests that the conclusion that "the Article and the Commentary recognise that the distinction between residents and non-residents is a normal and common feature of income tax systems and should be respected"[472] is uncontroversial.

(c) Indirect Discrimination against Non-Residents

The OECD Model Commentary suggests that Article 24 should not be unduly extended to cover what it describes as situations of "indirect" or covert discrimination. These are situations where tax rules affect a group of taxpayers who are substantially non-resident but not on the basis of their non-residence. For example, a thin capitalisation regime may apply to disallow interest deductions to parties in circumstances where the interest is not subject to full domestic taxation. This might predominantly affect non-resident lenders, but the regime will also apply to charities and exempt domestic entities.

It might be alleged, for instance, that the level of thresholds set by jurisdictions imposing interim taxes are set having in mind the application to major multinational businesses involved in the digital economy,

---

[470] *Commissioner of Inland Revenue v United Dominions Trust Ltd* [1973] 2 NZLR 555 (CA).
[471] Ibid at 562.
[472] OECD/G20, above n 368, [426] at 183.

most of whom are based in the United States and not in the domestic jurisdiction imposing the new tax. The argument is that although on the face of the unilateral tax it applies equally to residents and non-residents, in substance it is designed to apply only to large multinational non-residents.

The question of whether or not only direct discrimination, and not covert or indirect discrimination, is relevant to Article 24 was expressly considered by the Committee on Fiscal Affairs in its 2008 report,[473] which led to the introduction and insertion of paragraph 1 of the OECD Model Commentary on Article 24 as follows:[474]

> The non-discrimination provisions of the Article seek to balance the need to prevent unjustified discrimination with the need to take account of these legitimate distinctions. For that reason, the Article should not be *unduly extended to cover so-called "indirect" discrimination.*

(d) Conclusion on Article 24(1)

The non-discrimination provisions of the OECD Model do not provide a basis to challenge the introduction of the unilateral interim taxes discussed earlier in this chapter. Even if such unilateral interim taxes were designed to uniquely apply to non-resident taxpayers, then they would still not offend against Article 24 as such discrimination on the basis of residency is expressly permitted. Given that direct discrimination is permissible, indirect discrimination is no additional problem.

Discrimination against non-residents may be more problematic in the context of international obligations arising under the WTO and free trade agreements, or for member states of the European Union and parties to the Agreement on the European Economic Area (EEA Agreement). Focus is now turned to the international obligations imposed by the membership and legal agreements made as part of the WTO.

4.6 Constraints Imposed by the Membership of the WTO

The WTO consists of over 160 countries and represents some 98 per cent of global trade.[475] Additionally, as of 2019 a further twenty countries

---

[473] OECD Committee on Fiscal Affairs *Application and Interpretation of Article 24 (Non-Discrimination): Public Discussion Draft* (OECD Publications, June 2008).
[474] OECD, above n 394, Commentary on Article 24 at [1].
[475] World Trade Organization "The WTO" <www.wto.org>.

have applied for membership, so it is fair to say the organisation is a very substantial and important vehicle to promote and encourage world trade. The WTO has as its principal objective open trade for the benefit of all. According to its website, it operates a global system of trade rules, acts as a forum for negotiating trade agreements, settles trade disputes between its members and supports the needs of developing countries.

Any country considering the introduction of interim unilateral taxes will need to consider the WTO implications carefully as these obligations seem to apply more broadly than the non-discrimination provisions in DTAs as referred to above (Section 4.4.6). The OECD suggests that the imposition of a "standalone gross-basis final withholding tax on foreign suppliers for remote sales of goods and services is likely to raise substantial conflicts with trade obligations".[476]

There are many unanswered and quite fundamental questions in this area, such as which WTO rules apply. Should we examine those dealing with goods or services? Other questions are more specific and legal. These are questions such as whether various exemptions apply. If the OECD's multilateral solution fails and interim taxes proliferate, then it seems highly possible that a WTO challenge will occur to say that such interim taxes are in breach of WTO obligations, but it will take many years of litigation to reach the sanctions stage. Furthermore, a detailed analysis of legal obligations must be made on a country-by-country basis, so any discussion here is limited to more general observations.

An appropriate starting point is to examine the purpose of the WTO rules.

4.6.1 Contrasting the Economic Purpose of the WTO Rules to International Tax Arrangements

The Marrakesh Agreement (establishing the WTO) proclaimed that trade and economic relations should be established with the following objectives in mind:[477]

> Recognising that their relations in the field of trade and economic endeavour should be conducted with a view to raising standards of living, ensuring full employment and a large and steadily growing volume of real income and effective demand, and expanding the production of and trade

---

[476] OECD/G20, above n 365, [299] at 115.
[477] WTO "Marrakesh Agreement Establishing the World Trade Organization" (15 April 1994) <www.wto.org>.

in goods and services while allowing for the optimal use of the world's resources in accordance with the objective of sustainable development, seeking both to protect and preserve the environment and to enhance the means for doing so in a manner consistent with their respective needs and concerns at different levels of economic development.

In common with the WTO rules, the OECD Model Commentary confirms that: "The principal purpose of double taxation conventions is to promote, by eliminating international double taxation, exchanges of goods and services, and the movement of capital and persons."[478] The second part of the paragraph goes on to add, in a completely different vein of thinking and purpose: "As confirmed in the preamble of the Convention, it is also a part of the purposes of tax conventions to prevent tax avoidance and evasion."[479] It is possible to reflect, therefore, on both the similarities and differences of the WTO and OECD tax instruments from these brief statements of purpose. Clearly, they are both designed to encourage trade and economic development on one level. As discussed by Michael Daly,[480] however, the economic rationale behind WTO and other trade agreements arises from the so-called traditional economic approach to trade agreements. As Daly explains, the standard economic theory which suggests that unilateral free trade is the optimal policy for a government does not actually manifest itself in the real world. The government of a large country is assumed to set its import tariff "in order to maximise national welfare, while recognising that some of the burden of the tariff is shifted onto foreign exporters whose products sell at a lower world price".[481] The consequence of this behaviour is a "terms of trade externality" which leads governments to set unilateral tariffs based on their own national welfare which are higher than would be efficient from a global perspective. What the WTO agreements do is to reduce these terms of trade externalities by offering governments a means of escape from a "prisoners' dilemma". The prisoners' dilemma is that situation in which two players both gain individually (seemingly maxi-

---

[478] OECD, above n 394, Commentary on Article 1 at [54].
[479] Ibid, Commentary on Article 1 at [54]. The Committee of Fiscal Affairs of the OECD has substantially reformed the OECD Model Commentary in this section relating to Article 1. For a discussion of the history of these changes see C. Elliffe "The Lesser of Two Evils: Double Tax Treaty Override or Treaty Abuse?" (2016) 1 BTR at 62–88.
[480] Michael Daly *The WTO and Direct Taxation* (WTO Publications, Discussion Paper Number 9, June 2005) at 16.
[481] Ibid at 16.

4.6 CONSTRAINTS IMPOSED BY THE WTO

mising their own national welfare) by not cooperating,[482] but in reality, both are worse off than if they had cooperated (and increased trade volumes through unilateral free trade). Another way to explain these terms of trade-driven restrictions is to express them as "market access" issues, which dominate world trade negotiations. When a country raises its tariffs, the loss in market access that home country exporters experience is simply the "price effect" of a deterioration in the home country's terms of trade.[483]

According to Daly, "this rationale for multilateral trade agreements has become the conventional wisdom among international trade theorists".[484]

A very similar analysis could be applied to DTAs. As has been previously discussed,[485] the 1920s compromise was an allocation of taxing rights necessitated because countries simply refused to give up their right to tax income sourced in their jurisdiction. The theory is that reduced source taxation will lead to increased investment through the reduction of a source tax externality. This theory posits that unrelieved source taxation creates a tax impost which dis-incentivises cross-border investment by creating barriers to investment. Reduced source taxation will, therefore, lead to increased foreign direct investment. Additionally, multinationals might be concerned about increased compliance and administrative costs.

The claim that DTAs eliminate double tax and encourage cross-border investment has been questioned because relief for international double taxation is very frequently provided on a unilateral basis. The home country provides either a credit for foreign tax or an exemption for foreign earnings. Many jurisdictions offer such a unilateral credit system and so, Daly argues, "a negotiated reduction in tax rates on bilateral flows of income from capital may have little, if any, effect on the economic behaviour of foreign investors".[486] Tsilly Dagan describes the argument

---

[482] The prisoner's dilemma involves one of the most well-known concepts in modern game theory in which two individuals acting in their own self-interests do not produce the optimal outcome. The typical prisoners' dilemma is set up in such a way that both parties choose to protect themselves at the expense of the other participant. As a result, both participants find themselves in a worse state than if they had cooperated with each other in the decision-making process.

[483] K Bagwell and R Staiger *The Economics of the World Trading System* (The MIT Press, 2002).

[484] Daly, above n 480 at 17.

[485] See Chapter 1 at Section 1.3 "The History of International Double Taxation: The '1920s Compromise'".

[486] Daly, above n 480 at 17.

that DTAs promote cross-border investment as mythical.[487] Empirical evidence suggests that a negotiated reduction in tax rates on bilateral flows of income may have little, if any, effect on the economic behaviour of foreign investors.[488] Even if the reduction in source taxation and the claimed increase in foreign direct investment is overstated, there is no denying the administrative benefits that can emerge from a DTA such as increased certainty for taxpayers, the supply of information between tax authorities and the potential for dispute resolution.

This has led Daly to assert that the rationale "underlying tax treaties may lie more in preventing 'aggressive' tax planning, if not evasion (often by means of deferral, transfer pricing or treaty shopping), which, if not addressed, could result in little, if any, taxes being paid in either the ' source' or 'residence' country".[489] All of this goes to suggest that the second purpose of tax treaties is one of the key rationales for DTAs – the prevention of tax avoidance and evasion. History would suggest, through the evolution and changes made to the OECD Model Commentary on Article 1, that this purpose of tax treaties has become increasingly elevated and may indeed, post-BEPS, be the most significant purpose.

Tax law and trade law may, therefore, have less overlap than it first appears, and perhaps less than the OECD suggests when it talks about the likelihood of substantial conflicts. Reuven Avi-Yonah suggests that the two spheres of trade and tax law do not substantially "overlap, much less clash in their objectives".[490] Fundamentally, the objectives are different, with the goal of trade law being to facilitate trade, whilst the goal of tax law is to raise revenue. Accordingly, Avi-Yonah says: "Thus, for example, an ideal tariff under trade law is set at zero, but an ideal tax under tax law is set at some positive rate. It, therefore, should not be surprising that there is a large measure of non-overlap between trade and tax law."[491] Paul McDaniel clarified the relationship between trade law and tax law with three important observations:[492]

---

[487] Tsilly Dagan "The Tax Treaties Myth" (2000) 32(939) Journal of Int' Law and Politics.
[488] BA Blonigen and RB Davies *Do Bilateral Tax Treaties Promote Foreign Direct Investment?* (NBER, Working Paper 8834, March 2002).
[489] Daly, above n 480 at 17.
[490] RS Avi-Yonah "Treating Tax Issues through Trade Regimes" (2001) 26(4) Brooklyn Journal of Int' Law 1683 at 1683.
[491] Ibid at 1683.
[492] P McDaniel "The David R. Tillinghast Lecture: Trade Agreements and Income Taxation: Interactions, Conflicts, and Resolutions" (2004) 57(2) TLR 275 at 276 and 276.

- A normative income tax structure and free trade principles are not in conflict with each other. By normative income tax structure, he meant those provisions that comprise the normal or benchmark structure of a tax system. Namely, those that (1) define the tax base; (2) establish the tax rates; (3) determine the taxable unit; (4) establish accounting rules and methods; (5) determine the tax treatment of cross-border flows of trade and investment; and (6) provide the rules necessary to administer the tax.
- The provisions of a country's tax system that comprise its normative or benchmark structure should be outside the scope of trade agreements and procedures. These are true "tax" provisions, and not substitutes for direct subsidies, and thus should be governed exclusively by bilateral tax treaties.
- Subsidies provided through a tax system (tax expenditures) should be subject to scrutiny under trade agreements just as are direct subsidies that may adversely affect free flows of trade. Subsidies cannot be removed from the scrutiny of trade agreements just because they are provided through the tax system.

The current environment is one where the spectre of the WTO rule incompatibility with new tax measures is commonplace. Various measures in the United States Tax Cuts and Jobs Act, adopted at the end of 2017, have been criticised for being in violation of WTO agreements and certainly there was criticism of the EU's proposal to adopt a digital services tax. Commentators remind us that of course WTO members should consider the risks of challenges under WTO law but also that WTO law should not be used as "some sort of 'tax scarecrow' to ward off attempts by WTO members to adopt new types of tax measures or to fundamentally reform their tax systems".[493] Alice Pirlot reminds us that, "generally speaking, WTO law does not operate to prevent WTO members from adopting new tax measures, including tax measures that represent a radical departure from the established norm".[494]

It is possible from the above analysis to conclude that the overall purposes and objectives behind tax law and trade law are not as aligned as a superficial examination might suggest. True tax provisions which are

---

[493] A Pirlot "The WTO as Tax Scarecrow?" (2019) 1427 Tax Journal.
[494] Ibid.

designed to collect tax rather than to distort international trade ought not to be problematic under international trade law. Having established the 'big picture' purpose and objectives of trade law and tax law it is now appropriate to focus on the particular areas where WTO rules could affect interim taxes.

4.6.2 Goods or Services? The GATS Provisions That Affect Direct Taxation

The OECD briefly discusses the WTO obligations in the Action 1 Final Report.[495] It notes that there is a significant difference in the trade law dealing with goods; the Organisation describes it as "a product" versus a service. In the case of a product, the General Agreement on Tariffs and Trade (GATT) applies, whereas with services the General Agreement on Trade in Services (GATS) applies. Quite significant differences arise in the obligations under the GATT and GATS rules. These are detailed below (Sections 4.6.3–4.6.7), but in summary, the GATS rules have much broader exceptions in the area of taxation.[496]

As detailed in Chapter 2 of this book, the vast majority of digitalised businesses involve income streams which are characterised as services. These include subscriptions for digital programs, income from advertising, and in particular commission arising from introducing parties to each other on a multi-sided platform. It therefore seems likely that the relevant WTO rules applicable to interim taxes will be contained in the GATS provisions for the vast majority of situations in which the interim digital (services) taxes will apply.

There are three Articles of the GATS that are particularly relevant to taxation. These are the Most-Favoured-Nation (MFN) obligations in Article II, the National Treatment (NT) obligation in Article XVII, and the consultation and dispute settlement provisions in Article XXII. As briefly indicated above in this section, many of these obligations have important carve-outs with respect to taxation.

---

[495] OECD/G20, above n 365 [299] at 115.
[496] The OECD notes that the GATS rules provide broad exceptions for the application of the provisions of tax treaties and for the imposition of direct tax provisions aimed at ensuring the equitable or effective imposition of direct taxes. In contrast, the GATT rules are stricter and contain no exceptions in respect of NT obligations, meaning that the home country cannot subject imported products to taxes on importation in excess of what they would apply to similar products domestically produced.

4.6.3 The GATS Provisions That Affect Direct Taxation: MFN Obligations

Article II paragraph 1 provides as follows:[497]

> With respect to any measure covered by this Agreement, each Member shall accord immediately and unconditionally to services and service suppliers of any other Member treatment no less favourable than that it accords to like services and service suppliers of any other country.

MFN treatment essentially extends any concessions or advantages given to one trading partner to every other trading partner. It can be immediately noted that the MFN obligation applies to both services and suppliers alike. The term "measures" is broadly defined,[498] and means "any measure by a Member, whether in the form of a law, regulation, rule, procedure decision, administrative action, or any other form". On the face of paragraph 1, any tax (such as an interim tax) would be a measure imposed on either the services supplied (more likely in this case and consistent with the view of the OECD when discussing whether the interim tax was a tax on "income"[499]) or on the MNE supplier itself.

The full consequences of this obligation are, however, watered down by a number of exceptions. The most relevant of these are as follows:

(a) Specific Member Exemptions

Paragraph 2 of Article II provides: "A Member may maintain a measure inconsistent with paragraph 1 provided that such a measure is listed in, and meets the conditions of, the Annex on Article II Exemptions."[500] The Annex on Article II Exemptions allows members to deviate from the standard position in paragraph 1 if they list areas in which they want to maintain the existing regulations or agreements inconsistent with the MFN obligation or alternatively they wish to preserve a prospective right to use unilateral measures. Most countries claim MFN exemptions in the area of civil and maritime aviation, telecommunications and financial services, but some countries claim particular tax exemptions. For example, the United States provides an exemption for certain

---

[497] General Agreement on Trade in Services, found in Annex 1B of the legal texts negotiated during the 1986–94 Uruguay Round negotiations, and signed at the Marrakesh ministerial meeting in April 1994; WTO "General Agreement on Trade in Services" <www.wto.org> at Article III.
[498] Ibid at Article XXVIII(a).
[499] See Section 4.4 "Constraints Imposed by the Scope of Double Tax Agreements (DTAs)".
[500] GATS, above n 497 at Article II: 2.

"differential treatment under direct tax measures at the federal level". In its schedule it then lists more than a handful of specific exemptions under the Internal Revenue Code and a further list of sub-federal exemptions. In the case of the United States, for example, countries contiguous to the US border may be given certain more favourable taxation concessions, and in return, US companies may be given more favourable taxation measures in their dealings with those contiguous countries. Such actions are not subject to the MFN obligations.

The Annex on Article II exemption is theoretically subject to review and in principle should not exceed a period of ten years from the date of entry of the WTO agreement into force. There is, however, no obligation to eliminate the exemptions.[501]

This means that prior to examining any MFN claim, it is essential to review the specific exemptions made by any member. Details of the exemptions are provided on the WTO website.[502]

(b) General Exemptions

A range of general exemptions are contained in Article XIV. This Article reads as follows:

> Subject to the requirement that such measures are not applied in a manner which would constitute a means of arbitrary or unjustifiable discrimination between countries where like conditions prevail, or a disguised restriction on trade in services, nothing in this Agreement shall be construed to prevent the adoption or enforcement by any Member of measures:
>
> necessary to protect public morals or to maintain public order, etc.

WTO members may adopt and enforce measures which would otherwise offend against the MFN principle provided they are for the protection of public morals, maintain public order, protect human, animal or plant life or health and include any measures necessary to secure compliance with other laws which are themselves consistent with the GATS.

The most important general exemption, from a tax perspective, is contained in Article XIV paragraph (e), which states that the member can adopt laws:

---

[501] Ibid at Article XXIX(6).
[502] A detailed list of exemptions for each member country is available at WTO "Schedules of Specific Commitments and Lists of Article II Exemptions" <www.wto.org>.

(e) inconsistent with Article II, provided that the difference in treatment is the result of an agreement on the avoidance of double taxation or provisions on the avoidance of double taxation in any other international agreement or arrangement by which the Member is bound.

4.6.4 Observations on the Applicability of the MFN Provisions

The MFN rules are designed to circumvent trading practices whereby a member country would allow trading which prefers one country to another. The obligation, therefore, is to ensure that no one country is accorded treatment less favourable than any other country. The introduction of a new tax based on services supplied in a digital context does not seem to result in any country being provided with favourable treatment. Of course, that depends upon the circumstances. A tax which applies equally to residents and non-residents, and taxes both, does not seem to offend the MFN principle. It therefore seems less likely that it could be meaningfully argued in a WTO dispute.

In examining the potential application of the MFN provisions to interim taxes it is important to look at the general principle behind trade law rules. The specific exemption provided in the case of the United States helpfully illuminates the real reason for the MFN provision. It is designed to prevent a particular tax regime being introduced (or which already exists) which would provide a particular incentive to one country when other countries do not receive the same privilege. The US-specific exclusion for those neighbouring and contiguous countries to the United States which receive preferential tax treatment highlights the operation of the exclusion to the MFN in such a tax context and in doing so demonstrates the normal operation of the rule.

This leads to the conclusion that a unilateral interim tax which applies to all countries does not naturally fall within the scope of Article II. Such an outcome would be consistent with Paul McDaniel's view that trade law ought not to interfere with normative taxation provisions unless there are special features of the tax rules which are designed to assist or disrupt trade. Notwithstanding, it is likely to be argued in a dispute, in addition to the National Treatment obligation (discussed below, Section 4.6.5).

There are many difficult questions in this intersection of trade and tax law. One of them is whether the general exclusion in Article XIV(e) applies in a situation such as the application of the MFN rule. There are several different points that need to be considered.

The first is that the exclusion in paragraph (e) does not apply at all. The provisions in the DTA relating to the substantive allocation of taxing rights arguably do not apply because an interim tax is outside the scope of Article 2 of the DTA due to it not being a tax on income.[503] Since the argument is that the DTA does not apply to interim taxes in terms of allocating taxing rights, the general exclusion contained in Article XIV(e) also cannot apply.

That, however, is not the full picture, as the DTA does apply more generally to other forms of tax and, in particular, it has a potential application under Article 24 (the non-discrimination article) of the DTA.[504] So it could be argued that the DTA has potential scope in the very important area of non-discrimination. As discussed, the tax rules are significantly more liberal in this area than the trade law, tax law permitting discrimination on the basis of residency and largely ignoring indirect discrimination. So, in theory, Article 24 is in scope to potentially apply to the interim taxes (i.e. they are applicable "taxes" to which Article 24 could potentially apply) but does not "bite" because Article 24 actually does not engage discrimination on the basis of residence and so does not have any real consequences arising on application.

The general exclusion in Article XIV(e) requires that the difference in treatment is the *result* of the operation of the DTA. That would seem to require its application to allocate or reduce taxing rights rather than the non-application of the non-discrimination article. In other words, the DTA does not result in prescribing a course of action that is in breach of the MFN trade obligations. Accordingly, the general exclusion does not seem applicable.

To conclude, although the matter is not free from doubt, the MFN provisions arguably do not apply, but neither does the general exclusion in paragraph (e).

4.6.5 The GATS Provisions That Affect Direct Taxation: National Treatment (NT)

The NT obligation is contained in Article XVII of the GATS. This requirement is that "each Member shall accord to services and service suppliers of any other Member, in respect of all measures affecting the

---

[503] See Section 4.4 "Constraints Imposed by the Scope of Double Tax Agreements (DTAs)".
[504] See Section 4.4.6 "Restrictions within the DTA: Application of the Non-Discrimination Article in the DTA".

supply of services, treatment no less favourable than that it accords to its own like services and service suppliers".[505] The trade distortion or discrimination aimed at is the disadvantaging of foreign services (and service providers) in comparison to domestic service and their providers.

(a) Specific Exemptions

As was the case for the MFN commitments, members of the WTO can claim NT qualifications for different services. The WTO Guide explains:[506]

> The national treatment obligation under Article XVII of the GATS is to accord to the services and service suppliers of any other Member treatment no less favourable than is accorded to domestic services and service suppliers. A Member wishing to maintain any limitations on national treatment – that is any measures which result in less-favourable treatment of foreign services or service suppliers – must indicate these limitations in the third column of its schedule.

The schedules referred to in the Guide are complex documents in which each country identifies the service sectors to which it will apply the market access and national treatment obligations of the GATS and any exceptions from those obligations it wishes to maintain. The commitments and limitations are in every case entered with respect to each of the four modes of supply which constitute the definition of trade in services in Article I of the GATS: these are cross-border supply; consumption abroad; commercial presence; and the presence of natural persons.

An example of how this operates in the context of taxation is the Specific Commitment that Canada has registered in respect of the first two modes of supply, namely cross-border supply[507] and consumption abroad.[508] As a result of its policy, and as one of many exclusions for taxation, Canada advises that: "Tax measures that result in differences of treatment with respect to expenditures made on scientific research and experimental development services are excluded from their obligations to

---

[505] GATS, above n 497, Article XVII: National Treatment at [1].
[506] WTO "WTO Guide to Reading the GATS Schedules of Specific Commitments and the List of Article II (MFN) Exemptions" <www.wto.org>.
[507] Cross-border supply is identified as the possibility for non-resident service suppliers to supply services across the border into the member's territory.
[508] Consumption abroad means the freedom for the member's residents to purchase services in the territory of another member.

otherwise observe NT."[509] In addition to these specific exemptions, a departure from the NT obligation is permitted under the general exemptions from GATS.

(b) General Exemptions

The general exemptions contained in Article XIV which are applicable to MFN are also applicable to the NT obligation. These include general exclusions for the protection of public morals, the maintenance of public order etc.

Article XIV requires that "such measures are not applied in a manner which would constitute a means of arbitrary or unjustifiable discrimination between countries where like conditions prevail, or a disguised restriction on trade in services".[510]

In addition, there is a specific exemption aimed at direct tax. This is contained in Article XIV (d):

> (d) inconsistent with Article XVII, provided that the difference in treatment is aimed at ensuring the equitable or effective imposition or collection of direct taxes in respect of services or service suppliers of other Members.

The terms "equitable or effective" are footnoted in the GATS with a further explanation of their meaning. This is as follows:

> Measures that are aimed at ensuring the equitable or effective imposition or collection of direct taxes include measures taken by a Member under its taxation system which: (i) apply to non-resident service suppliers in recognition of the fact that the tax obligation of non-residents is determined with respect to taxable items sourced or located in the Member's territory; or (ii) apply to non-residents in order to ensure the imposition or collection of taxes in the Member's territory; or (iii) apply to non-residents or residents in order to prevent the avoidance or evasion of taxes, including compliance measures; or (iv) apply to consumers of services supplied in or from the territory of another Member in order to ensure the imposition or collection of taxes on such consumers derived from sources in the Member's territory; or (v) distinguish service suppliers subject to tax on worldwide taxable items from other service suppliers, in recognition of the difference in the nature of the tax base

---

[509] There are many other Canadian tax exemptions taken by Canada in its Schedule of Specific Commitments; Canada – Trade in Services S/DCS/W/CAN, 24 January 2003 (Draft Consolidated Schedule of Specific Commitments) at GATS/SC/16; PC/SCS/SP/1; S/L/34; GATS/SC/16/Suppl.2/Rev.1; GATS/SC/16/Suppl.3; GATS/SC/16/Suppl.4/Rev.1.
[510] GATS, above n 497 at Article XIV.

between them; or (vi) determine, allocate or apportion income, profit, gain, loss, deduction or credit of resident persons or branches, or between related persons or branches of the same person, in order to safeguard the Member's tax base. Tax terms or concepts in paragraph (d) of Article XIV and in this footnote are determined according to tax definitions and concepts, or equivalent or similar definitions and concepts, under the domestic law of the Member taking the measure.

On the face of paragraph (d), this carve-out for direct tax is broad. It applies both to the imposition of tax and the process of collection. The footnoted description details the classic imposition of a withholding tax which is often imposed on non-resident taxpayers on a gross basis in contrast to the net taxation imposed on residents. The various components in the footnote "speak" to a difference in taxation for non-residents commonly found in low-rate withholding tax based on gross income.

What is meant by including paragraph (d)? Was it intended to be as broad as the language actually is? According to Michael Lennard, "the negotiating history of the GATS provisions is, unfortunately, not readily available".[511] Nonetheless, he refers to historical documents available on the WTO website to piece it together. According to Leonard, the taxation concerns about the GATS NT Article were significant during the Uruguay Round:[512]

> The tax experts, who were not the chief GATS negotiators, felt so strongly about the matter that they were able to force late changes to the text to meet their needs despite concerns from some GATS negotiators that this demand could unravel the GATS as a whole.

This is substantiated by two other highly respected commentators. Robert Green suggests that giving the WTO authority over taxes is unlikely to be an easy matter because countries simply do not give up their sovereignty over tax matters.[513] To do so goes to the heart of a country's ability to exercise national power. Reuven Avi Yonah references Green's viewpoint,[514] suggesting that it was the United States that was at the forefront of asserting this point of sovereignty: "This concern is

---

[511] M Lennard "The GATT 1994 and Direct Taxes: Some National Treatment and Related Issues" (2005) 73 WTO and Direct Taxation at 81.
[512] Ibid at 81.
[513] RA Green "Antilegalistic Approaches to Resolving Disputes Between Governments: A Comparison of the International Tax and Trade Regimes" (1995) 23(1) Yale Journal of Int' Law at 81.
[514] Ibid.

particularly acute in the US and almost led to the failure of the entire Uruguay Round as the US insisted upon, at the last minute, excluding direct taxes from the purview of the GATS."[515] Because the GATS were designed to have a wide coverage of services and service suppliers, they would "undoubtedly apply to a wide range of tax-related measures, were it not for the 'carve-outs' relating to substantive coverage and dispute resolution".[516]

It would therefore appear likely that the intention was to largely "take tax off the table" in the GATS negotiations. Accordingly, as Lennard says, "the 'carve-outs' for tax measures in the GATS are meant to recognise that in some respects these issues are better dealt with by well-established and sophisticated international tax policies and approaches".[517]

4.6.6 Cases on GATS and Tax

The WTO database[518] illustrates that tax is not often the reason for a dispute. Across all WTO agreements, thirty-four disputes have involved tax, which is approximately 6 per cent of the total number of disputes.[519] Many of these disputes involve the Agreement on Subsidies and Countervailing Measures, various articles of which prohibit the provision of subsidies that are contingent upon export performance or upon the use of domestic over imported goods. Accordingly, they have little to do with services and most seem to focus on particular regimes that provide domestic subsidies.

Only one case involving indirect tax has been brought up to and including 2019. This was a dispute under Article XVII (NT) of the GATS agreement, inter alia with other provisions of the GATT.[520]

Under this dispute, the United States claimed that, although China provided for a 17 per cent VAT on Integrated Circuits (ICs), enterprises in China were entitled to a partial refund of the VAT on ICs that they have produced, resulting in a lower VAT rate on their products. In the United States' view, China thus appears to be subjecting imported ICs to

---

[515] Avi-Yonah, above n 490 at 1691.
[516] Green, above n 513 at 81.
[517] Lennard, above n 511 at 81.
[518] World Trade Organization "Follow disputes and create alerts" <www.wto.org>.
[519] At the beginning of October 2019, a total of 590 disputes had been raised at the WTO.
[520] *China – Value-Added Tax on Integrated Circuits* WT/DS309/8, 5 October 2005 (Notification of Mutually Agreed Solution).

higher taxes than applied to domestically produced ICs and to be according less favourable treatment to imported ICs.

In addition, the United States claims that China allows for a partial refund of VAT for domestically designed ICs that, because of technological limitations, are manufactured outside of China. In the United States' view, China thus appears to be providing for more favourable treatment of imports from one member than from others, and also is discriminating against services and service suppliers of other members.

On 14 July 2004, China and the United States notified the Dispute Settlement Body of the WTO (DSB) that they had reached an agreement with respect to the matter raised by the United States in its request for consultations. According to the notification, China agreed to amend or revoke the measures at issue to eliminate the availability of VAT refunds on ICs produced and sold in China and on ICs designed in China but manufactured abroad.

This case is neither particularly relevant nor insightful from the perspective of relevant WTO law. The implications that can be drawn from it are broader, when examined from the perspective of the frequency and nature of disputes, suggesting that it is difficult to raise such tax disputes under the GATS rules. This may not be that surprising considering the history of the WTO and given the attempts to minimise the impact on sovereignty and taxation when introducing the GATS provisions.

4.6.7 Observations on the Applicability of the NT Provisions

The first, and most obvious, observation is that these interim taxes have been designed to apply equally to residents and non-residents. Accordingly, at least on a superficial level, it does not discriminate against foreign firms and service providers. Whilst the de jure position is one of clear non-discrimination on the perspective of NT, it has been asserted that such unilateral taxes represent de facto discrimination. Based in Washington DC, the Peterson Institute for International Economics suggests that the EU's proposed DST (upon which the vast majority of the current interim taxes are based) is a de facto tariff and in breach of Article XVII.[521]

---

[521] GC Hufbauer and Z Lu *The European Union's Proposed Digital Services Tax: A De Facto Tariff* (online ed, Peterson Institute for International Economics) at 18–15.

The Peterson Institute argues that discrimination occurs in three ways:[522]

- the EU set the DST thresholds (€750 million in global gross revenue and at least €50 million in EU gross revenue) to capture successful US digital firms (such as Google, Facebook, Amazon, eBay, Uber and Airbnb) whilst leaving EU firms outside the net; and
- that the design, based on "taxable revenues", included digital advertising, digital platforms and marketplaces to sell goods and services and the transmission of users' data to other users were targeting US firms, whereas excluding subscription fees (which was the main revenue of Spotify, based in Sweden) had the same effect, that is to discriminate against US digital firms and not EU providers; and
- the proposal allows value-added taxes and other indirect taxes to be subtracted from "taxable revenue". Given that the United States, almost exclusively, does not have a form of indirect tax applied at the federal level, the tax base for US firms is higher than for identical EU digital suppliers.

The Peterson Institute goes on to highlight that the EU does not provide any specific commitments to preserve its position under the NT obligation for "computer-Related Services" and "Advertising", whether under the modes of cross-border sales or consumption abroad.

Accordingly, the Institute concludes that this is a case of de facto discrimination and the United States should take a WTO complaint to the Disputes Appellate Body.

With the European Union abandoning its proposals for a DST, and with the subsequent adoption by European countries independent of the EU, such as France and Italy (and at the time of writing proposals in other European countries and other jurisdictions) the United States may, in the absence of a multilateral agreement, pursue this avenue of disputes claim.

The arguments that will be made on the other side of the dispute include:

- That the thresholds do not discriminate on residence grounds, but simply the size and market dominance of any company. The logic is that such dominant organisations are profitable and that a gross tax on turnover should only apply to profitable entities and not smaller

---

[522] Ibid at 8–9.

4.6 CONSTRAINTS IMPOSED BY THE WTO

companies which are building up market share and expending substantial sums in research and development. This is not to say that large organisations are always profitable but simply that the likelihood of profitability increases dramatically with size.

- That the design of the tax is targeted to the major suppliers of digital services wherever they are based. In the design of any tax there is usually careful consideration of the tax base with decisions being made at the threshold of what to include and what to exclude.
- It makes no sense whatsoever to include value-added taxes in the calculation of taxable revenue. To suggest otherwise shows a misunderstanding of the nature of such indirect taxes. The firm, of course, would never get to "keep" the indirect tax which it collects from the consumer. It is a tax paid by the consumer on the consumption of the digital services. It is absolutely correct to exclude it from the calculation as otherwise, if it formed part of the calculation, it would constitute a tax on a tax.

Whether these arguments play out in the Dispute Settlement Body of the WTO depends on whether these interim taxes proceed, the likelihood of success, and many other matters including political concerns. A dispute could be lengthy – the arbitration (in the matter of the European Union and United States on whether members of the EU were subsidising Airbus contrary to the WTO rules) resulted in a decision in October 2019 when the original consultation request took place in October 2004.

The legal position is far from clear and opinions are divided on the application of the WTO rules to different types of taxes.[523] A learned commentator describes it thus, in coming to the conclusion that it is nowhere near as certain a problem as bodies such as the Peterson Institute have proclaimed:[524]

> Ultimately, none of the currently discussed and variously proposed measures (be they additional WHTs [withholding taxes], extended VPEs

---

[523] A careful examination of the WTO rules suggest that they do not apply to destination-based taxes, see A Pirlot *Don't Blame It on WTO Law: An Analysis of the Alleged WTO Law Incompatibility of Destination-Based Taxes*. University of Oxford Centre for Business Taxation, WP 19/16, November 2019, <https://ssrn.com/abstract=3551877> or <http://dx.doi.org/10.2139/ssrn.3551877>.

[524] W Haslehner "EU and WTO Law Limits on Digital Business Taxation" in W Haslehner and others (eds) *Tax and the Digital Economy: Challenges and Proposals for Reform* (Kluwer Law International, 2019) at 3.05.

[virtual permanent establishments] thresholds or special DSTs) are definitively prohibited or entirely legal in all circumstances. Inevitably, the detailed features of each and every concrete proposal with respect to digital economy taxation must be carefully and fully considered against both the EU and international-level prohibitions on discrimination and inappropriate subsidies.

For these reasons, if the issue primarily involves the NT obligations under the GATS, then there is a significant question as to whether the direct tax rules involving the introduction of a normative new tax are expressly excluded from the scope of the WTO rules under paragraph (d) of Article XIV. On balance, there is a reasonable case to suggest that the WTO rules might well fail to have application to these interim unilateral taxes. Such a conclusion could be justified on broad policy grounds that the WTO rules ought not to apply to normative taxation, together with, and as explained above (Section 4.6.5(b)), the specific carve-out for taxes under paragraph (d) of Article XIV.

(a) Consultation and Dispute Settlement

In addition, a member may not invoke the NT obligation if a measure of another member comes within paragraph 3 of Article XXII. This reads:

> 3. A Member may not invoke Article XVII, either under this Article or Article XXIII, with respect to a measure of another Member that falls within the scope of **an international agreement between them relating to the avoidance of double taxation.** In case of disagreement between Members as to whether a measure falls within the scope of such an agreement between them, it shall be open to either Member to bring this matter before the Council for Trade in Services.

Accordingly, if there is a tax treaty between the members, it may not be possible to argue that there is a violation of the NT obligation under the GATS if the measure falls within the DTA. As discussed above (Section 4.4.6), the measure may well fall within the *scope* of Article 24 (being a tax to which Article 24 applies) even though it is not discriminatory under that article.

Part II

5

The OECD Secretariat's and Inclusive Framework's Proposals for Multilateral Reforms

5.1 Introduction

Part I of this book considered the landscape and framework of the international tax system in the context of the emerging threat from the digitalisation of business. This emerging threat has arisen because certain types of business models are facilitated by technology (discussed in Chapter 2). Chapter 3 detailed specific problems with the current international tax system.

The second part of this book looks at the possible responses to these threats. As identified in Chapter 4, the international tax system is currently at a crossroads. The alternatives for change loosely fall into two categories: a multilateral solution which is a revision to the 1920s compromise – this can be termed "the 2020s compromise" – or a plethora of unilateral digital taxes imposed by a variety of countries in a much less coordinated fashion.

Two substantial work streams which the OECD is undertaking were introduced in Chapter 4. The OECD has termed these work streams "pillars", presumably to denote that they are both quite significant and fundamental to the tax system. This chapter discusses the key elements proposed in both Pillar One and Pillar Two. The objective is to identify these fundamental changes and to assess them in the context of the theory of cross-border taxation, the existing framework of the international tax rules, and the challenges identified by the digitalisation of business.

5.2 Pillar One: Allocation of Taxing Rights and Nexus

5.2.1 *The Unified Approach to Seek to Achieve a 2020s Compromise: A Brief History*

In October 2019 the OECD Secretariat released its proposal for public consultation "Secretariat Proposal for a 'Unified Approach' under Pillar

One".[525] Consultation with the public was invited on a series of proposals drawn together into one unified approach.[526] The objective of the consultation was to assist the members of the Inclusive Framework in the development of their report to the G20 in 2020. The timeline recognises "that for a solution to be delivered in 2020, the outlines of a unified approach would need to be agreed by January 2020".[527] The intention is that there is an agreed solution by late 2020.

The OECD was acting in accordance with the Programme of Work[528] which had been adopted by the Inclusive Framework on BEPS at its meeting of 28–29 May 2019, and approved by the G20 Finance Ministers and Leaders at their respective meetings in Japan in June 2019. This programme of work was hailed as "a major step forward" by the OECD Secretary-General in the report to the G20 Finance Ministers and Central Bank Governors.[529]

That it was so described as a major advancement indicates that there was a comparatively recent but significant congruence amongst countries in attempting to achieve a global, consensus-based solution. Previously, and as late as June 2018, the OECD/G20 Inclusive Framework on BEPS had described three distinct groups of countries:[530]

- a group of countries that regarded reliance on data and user participation as creating a misalignment between the location where profits are taxed and the location in which value is created. This group wanted new targeted tax rules focused on the digital economy; and
- a group of countries that regarded the digital transformation of the economy as more systemic, presenting challenges to the effectiveness of the international tax framework for business profits in a much broader manner and so not specific to highly digitalised business models; and

---

[525] OECD *Public Consultation Document: Secretariat Proposal for a "Unified Approach" under Pillar One* (OECD Publishing, October 2019). OECD Public Consultation Document ("OECD Unified Approach").

[526] This public consultation took place on 21 and 22 November 2019 at the OECD Conference Centre in Paris.

[527] OECD Unified Approach, above n 525 at [2].

[528] OECD/G20 *Inclusive Framework on BEPS: Programme of Work to Develop a Consensus Solution to the Tax Challenges Arising from the Digitalisation of the Economy* (OECD Publishing, May 2019) ("OECD Programme of Work").

[529] OECD Secretary-General *Report to G20 Finance Ministers and Central Bank Governors* (OECD Publishing, June 2019) at [12].

[530] OECD/G20 *Inclusive Framework on BEPS: Progress Report July 2017–June 2018* (OECD Publishing, July 2018) at [13].

- α group of countries for which the BEPS package was sufficient. This group saw no need for any further significant reform (outside of the BEPS measures to address double non-taxation) and so was opposed to any changes.

In other words, in the middle of 2018 there was no real consensus about the need for change, let alone a preferred or common direction of travel.

By 2019, however, something had changed, and the Inclusive Framework had identified three proposals for revising the profit allocation and nexus rules and most significantly had "committed to continue working together towards a consensus-based solution with the goal of producing a final report in 2020, with an update to the G20 in 2019".[531] The three proposals, described in some detail in the Inclusive Framework's Public Consultation Document, "Addressing the Tax Challenges of the Digitalisation of the Economy", were:[532]

- the "user participation" proposal; and
- the "marketing intangibles" proposal; and
- the "significant economic presence" proposal.

5.2.2 The "User Participation" Proposal

(a) Policy Rationale

The user participation proposal[533] is founded on the concept that the active and sustained engagement of users creates significant value for certain highly digitalised businesses. Essentially, it is the interaction of users which creates (at least in part) the brand of the business and generates valuable data (which is often able to be sold immediately). Additionally, users help to establish a critical mass allowing the digitalised business to achieve significant network effects. Examples of such digitalised businesses include social media platforms, search engines and online marketplaces. Each of these multi-sided platforms benefits from a key role played by users on one of the, if not both, sides of the platform.

In the case of social media platforms, users provide content and play a key role in building a network of platform users. These contributions

---

[531] OECD/G20 *Base Erosion and Profit Shifting Project: Public Consultation Document: Addressing the Tax Challenges of the Digitalisation of the Economy* (OECD Publishing, February 2019) at 7 ("OECD Public Consultation Document").
[532] Ibid at 9–17.
[533] Ibid at [17]–[21] on 9–10.

generate revenue for the platform operator through advertising sold on the other side of the platform or sometimes through subscription.

In the case of search engines, the users' searches are monitored and analysed, enabling the platform operator to earn revenue by selling targeted advertisements.

Users are also critical to an online marketplace. In addition to the network effect created by more users on both sides of a marketplace (buy/sell, lease/rent etc.), users frequently offer public reviews and feedback which acts as a valuable quality control/recommendation.

Under the current international tax framework, the activities of the user and any value generated through user participation are ignored in determining the profits of the platform operator. Only the physical activities of the multi-sided platform operator are assessed (in the more general sense of that word) in determining the platform's income. This results "in businesses being able to generate significant value from a jurisdiction with a significant and engaged user base (user jurisdiction) without the profits they derive from that value being subject to local tax".[534]

In order to align profit allocation outcomes with this value creation by users, the proposal seeks to attribute profits made by the multi-sided platform operator to the jurisdiction of the user. An additional requirement of the proposal is to change the nexus rules so that the user jurisdiction would have the right to tax this additional profit in circumstances where the platform operator does not have a physical presence or permanent establishment.

(b) Profit Allocation Rules

The current profit allocation rules are changed in order to allocate profit to those jurisdictions where a business (most likely a platform operator) has active and participatory users. This reallocation of profit occurs regardless of whether the platform firm has a physical presence in the jurisdiction where the users reside or indeed a permanent establishment.

The proposal suggests that this profit should be allocated using a non-routine or residual profit split approach rather than traditional transfer pricing models. It recognises that trying to consider the user base as a separate enterprise and asking what return it would receive on an arm's length dealing is a difficult, if not impossible, calculation.

---

[534] Ibid at [20] on 10.

Accordingly, the broad approach to profit allocation takes the following steps:

1 Calculate the residual profit of the business. That is, the profits that remain after routine activities have been allocated an arm's-length return.
2 Attribute a proportion of these residual profits to the value created by the activity of users. The Inclusive Framework suggests this could be determined through quantitative/qualitative information or a simple pre-agreed percentage.
3 Allocate the profits between the jurisdictions in which the business has users, based on an agreed formula such as revenues.
4 Provide the legal basis to give jurisdictions the right to tax this profit, irrespective of the absence of any physical presence or PE threshold.

Certain features of this approach are apparent. Some of these features might be regarded as advantages in some jurisdictions, but disadvantages in others. For example, the user participation proposal would only affect certain highly digitalised businesses. It would, therefore, focus on certain targeted activities (social media, search engines and online markets) and also have a threshold so that only large businesses in this category were affected. The limited application is likely to currently affect highly digitalised businesses. Most of these types of business are headquartered in the United States.

The calculation of routine profits would use existing transfer pricing rules. The allocation of non-routine profits (the residual profit split) would necessitate some complexity in the allocation of profits within an entity where there are several business lines. Furthermore, because of the complexity in determining profits to the value created by the activity of users (step 2 above), it is suggested that formulas and percentages be used. These are likely to be a pragmatic and potentially arbitrary solution. The Inclusive Framework was envisaging the need for strong dispute resolution as part of the proposal.

5.2.3 *The "Marketing Intangibles" Proposal*

(a) Policy Rationale

The marketing intangibles proposal[535] recognises a link between the market jurisdiction and marketing intangibles which enables successful

---

[535] Ibid at [29]–[49] on 11–16.

multinational businesses to establish and develop marketing intangibles even though they might have a limited local presence (such as a limited risk distributor) or no local physical presence at all. This manifests itself in two areas: first, in the area of intellectual property such as brands and trade names which are created by virtue of the favourable disposition of consumers and customers in the market jurisdiction. The second is other marketing intangibles, such as customer data, customer relationships and customer lists, all of which are derived from the interaction with consumers in the market jurisdiction.

The Inclusive Framework proposal suggests modifying current transfer pricing rules to require the marketing intangibles (and risks associated with these intangibles) to be allocated to the market jurisdiction. Like the user participation proposal, this proposal allows the market jurisdiction to tax some or all of the non-routine income associated with marketing intangibles, whilst other income would be allocated to members of the group based on existing transfer pricing principles. Some, or all, of the profit attributable to the marketing intangibles could be allocated depending on decisions made.

It is not intended that this would allow the market jurisdiction to benefit from profits which are features of the market jurisdiction rather than the independent actions of the non-resident multinational firm. The principle is based instead on the value created by the firm through the positive consumer mindset created by the brand, together with customer information and data acquired through the action of the firm in the marketplace.

Marketing intangibles can be differentiated. Therefore, something like "a patent used to build an efficient car engine will allow it to achieve the same mileage in one country as it does in another, and does so regardless of who made it or who bought it".[536] Value created by such trade intangibles would be retained in the country where they were developed.

This proposal overcomes one of the most significant risks to the international tax framework posed by the digitalisation of the economy. This is that modern firms can reach into and interact with customers either remotely or with limited physical presence in the market jurisdiction. As customers increasingly buy online, consumer businesses no longer have to invest in physical proximity and local presence but can instead deal with the sales and marketing side of the business remotely.

---

[536] Ibid at [34] on 12.

5.2 PILLAR ONE: ALLOCATION OF TAXING RIGHTS

Only shipment and fulfilment need to be handled in the jurisdiction and this might be done through third parties or limited risk distributors. The allocation of profits to the market jurisdiction can accordingly be substantially reduced.

The Inclusive Framework document goes on to describe three "key fact patterns" which it uses to further explain the concept of marketing intangibles. The first is a highly digitalised business which derives revenue from sales and marketing activities in a particular market jurisdiction where it does not have a taxable presence. The marketing intangibles could include those generated by the operation of free search services, free email, free digital storage and other similar interactions with consumers. The Inclusive Framework Document notes "thus, despite a different conceptual starting point, it would get to a result similar to that which would be achieved using the user participation proposal".[537]

A second example is where the same highly digitalised business has a local presence but operates it as a limited risk distributor. Under the existing rules, the resulting profit allocable to the market jurisdiction is considered inappropriately small".[538] In comparison, the marketing intangibles proposal would provide that some or all of the non-routine profit allocable to marketing intangibles associated with the market jurisdiction would be taxable by that market jurisdiction.

The third example is that of a non-highly digitalised business. As a matter of consistency and equity, the proposal contemplates changes to the profit allocation and nexus rules where traditional consumer businesses operate with the sale of goods and services to consumers in the market jurisdiction. Profits attributable to the marketing intangibles would be assessable in the market jurisdiction. This is a point of differentiation between the user participation proposal and the marketing intangibles proposal. That is, the marketing intangibles proposal applies to all businesses, not just those that are highly digitalised.

(b) Profit Allocation Rules

The essential difference between current international tax rules and this proposal is that the non-routine or residual income of the multinational group attributable to marketing intangibles would be allocated to the market jurisdiction. All other income, such as income attributable to

---

[537] Ibid at [40] on 14.
[538] Ibid at [41] on 14.

technology-related intangibles and routine marketing and distribution functions would be allocated on existing profit allocation principles.

This new allocation of (some or) all non-routine returns from marketing intangibles takes place notwithstanding which entity owns legal title to the marketing intangibles or regardless of which entities in the group factually perform or control DEMPE functions[539] related to these intangibles.

The calculation of the non-routine or residual income could be calculated using different methods. The first method splits out the profit adjustment attributable to marketing intangibles allocated to the market jurisdiction. It would then make this adjustment from the "normal" calculation of profit under the existing rules. In order to perform this calculation, marketing intangibles would need to be determined together with their contribution to profit using two sets of assumptions: (i) an assumption that marketing intangibles are allocated under the current rules (together with risks) and (ii) an assumption that the marketing intangibles are allocated to the market jurisdiction.

An alternative calculation is to use a residual profit split analysis. This involves determining the relevant profit, deducting routine profit and calculating the remaining or residual profit and then allocating a portion of this to marketing intangibles (either on cost-based methods or using more formulaic and pragmatic contributions such as fixed percentages).

Under either method, having determined the income attributable to marketing intangibles, it is then allocated to each market jurisdiction on an agreed formula, such as sales or revenue. With respect to platforms which derive substantial revenue from advertising, it would be necessary to reference the customers targeted by the advertisement and not necessarily the residence of the payer of the advertising fee.

5.2.4 The "Significant Economic Presence" Proposal

The significant economic presence proposal,[540] which was part of the 2019 Public Consultation Document, had already been discussed in the

---

[539] DEMPE stands for the development, enhancement, maintenance, protection and exploitation of intangibles and is designed to ensure that allocation of the returns from the exploitation of intangibles, and also allocation of costs related to intangibles, is performed by compensating MNE group entities for functions performed, assets used, and risks assumed in their development, enhancement, maintenance, protection and exploitation.

[540] OECD Public Consultation Document, above n 531 at [50]–[55] on 16–17.

5.2 PILLAR ONE: ALLOCATION OF TAXING RIGHTS 175

Action 1 Final Report, "Addressing the Tax Challenges of the Digital Economy".[541]

(a) Policy Rationale

The key concept here is that technological advances have enabled businesses to be involved in the economic life of another jurisdiction without physical presence. Accordingly, the new business developments have rendered the rules largely useless. This proposal focuses on "expanding" the concept of what constitutes a taxable presence in a jurisdiction away from the traditional permanent establishment. Instead, "factors that evidence a purposeful and sustained interaction with the jurisdiction via digital technology and other automated means" could constitute a "significant economic presence" when combined with revenue generated on a sustained basis.[542]

What sort of factors could establish a "significant economic presence" in a country? The Inclusive Framework Public Consultation Document suggests that the following would be sufficient:

- the existence of a user base and the use of data from those users;
- the volume of digital content derived from the jurisdiction;
- billing and collection in the local currency, or with a local form of payment;
- the maintenance of a website in a local language;
- responsibility for the final delivery of goods to customers, or the provision by the enterprise of other support services such as after-sales service or repairs and maintenance; and
- sustained marketing and sales promotion activities.

These factors would need to be present so that "a link would have to be created between the revenue-generating activities of the non-resident enterprise and its significant economic presence in the country".[543]

(b) Profit Allocation Rules

In the 2015 Final Report, several possible methods of profit allocation were discussed.[544] The method involving fractional apportionment,

---

[541] OECD/G20 *Base Erosion and Profit Shifting Project: Addressing the Tax Challenges of the Digital Economy, Action 1 – 2015 Final Report* (OECD Publishing, October 2015) ch 7 at 7.6.1 at 107 ("OECD Final Report").
[542] OECD Public Consultation Document, above n 531 at [51] at 16.
[543] OECD Final Report, n 541, ch 7, 7.6.1.4 at [282] on 111.
[544] Ibid, modifications to existing rules (at [285]), a modified deemed profit method (at [289]), and methods based on fractional apportionment (at [287]). The use of withholding taxes was also considered (at [292]).

however, received greater consideration than the others as part of the proposal explored by the Inclusive Framework in 2019.[545] This is how it works:

- define the tax base to be divided (one possible way to do this is to apply the global profit rate of the multinational group to the revenue (sales) generated from a particular jurisdiction); then
- determine the allocation keys to divide the tax base (these are factors such as sales, assets, employees and where users are meaningfully involved in the business they would form part of the allocation); and
- weigh the allocation keys (some factors may be given more importance than others).

It was from these three proposals that the unified approach was devised, not as a final solution but as a proposition which was meant again for public consultation.[546] The unified approach is intended to utilise elements of all three of the above proposals in that it:[547]

> addresses the allocation of taxing rights between jurisdictions and describes proposals for new profit allocation and nexus rules based on the concepts of "significant economic presence" and the exploitation of "user participation" and "marketing intangibles" in a jurisdiction.

5.3 Pillar One: What Is Proposed in the Unified Approach Proposal? Three Components of Income: Amount A

The unified approach proposal put forward a possible 2020s compromise because none of the three options proposed in the Public Consultation Document could be agreed upon.[548] It has new nexus rules, eliminating the requirement that it is necessary to have a physical presence in a jurisdiction in order to establish a taxing right. It also has new profit allocation rules made up of a three-tier combination of amounts (A, B and C).

---

[545] OECD Public Consultation Document, above n 531 at [52], at 16.
[546] As previously discussed in the introduction to this section, a two-day public forum was held in Paris on 21 and 22 November 2019.
[547] OECD *Public Consultation Document: Global Anti-Base Erosion Proposal ("GloBE") – Pillar Two* (OECD Publishing, November 2019) at [1] ("OECD GloBE").
[548] Richard Collier "Public Consultation Meeting on the Secretariat Proposal for a 'Unified Approach' under Pillar One" (presented at OECD Public Conference, Paris, November 2019).

5.3.1 Amount A: The Conceptual Relationship between Amounts A, B and C

It is important to understand that the three amounts are somewhat unrelated to each other in that there is no strategic rationale other than that they are the components of the package. A more accurate description is perhaps that they are related only by the fact that they are part of the same international tax compromise agreement and that they are designed to operate together as a new framework. As will be explained subsequently,[549] the three components of Pillar One and the rules in Pillar Two are aimed at different features of the international tax system.

Amount A is the most controversial, and it is focused on providing a solution to the existing problem in the 1920s compromise, which has been highlighted by highly digitalised businesses such as multi-sided platforms. Accordingly, Amount A breaks new ground in proposing new taxing rights without the requirement of a physical presence in the source or market jurisdiction. Amounts B and C continue to require a taxable physical presence in the source jurisdiction which has long been the case under the existing international tax framework.[550] That said, the computation of income under Amount B can also be seen as quite a significant reinforcement to the new taxing right created by Amount A. The reason for this is that whilst Amount A deals with both the issue of nexus (the creation of the ability to tax without physical presence) and the allocation of profit using a formula to attribute some of the non-routine profits to the new taxing right, Amount B also deals with the issue of profit allocation but more as a backstop.

The logic behind Amount B is to deal with the problem where modest (some would say overly modest) returns are allocated to "limited risk distributors" or LRDs. In other words, without addressing the issue of profit allocation using Amount B, multinationals could sidestep the nexus issue that Amount A deals with and establish an LRD which under current rules would earn a very small proportion of the multinational group's profit.[551] Amount C has a similar relationship to Amount B. It provides the ability to use an arm's length assessment of the risks and functions carried out by a marketing and distribution entity in order to

---

[549] In Chapter 6 "Examining the Proposals for Multilateral Reforms".
[550] OECD Unified Approach, above n 525 at [50] on 13.
[551] OECD Public Consultation Document, above n 531 at [13] on 8.

adjust the standardised Amount B with a "top up" to reflect additional risk and function features found in the entity.

These profit allocation rules radically depart from the existing international tax framework in several ways which are explained below (Section 5.3.8): using formulaic calculations in a modified residual profit split methodology and elements of formulary apportionment, allocating profits to the marketplace jurisdiction, ignoring the single-entity concept, and departing from the arm's length principle.

5.3.2 What Is the Policy Rationale behind Amount A?

While the OECD Secretariat's Proposal did not expressly draw on a policy rationale,[552] the subsequent Inclusive Framework statement addresses this issue. The allocation of taxing rights and taxable profits are no longer appropriately constrained by physical presence. The combination of globalisation and the digitalisation of the economy have enabled businesses to develop "an active and sustained engagement in a market jurisdiction, beyond the mere conclusion of sales, without necessarily investing in local infrastructure and operations."[553]

There is some helpful background to some of the policy rationale for Amount A described in the marketing intangibles proposal back at the beginning of 2019.[554] In the previous discussion outlining the policy rationale for marketing intangibles it was stated that there is a link, described as an "intrinsic functional link",[555] between marketing intangibles in the market jurisdiction and the value created by their business in the market jurisdiction.[556] The connection is one of a positive attitude in

---

[552] OECD Unified Approach, above n 525. This is not expressly detailed in the Secretariat Proposal for a "Unified Approach" under Pillar One, so one is left to draw this implication. This conclusion is also made in Letter from RJ Danon and V Chand (on behalf of the Tax Policy Center of the University of Lausanne (Switzerland)) to David Bradbury (Tax Policy and Statistics Division Centre for Tax Policy and Administration Organisation for Economic Co-operation and Development) regarding comments to public consultation document: "Secretariat Proposal for a 'Unified Approach' Under Pillar One" (12 November 2019) at [5]: "Although not explicitly stated, out of the three proposals that were presented earlier this year, from a conceptual perspective, the Unified Approach seems to be built on the market-related intangibles idea."

[553] OECD Public Consultation Document, above n 531 at [15] on 9.

[554] Ibid at [30]–[39] on 12–13.

[555] Ibid at [30], on 12.

[556] See the description under Section 5.2.3(a) "The 'Marketing Intangibles' Proposal: Policy Rationale".

the minds of customers reflecting the active intervention of the firm in the market in creating product or service brands and tradenames. Added to these intellectual property assets are other marketing intangibles, such as customer data, customer relationships and customer lists. These are derived from activities targeted at customers and users in the market jurisdiction suggesting that such intellectual property and other marketing intangibles are created in the market jurisdiction.[557] It is also enlightening to include some of the policy rationale for the user participation proposal, suggesting that taxation might be justified to the extent that the digital businesses generate value from the "engagement, interaction and contribution of users, including content, data and powerful network effects".[558]

(a) A Focus on Value Creation Associated with the Marketing Intangibles?

It certainly does make sense to align the scope and range of businesses affected by the creation of this new taxing right to a clear policy rationale for the exercise of the taxing right by the market jurisdiction. The OECD Secretariat Proposal suggests that the focus should be on those businesses "that can project themselves into the daily lives of consumers (including users), interact with their consumer base and create meaningful value without a traditional physical presence in the market".[559] The OECD Secretariat goes on to discuss, by way of footnote, what is meant by the terms "consumer" versus the term "customer":[560]

> The term "consumer" generally refers to individuals who acquire or use goods or services for personal purposes (i.e. outside the scope of a professional or business activity), while the term "customer" generally includes all recipients of a good or service (including business customers that are not end-users).

This led Danon and Chand to conclude that one possible approach is to identify businesses that are creating products and services for individual consumers and they use the following criterion, together with certain international benchmarks to establish a potential list of businesses:[561]

---

[557] OECD Public Consultation Document, above n 531 at [31]–[33] on 12.
[558] Ibid at [59] on 17.
[559] OECD Unified Approach, above n 525 at [19] on 7.
[560] Ibid at [19] (see note 7).
[561] Danon and Chand, above n 552 at [10] on 7.

If the business makes the product/service primarily for consumption by an individual, then it should be carved in. For example, an MNE which is in the business of making branded chocolates should be carved in. It should not matter whether the MNE sells branded chocolates directly to an individual (through its own store) or to another business that gives it to its employees for consumption. By contrast, businesses that do not create products or provide services targeted at consumers should not be carved in.

(b) What Are the Types of Businesses Included within the Scope of Amount A?

The first of the three components described in the OECD Secretariat's proposal[562] and the Inclusive Framework's statement[563] is Amount A.

The proposition of Amount A is the primary response to the tax challenges created by the digitalisation of business. It is without question the most radical change proposed by the Secretariat and the Inclusive Framework. The income deemed to arise under Amount A responds to the challenge that the new digitalised businesses can successfully interact with their customers (consumers) and users without the need to establish any form of physical presence in the jurisdiction in which the customers are based (disintermediation).

This disintermediation (removal of a physical presence or trading entity) enables the digitalised business to carry on its activities without triggering the taxation threshold under the concept of permanent establishment for the purposes of a DTA and business profits under Articles 5 and 7, and potentially under domestic law as well.

Originally, Amount A was conceived as the component of income deemed to be derived (or allocated) to the market jurisdiction where the MNE does not have a physical presence in the jurisdiction but is carrying on a "consumer-facing business" in a remote manner. The conception of a consumer-facing business included highly digitalised businesses like multi-sided platforms, so highly automated businesses were definitely in the scope of the "all-encompassing" consumer-facing business definition.[564] Subsequently, the scope of the businesses targeted for the

---

[562] OECD Unified Approach, above n 525 at [15] and [30] on 6 and 9.
[563] OECD/G20 *Inclusive Framework on BEPS: Statement by the OECD/G20 Inclusive Framework on BEPS on the Two-Pillar Approach to Address the Tax Challenges Arising from the Digitalisation of the Economy* (OECD Publishing, January 2020) ("OECD IF 2020").
[564] OECD Unified Approach, above n 525 at [15] on 5, where it says: "The approach covers highly digital business models but goes wider – broadly focusing on consumer-facing

application of Amount A has been refined, so as to split these out into "two broad sets of businesses".[565]

5.3.3 Scope of Amount A: Highly Digitalised Businesses

The first set or type of business is those businesses "that provide automated and standardised digital services to a large and global customer or user base".[566] Highly digitalised businesses such as these provide their services to customers remotely using little or no local infrastructure or physical presence. As discussed in Chapter 2, these businesses frequently use customer or user networks, generating "substantial value from interaction with users and customers", while benefiting from data and content contributions made by users and the interaction of users with the suppliers' businesses.

(a) Examples of Automated Digital Services

As highly digitalised businesses, they provide services that generate revenue from the provision of automated digital services on a standardised basis to a large population of customers or users across multiple jurisdictions.[567] The Inclusive Framework expects that Amount A would apply to include the following non-exhaustive list of business models:

- online search engines;
- social media platforms;
- online intermediation platforms, including the operation of online marketplaces, irrespective of whether used by businesses or consumers;
- digital content streaming;
- online gaming;
- cloud computing services; and
- online advertising services.

The Inclusive Framework's statement indicates that the definition of automated digital services will require further work, especially in the areas of businesses that deal mostly with other businesses (B2B transactions) and those services which are delivered online but involve a high

---

businesses with further work to be carried out on scope and carveouts. Extractive industries are assumed to be out of the scope."
[565] OECD IF 2020, above n 563 at [17] on 9.
[566] Ibid at [18].
[567] Ibid at [21] on 10.

degree of human intervention and judgement (such as professional services in law, accounting, architecture, engineering and consulting). These latter professional services-type businesses were not in the scope of the Inclusive Framework's statements architecture.

5.3.4 Scope of Amount A: Consumer-Facing Businesses

The second type of "in-scope" businesses are those businesses that generate revenues from selling goods or services, directly or indirectly, to consumers. These are known as "consumer-facing businesses", but under the Inclusive Framework's statement of January 2020, this group of businesses is now separated from the highly digitalised group referred to above.[568] These businesses are more traditional businesses, less affected and disrupted by digitalisation. They manufacture and sell products through physical distribution channels as they have done for many decades. In order to enhance their business offering, these businesses increasingly use "digital technology to more heavily interact and engage with their customer base".[569] Accordingly, these consumer-facing businesses focus on building and sustaining relationships with individual customers, targeting their marketing and branding to these customers, frequently by collecting and exploiting individual customer data. The Inclusive Framework statement highlights that good examples of such consumer-facing businesses are more heavily interacting with their customers rather than those selling connected products and/or using online platforms as a principal mechanism for their sales and marketing.[570]

(a) Examples of Consumer-Facing Businesses

One of the key aspects of consumer-facing businesses is that the goods and services they sell are commonly sold to individual consumers for personal use and not for commercial or professional purposes.[571] As discussed subsequently, when discussing B2B transactions,[572] this could include businesses that sell consumer products to end-consumers via third-party resellers or intermediaries when they perform routine tasks such as minor assembly and packaging. In contrast, businesses that sell

---

[568] Ibid at [18]–[19], on 10.
[569] Ibid at [19].
[570] Ibid at [19].
[571] Ibid at [24]–[29] on 11.
[572] See the discussion at Section 5.3.5(a) "May Also Include B2B Transactions".

components or intermediate products which are incorporated into finished goods that are then sold to consumers would be out of scope.

The definition of a consumer-facing business would be expected to bring into scope the following non-exhaustive list of businesses:

- personal computing products (e.g. software, home appliances, mobile phones);
- clothes, toiletries, cosmetics, luxury goods;
- branded foods and refreshments;
- franchise models, such as licensing arrangements involving the restaurant and hotel sector; and
- automobiles.

As can be seen, the intention is to bring within the scope those businesses that generate revenue: (i) from licensing rights over trademarked consumer products or (ii) from licensing a consumer brand, such as under a franchise model.[573]

5.3.5 Further Consideration on What Businesses Are Affected?

At the time of writing, the decision on what businesses are included within the scope of Amount A has not been finalised. There are some indications arising from the various discussion documents.

(a) May Also Include B2B Transactions

As noted, the Inclusive Framework's statement indicates there is careful consideration required on the definition of whether business models that deal with other businesses, rather than directly with consumers, will be included within both the automated digital services definition and the consumer-facing businesses definition.[574]

Prior to the Inclusive Framework's statement, the Secretariat's Proposal suggested that:[575]

> These features could be said to be relevant for any business, but they are most relevant for digital-centric businesses which interact remotely with users, *who may or may not be their primary customers* and other consumer-facing businesses for which customer engagement and interaction, data collection and exploitation, and marketing and branding is

---

[573] OECD IF 2020, above n 563 at [27] on 11.
[574] Ibid at [23] and [25] on 11.
[575] OECD Unified Approach, above n 525 at [19] on 7 (emphasis added).

significant, and can more easily be carried out from a remote location. This would include highly digitalised businesses which interact remotely with users, *who may or may not be their primary customers*, as well as other businesses that market their products to consumers and may use digital technology to develop a consumer base.

This comment would tend to suggest that certain B2B businesses/transactions might be caught in addition to "in-scope" B2C businesses/transactions.

This conclusion is supported by commentators examining the justification for Amount A. Danon and Chand, on behalf of the Tax Policy Centre of the University of Lausanne (Switzerland), suggested in their submission (as part of the public comments on the Secretariat's Proposal on the Unified Approach) that one should consider scope in the context of the implied policy rationale of the marketing intangibles proposal:[576]

> Moreover, seen from the perspective of the business, the objective of the enterprise should be to create a final product/or provide a service for an individual consumer. In this sense, a difference should not be made as to whether the product/service is sold in a business to consumer (B2C) or Business to Business (B2B) context. The controlling criteria is – for whom does the business develop the product/service?

(b) Extractive Industries and Producers and Sellers of Raw Materials and Commodities

The Inclusive Framework's statement is clear that extractive industries and the producers and sellers of raw materials and commodities will not be within the definition of consumer-facing businesses.[577] The reason given for this is that "taxes on profits from the extraction of a nation's natural resources can be considered to be part of the price paid by the exploiting company for those national assets, a price which is properly paid to the resource owner".[578] Generally speaking, extractives and commodities are usually generic goods whose price is determined on the inherent nature of the product. Accordingly, they do not have the characteristics of some of the consumer-facing businesses which have substantial marketing intangibles. Such extractive and commodity businesses can, therefore, refute that part of the price paid for their

---

[576] Danon and Chand, above n 552 at [10] on 7.
[577] OECD IF 2020, above n 563 at [30] on 11.
[578] Ibid at [30].

products is attributable to the market jurisdiction or consumer demand. An important observation qualifies this proposition: the comment by the Inclusive Framework's statement is as follows: "For example, the sale of sacks of green coffee beans will not be within the scope of the new taxing right, whereas the sale of branded jars of coffee will be."[579]

(c) Other Industries and Sectors outside the Scope

The financial services sector mostly deals with commercial customers and therefore will be outside the scope of Amount A calculations, but even those dealing with individual consumers are heavily regulated (for example, bank and insurance licensing requirements and protection of deposit and policy-holders in the market jurisdiction). According to the Inclusive Framework's statement this ensures that ordinarily the residual profits are largely realised in the local customers' marketplace and that, therefore, there is no need for the application of the new rules to these industries.

Likewise, the operation of ships and aircraft in international traffic has been subject to the long-standing practice of taxing the operator (of the aircraft or ship) in its country of residence. The view of the Inclusive Framework is that there is no need to make changes in this area so international traffic would be outside the scope of Amount A.[580]

(d) Favourable Demand Conditions Excluded

Another key and logical exclusion relates to those businesses in scope solely because of a consumer-facing rationale. In other words, the exclusion would not apply to the automated digitalised business models. With respect to consumer-facing businesses, the Inclusive Framework suggests that it is desirable that the scope of businesses be required to perform a calculation of Amount A having due consideration of whether value for the business has been created in the marketplace due to the use of marketing intangibles or whether there are other factors.

Why is this desirable? This reference into the policy behind Amount A is useful because it can exclude certain features or attributes of the market jurisdiction which may be unrelated to the marketing intangible and therefore not appropriately within the scope. An example of this was provided in the OECD's Secretariat Proposal where it was made clear that favourable demand conditions in the market jurisdiction "that exist

---

[579] Ibid at [30].
[580] Ibid at [32] on 12.

independent of the actions of the firm – such as the existence of a stable population benefiting from a successful economy that provides them with the financial means to be able to buy the relevant product" should not be within the scope of those businesses required to perform the calculation of Amount A.[581]

5.3.6 *Relevant Thresholds*

Concerned about unnecessary compliance costs for smaller businesses and seeking to target the rules to profitable digital multinational enterprises operating a cross-border business, the new taxing right created through the calculation of Amount A will only apply to multinational groups that meet certain gross revenue thresholds. This could be set at the same level of the reporting requirement for country-by-country (CbC) reporting under BEPS Action 13. This would mean that only those multinational groups that have gross revenue above €750 million would be affected.

There is also an indication that even if the gross revenue exceeds €750 million then the multinational will not necessarily be within the rules unless it is carrying on a certain (currently unspecified) level of in-scope activities (for instance, X amount of automated digital services and consumer-facing business activities). Lastly, there is also consideration being given to a carve-out in circumstances where the total profit to be allocated under the new taxing right does not meet a certain *de minimis* amount. This would have the potential to exclude a large domestic business which had a small amount of in-scope foreign income.

5.3.7 *Nexus Rules*

There are effectively two major thresholds in respect of Amount A. As indicated in Section 5.3.6, there are qualifying thresholds as to the size of the multinational enterprise with the focus being to include only large businesses which have significant (and possibly profitable) in-scope digital or consumer-facing activities. For clarity, this can be described as the included company threshold.

The second threshold relates to the nexus as it creates a new taxing right in the market jurisdiction. As previously indicated in the policy

---

[581] OECD Public Consultation Document, above n 531 at [33] on 12.

5.3 AMOUNT A

section and types of businesses part of this discussion (Sections 5.3.1 and 5.3.2), the key is to allocate taxation to those multinationals that develop "an active and sustained engagement in a market jurisdiction, beyond the mere conclusion of sales, without necessarily investing in local infrastructure and operations".[582] In order to do that, the Inclusive Framework suggests creating a new nexus rule "based on indicators of significant and sustained engagement with market jurisdictions".[583] It is thought that the generation of in-scope revenue is the primary evidence of such significant and sustained engagement and thus a nexus will be based on a revenue threshold in the market jurisdiction – the included jurisdiction threshold. The final figures are a matter of negotiation but will reflect a variation according to the size of the market jurisdiction.

With respect to automated digitalised businesses, the revenue threshold is the only test. This reflects the nature of the automated digitalised business, namely that the level of active and sustained engagement with customers or users has an outcome in the business model which results directly in revenue for the digital provider (for example, a multi-sided platform) regardless of any other factors.[584]

With consumer-facing businesses, there are some additional requirements in order to establish a taxable nexus. This is because the Inclusive Framework's Statement recognises that "the proposal will not create a new nexus if the MNE is merely selling consumer goods into a market jurisdiction without a sustained interaction with the market".[585] This is the exclusion for merely favourable market demand factors referred to above.[586] Further work will consider these factors, but they are likely to include (i) the existence of a physical presence of the multinational enterprise in the market jurisdiction and/or (ii) targeted advertising directed at the market jurisdiction. The intention is to avoid capturing mere sales in circumstances where the multinational is not present in the market or has not targeted specifically that market from abroad.[587]

---

[582] Ibid at [15] on 9.
[583] OECD IF 2020, above n 563 at [36] on 12.
[584] Reflecting also the power of the network effect, the use of data and intangibles and other key features are described in Chapter 2 as part of the highly digitalised business model.
[585] OECD IF 2020, above n 563 at [39] on 13.
[586] See the discussion at Section 5.3.4(d) "Favourable Demand Conditions Excluded".
[587] OECD IF 2020, above n 563 at [39] on 13.

5.3.8 Application of Amount A by Way of an Example

Under this proposal, certain businesses will have a share of deemed residual profit allocated to market jurisdictions using a formulaic approach, i.e. the new taxing right. The intention behind this part of the book is simply to illustrate how Amount A might be calculated (in a general rather than a detailed way).

(a) Calculation of the Deemed Income under Amount A Scope of the Rules (Thresholds)

For example, a company resident in country A (company A) is making sales of certain consumer-orientated products or services in a country (country B), but it does not have a taxable presence in country B. The business is a highly digitalised one operated through a multi-sided platform. The level of sales of the multinational group of which company A is a member is €1 billion and so exceeds a threshold both in terms of the company's worldwide turnover (the included company threshold – say €750 million) and any requisite in-scope business turnover. Additionally, the sales in country B are €150 million and so exceed €50 million. The €50 million is an assumed and hypothetical threshold (the included jurisdiction threshold) – a certain minimum in that particular jurisdiction (country B) to reflect a level of sales connection by reference to the size of the country B jurisdiction. In other words, a larger country would have a larger included jurisdiction threshold, and a smaller country would have a lesser jurisdiction threshold.

Step One: Identify the Multinational Group's Profits Irrespective of the profits of company A, the calculation of Amount A begins with the group profits of the whole of the multinational.[588] It is expected that this will be able to be drawn from the consolidated group financial accounts[589] prepared under Generally Accepted Accounting Principles (GAAP) or International Financial Reporting Standards (IFRS).[590] Such financial statements are easily available, almost invariably audited, and prepared in a reasonably standard way to satisfy reporting and regulatory

---

[588] OECD Unified Approach, above n 525 at [53], and largely confirmed under the approach of the Inclusive Framework's Statement in OECD IF 2020, above n 563 at [43].
[589] OECD IF 2020, above n 563 at [43].
[590] OECD Unified Approach, above n 525.

requirements (such as stock exchange listing or a country's domestic companies' office requirements)

As recognised by the later Inclusive Framework's Statement, if in-scope business activities do not exceed a certain level of profitability, then they may be excluded from the calculation of Amount A.[591] Originally the OECD Secretariat Proposal recognised that where losses are concerned, it is likely that there will be a need to provide for these losses to be carried forward (in circumstances where the group's losses proceed the group's profits, described as an "earn-out" by the OECD) or clawed back (in circumstances where the group's losses are subsequent to the group's profits).[592]

Even though accounting standards usually require reporting on the basis of operating segments such as business line or regional operations, the OECD Secretariat Proposal recognises it may be necessary to further require a separation of the multinational enterprise's business into a business line, regional or market bases. The reason for doing so is to prevent profit distortion through the averaging of business lines (an example given is the integration of a low-margin retail business into the results from a high-margin digital business).[593] The subsequent comments by the Inclusive Framework's Statement indicate this work is continuing.[594]

In this case, let us assume two things: first, that there is only one line of business and it is within scope, and secondly, that the profit margin (profit as a percentage of sales) is 20 per cent, so the net profit for the multinational is €200 million.

Step Two: Separate Out the Amount of Profits Attributable to Routine Functions The second step involves separating out those profits attributable to routine functions in an approach broadly consistent with rewarding routine functions performed under the residual profit split method in conventional transfer pricing.[595] This second step preserves the ability of jurisdictions to tax routine business functions performed in their jurisdiction and attributable to activities physically

---

[591] OECD IF 2020, above n 563 at [42] on 13.
[592] Ibid at [51] on 13.
[593] OECD Unified Approach, above n 525 at [53] on 14.
[594] OECD IF 2020, above n 563 at [45] on 14.
[595] OECD Unified Approach, above n 525 at [54] on 14.

located in their jurisdiction. It retains some elements of the existing status quo in the current international tax rules, namely the ability of the source and residence jurisdictions to tax routine functions under a method "broadly analogous" to the residual profit split method.[596]

The words "broadly analogous" are an amalgamation of terms as the exact words of the Secretariat's Proposal are: "In broad terms, these are profits which, by analogy to the residual profit split method, would be regarded as rewarding routine functions."[597] The actual mechanism is to allocate a portion (as a percentage) of the net profits to routine functions and the balance to non-routine functions. In this way Amount A applies only to the portion of profit exceeding a certain level of profitability (the routine profits).[598] The percentage is an estimate and may be varied industry by industry. For example, the quantum of Amount A could be weighted for different degrees of digitalisation (described in the Inclusive Framework's Statement as "digital differentiation").[599] It is a simplification designed to "facilitate the administration of the new profit allocation approach alongside the current transfer pricing rules and reduce the scope for disputes".[600] It is not:[601]

> intended to disturb the actual allocation of the remuneration derived from actual routine activities under the current transfer pricing framework. Instead, the purpose of the simplifying conventions would be merely to simplify the calculation of the deemed non-routine profit subject to the new taxing right.

The method of using a percentage or proportion of profit is designed to be administratively simple. As an agreed percentage it would be anticipated that there would be fewer disputes as taxing jurisdictions would understand and have agreed to this allocation in advance.

Let us assume that the proportion of net profit attributable to routine functions is 5 per cent, meaning that the balance of 15 per cent (20 per cent net profit less the 5 per cent) is attributable to non-routine profit. In the case of company A, the non-routine profits of the group are €150 million.

---

[596] Ibid at [52] on 13.
[597] Ibid at [54] on 14.
[598] OECD IF 2020, above n 563 at [46] on 14.
[599] Ibid at [46].
[600] OECD Unified Approach, above n 525 at [52] on 13.
[601] Ibid at [56] on 14.

5.3 AMOUNT A

Step Three: Attribute a Portion of the Non-Routine Profits to the Market Jurisdiction The third step in determining Amount A is to identify the portion of the non-routine profits, which are attributed to the market jurisdiction.[602] The split is between those factors attributable to the market. These are marketing intangibles as discussed above, such as brand and customer loyalty, and other market-related intangibles such as customer lists, customer data and elements related to the customer relationship. They would also include, in the digital environment, matters relating to users. Accordingly, factors associated with users' engagement, contribution and network effect might form part of this attribution.

In contrast, the portion of the non-routine profits attributable to other factors such as trade intangibles, capital and risk would not be included in Amount A.

For illustrative purposes, let us assume that it is agreed that in the case of this industry/business, the marketing/user portion of the non-routine profits is 40 per cent. In other words, the non-routine profits attributed to the various market jurisdictions of the multinational group are €60 million (€150 million times 40 per cent); 60 per cent of the non-routine profits (€90 million) are attributable to other factors such as capital and trade intangibles.

The portion (40 per cent) is an internationally negotiated percentage and may be varied for different industries/businesses. Highly digitalised businesses such as social media platforms may generate income from very different activities, some of which can be attributed to the market jurisdiction (such as the monetisation of the customers' data and networking, and the value created from its brand) and some of which are attributed to non-market, non-routine profits (such as innovative algorithms and software).[603]

Step Four: Allocate the Deemed Income Based on the Non-Routine Profits Attributable to Market Jurisdictions to Those Eligible Jurisdictions The final step in the calculation of Amount A involves allocating the non-routine profits attributable to market jurisdictions to the various jurisdictions based on factors, such as sales.[604]

In the case of company A, it has 15 per cent of its total worldwide sales in country B (€150 million divided by €1 billion). Accordingly, 15 per

---

[602] Ibid at [57] on 15.
[603] Ibid at [57].
[604] Ibid at [60] on 15.

cent of the non-routine profits attributable to market jurisdictions, or €9 million (€60 million times 15 per cent), is the deemed income of company A[605] and subject to tax in country B.

5.3.9 Summary of Amount A

As is clear, Amount A is, therefore, a new taxing right over a portion of "in-scope" multinational groups' deemed non-routine or residual profits. This means that the existing international tax framework rules (the 1920s compromise) will apply to the deemed routine profits applicable to the activities performed by the companies in the countries concerned.

There are several highly innovative features to the new "2020 international tax compromise" with respect to the deemed income under Amount A. These include:

- The creation of a new taxing right which reaches into the market jurisdiction and reflects activities (to do with marketing intangibles and the user base) carried on by certain businesses in that jurisdiction. This is obviously a fundamental change from the position reached in the OECD Model Treaty as a result of the 1920s compromise (taxation rights did not extend to the market on the sale of goods and services but were essentially retained by the country of residence and production).
- The consequential need to change the nexus requirements for taxation so that the new taxing right could be established even in the absence of any physical presence in the market jurisdiction. This enables the taxation of remote sales of goods and services.
- The starting point for the calculation of Amount A is the multinational groups consolidated profits. This is a fundamental difference as previously the international tax system operated on a strict separate entity accounting system attributing worldwide profits to particular entities (usually companies) in the multinational group located in particular jurisdictions.
- The use of formulas and agreed proportions to allocate taxing rights rather than individual arm's length computations. For example, as detailed above, there is a split between routine and non-routine profits which will be agreed (perhaps on an industry by industry basis) as part of the new consensus. This purports to be broadly analogous to the existing transfer pricing rules with respect to routine profits and, in

---

[605] Or as determined, any member of the multinational group of which company A is a member.

that sense, attempts to keep a status quo with existing international transfer pricing rules. The use of agreed percentages is an innovative and controversial measure, but if it can be implemented it is possible to see significant improvement in reduced international compliance costs for business, easier administration by tax authorities, and the possibility of a better regime for dispute resolution.

- Consistent with the above innovative suggestions for reform, the overriding impression from participants in the public consultation facilitated by the OECD in late November 2019 was that it was necessary to develop a new regime for the calculation, assessment and payment of tax on the deemed income arising from these Amount A calculations.[606] There was reference to the need to have "a one-stop shop" so that the parent company would be the entity performing the calculations and providing the information to the market jurisdictions. There were several administrative advantages to this, including the significant lessening of the possibility of double taxation because all the calculations would be performed in a single location and with a consistent approach. Furthermore, in addition to this central coordinated jurisdictional approach for the calculation of Amount A, there was support for having a process involving a binding disputes panel with independent panel members in order to facilitate dispute resolution. Another aspect for consideration raised at the public consultation was how to prevent double taxation because, of course, the allocation of the deemed amount of income to the market jurisdiction should mean either a reduction of income for the residence jurisdiction or a foreign tax credit. Many commentators made the plea for a tax base correction rather than the foreign tax credit – that is, a preference to a deduction for the deemed income of Amount A in the residence jurisdiction.

5.4 Amount B: Fixed Remuneration for Marketing and Distribution

The second component in the Inclusive Framework's Statement and the OECD Secretariat's Proposal is also controversial but for different reasons. This part of the proposal suggests making a new fixed remuneration for baseline marketing and distribution functions that take place in the market jurisdiction. Amount B is best seen as a compatible part of the overall package. It seems to have emerged from practical solutions proposed by

---

[606] As discussed in the sessions on "Computation of Amount A" and "Elimination of Double Taxation" (Public Consultation Meeting on the Secretariat Proposal for a "Unified Approach" Under Pillar One, Paris, November 2019).

business to the original Public Conference on the Taxation of the Digital Economy which took place in Paris in March 2019; these included submissions by major multinationals such as Johnson & Johnson.[607]

5.4.1 Scope of Amount B

The original proposals on marketing intangibles discussed fixed remuneration for marketing and distribution functions for both highly digitalised businesses and ordinary businesses, and so were an amalgamation of both Amounts A and B.[608] In their submission of 3 March 2019, Johnson & Johnson wrote:[609]

> If we understand the key goals to be an increase in taxable profits to the local market sales and marketing companies (including markets with users but no physical presence in the case of highly digitalized companies in a local market), use of a formulaic method rather than a pure arm's length standard, and a solution that countries and companies will find easy to administer, then we recommend a solution that targets local market profitability in a simple manner.

The OECD Secretariat's Proposal splits out the amount of income attributable to highly digitalised businesses (in Amount A) and categorises this as a new taxation right in circumstances where the multinational has no physical presence in the market jurisdiction. The component relating to Amount B applies to a much broader type of business model – all distributors – and it is particularly relevant for a commonly utilised model, that involving limited risk distributors.

The exact definition of which distributors are affected by Amount B requires careful consideration because there does not appear to be any *de minimis* exemptions. As a result, the number of multinationals affected by this methodology for calculation of income will be exponentially greater than those affected by the requirements to perform the Amount

---

[607] OECD "*Public Conference on the Possible Solutions to the Tax Challenges of Digitalisation*" (OECD Public Consultation, March 2019).
[608] OECD Public Consultation Document, above n 531 at [30] on 12: "The marketing intangibles proposal addresses a situation where an MNE group can essentially 'reach into' a jurisdiction, either remotely or through a limited local presence (such as an LRD) to develop a user/customer base and other marketing intangibles."
[609] OECD Public Consultation Document, above n 531 at [30] on 12; and Letter from K Amos and L Weingrod (on behalf of Johnson & Johnson) to Tax Policy and Statistics Division, Centre for Tax Policy and Administration, regarding public comments on the possible solutions to the tax challenges of digitalisation (3 March 2019).

A calculation. The Inclusive Framework's Statement indicates that the definition of baseline distribution activities "will likely include distribution arrangements with routine levels of functionality, no ownership of intangibles and no or limited risks".[610]

5.4.2 Policy Rationale in Respect of Amount B

The logic behind the use of formulas is simple pragmatism. A fixed return reduces compliance costs and provides certainty:[611]

> The fixed return under Amount B would seek to reduce disputes in this area, where tensions are important as a result of applying the transfer pricing rules. The intention would be to benefit taxpayers and tax administrations, as it would reduce the risk of double taxation as well as the substantial compliance costs arising from the aggressive enforcement of current transfer pricing rules.

Subsequent statements by the Inclusive Framework mirror the OECD Secretariat's view on the purpose of Amount B.[612]

There does seem to be considerable business support for the proposal, and it confirms the policy rationale.[613] In their submission, Procter & Gamble says:[614]

---

[610] OECD IF 2020, above n 563 at [61] on 17; The Inclusive Framework document goes on to say in this same paragraph: "Defining what entities and activities would qualify could be achieved by using a positive definition based on qualitative and quantitative factors, together with a list of activities and entities that would be out of scope."
[611] OECD Unified Approach, above n 525 at [62] on 15.
[612] OECD IF 2020, above n 563 at [58] on 16; where they state:

> The overall purpose of amount B is therefore to:
>
> achieve a greater degree of simplification in the administration of transfer pricing rules for tax administrations and lower compliance costs for taxpayers; and
> enhance tax certainty about the pricing of transactions, which should lead to a reduction of controversies between tax authorities and taxpayers.

[613] Letter from TM McDonald (on behalf of the Procter & Gamble Company) to Tax Policy and Statistics Division, Centre for Tax Policy and Administration, Organisation for Economic Co-operation and Development regarding public comments on the Secretariat Proposal for a "Unified Approach" Under Pillar One (11 November 2019); and Letter from K Amos and L Weingrod (on behalf of Johnson & Johnson) to Tax Policy and Statistics Division, Centre for Tax Policy and Administration, regarding public comments on the Secretariat Proposal for a "Unified Approach" Under Pillar One (11 November 2019).
[614] McDonald, above n 613, executive summary at 2.

> We view "Amount B" as critical to the project and see a successful resolution as highly beneficial for all MNEs and tax administrations, especially for many developing countries. "Amount B" addresses the area where most transfer pricing disputes arise. It is, therefore, critical for tax certainty and the avoidance of double taxation.

Some commentators[615] suggest that taxpayers may end up paying more tax under Amount B to achieve greater certainty and reduce the risk of disputes and double tax.

5.4.3 Calculation of the Deemed Income under Amount B

Multinational business has contributed in a very positive way to this discussion. It has been suggested by Johnson & Johnson that one approach to the calculation of this deemed income under Amount B is simply to take a percentage of sales (say 3 per cent) and then adjust this amount dependent on the profitability (or other factors) of the particular industry/region of the multinational enterprise.[616] Another approach is to take a percentage of the "earnings before tax, calculated using an allocation and segmentation approach consistent with "Amount A".[617] Procter & Gamble submitted that a distributor's share of profitability (based on feedback from transfer pricing experts from firms in different regions) is between 15 and 18 per cent of total pre-tax profitability.[618] They recommended, in a manner broadly consistent with the Johnson & Johnson proposal, that this amount be adjusted depending on the actual profitability of the global multinational.

In essence, the quantum of income calculated under Amount B is thought to be a fixed return on either sales or earnings before tax. It is a matter of negotiation with the OECD Secretariat Proposal suggesting:[619]

> Whilst the distinction between marketing and distribution activities and others performed by an MNE group will, in most cases, be clear, there will be some borderline issues. Therefore, a clear definition of the activities

---

[615] Such as T McDonald (on behalf of the Procter & Gamble Company) "Fixed Remunerations (Amount B)" (Public Consultation Meeting on the Secretariat Proposal for a "Unified Approach" Under Pillar One, Paris, November 2019).
[616] OECD "Public Conference on the Possible Solutions to the Tax Challenges of Digitalisation" (OECD Public Consultation, March 2019); and Amos and Weingrod, above n 613.
[617] McDonald, above n 613 at 12.
[618] Ibid at 12.
[619] OECD Unified Approach, above n 525 at [63] on 15, 16.

that qualify for the fixed return would be required. The quantum of the fixed return could be determined in a variety of ways: it could be (1) a single fixed percentage; (2) a fixed percentage that varied by industry and/or region; or (3) some other agreed method.

5.4.4 Summary

It is suggested by the OECD Secretariat Proposal that the use of this simpler formulaic approach, while still being broadly consistent with the arm's length principle and the existing calculation of profits under Article 7 of the OECD Model Treaty, would overcome some of the areas where tension has increased.[620] The tensions are different for Amount A and Amount B. In the case of the former, it is an intense pressure caused by non-taxation for remote highly digitalised activities. In the latter, the tensions are concerned with the lack of precision in transfer pricing and the consequential disputes arising.

The cost of applying the existing rules and their complexity, particularly for developing countries, has led to considerable pressure for change to make the system more user-friendly in the twenty-first century. At the Public Conference held in Paris in late November 2019 it was suggested that, for example, of the (approximately) 135 countries that were members of the Inclusive Framework, seventy or eighty had no transfer pricing economists or access to a licensed transfer pricing database.[621] It is hardly surprising that this larger group of countries is, therefore, looking for another more pragmatic solution whilst at the same time expressing dissatisfaction with the current regime.

The OECD summarises this practical problem as follows:[622]

> Moreover, there seems to be agreement that the arm's length principle is becoming an increasing source of complexity and that simplification would be desirable to contain the increasing administration and compliance costs of trying to apply it. Thus, an "administrable" solution is essential, especially for emerging and developing countries. And a simple system will lower the risks of disputes, which currently endanger the cohesion of the international tax system.

These proposed changes can be seen as a further development in the work by the OECD on safe harbours for certain categories of taxpayers.

---

[620] Ibid at [18] on 6.
[621] McDonald, above n 613.
[622] Ibid at [17] on 6.

For example, in the OECD Transfer Pricing Guidelines,[623] there is considerable discussion about the merits of using safe harbours, with the Guidelines suggesting that much of the original 1995 feedback was negative about the practice.[624] Over time, there appears to be growing acceptance that the use of safe harbours, rather than presenting undue risk, presents significant opportunity to simplify and reduce compliance costs for eligible taxpayers, provides certainty to such taxpayers that their tax positions will be accepted by tax administrations, and permit tax administrations to redirect their administrative resources from lower risk to more complex or higher risk transactions.[625]

5.5 Amount C: The "Top-Up"

The final component in the Unified Approach is the proposal to have an Amount C, which represents the ability to "correct" the outcome arrived at through the application of Amount B in situations where Amount B has been too arbitrary and come to an unacceptable position from an arm's length perspective. The OECD described the application of Amount C as follows:[626]

> 64. Taxpayers and tax administrations would retain the ability to argue that the marketing and distribution activities taking place in the market jurisdiction go beyond the baseline level of functionality and, therefore, warrant a profit in excess of the fixed return contemplated under Amount B, or that the MNE group or company perform other business activities in the jurisdiction unrelated to marketing and distribution.

5.5.1 Scope of Amount C

The scope of Amount C appears identical to that of Amount B, having application to the same type of entities which are performing the functions of a limited risk distributor. Essentially, it is intended to apply "where there are more functions in the market jurisdiction than have been accounted for by reference to the local entity's assumed baseline activity (which is subject to the fixed return in B(ii) above), and that

---

[623] OECD *Transfer Pricing Guidelines for Multinational Enterprises and Tax Administration* (OECD Publishing, July 2017).
[624] Ibid at [4.96] on 204.
[625] Ibid at [4.105], [4.108] and [4.109] on 206-7.
[626] OECD Unified Approach, above n 523 at [64] on 16.

5.5 AMOUNT C

jurisdiction seeks to tax an additional profit on those extra functions in accordance with the existing transfer pricing rules".[627]

It is interesting to note that the OECD Secretariat's Proposal only seems to contemplate that Amount C is a positive number. The implications from this observation are that it is only the tax authority which will assert that there is a need to adjust Amount B to establish an arm's length amount under Amount C. In other words, there is no discussion in the proposal about the taxpayer demonstrating that their marketing and distribution activities are below the baseline contemplated by Amount B and that therefore the adjustment under Amount C should be that Amount B is reduced.[628]

The function of Amount C is, therefore, to "top up" situations where the baseline activity is exceeded by the taxpayer and the tax authority is asserting that their return in the source jurisdiction is inadequate under Amount B. This will necessarily lead to the possibility of disputes, and there is quite a significant focus on this aspect of Amount C, with the OECD suggesting that "any dispute between the market jurisdiction and the taxpayer over any element of the proposal should be subject to legally binding and effective dispute prevention and resolution mechanisms".[629]

5.5.2 Policy Rationale under Amount C

The policy rationale behind Amount C is simply adherence to the arm's length principle. In that sense, it can be seen as the least controversial of any of the proposed changes. What Amount C is effectively doing is ensuring that there is no undertaxation of multinationals in the market jurisdiction in circumstances where there are more significant marketing and distribution functions than those contemplated by the fixed amounts in Amount B. One major policy concern with Amount C is that it "unwinds" the certainty of Amount B.[630]

---

[627] Ibid at [30] on 9.
[628] Ibid at [64] on 16; and OECD Public Consultation Document, above n 531 at [30] on 9 which says: "This would include those cases where there are more functions in the market jurisdiction than have been accounted for by reference to the local entity's assumed baseline activity (which is subject to the fixed return in B above), and that jurisdiction seeks to tax an additional profit on those extra functions in accordance with the existing transfer pricing rules."
[629] OECD Unified Approach, above n 523 at [30] on 9.
[630] G Perez-Navarro "Conclusion", Public Consultation Meeting on the Secretariat Proposal for a "Unified Approach" Under Pillar One, Paris, November 2019).

5.5.3 Calculation of Income under Amount C

A distributor (which is a company incorporated in the market jurisdiction), owned by a foreign multinational, has deemed income under Amount B of €1 million. The functions performed by the local distributor are substantial (and go beyond those contemplated in the formulation of the agreed fixed amounts in Amount B). Accordingly, the market country's tax administration performs an analysis which suggests that the arm's length amount of profit is €2 million. Amount C, being income of €1 million (€2 million arm's-length amount less €1 million being Amount B), is raised as an assessment as a result.

5.6 Dispute Prevention and Resolution

5.6.1 Amount A

To this end objective of either preventing disputes or resolving them, the OECD Secretariat's Proposal discusses the need for new rules to provide for: "dispute prevention and resolution, including mandatory and effective dispute prevention and resolution mechanisms to ensure the elimination of protracted disputes and double taxation".[631] The OECD Secretariat listened to comments made at the Public Conference in Paris in November 2019 about mandatory arbitration and indicated that they are working towards something other than binding arbitration although having some level of binding dispute resolution.[632]

Certain fundamental requirements are identified in the Inclusive Framework's Statement for this new dispute prevention and resolution framework.[633] These include (i) securing certainty for taxpayers and tax administrations alike; (ii) drawing on existing models of multilateral processes; (iii) taking into account domestic legal constraints; and (iv) ensuring an inclusive and fair process for both developed and developing countries. The Inclusive Framework is considering innovative and inclusive processes to develop a new enhanced dispute resolution process as a key component of Pillar One.

The preliminary considerations were identified as follows:[634]

- There is a need to design clear and simple rules. The new approach proposed in the 2020s compromise adopts formulas in order to allocate

---

[631] OECD Unified Approach, above n 525 at [64] on 16.
[632] Perez-Navarro, above n 630.
[633] OECD IF 2020, above n 563 at [65] on 17.
[634] Ibid at [65]–[82] on 17–19.

taxing rights and does not rely on the arm's-length principle. This will reduce the risk of disputes but not eliminate them completely.
- Tax administrations must be allowed to assess and audit a multinational entity's calculation and allocation of Amount A. A dispute between two jurisdictions over Amount A will have consequential flow on implications to other jurisdictions (because the allocation of taxing rights extends on a formula where the calculation of Amount A is spread to multiple jurisdictions). If you try to resolve the differences using the existing bilateral system, it would be necessary to have multiple mutual agreement procedures, which the Inclusive Framework would regard as "uncoordinated, inefficient and lengthy".[635]
- This new process is designed to provide early certainty, before tax assessments are made, to prevent disputes arising. The intention is to have certainty over all aspects of the calculation of Amount A. These include whether the multinational is in scope, the delineation of business lines, allocation of central costs and tax losses to business lines, whether a nexus exists in a particular jurisdiction, and identification of the relieving jurisdictions for the purposes of eliminating double taxation.[636]
- It is proposed to explore innovative approaches to prevent the possibilities of dispute, particularly focusing on early tax certainty for Amount A. One possibility is the establishment of representative panels made up of appropriate members of the Inclusive Framework and having a transparent and inclusive process for computation and dispute resolution. There is discussion about the possibility of providing expert commentary and assistance to those tax administrations with resource constraints.
- The use of standardised administration (information reporting, filing of returns and collection of taxes) would ensure consistent application and minimise administrative costs.
- A key issue is the question of binding agreements. It is suggested that if a dispute is not prevented by the preceding process, then an appropriate mandatory binding dispute resolution mechanism be agreed and available.

---

[635] Ibid at [68] on 18.
[636] Ibid at [70] on 18.

5.6.2 Amounts B and C

The objective behind Amount B is to limit disputes and to increase certainty for taxpayers and administrators. Notwithstanding, there is an obvious tension between the policy objectives of Amounts B and C. The question remains: how can these differing objectives be resolved? The ideal solution is that the taxpayer certainty and administrative convenience of Amount B is retained whilst preventing the obvious abuse of "undertaxation" in the market jurisdiction in circumstances where the functions performed are significantly higher than the baseline marketing and distribution functions contemplated by Amount B.

It seems there are two possible solutions. One is to keep Amount B relatively simple and to deal with the complexity of either more complicated industries or multinationals that decide to decentralise marketing and distribution functions to local market entities by increased use of Amount C. This may well be an answer, but there will be a huge tax planning-orientated focus on the definition of routine marketing and distribution activities. One suggestion, from Procter & Gamble, is to carefully work through the list of functions dealt with under Amount B and therefore: "'Amount C' should apply to scenarios when functions in a market exceed a well-defined list of routine marketing and distribution activities."[637]

The other alternative would be to conceptually deal with the differences in functions to a much greater extent in the formulation of Amount B. If a multilateral agreement is reached in respect of Amount B to deal with a range of different circumstances so that there is clear recognition that "one size does not fit all" then Amount B might deal with variations in types of industry or decisions on decentralisation. An example, again provided by Procter & Gamble,[638] is that of the regulatory expertise and medical training required to be an effective distributor in the medical device or pharmaceutical industry, which generally commands a higher distributor return. If Amount B provides for greater functions being performed by such distributors of medical device or pharmaceutical industry businesses and hence increased profitability, then recourse to Amount C's arm's-length amount might be significantly restricted. This would accord with the sentiment of quite a few

---

[637] McDonald, above n 613 at 3.
[638] Ibid at 13.

commentators in the OECD's Public Conference in Paris in late November 2019 who advocated against the need (or widespread use) of Amount C.

Whether the complexity of different industries and different business models are dealt with in a more prescriptive but formulaic way in Amount B or by way of adjustment to different facts and circumstances to the arm's-length standard in Amount C, this affects the potential for tax disputes.

Arguably, the more that the sophistication of Amount B deals with different situations adequately the more disputes will be prevented. If the amount determined under Amount B is inadequate and adjustments under Amount C are common, then:

- Taxpayers will face greater uncertainty and the possibility of costs and litigation through disputes relating to the amount of income under Amount C; and
- The various tax administrations in different jurisdictions will have to dedicate resources not only to making and defending their assessments under Amount C, but also to adjustments made by other jurisdictions who have similar claims (in respect of Amount C).

This leads to the likelihood of double taxation with other jurisdictions (double jurisdictional taxation) as the amount of income under Amount C will probably already be assessed by the residence country or another jurisdiction (double taxation caused by the delayed assessment under a dispute relating to Amount C). The consequence would be the burgeoning costs of multiple dispute resolution.

- There is also the possibility of double taxation (double same jurisdiction taxation) under the new framework as amounts already included under Amount A could be assessed through the arm's-length amount in Amount C. This was identified in the OECD Secretariat's Proposal as follows:[639]

> In relation to Amount C, it would also be important to ensure that the profit under Amount A could not (whether in whole or part) be duplicated in the market jurisdiction, for example, based on an argument that some or all of the profit under Amount A is also in some way referable to the functional activity in the market jurisdiction which is rewarded by Amount C

---

[639] OECD Unified Approach, above n 525 at [65], on 16.

The Inclusive Framework's Statement suggests that some of the innovative approaches discussed above with respect to Amount A could be put in place to ensure enhanced dispute resolution mechanisms to transfer pricing and PE disputes under Amount B.[640] If the routine "baseline" marketing and distribution activities under Amount B are challenged by tax administrations taking the view that an additional amount should be charged under Amount C, then a new dispute resolution process will be required. Although this dispute mechanism is a backstop (competent authorities should resolve disputes in a timely way under the mutual agreement procedures), the Inclusive Framework indicates that specific enhancing measures can be enacted domestically to improve tax certainty and dispute resolution. In particular, in relation to Amount C:[641]

- jurisdictions can explore limiting the time during which adjustments to Amount C can be made; and
- the collection of tax could be limited or suspended for the duration of any disputes related to Amount C (subject to conditions being agreed).

5.7 Pillar Two: Global Anti-Base Erosion Proposal

5.7.1 Profit Shifting Revisited

The second pillar of the OECD's Programme of Work,[642] which was adopted by the Inclusive Framework on BEPS at its meeting of 28–29 May 2019,[643] focuses on unresolved base erosion and profit shifting (BEPS) issues.[644] Even after the comprehensive reforms proposed by the BEPS project, there was a desire amongst members of the Inclusive Framework to go further to combat the continued risk of profit shifting to entities subject to no or very low taxation. Accordingly, in the Policy Note approved by the Inclusive Framework, agreement was reached: "to explore on a 'without prejudice' basis taxing rights that would strengthen the ability of jurisdictions to tax profits where the other jurisdiction with

---

[640] OECD IF 2020, above n 563 at [76]–[82] on 18–19.
[641] Ibid at [82] on 19.
[642] OECD Programme of Work, above n 528.
[643] Subsequently approved by the G20 Finance Ministers and Leaders at their respective meetings in Japan in June 2019.
[644] OECD/G20 *Base Erosion and Profit Shifting Project: Addressing the Tax Challenges of the Digitalisation of the Economy – Policy Note* (OECD Publishing, January 2019) at [1.2] on 1 ("OECD Policy Note").

taxing rights supplies a low effective rate of tax to those profits".[645] The Policy Note highlights that the tax issues concerning problems arising from the rapidly growing digitalised economy (discussed in Chapter 3) are more than the allocation of taxing rights between residence and source countries. Although this is the primary focus of Pillar One, it extends to the "larger landscape"[646] picture where multinationals have been legitimately structuring their affairs to take advantage of no or very low taxation. Under Pillar Two, the continued risk of profit shifting is countered through two new (but interrelated) rules which "provide jurisdictions with the right to 'tax back' where other jurisdictions have not exercised their primary taxing rights or the payment is otherwise subject to low levels of effective taxation".[647] These new rules are an income inclusion rule and a tax on base eroding payments.

5.7.2 Policy Rationale for the New Pillar Two Rules

The policy rationale is essentially one of anti-avoidance and, in particular, focused on preventing profit shifting. Members of the Inclusive Framework (or at least a subset group of members – described in the Program of Work as "certain members"[648]) believe that profit shifting occurs through the use of intangibles as well as in more fundamental ways such as capital structuring and intragroup financing. Whilst the use of intangibles to shift profits is particularly prevalent in the digital economy, the other capital and financing activities are not so limited but extend to all multinational businesses.

The new rules are, therefore, designed to protect corporate income tax bases around the world and restrict countries from competing with each other. In the alternative, unless these measures are considered:[649]

> there is a risk of uncoordinated, unilateral action, both to attract more tax base and to protect the existing tax base, with adverse consequences for all countries, large and small, developed and developing as well as taxpayers. It posits that global action is needed to stop a harmful race to the bottom, which otherwise risks shifting taxes to fund public goods onto less mobile bases including labour and consumption, effectively undermining the tax sovereignty of nations and their elected legislators.

---

[645] Ibid at [1.2] on 1.
[646] Ibid at [1.2].
[647] OECD Programme of Work, above n 528 at [7] on 6.
[648] OECD Programme of Work, above n 527 at [53], on 25.
[649] Ibid at [54] on 25.

Clearly, the OECD/G20 Inclusive Framework is concerned about the erosion of corporate income tax bases in all types of economies, but they have a particular concern that the types of tax incentives becoming more widespread in developing countries are undesirable. Not only do they not achieve their goal of attracting investment,[650] the tax expenditure revenue forgone reduce opportunities for "public spending on infrastructure, public services or social support".[651] The Inclusive Framework pointed to evidence to suggest that such tax incentives are frequently provided in developing countries in circumstances where governments are pressured by businesses to grant them.[652]

The Pillar Two proposal could, therefore, "effectively shield developing countries from the pressure to offer inefficient incentives and in doing so help them in better mobilising domestic resources by ensuring that they will be able to effectively tax returns on investments made in their countries".[653]

The policy rationale is, therefore, twofold. As briefly described, it is intended that the new rules will limit the opportunity for countries to offer tax incentives or other forms of tax competition to prevent the "distortive impact of direct taxes on investment and business location decisions".[654] A secondary rationale is that these rules will act as a backstop in a complementary way to the Pillar One proposals, ensuring that the profits under those proposals are booked at an appropriate tax rate. That is, and by way of example, having redesigned the new taxing rights under Pillar One, Amount A, the income is not then diverted to another low-tax jurisdiction through the use of profit-shifting techniques such as payments made for the use of intellectual property.

The proposals under Pillar Two contemplate a minimum level of tax paid on all internationally operating businesses. In that sense, and just like their Pillar One counterparts, these proposals have a much broader concept than the original Action 1 plan which started with a much sharper focus on the digital economy. They now extend to the whole economy, although the challenges posed by digitalisation are extensive and it is accepted that it may not be possible to ring-fence the digital side

---

[650] Ibid at note 7; and IMF, OECD, UN and World Bank *Options for Low Income Countries' Effective and Efficient Use of Tax Incentives for Investment* (International Monetary Fund, October 2015) at 11–12.
[651] OECD Programme of Work, above n 528 at [54].
[652] IMF, OECD, UN and World Bank, above n 650 at 35–6.
[653] OECD Programme of Work, above n 528 at [54] on 26.
[654] Ibid at [54] on 26.

of business. Not only do these Pillar Two proposed changes extend beyond digital business, but they confront the international tax framework norm in the areas of transfer pricing, the use of intellectual property, residence taxation and tax competition.

5.7.3 An Income Inclusion Rule

(a) The Scope of the Rule

The income inclusion rule extends residence-based taxation so that the income of a foreign branch or a controlled entity becomes subject to tax in circumstances where the effective rate of tax in the source jurisdiction is below a minimum rate.

In broad terms, it is envisaged that the income inclusion rule would operate as a minimum tax. It is envisaged that it would operate in a similar, but supplementary, way to a jurisdiction's controlled foreign company (CFC) rules. A shareholder in a foreign corporation which was not subject to an effective rate of tax above a minimum rate would be required to "top up" the proportionate share of tax liability for the underlying foreign corporation's profits.

The effect of the income inclusion rule is to ensure that the income of the multinational group is subject to tax at a minimum rate which reduces the incentive for the group to allocate profits for tax reasons to low-tax entities. Thus, according to the Pillar Two Public Consultation document:[655]

> The income inclusion rule would have the effect of protecting the tax base of the parent jurisdiction as well as other jurisdictions where the group operates by reducing the incentive to put in place intra-group financing, such as thick capitalisation, or other planning structures that shift profit to those group entities that are taxed at an effective rate of tax below the minimum rate.

(b) How It Operates

The proposal contemplates a minimum tax rate which would be consistently applied irrespective of the jurisdiction of the headquarters of the multinational enterprise.[656] There is an indication that there is a

---

[655] OECD GloBE, above n 547 at [11] on 29.
[656] Ibid at [12] on 30; the OECD Secretariat's Proposal suggests that consideration be given to an exception to this blanket minimum tax: namely, where income is taxed below the

preference for this to be a fixed rate rather than a percentage of the parent jurisdiction's corporate income tax rate. Using a percentage of the parent jurisdiction's rate could result in "a more complex and opaque international framework given the significant variance in CIT rates across Inclusive Framework members".[657] This proliferation of rates might make it difficult to coordinate the rule with the undertaxed payments rule, significantly increasing the risk of double taxation. In addition to the benefits of transparency and coordination with other rules, using a fixed rate also has administrative and compliance cost benefits.[658] Indications from the Inclusive Framework's Statement are that "the inclusion rule would operate as a top-up tax to a minimum rate calculated as a fixed percentage".[659]

By way of a very high-level example,[660] assume a parent company (with a tax rate of 25 per cent) operates a business in a local jurisdiction where there is a substantial incentive regime (not compliant with the BEPS Action 5 on harmful tax practices) which means it enjoys a reduced rate of tax. The rules could operate as follows:

1 Take the relevant accounting rules and adjust according to agreed-upon changes to reflect timing and permanent differences customarily found between tax and financial accounting rules and consistent with the normal CFC rules (in other words, the tax base is determined by reference to the rules applicable in the shareholder jurisdiction). Let's assume this is €1 million for the local entity concerned.
2 Multiply the adjusted profits by the agreed standardised international tax rate (let us say this is 15 per cent so the minimum tax is €150,000).
3 Subtract the corporate income tax actually paid in the local jurisdiction (in this case, let us assume this was zero), so the income inclusion rule

---

minimum rate and benefiting from a harmful preferential regime, then the tax rate could be the higher of the minimum rate or the full domestic tax rate (if this is greater).
[657] Ibid at [14] on 30.
[658] Ibid at [18] on 30.
[659] OECD IF 2020, above n 563, Annex 2 at [9] on 28.
[660] OECD GloBE, above n 547; and OECD Programme of Work, above n 528, illustrate the significant complexity potential for these calculations. These will include, inter alia, adjustments to the taxable base (i.e. rules applicable in the shareholder jurisdiction adjusted with simplifications to reduce compliance costs with the intention of using financial accounting rules as a basis for determining net income (with adjustments for losses and the timing of recognition of income and expenses), exemptions and carve-outs, options for blending high-tax and low-tax income and rules relating to tiered ownership).

would require €150,000 tax to be paid by the parent company in the parent jurisdiction.

Expressed in this simplified way, the concept is straightforward, but the reality of the actual calculation is that it is anything but straightforward.[661] Anyone who has advised, complied with or written about CFC rules will know that there are numerous problems in trying to determine a sensible tax base upon which to apply the fixed tax rate. For example, the local jurisdiction to which the calculations apply may have different loss carry-forward rules or timing rules for the recognition of expenditure or depreciation. These differences not only result in significant compliance costs but of more concern is that they may "lead to situations where technical and structural differences between the calculation of the tax base and the parent and subsidiary jurisdiction could result in an otherwise highly taxed subsidiary being treated as having a low effective rate of tax for reasons unrelated to the policy drivers under the GloBE proposal".[662]

Insofar as it is possible, the intention is to simplify the calculation by starting with financial accounts prepared in accordance with legal, regulatory and the relevant accounting standards. The Inclusive Framework has done extensive work on the use of financial accounts, examining different mechanisms to address temporary (timing) differences between tax and financial accounting. The objective is to "limit adjustments for permanent differences to reduce complexity and compliance costs, benefits for both taxpayers and tax administrations".[663]

In order to achieve neutrality between subsidiaries and branches, the income inclusion rule would need to apply to foreign branches. Many jurisdictions exempt foreign branches rather than providing a foreign tax credit. The income inclusion rule could be implemented by way of a switch-over rule which turns off the exemption and implements a tax credit mechanism in circumstances where the income is subject to a low effective tax rate. A simple switch-over rule is being developed in conjunction with the income inclusion rule (to ensure consistency in scope).[664]

---

[661] OECD GloBE, above n 547 at [19]–[24] on 30–3.
[662] Ibid at [19] on 31.
[663] OECD IF 2020, above n 563, Annex 2 at [10] on 28.
[664] Ibid, Annex 2 at [15] on 29.

5.7.4 Taxing Base Eroding Payments

(a) The Scope of the Rule

The proposed second new rule is a tax on base eroding payments. Broadly, these types of rules operate to reduce the risk of tax-free deductible payments being made from a jurisdiction to another related party in a low-tax jurisdiction. Existing examples of such rules are those contained in many domestic rules dealing with thin capitalisation, interest allocation and earnings-stripping regimes, all of which are designed to place limitations on the amount of interest income allowable as an expense in the jurisdiction of the paying entity.

These proposals are broader and they contemplate two components:

- *an undertaxed payments rule.* This rule would either deny a deduction for a payment or impose source-based taxation such as withholding tax in respect of any payment made to a related party where the related party does not pay tax at a minimum rate; and
- *a subject to tax rule.* This rule would apply to tax treaties which would have the effect of only granting treaty benefits if the item of income was subject to tax at a minimum rate. While the subject-to-tax rule would apply to related parties, the OECD Secretariat's proposal also contemplates exploring its application to payments made to unrelated parties insofar as Articles 11 and 12 (interest and royalties) of the OECD Model Convention are concerned.[665]

(b) How It Operates

A multinational makes a payment of €1 million for the right to use certain intellectual property rights to a subsidiary based in a low/no-tax jurisdiction. There is a double tax agreement between the parent company jurisdiction and the subsidiary jurisdiction. It provides for zero withholding tax and gives no source taxing rights. Under domestic law in the parent country the withholding tax on royalties would normally be 15 per cent.

Under the undertaxed payments rule, it is determined that the payment is "undertaxed". The rule would deny a deduction for the €1 million payment.

An alternative to the application of the undertaxed payments rule, is that the subject to tax rule applies, denying the limitation on the taxation

---

[665] OECD GloBE, above n 547 at [29] on 34.

of royalties in the source state under Article 12 of the parent/subsidiary country double tax agreement. Under the domestic law in the parent company jurisdiction withholding tax at the rate of 15 per cent would be required (or €150,000).

(c) Other Issues

There are other matters relating to coordination, simplification and compatibility with international obligations (such as non-discrimination) being performed under the auspices of the Inclusive Framework.[666] There are also some important issues looking at the use of thresholds (such as the €750 million revenue threshold) and carve-outs to restrict the application of the rules in Pillar Two.

5.8 Conclusion

This chapter has examined the reasons for, and policy behind, the programme of work to develop a new international tax framework consensus. It then discussed the broad direction of these changes. The next chapter looks at the key features of the 2020s proposed compromise and seeks to assess the suitability of these changes against the challenges posed to the existing tax framework caused by changes in the way in which business is carried on in the digital era.

David Bradbury, Head of the Tax Policy and Statistics Division of the OECD,[667] described the likely changes which might arise as a result of the OECD's work as "modest but significant". He did not further elaborate on which elements were "modest" and which were "significant". It may well be that the amounts involved in some of the adjustments proposed are relatively modest and this accords with some of the expectations of the business community. Tim McDonald, Vice President, Finance & Accounting Global Taxes of Procter & Gamble, illustrated this expectation, together with a strong desire to embrace the changes if they are broadly consistent with what has been proposed prior to the November 2019 Public Conference. In P&G's submission, he said:[668]

---

[666] OECD IF 2020, above n 563, Annex 2 at [20] on 30.
[667] D Bradbury, Head of the Tax Policy and Statistics Division, Centre for Tax Policy and Administration "Keynote Presentation – Tax and the Digital Global Economy – Issues for the Region and Globally" (International Fiscal Association Conference, Melbourne, June 2019).
[668] McDonald, above n 613 at 3.

> If a consensus solution can be reached (as broadly described above), we expect that P&G's global income tax liability will increase. However, we (and we believe most other MNEs) are willing to pay a modest amount of incremental income tax in exchange for an easier to administer, economically rational, and stable taxation system which minimizes the cost and effort caused by tax disputes and unresolved incidences of multiple taxation of the same income.

Even if the amounts of tax involved are relatively modest, no one should underestimate the importance of the proposed changes because of their nature. The principles and the rationale behind the proposed changes are most certainly "significant" and represent a fundamental change to the international tax system in the ways now discussed.

As part of the work by the G20/Inclusive Framework, the OECD presented an Update on the Economic Analysis and Impact Assessment on the overall impact on global tax revenues of Pillars One and Two.[669] The combined effects of Pillars One and Two is an estimated global net revenue gain of 4 per cent of global corporate income tax which amounts to some US$100 billion, shared in a broadly similar way across high-, middle- and low-income economies. For high- and middle-income economies, the lion's share of these forecast revenue gains will be made up from the contribution from the Pillar Two initiative.[670] If these calculations prove accurate, it might be an understatement to suggest that they are modest amounts of revenue.

---

[669] OECD "Update on Economic Analysis and Impact Assessment" (webcast, 13 February 2020) OECD <www.oecd.org.>.
[670] Ibid at slide 20.

6

Examining the Proposals for Multilateral Reforms

6.1 Does the 2020s Compromise Address the Challenges of the Digital Economy to the International Tax Framework?

6.1.1 Introduction

As discussed in the previous chapter, the OECD Secretariat has prepared proposals under its Programme of Work under two Pillars to try to reach a 2020s compromise and develop a new international tax framework.[671] This chapter examines and critiques the OECD Secretariat's proposals in light of the tax challenges arising from the increasing use of highly digitalised business models.

6.1.2 Broader than Digital

The first point to be made is that the OECD has, correctly, taken quite a broad approach in its proposals for tax reform. It is not just a case of the OECD Secretariat attempting to deal just with the consequences of digitalisation and the challenges posed to the tax system in itself. As already discussed, it is not possible to ring-fence the digital economy.[672]

Business already uses technology to a greater or lesser extent but there is an increasing trend to utilise highly digitalised business models. For example, and there are many, take the way airlines carry on business. They provide a classic service of passenger travel, physically carrying people. This is not, at least at this stage, remotely digital. Their booking

---

[671] OECD *Programme of Work to Develop a Consensus Solution to the Tax Challenges Arising from the Digitalisation of the Economy* (OECD, May 2019) ("OECD Programme of Work"); and OECD *Tax Challenges Arising from Digitalisation – Interim Report 2018: Inclusive Framework on BEPS* (OECD Publishing, 2018). See also OECD *Statement by the OECD/G20 Inclusive Framework on BEPS on the Two-Pillar Approach to Address the Tax Challenges Arising from the Digitalisation of the Economy* (OECD, January 2020).

[672] See Section 2.1.1(b) "The Difficulty of Separating the Digital Economy from the Rest of the Economy".

services, however, together with ticketing, boarding passes, pricing, luggage and loyalty schemes, all employ highly digitalised features. Airlines also use multi-sided platforms to enable you to book other services such as hotel accommodation, rental cars, parking and taxis, none of which are directly provided by them. This is a good example of a modern business integrating traditional services and multi-sided platforms which can enable remote sales and the generation of income without physical presence. There is no limitation on the possibility of connecting customers on one side of the multi-sided platform (passengers booking airline tickets) to service or goods providers on the other side of the platform (hotel accommodation providers).

Accordingly, the proposed reforms are broader than a response to a purely digital challenge would suggest. The OECD, on behalf of the Inclusive Framework, are making suggestions about a tax system better suited to the twenty-first century.

Why would there be a need to suggest an arbitrary fixed rate percentage return for limited risk distributors under Amount B in Pillar One? This is not a response to highly digitalised businesses. The answer is for other reasons such as administrative compliance, lower costs, improved certainty and dispute prevention and resolution and not because of challenges posed by the digital economy. So, whilst highly digitalised businesses may well be the principal reason for these changes, they are not the only rationale in the "smorgasbord" of changes suggested in the proposals.

6.1.3 A Direction of Travel

The previous international tax compromise of the 1920s has been remarkably stable, defying the Greek philosopher Heraclitus's observation that "change is the only constant in life". Given the extraordinary changes in business, it may well be that the tax reforms of the 2020s are about a "direction of travel" in the sense of emerging tax policies and principles and that further significant changes will be required as new developments in technology and the consequential change in business models occurs. As will be discussed in Chapter 8, the direction of travel for these reforms is most clearly a trend towards destination-based taxation: taxation in the place of destination rather than taxation in the place of origin.

This chapter, therefore, seeks to identify not only the response to the challenges posed by the digital economy but also other areas of significant change proposed in the Programme of Work and the associated two Pillars.

6.1.4 The Approach Taken in This Analysis

Earlier in this book we considered how highly digitalised businesses operated and what unique features were being employed in their business models.[673] As a result, the following significant challenges were identified as arising from the development of these business models:[674]

1 "The Vanishing Ability to Tax Business Profits" (Section 3.2);
2 "The Use of Data, the Contribution of Users, and the Measurement of their Value" (Section 3.3);
3 "The Reliance on, and Mobility of, Intellectual Property" (Section 3.4);
4 "The Characterisation of Transactions and Income" (Section 3.5);
5 "The Failure of Transfer Pricing with Certain Multinational Enterprises and their Transactions" (Section 3.6);
6 "The Inadequacy of Residence-Based Taxation" (Section 3.7); and
7 "Competition by States" (Section 3.8).

Each of these challenges will now be examined in light of the Programme of Work. This will identify which of the proposals are designed to address particular challenges and also situations where the proposals "go further" than the challenges identified. For example, one can immediately see that the proposals in Pillar One address some of the problems, such as the vanishing ability to tax business profits through the lack of physical presence (and the inadequacy of the permanent establishment rules in the twenty-first century). Furthermore, the proposal in Pillar One also addresses how users, arguably, form a significant and integral part of a business model through their establishment of content, participation in the network effect, validation and review work as well as contributing their data.

The proposals in Pillar One seek to address these first two significant challenges (1 and 2 above) and they also assist in two of the other challenges, namely the characterisation of transactions and income and to a certain extent the failure of transfer pricing, but there are many challenges which Pillar One does not address which, arguably, Pillar Two

---

[673] See Section 2.2.2 "New Business Models".
[674] See the main challenges described in detail in Chapter 3.

does. Overlaying the proposed solution on the challenges shows us which areas are being addressed by which proposals together with any possible omissions.

6.2 Dealing with the Vanishing Ability to Tax Business Profits

6.2.1 The Challenge: Nexus to a Taxable Presence

The vanishing ability to tax business profits is a compound challenge. It can be split into two components. The first is one of nexus or taxing rights. Without a taxable presence in a jurisdiction, there is no taxation under existing rules. The second component concerns the allocation of income. Even if the first challenge is overcome, it is important that a fair allocation of income occurs, so that the source or market jurisdiction receives a sensible allocation of income.

The 1920s compromise was based, in part, on the concept of a permanent establishment which had its roots in continental Europe but was adopted by the 1925 and 1927 Technical Expert Reports.[675] The commonly held view is that the permanent establishment (PE) definition has not kept pace with technological developments and that a nineteenth-century concept is not fit for purpose in the twenty-first century.[676]

The challenge identified for the international tax system is that digitalisation allows business activities to be carried out remotely, enabling a multinational business to operate in a reasonably comprehensive way in a jurisdiction without maintaining a physical presence or triggering any of the other PE thresholds. This carrying on business includes processing, analysing and utilising information where these processes can be performed across the border or automatically by machines. The expanding customer base which is now worldwide (distance being a limited, or no, barrier to international trade using the Internet) together with the changing roles of staff has led to significant disintermediation of entities based in the customers' jurisdiction. This removal of the trading entity (disintermediation removing the need for a subsidiary or branch in the source jurisdiction) has significantly diminished the utility of the

---

[675] See the discussion in Sections 1.3 "The History of International Double Taxation: The '1920s Compromise'" and 3.2 "The Vanishing Ability to Tax Business Profits".

[676] Wolfgang Schön "10 Questions about Why and How to Tax the Digitalised Economy" (2018) 72 Bull For Int' Tax 278 at 278.

traditional method, which required physical presence for imposing corporate income tax.

6.2.2 The Programme of Work Response

The response to this problem is without a doubt the most significant development in international tax in 100 years. Very clearly, the deemed income arising under Amount A[677] is designed as the response to the challenges posed by highly digitalised businesses and multi-sided platforms. As previously discussed, Amount A is the most revolutionary part of the OECD Secretariat's proposal because it posits new taxing rights without the requirement of physical presence in the source or market jurisdiction.

The calculation of the deemed income arising under Amount A is the four-step process detailed in Chapter 5. Essentially, from the starting point of the overall multinational group profits, the second step involves determining the routine profits which are subsequently subtracted from the total profits to determine non-routine profits. These non-routine profits are then further split, with a proportion allocated to the "parent jurisdiction", and a proportion allocated to the market jurisdictions. The final step involves allocating the proportion of profits attributable to the market jurisdictions to individual countries using an appropriate "allocation key" (such as sales, which seems most likely in these circumstances).

6.2.3 Does the Response Address the Challenge?

In simple terms, the answer to the above question is a "yes". Amount A is specifically targeted at the vanishing ability to tax business profits. It does so by using formulae to allocate income to the market jurisdiction based on a portion of the residual "super-profit" after the allocation of all routine profits.

To make sense of the unified approach proposal to introduce a concept such as Amount A, it is helpful to compare the approach under Amount A to the three original Inclusive Framework proposals (namely, user participation, marketing intangibles and significant economic presence).[678]

---

[677] For the detailed discussion, see Chapter 5, at Section 5.3 "Pillar One: What Is Proposed in the Unified Approach Proposal? Three Components of Income: Amount A".
[678] Discussed in greater detail in Chapter 5.

All three proposals had the same "over-arching objective" which was "to recognise ... value created by business's activity or participation in user/market jurisdictions that are not recognised in the current framework for allocating profits".[679] The different solutions considered the problem from different perspectives, one emphasising the contribution made by users, another the contribution made by marketing intangibles, whilst the third considered that sustained interaction with the jurisdiction via digital technology and other automated means could constitute a significant economic presence.

All three proposals recognise that it is possible to have active participation in a business in a jurisdiction without physical presence due to technological advancement in the business models. The characteristics of highly digitalised businesses, being able to achieve "scale without mass" through the utilisation of the network effect, the reliance on intangible assets and the role of data and user participation enable "remote" participation in a domestic economy through digital means without a taxable physical presence.[680] The OECD justify taxation on the principle that business profits should be taxed in the countries in which value is created.[681]

As previously discussed, value creation is an imprecise and difficult concept to use as a principle for taxation.[682] Arguably, it is not a principle per se but it could be used as a justification for taxation (the "forgotten question" in the words of Klaus Vogel).[683] If the Inclusive Framework is seeing the value creation concept simply as justifying the right to consider the taxation of entities deriving income from cross-border activities in the digital age (establishing a nexus) in the absence of physical presence, and at the same time recognising that the existing rules do not permit this due to the consequences of constraint arising from the 1920s compromise, then it is submitted that this is an acceptable policy from a theoretical perspective.

---

[679] OECD *Addressing the Tax Challenges of the Digitalisation of the Economy Public Consultation Document* (OECD Publishing, February 2019) at [11], on 8 ("OECD Public Consultation").

[680] Ibid at [12].

[681] Ibid at [58], on 17.

[682] See Section 1.5.5 "The Relationship between Value Creation and the International Tax Framework".

[683] Klaus Vogel "The Justification for Taxation: A Forgotten Question" (1988) 33 Am J Juris 19 at 19.

One of the problems for the Inclusive Framework is that none of the three proposals were universally acceptable and hence the need to have a unified approach which incorporates key features of all three individual approaches. The approach in Amount A, without ascribing a policy rationale from any one of the three alternatives, deals with the first challenge of nexus. The further refinement proposed in early 2020, which splits automated digital services and consumer-facing businesses, refines this nexus requirement, making the former subject to tax after meeting a revenue threshold, while the latter requires some additional requirements such as physical presence or targeted advertising. In this respect, it is possible to see more influence in the automated digital services limb coming from the "user participation" proposal. In the alternative concerning consumer-facing businesses, one can see the influence coming from the "marketing intangibles" proposal.[684]

6.2.4 Does the Response Go Further Than the Challenge?

As previously identified in Chapter 5 the scope of Amount A is not limited by some type of highly digitalised business definition but envisages a much broader set of businesses. Amount A is the component of income deemed to be derived (or allocated) to the market jurisdiction where the MNE does not have a physical presence in the jurisdiction but is carrying on a "consumer-facing business" in a remote manner.[685] The logic of expanding these taxing rights beyond the digital economy owes much to the policy rationale of the marketing intangibles option.[686] It was flagged as an issue as part of the Public Consultation Document issued in February 2019 as follows:[687]

> Finally, if "remote" participation in the absence of a taxable physical presence, or in the absence of one that attracts substantial taxable profits,

---

[684] See Section 5.2 "Pillar One: Allocation of Taxing Rights and Nexus", with respect to the three alternative proposals at Sections 5.2.2–5.2.4, and with respect to the requirements of nexus at Section 5.3.7.

[685] OECD *Public Consultation Document Secretariat Proposal for a "Unified Approach" Under Pillar One* (OECD, October 2019), where it says: "The approach covers highly digital business models but goes wider – broadly focusing on consumer-facing businesses with further work to be carried out on scope and carve-outs. Extractive industries are assumed to be out of the scope" ("OECD Unified Approach").

[686] Ibid, and see further discussion in Section 5.3.2 "What Is the Policy Rationale behind Amount A ?"

[687] OECD Public Consultation, above n 679 at [14], on 9.

is considered to be a concern in relation to certain highly digitalised businesses, there is an important question as to whether this concern is not relevant to a broader set of businesses ... In other words, to the extent the current rules are seen as under-allocating income to particular jurisdictions due to the ability of highly digitalised businesses to remotely and non-physically participate in those jurisdictions, horizontal equity, design coherence and a level playing field suggest consideration should be given to whether that policy concern (and reforms to address the concern) are relevant also to more traditional businesses.

Quite clearly this analysis shows that Amount A not only answers the challenge of nexus posed by the digitalisation of the economy, but goes further into other businesses involved in utilising marketing intangibles with consumer-facing businesses.

6.2.5 The Challenge: Allocation of Profits

Unlike the nexus issue, the second part of the challenge posed by the vanishing ability to tax business profits is not caused by a gap in the existing rules (which is one way to view the lack of physical presence/PE threshold problem), but more with a concern with the current international tax framework rules concerning the allocation of profits.

The allocation of profits is a twofold issue which is described below. The first and most difficult problem is trying to work out how much profit should be allocated to the market jurisdiction in respect of activities carried on by the multinational there. This is relatively uncharted territory as we have a new taxing right deemed under the introduction of the nexus rules described above. Furthermore, as this new taxing right is introduced it is also necessary to ensure that the existing rules work adequately insofar as the current transfer pricing regime allocates profits to low-risk distributing entities.

The problem can be illustrated as follows: a multinational enterprise with a highly digitalised model has been making remote sales to a large consumer market. Concerned about the tax risk associated with its structure and the possibility of attack under expanded definitions of permanent establishment and the amendments to the PE article brought about by Action 7 of the BEPS Action Plan, the multinational restructures and establishes a limited risk distributor (LRD) in the large consumer jurisdiction. This local affiliate is structured so as to have no ownership interest in intangible assets, does not perform DEMPE functions, and does not assume any risks related to assets. A modest allocation of profit is allocated to this LRD entity.[688] One can immediately see that addressing the nexus problem through the allocation of an Amount A must be supported by actions to deal with the allocation of profits to entities such as LRDs (referred to subsequently as "the restructuring risk") but the issue is more fundamental, namely how much profit do you attribute to the activities carried on in the market jurisdiction (referred to subsequently as "the fundamental taxing right")? In other words, it is necessary to consider both the restructuring risk and a sensible basis for determining the fundamental taxing right so that the correct amount of profit is allocated to the market jurisdiction in circumstances where there is activity over a certain threshold justifying taxation.

6.2.6 The Programme of Work Response

As the OECD notes, the establishment of a new taxing right in respect of remote sales requires a new method for quantifying the appropriate amount of profit reallocated to the market jurisdiction (furthermore, to be split amongst the market jurisdictions if the multinational is trading in more than one jurisdiction, which of course is highly likely).[689] The Programme of Work considered three separate "conceptually underpinned" methods for determining the amount of profit and loss subject to the new taxing right.[690] These are:

1 the modified residual profit split method;
2 the fractional apportionment method; and
3 distribution-based approaches.

The modified residual profit split method (MRPS), according to the OECD, "allocates to market jurisdictions a portion of an MNE group's non-routine profit that reflects the value created in markets that is not recognised under the existing profit allocation rules".[691] The steps in the MRPS are exactly (or resemble very closely) those carried out under Amount A: (i) determine the total profit to be split; (ii) remove routine profits; (iii) determine the portion of the non-routine profits attributable to the market jurisdictions; and (iv) allocate (iii) to the relevant market jurisdictions using an allocation key.

---

[688] Ibid at [13], on 9, see the description of the issue.
[689] OECD Programme of Work, above n 671.
[690] Ibid at [22–35], on 11–16.
[691] Ibid at [28], on 12.

The fractional apportionment method is represented in parts of the above steps (particularly (i), (iii) and (iv)), allocating part of the global non-routine profits to a particular market jurisdiction using an allocation key.

The distribution-based method applies a simplified approach to specify a baseline profit in the market jurisdiction for marketing, distribution and user-related activities. The proposal in suggesting Amount B involves making a new fixed remuneration for baseline marketing and distribution functions that take place in the market jurisdiction and accords with this method.

Therefore, it is clear that Amount A has elements of the first two methods (MRPS and fractional apportionment), while Amount B utilises the third method on a distribution basis.

6.2.7 Does the Response Address the Challenge?

The challenge of allocating profits to the new taxing right is embraced by the formulation of Amount A. In allocating a proportion of these residual profits to the market jurisdiction this breaks new ground. Furthermore, the proposal relating to Amount B has numerous administrative and certainty-related benefits but can also deal with the restructuring risk and enables the international tax work framework to draw a baseline on profitability for LRD entities.

Together as a combination, Amounts A and B present a viable solution to both the restructuring risk and the fundamental taxing right.

6.2.8 Does the Response Go Further Than the Challenge?

The answer to this question, like the answer to the question posed in Section 6.2.7, is yes. Amount A is not targeted exclusively at digital businesses but extends to customer-facing entities. This is justified on the grounds of neutrality (that it is not just highly digitalised businesses exclusively that carry on remote sales) and reflects the idea that a multinational investing in its brand in the market jurisdiction (or investing in users located in a market jurisdiction) can be subject to tax based on that activity in the market jurisdiction.

Under the current proposals, the application of Amount B to distributors is limited neither by threshold nor by activity.[692] Accordingly, this is

---

[692] OECD Unified Approach, above n 685.

a much more significant change than the one proposed to deal with the restructuring risk referred to above (Section 6.2.5). As discussed in Chapter 5 the reasons for making this change are pragmatic and driven by the business community with the trade-off of the possibility of increased tax in return for certainty and dispute prevention and resolution.[693]

Even though the restructuring risk would necessitate something similar to the application of Amount B to limited risk distributors involved in highly digitalised businesses, nonetheless it is clear that the wide application of Amount B goes way beyond dealing with the challenges of the digitalised economy and highly digitalised business models. It should therefore be seen as part of a broader 2020s compromise involving a newly negotiated deal.

6.3 The Use of Data, the Contribution of Users and the Measurement of Their Value

6.3.1 The Challenge: How Data and the Contributions of Users Are Used in Highly Digitalised Businesses

In Chapter 3 the creation, analysis and use of data were described, together with the independent contribution of users. They are seen as a critical part of highly digitalised businesses.[694] This challenge is one of the most "specifically" digital challenges and it is (at least) three challenges which are all interconnected. The first is the use of data. Technology permits the remote collection, storage and use of data. Sometimes this is subject to analysis or analytics and can occur directly with the user or indirectly through a third party. Additionally, as described in Chapter 3, this can either be with the express consent of the user, or their consent may be implicit. However it is collected, the use of data has enabled highly digitalised multinational enterprises to deliver superior customer experiences. The best example of this is highly targeted advertising to those people who have identified themselves through their data as "great targets" for the product or service of the advertiser.

---

[693] See the discussion on "Amount B" in Section 5.4 "Amount B: Fixed Remuneration for Marketing and Distribution".
[694] See Section 3.3 "The Use of Data, the Contribution of Users and the Measurement of Their Value".

Integral to this capture and use of data is the role of the user, which is the second challenge. This has been a particular feature of some of the already implemented or planned digital services taxes. They have regarded the participation of the user as a critical part of the digital services model. This is because, in many cases, they are not under the control of the multi-sided platform but operating independently, and yet they are still:

- contributing to the creation of the brand of the multi-sided platform (examples of this include quality reviews, feedback and endorsements); and
- generating valuable data through their active interaction and depth of engagement with the platform; and
- expanding the customer base through their social networks, which has the effect of increasing potential users while reducing marginal costs (also known as the direct and indirect network effects).

Finally, the third part of this challenge is the difficulty in measuring what profits or value are created by these activities. Considerable complexity and uncertainty exists on this matter. Lines have been drawn between active and passive users as discussed in Chapter 3, while some academics have helpfully commented on this.[695] In the design of the UK Government's digital services tax, for instance, the mere collection of data was excluded from the scope of the tax, preferring to concentrate on more active user participation and the depth of engagement of users.[696]

6.3.2 The Programme of Work Response

As discussed in Chapter 5, one of the three proposals put forward in the Public Consultation Document for consideration by the Inclusive Framework was the user participation proposal.[697] The user participation proposal was very firmly focused on dealing with these particular user data and participation challenges. What has become clear is that no single proposal of the three put forward in the Public Consultation Document was universally accepted and that accordingly the Unified

---

[695] Johannes Becker and Joachim Englisch "Taxing Where Value Is Created: What's 'User Involvement' Got to Do with It?" (2019) 47 Intertax 161 at 162.
[696] HM Treasury *Corporate Tax and the Digital Economy: Position Paper Update* (HM Treasury, March 2018) at [2.37–2.40].
[697] OECD Unified Approach, above n 685 at [17–21], on 9–10.

Approach on Pillar One was a compromised amalgamation dealing with parts of each of the three proposals.[698] Amount A is, therefore, the component of income deemed to be derived (or allocated) to the market jurisdiction where the MNE does not have a physical presence in the jurisdiction but is carrying on a "consumer-facing business" in a remote manner. The OECD Secretariat's Proposal makes it clear that it is intended to address the challenge of the use, creation and valuation of data:[699]

> The approach covers highly digital business models but goes wider – broadly focusing on consumer-facing businesses with further work to be carried out on scope and carve-outs. Extractive industries are assumed to be out of the scope. (Emphasis added)

This deemed income responds to the challenge that these new digitalised businesses can successfully interact with their customers (consumers) and users without the need to establish any form of physical presence in the jurisdiction in which the customers are based.

The Secretariat's Proposal suggests that:[700]

> These features could be said to be relevant for any business, *but they are most relevant for digital centric businesses which interact remotely with users*, who may or may not be their primary customers, and other consumer-facing businesses for which *customer engagement and interaction, data collection and exploitation*, and marketing and branding is significant, and can more easily be carried out from a remote location. *This would include highly digitalised businesses which interact remotely with users, who may or may not be their primary customers, as well as other businesses that market their products to consumers and may use digital technology to develop a consumer base.*

The Unified Approach attempts to address this challenge, although, as indicated above, it goes further.

6.3.3 *Does the Response Go Further Than the Challenge?*

As discussed in Section 6.3.2, Amount A goes significantly beyond the concept envisaged in the user participation proposal and in this respect goes beyond this data/user challenge.

---

[698] OECD Public Conference, 21 November 2019 in the discussion by Richard Collier.
[699] OECD Unified Approach, above n 685 at [15], on 5.
[700] Ibid at [19], on 7 (emphasis added).

6.4 The Reliance on, and Mobility of, Intellectual Property

6.4.1 The Challenge: The Role of Intellectual Property in Highly Digitalised Businesses

The enormous growth in many highly digitalised businesses, according to Wolfgang Schön, is attributable to two major factors.[701] The first factor is the economies of scale created by these businesses particularly as relates to the network effect. Often this is achieved through the role of user participation in the business, which is discussed in Section 6.3 above. The second major factor is the use of, or reliance upon, intellectual property that is used to analyse data and create complex algorithms (a process or set of rules to be followed in calculations or other problem-solving operations). Using intellectual property in this way to process information enables highly digitalised (and other) businesses to interact with customers in a tailored and individually responsive way. The problem from a tax perspective is that this intellectual property is extremely hard to value and can be transferred from one jurisdiction to another without a great deal of legal, financial or physical effort.

This is very problematic from a tax perspective and, as discussed in Section 3.3, leads Schön to observe that: "multinational firms are therefore able to choose at will the location of central functions and value drivers, including jurisdictions which are neither the country where the ultimate consumer resides nor the country where the parent company is resident".[702] The obvious tax consequence is that intellectual property is located in, and sometimes moved to, entities based in low or no tax jurisdictions within the multinational group.

6.4.2 The Programme of Work Response

The major heavy lifting on this challenge is provided by Pillar Two and not Pillar One. This is because the challenge is not so much related to the allocation of income or questions of nexus but relates to profit shifting and the location of profits. As discussed in Chapter 5, "certain members"[703] of the Inclusive Framework believe that profit shifting occurs through the use of intangibles, as well as in other ways such as capital structuring and intragroup financing. Whilst the use of intangibles to shift profits is

---

[701] Wolfgang Schön "10 Questions About Why and How to Tax the Digitalised Economy" (2018) 72 Bull For Int' Tax 278 at 278.
[702] Ibid at 278.
[703] OECD Programme of Work, above n 671 at [53], on 25.

6.5 TRANSACTIONS AND INCOME

particularly prevalent in the digital economy, the practice extends to all types of multinational businesses.

Both the rules of Pillar Two can be of assistance in response to the challenge regarding the use, and mobility, of intellectual property. If intellectual property is located in a low-tax jurisdiction and held by a related entity there (owned by the parent multinational), then the income inclusion rule could apply.

Alternatively, if a deduction is claimed by the multinational in respect of a royalty paid for the use of intellectual property where the IP is owned by a related party then the undertaxed payments rule (or the switch-over rule if a treaty benefit, such as reduced withholding tax, is being utilised) could apply.

As currently proposed, these rules will deal with some aspects of current concerns with the location of intellectual property in low/no-tax jurisdictions. If the intellectual property is located in a high-tax jurisdiction then Pillar Two will not apply.

6.4.3 Does the Response Go Further Than the Challenge?

As indicated in the previous section, the two major rules of Pillar Two are not exclusively focused on the challenge caused to the international tax rules by the profit-shifting ability and inherent mobility of intellectual property. These rules are much broader than just intellectual property but, that said, they do deal with the issue of profits moved to low-tax jurisdictions caused both by intellectual property as well as other mechanisms.

6.5 The Characterisation of Transactions and Income

6.5.1 The Challenge: The Characterisation of Different New Categories of Income

This challenge, described in Chapter 3,[704] recognises that many new digital products and services have a question mark over their classification and this characterisation is frequently both a matter of domestic law and the definition of various categories contained in the relevant treaty. Accordingly, transactions might be classified as business profits (if they are regarded as the provision of goods or services), technical services (in which case some treaties may regard them in a special category as royalties, or in the alternative as ordinary services and so business profits) or royalties

---

[704] See Section 3.5 "The Characterisation of Transactions and Income".

(this is particularly the case where the treaties define royalties to include payments for the rental of commercial, industrial or scientific equipment).

The tax treatment for these various types of characterisation differs enormously. Business profits, under the 1920s compromise, are not taxable in the source state unless there is a permanent establishment. Royalties may have domestic withholding taxes applied but they are conventionally deductible. Technical services may fall into either category (business profits or royalties) depending on both the domestic law and treaty analysis.

6.5.2 The Programme of Work Response

There does not appear to be any particular targeted work in this area by the Programme of Work, but it is interesting to reflect on the impact that both Pillar One and Pillar Two proposals will be likely to have on this issue. For example, where income has been characterised as business profits and previously not subject to tax because of the lack of nexus to a permanent establishment, then Amount A will lead to new taxing rights. The formulae used to determine the amount of the deemed income does not seem to be susceptible to this characterisation. Furthermore, if the income under any of these characterisations is derived by a related entity in the multinational group which is based in a low-tax jurisdiction, then the income inclusion rule should apply. Additionally, where the characterisation takes the form of a deductible payment and is made to a low-tax jurisdiction related party then the undertaxed payments rule may have application.

The 2020s compromise will necessitate further work and an in-depth examination of the consequences of the characterisation of transactions. At this stage, it seems that the OECD Secretariat's Proposals provide some solutions to these difficult problems of characterisation.

6.6 The Failure of Transfer Pricing with Certain Multinational Enterprises and Their Transactions

6.6.1 The Challenge: Are There Better Ways to Manage Some Areas of Transfer Pricing?

Transfer pricing and the arm's-length principle are discussed in Chapter 3.[705] In a nutshell, there are concerns that some transactions,

---

[705] See Section 3.6 "The Failure of Transfer Pricing with Certain Multinational Enterprises and Their Transactions".

particularly those involving hard to value intangible property, can always be appropriately priced under the arm's-length standard.

As discussed previously,[706] at the heart of these concerns is the fact that multinational enterprises employ complex value chain structures to generate profits beyond those that an independent, arm's-length and separate entity approach would realise. The profits attributable to such synergies and the economic rents created from such sophisticated ways of doing business cannot, therefore, be allocated under traditional arm's-length principles and, additionally, there are no arm's-length entities to allocate them to.

This breakdown of the ability to allocate profits is the theoretical problem, but the practical issue is equally problematic. Many countries, particularly in the developing world, are deeply distrustful of the methodology, regarding it more as an art than a science and one that they do not have the tools to interpret accurately. The costs involved in administering the regime and managing disputes are rapidly rising. Consequently, the likelihood of disputes and significant costs arising to both taxpayers and administrations is high.

There are concerns in many countries about the required expertise, databases and experience in dealing with complex transfer pricing matters. As discussed in Chapter 3, there are numerous transfer pricing problems, particularly dealing with highly digitalised businesses, but the concern is broader than the digital economy.

6.6.2 The Programme of Work Response

Both Pillar One and Pillar Two have components that have an impact on the challenges posed by transfer pricing. Concerning Pillar One, we have discussed that the profit allocation rules radically depart from the existing international tax framework in several ways, which are explained in Chapter 5.[707] These include using formulaic calculations in a modified residual profit split methodology and elements of formulary apportionment, allocating profits to the marketplace jurisdiction, ignoring the single-entity concept and, significant to this challenge, departing from the arm's-length principle.

---

[706] See ibid.
[707] See Section 5.3 "Pillar One: What Is Proposed in the Unified Approach Proposal? Three Components of Income: Amount A".

How does the 2020s proposal address the challenge of transfer pricing? We can see this in the various components as follows:

- Pillar One, Amount A. As already discussed, there are two principal objectives behind Amount A, the establishment of a new nexus together with a formulaic allocation of profit to the new taxing rights suggested for the market economy. It is the second component in particular which is relevant to this discussion. The "new" allocation of profit rules suggest that a part of the non-routine residual profit should be allocated to the market in which the product or service is consumed. Amount A can be seen as quite a radical change to the existing international tax framework which has traditionally suggested that there is no entity to which an arm's-length profit can be attributed. These traditional rules would also not necessarily identify any functions carried on in the market jurisdiction to which profit could be allocated. Amount A controversially suggests both the new taxing right and an amount of profit determined by way of a formula which may or, more likely, may not reflect an arm's-length amount of profit.
- Pillar One, Amount B. Amount B suggests making a new fixed remuneration for baseline marketing and distribution functions that take place in the market jurisdiction. Amount B, it will be remembered, emerged from practical solutions proposed by business to the original public conference on the taxation of the digital economy, and it pragmatically suggests the use of a formula or a fixed amount to determine such marketing and distribution functions. There are two major advantages to the use of Amount B – it can act as a backstop to the creation of a limited risk distributor introduced into a multinational structure to avoid the application of Amount A and, at the same time, it pragmatically provides for a relatively certain fixed amount of income, potentially avoiding disputes and expensive transfer pricing documentation and advice. In any event, the use of Amount B, whilst bearing a relationship to the determination of an arm's-length amount, is likely to be a simplified formula or proxy for a more detailed calculation and so a departure from the arm's-length principle.
- Pillar One, Amount C. The final component in the proposal by the OECD Secretariat is the additional amount (Amount C). This amount gives tax administrations, primarily, but also taxpayers, the ability to "correct" the outcome arrived at through the application of Amount B in situations where Amount B has been too arbitrary and come to an unacceptable position from an arm's-length perspective. Amount

6.6 THE FAILURE OF TRANSFER PRICING

C can be seen therefore as a retention of the arm's-length principle in certain circumstances. Some concerns have been raised that this component reopens the complexity and cost of the determination of an exact arm's-length amount.

- Pillar Two, the income inclusion rule. By introducing a requirement that income derived by entities within a controlled group (i.e. branches or subsidiaries which are related to the multinational parent) are taxed at a minimum rate, the international tax system would overcome the risk of transfer pricing profits to low-tax jurisdictions. Effectively, this income inclusion rule operates as a backstop to prevent the operation of profit-shifting structures or transactions to reallocate profit to related parties in low/no-tax jurisdictions. This is effectively a significant potential curtailment of aggressive tax planning using transfer pricing.
- Pillar Two, the undertaxed payments and subject to tax rules. By imposing a withholding tax (or in the case of a double tax treaty preventing favourable tax benefits of lower withholding tax rates) or denying deductions for payments made to a related entity in a low/no-tax jurisdiction, the use of arm's-length transfer pricing techniques to reduce taxable profits in higher tax jurisdictions is also impacted.

The comprehensive response across a range of different areas means that the OECD Secretariat's proposal goes a significant way to counter the challenge of transfer pricing posed by the digital economy.

6.6.3 Does the Response Go Further Than the Challenge?

There are specific problems relating to transfer pricing inherent in the digital economy such as:[708]

- How to address issues in the transfer pricing methodologies relating to the quantification of value associated with direct and indirect network effects?
- What about the role of users' sustained engagement, content creation and other previously discussed connections?

---

[708] For a further list of specific issues posed by the digital economy see Section 3.6 "The Failure of Transfer Pricing with Certain Multinational Enterprises and Their Transactions".

- What about multi-sided markets? In particular, where there are opportunities to non-neutrally price (prices on one side set below the marginal cost, while the other side subsidises the platform).

The Pillar One and Two responses are not focused on these types of specific issues but are far more generic and encompass all types of business, digital or not. The changes can be seen as far-reaching and potentially a significant response to the problems of transfer pricing in the digital economy (and beyond).

6.7 Tackling the Inadequacy of Residence-Based Taxation

6.7.1 The Challenge of Mobility and the Ease of Establishing Residence When There Is Tax on Both Companies and Shareholders

As discussed in Chapter 3,[709] the deficiencies of the 1920s compromise-based international tax framework were exposed by a combination of the lack of source taxation in respect of highly digitalised businesses (with no physical presence creating a taxable nexus) together with the inadequacy of residence-based taxation. The problems with residence-based taxation were twofold: the ease of establishing residence for a corporation and therefore the ability to locate it in a low-tax jurisdiction, together with the separation of taxation between shareholders and the company. This enabled large digital multinationals to establish entities (usually subsidiaries) in low/no-tax jurisdictions to derive profits which were not taxed by the country of source (no nexus), or the country of residence of the corporation (low or no tax in that jurisdiction), or the country of residence of the shareholders of the corporation (because of the inadequacy of controlled foreign company rules). The issues concerning residence-based taxation have been present for a significant time. So, while only the first part of this trifecta of tax phenomena owes much to the digital economy, the growth in highly digitalised businesses and the lack of source taxation made the residence tax issues more important than they have traditionally been.

6.7.2 The Programme of Work Response

Pillar One is primarily concerned with source-based taxation. Arguably, Pillar Two is primarily concerned with residence-based taxation. The

---

[709] See Section 3.7 "The Inadequacy of Residence-Based Taxation".

income inclusion rule operates as a type of worldwide controlled foreign company regime, meaning that the incentive to incorporate a subsidiary or establish a branch in a low-tax jurisdiction is removed because any profits that were not subject to a minimum tax (for example 15 per cent) are required to be included in the parent company's return and tax paid on a "top-up" basis. The consequence is that the income inclusion rule bolsters residence-based taxation and reduces the tax planning advantages of incorporating a subsidiary in a low-tax jurisdiction and diverting or shifting profits to it through a variety of different techniques.

Similarly, if deductible payments are made from the parent jurisdiction to a related entity based in a low-tax jurisdiction then the undertaxed payment rule or the subject to tax rule could apply. This would mean that either the payment would not be deductible or there would be withholding tax imposed (even overriding the reduced rates in a double tax agreement).

6.7.3 Does the Response Go Further Than the Challenge?

This challenge, as indicated above, is not particularly focused on the digital economy insofar as it particularly relates to residence-based corporate tax. Consequently, it is not surprising that the proposal by the OECD Secretariat is somewhat universal and concerned with base erosion and profit shifting in a broader frame than a purely digital focus.

6.8 Competition by States

6.8.1 The Challenge of Overcoming the Desire by States to Compete Using Their Tax Systems to Attract or Retain Investment

Tax competition by states is not necessarily seen as a problem by all people. It is sometimes seen as a healthy opportunity to attract investment to a jurisdiction, resulting in improved productive capacity, infrastructure, skills and output. When taken to its logical conclusion, however, tax competition can present the risk of the "race to the bottom" in corporate tax revenues. This necessarily means that the financial requirements of the state would need to come from other sources, such as consumption taxes, capital taxes and income taxes connected with labour and individual residence.[710] From the perspective of a so-called

---

[710] Assuming the expenditure is consistent between years and ignoring the effect of the government borrowing.

international tax framework, tax competition is a potentially destructive force because it does not encourage harmonisation or consistency. This challenge is discussed in greater detail in Chapter 3.[711]

6.8.2 The Programme of Work Response

The creation of a new taxing nexus and the allocation of taxing rights to the market or the source country might be viewed through one lens as a fundamental change to the international tax framework, which is largely about the taxation of highly digitalised businesses and the vanishing ability of the source state to tax business income generated in its jurisdiction (the first challenge described in this chapter). Pillar One focuses on this issue. It may also be possible to regard this potential change to the international tax framework through the lens of tax competition. Some multinationals based in highly developed countries have currently, or previously, structured their affairs to pay virtually no tax in the source jurisdiction, and little in their residence jurisdiction. Recent domestic legislative amendments in the United States have improved the position of that country to impose tax on their multinationals doing business overseas.

Looking at the proposed changes in Pillar One through the light of consistency in taxation between source and residence countries, and between consumer states and developing countries as opposed to highly digitalised and developed countries with significant multinational enterprises, the proposed response in this Pillar can be seen as one addressing tax competition. That is perhaps a surprising conclusion as superficially the changes have everything to do with the allocation of taxing rights and nothing to do with tax competition per se. It is just that the allocation of taxing rights under the existing regime favours certain highly digitalised and developed jurisdictions and not others, and the response proposed by the OECD Secretariat seeks to address that imbalance.

In the case of the proposed changes in Pillar Two, it is possible to see the challenge of tax competition addressed more directly.

The income inclusion rule, which is designed to eliminate the advantages of incorporating a subsidiary in a low-tax jurisdiction (or operating a branch in that jurisdiction) has the effect of bolstering the parent jurisdiction's residence-based taxation. One would expect this to reduce

---

[711] See Section 3.8 "Competition by States".

the opportunity for countries to offer low-tax or incentive-based regimes to attract profit and investment shifting through the operation of tax competition. A multinational may not see the same advantage in operating part of its international group through a low-tax jurisdiction if it is obliged to pay away some of the advantage gained through the structure to its parent jurisdiction by way of a "top-up" tax.

This is also a valid proposition for the second set of rules in Pillar Two. The undertaxed payments rule and the subject to tax rules are designed to discourage payments made to related entities in low-tax jurisdictions by either disallowing the deduction or imposing withholding tax. A classic example involves a multinational establishing a special-purpose subsidiary to hold intellectual property and then paying deductible royalties to that entity which would enjoy a deduction in the (high-tax) parent company or operating subsidiary's jurisdiction whilst the royalty income was subject to low or no tax in the subsidiary's jurisdiction that holds the intellectual property. If the deduction is disallowed, or withholding tax is imposed, then the benefits of the structure are largely eroded. The utilisation of such entities is likely to diminish as does the prospect of international tax competition.

6.8.3 Does the Response Go Further Than the Challenge?

When both Pillars are considered together, it can be seen that although part of the response to the tax competition by states is directed at those entities involved in the highly digitalised business economy, it is a much broader response. Accordingly, although the proposed changes to nexus and the allocation of taxing rights is a measure directly aimed at the digital economy, the other changes are significant and affect all business arrangements, both digital and non-digital.

6.9 Conclusion

This chapter examines the response proposed by the OECD Secretariat to the challenges to the international tax framework posed by the digital economy. The challenges are very different. Some challenges, such as the allocation of taxing rights and the taxable nexus, are relatively recent taxation consequences arising from the enormous success of the digitalisation of the economy and the massive business advantages that occur from phenomena such as the network effect, the use of data, the role of users and the ability of a business to identify customer needs and the value of the customer to the business. Other challenges, such as some issues in tax competition and transfer pricing, are more generic and long-standing. Many of the broader challenges are addressed by Pillar Two in its broad-brush remedies against base erosion and profit shifting – a backstop to the more specific actions detailed in the fifteen-point Actions adopted at the end of the first BEPS round.

The overriding impression is that it is difficult to address the specific challenges posed by the digital economy without reference to the broader issues. Therefore, the proposals need to be as broad as they currently are. That is, dealing with issues broader than those posed specifically by the digital economy.

To that extent, the controversial changes proposed in both Pillars are necessary to address the challenges detailed in the earlier part of this book.[712] At the time of writing it is uncertain whether all of the changes proposed by the OECD Secretariat will be adopted. All that can be said is that they represent a comprehensive and considered approach to meeting many of the challenges posed by the digitalisation of the economy. If a consensus cannot be achieved for political or other reasons, then the work the OECD has performed can be revisited in the future and examined to identify what changes could helpfully be made to the international tax framework.

---

[712] See Chapter 3 "Challenges to the Tax System Posed by the Digitalisation of Business".

7

Implementing the Proposals for Multilateral Reforms

7.1 Issues with the Implementation of the 2020s Compromise?

7.1.1 Introduction

The introduction of new taxing rights required by the revolutionary concept found in the OECD Secretariat's Proposal concerning Amount A necessarily dictates some significant tax "infrastructural" changes to the existing international tax framework. Such changes will be required at both the domestic law level dealing with the concept of income and its domestic source, and in the public international law arena of double tax treaties. This international dimension must address both the question of a right to tax (nexus) and the allocation of taxing rights and income.

In addition to considering the changes on new taxing rights, there are other matters to consider in the Secretariat's proposals. For example, adjustments (or refinements) to the other suggested changes (Amounts B and C, and the new Pillar Two income inclusion and deduction rules) will require amendments to both domestic law and tax treaties.

It will also be important to ensure that clear rules for the relief of double taxation are established as this may emerge to be a very significant issue. Given the extent of the changes, there has to be further considerable discussion on new rules relating to dispute resolution and dispute prevention.

Various choices present themselves as to the method of implementation. Should domestic law be amended in a relatively consistent way? Should existing articles in treaties be amended, or should new articles be introduced containing these new taxing rights? What is the best way to implement changes? Can withholding tax be usefully employed as a collection mechanism? Should the existing multilateral instrument used to implement the BEPS changes be utilised, or would a new multilateral instrument be preferable?

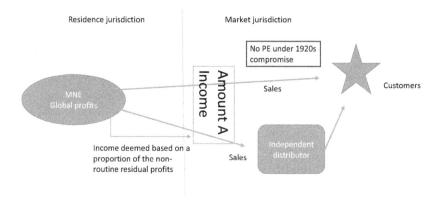

Figure 7.1 Establishing a new nexus and taxing rights

7.1.2 Implementing the New Taxing Rights Proposed by Amount A

By expanding countries' taxing rights from the previous international framework norm, Amount A is the greatest component of change in the OECD Secretariat's proposal. As previously discussed, in Chapters 5 and 6, Amount A has two separate elements. It establishes a new taxable nexus first, and then, secondly, allocates profits to the relevant market jurisdictions.

In examining Figure 7.1, two important features influence the design of the taxing right and thus the method of implementation. The first feature of the new regime is that for automated digitalised businesses the taxing right exists independent of whether there is a physical presence (or indeed a dependent agent or deemed legal presence) in the market jurisdiction.[713] For consumer-facing businesses, a nexus will be created if there is a sustained interaction with the market. This is likely to include additional factors such as the existence of a physical presence of the multinational in the market jurisdiction or advertising material targeted at the market jurisdiction.[714]

---

[713] See the discussion at Section 5.3.7 and OECD *Statement by the OECD/G20 Inclusive Framework on BEPS on the Two-Pillar Approach to Address the Tax Challenges Arising from the Digitalisation of the Economy* (OECD, January 2020) at [36]–[38] ("OECD Inclusive Framework 2020").

[714] OECD Inclusive Framework, above n 713 at [39].

The second feature is that the formulation of income (the deemed income comprising Amount A) is determined based on the gross income of the multinational enterprise. This is important for two reasons: first, allocating part of a global income is a fundamentally different basis for the allocation of profit and differs significantly from the separate entity approach found in the international tax framework; secondly, and as a consequence of the first reason, it departs from an arm's-length standard of determining profits based on transactions between independent entities. Both of these features influence the implementation of these taxing rights.

7.1.3 Taxation without Physical Presence

Turning first to the requirements of a new taxable nexus, the OECD has put forward that highly digitalised businesses currently (and in the future increasingly) carry on consumer and user-facing business transactions remotely with either no or little physical presence in the jurisdiction of the consumer/user.

The new nexus rules suggest that a taxable presence will exist for automated digitalised businesses based only on a revenue threshold. For consumer-facing businesses, the test will be where a business "has a sustained and significant involvement in the economy of a market jurisdiction, such as through consumer interaction and engagement".[715] Exactly what constitutes a significant and sustained engagement will be made clear but it is currently suggested that "the existence of a physical presence of the multinational enterprise in the market jurisdiction or targeted advertising directed at the market jurisdiction" are likely factors.[716]

Accordingly, the rule will establish a taxable nexus based on (1) the type of business (it seems automated digital and consumer-facing and marketing intangible-rich businesses are in scope as opposed to extractive industries and those that deal in commodities), together with (2) revenue thresholds (both absolute in terms of overall sales and those carried on in the market jurisdiction). Importantly, and for the first time in 100 years, there is for some automated digital businesses no

---

[715] OECD *Public Consultation Document Secretariat Proposal for a "Unified Approach" Under Pillar One* (OECD, October 2019) at [22] ("OECD Unified Approach").
[716] OECD Inclusive Framework 2020, above n 713 at [39].

requirement of physical presence or any deemed independent agency or contractual obligation:[717]

> The simplest way of operating the new rule would be to define a revenue threshold in the market (the amount of which could be adapted to the size of the market) as the primary indicator of a sustained and significant involvement in that jurisdiction. The revenue threshold would also take into account certain activities, such as online advertising services, which are directed at non-paying users in locations that are different from those in which the relevant revenues are booked.

As discussed above, the 2020 announcements confirm that for consumer-facing businesses, in addition to the revenue threshold there might need to be other "additional indicators" to demonstrate a link beyond mere selling and the multinational's interaction with the economy of a jurisdiction.[718] These indicators were some of the factors that emerged from the "significant economic presence" proposal, such as:

1 the existence of a user base and associated data input;
2 the volume of digital content derived from the jurisdiction;
3 billing and collection in local currency or with a local form of payment;
4 the maintenance of a website in a local language;
5 responsibility for the final delivery of goods to customers or the provision by the enterprise of other support services such as after-sales service or repairs and maintenance; or
6 sustained marketing and sales promotion activities, either online or otherwise, to attract customers.

7.1.4 Establishing a New Nexus Rule

Two alternative methods to bring into being the new nexus rules seem to have been on the agenda of the OECD.[719] In essence, the choice is between amending the existing definition by expanding the definition

---

[717] OECD *Addressing the Tax Challenges of the Digitalisation of the Economy – Policy Note* (OECD, 23 January 2019) at [1.2] ("OECD Policy Note"); and OECD Unified Approach, above n 715 at [22].

[718] OECD *Programme of Work to Develop a Consensus Solution to the Tax Challenges Arising from the Digitalisation of the Economy* (OECD Publishing, May 2019) at [2(b)] ("OECD Programme of Work").

[719] OECD Programme of Work, above n 718 at [40], on 18; and see the earlier version OECD *Addressing the Tax Challenges of the Digitalisation of the Economy Public Consultation Document* (OECD Publishing, February 2019) at [82], on 22 ("OECD Public Consultation").

of "permanent establishment" (PE), or to create entirely new nexus rules and taxing rights.

The first option is to amend (probably by supplementing) the definition of "permanent establishment" in Article 5 of the OECD Model Convention to expand the taxing rights to circumstances where the requisite type of business above the required threshold was carrying on its business irrespective of whether it had a physical presence or not. It was anticipated that this would also require changes to the distributive rules in Articles 7 and 9.[720] Changing the distributive rules in Articles 7 and 9 would not be an easy matter as they are predicated upon the determination of profits on a transactional basis between separate entities on an arm's-length basis. Article 7(2), for example, requires that profits be attributed to the PE based on its dealings with other parts of the enterprise as if the PE were a separate and independent enterprise (taking into account the functions performed, assets used and risks assumed by the PE).[721] Article 9, dealing with associated enterprises, enshrines the arm's-length principle enabling states to tax profits accruing to enterprises in circumstances where their dealings depart from "commercial or financial relations" between independent enterprises.[722] Other important distributive rules rely on the PE concept, for instance:

- Article 10 (dividends);
- Article 11 (interest);
- Article 12 (royalties);
- Article 13 (gains from the alienation of property);
- Article 15 (employment income);
- Article 21 (other income); and
- Article 22 (capital gains).

Even some of the special provisions such as those dealing with non-discrimination (Article 23) use the definition of PE in the establishment of the rules. A change to modify the definition of PE would, therefore, have very material significance across the whole structure of the OECD Model. This would suggest that if the first alternative was chosen, it would be necessary to have several categories of PE: one traditional and one expanded to reflect the new taxing right.

---

[720] OECD Public Consultation, above n 719 at [82].
[721] OECD *Model Tax Convention on Income and on Capital Condensed Version* (OECD, 21 November 2017) at Article 7(2) ("OECD Model").
[722] OECD Model, above n 721 at Article 9(1).

The second alternative of creating an entirely new nexus and taxing rights seems to be the preferred one because of the significant consequential effects that such a change to the definition of PE would cause. This disruption to the plethora of other Model Treaty Articles is not the only reason why a standalone new nexus rule seems to be preferred. Amount A is determined after considering the global profits of the multinational enterprise and then making adjustments to determine a portion of the non-routine residual global profits, not the arm's-length separate entity profits which are currently a central feature of the existing international tax framework. Given the fundamentally different nature of the formulation of profit and the relevant taxpayer, it would seem logical to prefer a new standalone provision.

If the proposals are accepted, the rule will, therefore, establish a separate taxing nexus presumably contained in a new article: "This new nexus would be introduced through a standalone rule – on top of the permanent establishment rule – to limit any unintended spill-over effect on other existing rules."[723]

This approach was confirmed in the January 2020 announcement: "The rule will be contained in a standalone rule to limit any unintended spill-over effects on other existing tax or non-tax rules."[724]

7.1.5 A New Taxable Presence or a New Concept of Source Income?

If the 2020s compromise establishes a new taxing right for certain categories of remote sales, a further question is whether this could be characterised as a new form of business profits for which the new article applies rather than Article 5 dealing with PEs, or whether it could be dealt with under a new category of income altogether. In the latter case, it would be similar to forms of passive income (such as royalties or interest). This question was raised in the Programme of Work document of the OECD back in May 2019.[725]

It is doubtful that this is a particularly important distinction. If it is a different category of business profits then it must be separate from the ordinary business profits dealt with under Articles 5 and 7. This is for the obvious reasons referred to above, namely that the definition of PE should remain consistent so that the other articles remain unaffected

---

[723] OECD Unified Approach, above n 715 at [22], on 8.
[724] OECD Inclusive Framework 2020, above n 713 at [36].
[725] OECD Programme of Work, above n 718 at [40], on 18.

by any potential change to the definition of PE. There is also the question of global profits rather than separate entity profits and the fact that Articles 5 and 7 are currently formulated on the latter concept.

In other words, if it is a category of business profits (let us call it remote sales business profits and say that it should have a taxing right under Article 5A and the ability to determine and tax profits attributable under Article 7A) then it would have separate distributive taxing rights allocated to the market jurisdiction.

It would also need to override the provisions in Article 7 in the same way as the other categories of income in Articles 8 to 21. Accordingly, Article 7(4) of the 2017 OECD Model would apply to make it clear that Articles 5A and 7A would override the ordinary business profits article so that such business profits from remote sales were not part of the income that Articles 5 and 7 dealt with.

7.1.6 Allocating Profits to the Market Jurisdiction: Rules That Do Not Comply with the Arm's-Length Standard

In addition to establishing a new taxing right through a new nexus, Amount A requires a provision which will enable market jurisdictions to exercise these taxing rights. This could be contained in the same Article 5A, perhaps by way of a separate paragraph, or as indicated above it could be contained in a new Article 7A. This would parallel the remote business profits Articles (5A and 7A) to the ordinary business profits articles (5 and 7).

There may be some drafting advantages in using the parallel provisions. The first advantage is that it would enable the methodology of the allocation of profits to be quite clearly set out, commencing with the global multinational net profit. The second advantage is that it would also enable market jurisdictions to establish their taxing rights which are not based on the arm's-length principle. This is why the existing framework, and in particular Article 7 does not work with the new concept of income in Amount A. Once it is recognised that "the new profit allocation rules would go beyond the arm's length principle and beyond the limitations on taxing rights determined by reference to a physical presence, two principles generally accepted as cornerstones of the current rules",[726] it becomes necessary to redefine these new profit allocation rules based on

---

[726] OECD Unified Approach, above n 715 at [28].

different concepts than the current regime which adheres to the concept of arm's-length pricing and profitability. These new profit allocation rules are focused on the taxing rights associated with Amount A:[727]

> given that the new taxing right would create a nexus for an MNE group even in the absence of a physical presence, it would be impossible to use the existing rules to allocate profit to this new nexus in cases where no functions are performed, no assets are used, and no risks are assumed in the market jurisdictions. Therefore, new profit allocation rules are required for Amount A.

As we will see, this is not a wholesale abandonment of the arm's-length principle. As far as the Unified Approach on Pillar One is concerned, the existing rules can be retained for those business profits not affected by Amount A, and also, materially, in respect of Amounts B and C. The OECD suggests that:[728]

> At the same time, while a number of criticisms of the arm's length principle have been voiced, there is a recognition that the current rules work reasonably well for most routine transactions. Therefore, the new rules would allow for the taxation at an appropriate level of business activities in market jurisdictions, while retaining transfer pricing rules where they work relatively well in that market jurisdiction.

For these business profits from remote sales, it will be necessary to amend Article 9 to reflect the extension of taxation rights beyond the arm's-length concept.[729] Presumably, this is only necessary for amounts of deemed income arising under Amount A.

7.1.7 Double Taxation and Losses

The possibility or likelihood of double taxation arises from two directions. The first is the double taxation of the amount of income deemed in Amount A just by itself. The second is the possibility of double taxation by the inclusion of income through the various cumulative changes to Amounts A, B and C and the rules potentially introduced by Pillar Two.

The formula in Amount A results in the allocation of some of the non-routine residual income of the multinational parent (or group) to the market jurisdiction. The market jurisdiction will impose tax (as discussed

---

[727] Ibid at [27].
[728] Ibid at [28].
[729] OECD Programme of Work, above n 718 at [3].

above this might be a combination of withholding taxes as an interim measure and then a final tax computation). While this income is deemed to arise in the market jurisdiction, as a matter of current accounting and existing tax law it is earned by the multinational parent (or a particular group entity which derives it). One of the problems is that the existing system for ameliorating the effects of double taxation in the international tax framework operates on single-entity profits determined on an arm's-length basis.

The same income cannot be taxed twice without some relief. The two obvious alternatives available to the multinational parent's jurisdiction are to include the income and give a credit for the tax paid in the market jurisdiction, or to exclude the income on the basis that it has already been earned (or deemed to be earned) in the market jurisdiction. In each case, it seems no easy matter to correctly identify the "match" between the deemed income and the actual income earned by one (or more) of the multinational group entities. Businesses, in their submissions at the OECD Public Conference,[730] seem to have a preference for the Amount A income to be excluded from the non-routine residual income derived in the "home" jurisdiction.

There is further work to be performed here by the OECD with the Unified Approach. The Inclusive Framework's Statement is looking for a system which is both "administrable and fair".[731] They suggest that one way to achieve this would be to take into account where profits reallocated under Amount A are currently recorded under the existing arm's-length principle system and allow the existing mechanisms of credit or exemption to eliminate double taxation.

A further complication involves circumstances where entities are making losses rather than profits. The OECD anticipates further work, simply saying: "Similarly, specific rules would need to be considered for the treatment of losses under Amount A (e.g. a claw-back or "earn-out" mechanism)".[732]

In the earlier Programme of Work document released in May 2019, the OECD had suggested that the profit allocation rules associated with Amount A would be symmetrical for both profits and losses.[733] One of the options considered was the development of an "earn-out" approach

---

[730] OECD Public Conference, 21 November 2019, held in Paris.
[731] OECD Inclusive Framework 2020, above n 713 at [52].
[732] OECD Unified Approach, above n 715 at [37].
[733] OECD Programme of Work, above n 718 at box 1.7.

to the recognition of losses, enabling a multinational group to calculate and record a notional cumulative loss. Only once this loss account had been utilised and the MNE moved to an overall profit position by making up the losses, would profits be subject to the new taxing right. More recently, consideration has been given to excluding the new taxing right in circumstances where losses exist, or where the total profit to be allocated does not meet a certain (currently unspecified) *de minimis* amount.[734]

Both these areas, namely the elimination or reduction of double taxation and the design of the system to deal with losses, may require both an international dimension in the change to tax treaties (concerning the allocation of taxing rights in the formulation of income/losses and credits/exemption) and a domestic law perspective (for example excluding Amount A income which is attributed to the market jurisdiction).

7.1.8 Domestic Law Changes: A Basis for Taxation? Can the Source Rules Just Be Changed?

In addition to the anticipated treaty changes referred to, it may be necessary for jurisdictions to change the domestic law relating to the source of income. For example, for the market jurisdiction to impose taxation on the deemed income under Amount A, the source rules of the jurisdiction concerned may need amendment.

An earlier part of this book examined the question as to whether domestic source-based taxation limits the right of states to exercise taxation.[735] In other words, are there any conventions in law (international law, principles in either common law jurisdictions or civil law jurisdictions) which would suggest that a source state ought to be constrained in taxing non-residents? Respected commentators believe that many domestic source rules are close to being a de facto harmonised international set of rules.[736] Taken to its logical conclusion, this gives rise to the possibility that under domestic law the ordinary meaning of income sourced in a jurisdiction has some customary international law flavour representing a consensus of views on what is domestically

---

[734] OECD Inclusive Framework 2020, above n 713 at [35].
[735] See Section 1.7 "Exploring the Limits of Domestic Source-Based Taxation".
[736] Reuven Avi-Yonah *International Tax as International Law* (Cambridge University Press, 2007) at 63; and Yariv Brauner "An International Tax Regime in Crystallization" (2003) 56 Tax L Rev 259 at 266.

sourced income across a range of jurisdictions. Theoretically, this might restrict a country from imposing a source rule outside a customary international legal norm.

After reviewing the authorities, however, and this is particularly true for common law countries based on the highest level of appellate decisions, the conclusion reached was that there is no practical limitation on states in respect of the imposition of a source-based tax, other than matters of enforcement.[737] Furthermore, should a relatively clear international consensus be reached by the discussions taking place in the Inclusive Framework and it emerges that the new taxing rights are the appropriate way forward for the design of a tax system in the twenty-first century, it would be strange if there was any historical international customary legal restriction to the introduction of new domestic source rules.

What is clear is that jurisdictions need to have the authority to impose tax under the domestic law and this would be particularly true of an amount of deemed income, such as that arising under Amount A.

7.1.9 Two Ways to Change Domestic Law

Generally, the source of income, as determined under tax laws, is identified first by domestic law. The source of income can be determined by a tax treaty, but this is unusual. Usually, the domestic law provides for a broad definition of the source rules while the treaty narrows down the taxing rights.[738] The most obvious way for countries to change the law relating to the source of income is for them to collectively adopt a reasonably consistent new sourcing rule.

Such a change could be something along the lines that "income shall be deemed to have a source in Country X, to the extent to which it is deemed to arise as remote sales business income in accordance with the defined formula". Another provision would then contain the formula for the calculation of Amount A. This would need to be adopted consistently across different countries. This appears to be what the OECD meant when it said: "Of course countries may also need to amend their domestic laws, such that any new article can become operational and there may be

---

[737] See Section 1.7 "Exploring the Limits of Domestic Source-Based Taxation".
[738] Porus Kaka "Source Taxation: Do We Really Know What We Mean?" (2017) 86 Tax Notes Int' 1221 at 1227.

benefits and coordinating the development of any such domestic rules."[739]

Another alternative is for countries to utilise provisions which generally adopt as domestic sourced income any income allocated to them by their tax treaties. Porus Kaka discusses this in his article in *Tax Notes International* and notes that three such countries, namely France, Japan and Australia, had followed this approach.[740] Other countries, such as New Zealand, have also followed this trend, recently (effective 1 July 2018) enacting the following provision:[741]

> Income of a non-resident that may be taxed in New Zealand under a double tax agreement and does not have a source under subsections (15) to (17) has a source in New Zealand, except if the income is a dividend from a share in a foreign company that is not revenue account property.

An illustration best demonstrates this approach. In France, for instance, the rule establishes a domestic source for any income allocated to France under a treaty, as follows: "Notwithstanding any provision to the contrary in the Code General des Impots, all income the taxation of which is allocated to France by a double taxation Convention is liable to income tax on natural persons or corporation tax in France."[742] Whilst the position in countries such as France eliminates the possibility of conflict between domestic law and treaties, it is not clear that such general rules adopting treaty allocated income as domestically sourced income will, from a constitutional law perspective, work in all countries. It may be best to adopt a consistent specific sourcing rule which makes it clear that the deemed income of Amount A is income for domestic law purposes.

7.1.10   Utilising a Withholding Tax?

One consideration that has been flagged by the OECD is whether a withholding tax makes sense as a collection mechanism. The reason for this is that the multinational entity conducting the remote sales does not have a physical presence in the market jurisdiction. This raises obvious questions about the

---

[739] OECD *Addressing the Tax Challenges of the Digitalisation of the Economy Public Consultation Document* (OECD Publishing, February 2019) at [82].
[740] Kaka, above n 738 at 1227.
[741] Income Tax Act 2007, s YD (17D), see the heading "Income Taxable under Double Tax Agreement".
[742] Act of 29 December 1959, codified in articles A-bis, 165-bis, 2019-I of Code General des Impots. French Constitution, Article 55.

7.1 ISSUES WITH THE IMPLEMENTATION 249

enforceability and collection of the tax. Accordingly, the OECD notes that "it is worth exploring whether a withholding tax would be an appropriate mechanism for the collection of the designated Amount A".[743]

On the one hand, the attractions of using a withholding tax are numerous. These include the familiarity of operation as well as many other important points discussed in a submission to the OECD on the Unified Approach by Professor William Byrnes:[744]

> A withholding based system offers the OECD the opportunity as a thought leader and influence agent to establish the parameters of an implementable regime built on legacy systems and procedural simplicity. A withholding based system offers: (a) better procedural certainty for taxpayer and tax authority based upon current withholding regimes for services, (b) better revenue estimation for tax authorities, (c) less complex and expensive audits by tax authorities of taxpayers, (d) better tax risk management for taxpayers, (e) an established procedural system for relief of double taxation, and finally, (f) less cause for requiring MAP.

On the other hand, and admittedly in a different context, Peter Hongler and Pasquale Pistone, in their paper written in 2015, advocated focusing on designing a new concept of a permanent establishment which would be redefined to include various activities undertaken by digital businesses.[745] They considered the alternative of withholding taxes on certain types of services, which they described as "cyber-based", but generally rejected the use of withholding taxes for several other important reasons. These included the lack of theoretical background, the lack of reference to the "ability to pay" (meaning that some businesses may be overtaxed in circumstances of low or no profitability) and, in the instance in front of the authors, they had concerns over the practicality and administrability of a proposal to impose withholding tax when there were no thresholds. These concerns are valid. Paul Oosterhuis and Amanda Parsons sounded a similar note of caution when discussing international reform alternatives:[746]

---

[743] OECD Unified Approach, above n 715 at [39].
[744] William Byrnes "Comments and Recommendations OECD Public Consultation Document Secretariat Proposal for a 'Unified Approach' under Pillar One" (12 November 2019) Social Science Research Network <https://papers.ssrn.com/sol3/papers.cfm?abstract_id=3487236> at 1.
[745] Peter Hongler and Pasquale Pistone *Blueprints for a New PE Nexus to Tax Business Income in the Era of the Digital Economy* (International Bureau of Fiscal Documentation, No 2015 – 15, 20 January 2015) at 43.
[746] Paul Oosterhuis and Amanda Parsons "Destination-Based Income Taxation: Neither Principled nor Practical?" (2018) 71 Tax L Rev 515 at 540.

> In the end, as many commentators have argued, it could be that, particularly with the rise of digital commerce, the avoidance possibilities of limiting any taxable presence standard to situations where an affiliated group of taxpayers (together with unrelated "captive" service providers) have a presence in the jurisdiction are too substantial to be ignored, and some sort of broader economic presence test accompanied by withholding tax enforcement mechanisms must be considered. But that should only be done with full recognition of the administration and enforcement costs and difficulties that inevitably follow.

However, the practicality of a withholding tax does improve when there are significant thresholds because it is more likely that the business concerned, if sufficiently large, is profitable. Furthermore, the scheme becomes much more administrable when there are only a few larger payees rather than a plethora of small recipients.

Another International Bureau of Fiscal Documentation (IBFD) paper, written by Yariv Brauner and Andrés Baez,[747] builds on the work of Hongler and Pistone, suggesting the use of withholding tax both in the context of a revised nexus and in the absence of obtaining agreement about what that revised nexus might be. While preferring the amended PE alternative, Brauner and Baez set out a withholding regime involving registration, which they suggested could be a simpler, if crude, response to the challenges of the digital economy.

Overall, the use of withholding tax becomes much clearer and a more viable option in circumstances where the nexus, allocation of income and thresholds are themselves clearly defined. While there would be transitional issues, such as understanding whether the multinational group is above the turnover threshold to be assured that the deemed income under Amount A definitively arises in the market jurisdiction, these can presumably be addressed.

The use of a withholding tax would have to be on an interim basis to deal with the over/under-taxation of the amount of deemed income. This is necessarily a complication. The final computation of the amount of deemed income arising under Amount A requires significant components of information held only by the recipient and not the payee (such as the global profit, the non-routine residual profit and the proportion of sales to the various market jurisdictions amongst other matters) so the

---

[747] Andrés Baez and Yariv Brauner *Withholding Taxes in the Service of BEPS Action 1: Address the Tax Challenges of the Digital Economy* (International Bureau of Fiscal Documentation, No 2015 – 14, 2 February 2015).

7.2 IMPLEMENTING THE CHANGES BY AMOUNT B

withholding tax would be available to offset against the final liability (or, if more than the final liability, would constitute a refund). The OECD makes the point that withholding taxes are matters of domestic law and are not part of the tax treaty arrangements (although of course limitation of the rates of taxes is a common feature of tax treaties). They suggest that any features of the domestic withholding tax should be agreed and, presumably, consistently applied, as indicated:[748]

> However, if countries choose to use it (and as an administrative mechanism to simplify and assure the collection of an underlying taxing right, it would be a matter for domestic law) it would be necessary to agree the features of the system of withholding that jurisdictions could commit to apply.

The Inclusive Framework's Statement most recently suggests a move away from withholding tax. There are suggestions that the "one-stop-shop" regime may be gathering momentum, enabling exclusive filing in the ultimate parent jurisdiction and therefore eliminating the filing obligations in multiple market jurisdictions.[749]

7.2 Implementing the Changes Proposed by Amount B

7.2.1 Introduction

While the practical implications of changes brought about by the proposed introduction of the new rules relating to Amount B are very significant, the infrastructural changes required to the international tax framework are nowhere near as major as those required for Amount A. As discussed in Chapters 5 and 6,[750] Amount B is designed to be a pragmatic solution to prevent disputes relating to the quantum of income attributable to a subsidiary or branch which is carrying on baseline distribution and marketing activities in the market jurisdiction. The key

---

[748] OECD Unified Approach, above n 714 at [39].
[749] OECD *Statement by the OECD/G20 Inclusive Framework on BEPS on the Two-Pillar Approach to Address the Tax Challenges Arising from the Digitalisation of the Economy* (OECD, January 2020) at annexure 1 at [36].
[750] See Section 5.4 "Amount B: Fixed Remuneration for Marketing and Distribution", and Section 6.6 "The Failure of Transfer Pricing with Certain Multinational Enterprises and Their Transactions".

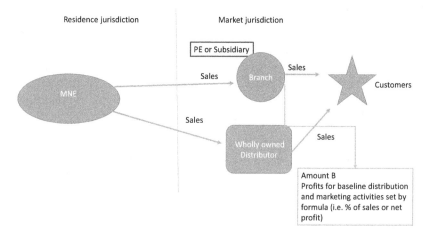

Figure 7.2 Determining the profits attributable to marketing and distribution taxable presence

point here is that this is a formulaic assessment of profitability within an existing framework (that taxation rights arise because there is a taxable presence in the jurisdiction being either a permanent establishment or a separate taxable entity such as a subsidiary).

As this can be viewed as a way or method of determining profits, rather than the establishment of new taxing rights, the question becomes how best to implement the changes proposed by Amount B (Figure 7.2).

7.2.2 What Needs to Be Amended?

Given that there is no fundamental change, and taxation takes place through the application of the nexus rules contained in Article 5 together with the business profits rule in Article 7, it would seem, at first glance, unnecessary to make a change in the OECD Model Treaty. The new determination of profits could potentially be introduced as a preferred method in the OECD Transfer Pricing Guidelines, or in the Commentary to Article 7. That said, to make it clear that it is a significant change which must be adopted, there would seem to be a case to include the method in one of the paragraphs to Article 7. This could be done on the basis that, unless it is a departure from the arm's-length principle (see the discussion on Amount C below, Section 7.2.3), the amount of profit for certain activities in distribution and marketing "is determined following the formula provided for in X". X can then be contained within either the Transfer Pricing Guidelines or the OECD Commentary as appropriate.

It would seem unnecessary to amend Article 9 in respect of Amount B. The discussion to date seems to be an agreement that Amount B operates as a proxy for the determination of an arm's-length amount of profit (or at least for a range of profits within an arm's-length quantum).

7.2.3 Implementing the Changes Proposed by Amount C

Amount C can be viewed as simply a "resumption in play" or as "business as usual" as far as the arm's-length principle is concerned. The situation where Amount C arises is where:[751]

> there are more functions in the market jurisdiction than have been accounted for by reference to the local entity's assumed baseline activity (which is subject to the fixed return in B above), and that jurisdiction seeks to tax an additional profit on those extra functions in accordance with the existing transfer pricing rules.

Accordingly, there would seem to be no need to make major changes to Articles 5, 7 and 9. As for the suggested changes in respect of Amount B, for the sake of clarity it might be best to acknowledge in a paragraph to Article 7 that the formulaic profits determined under Amount B are subject to the arm's-length principle in the formulation of an amount by Amount C.

The issue with implementing the changes proposed by Amount C therefore mostly are concerned with its relationship to the amounts calculated under Amounts A and B. This is referred to in the next section.

7.3 Issues with Implementing Amounts A, B and C

7.3.1 Establishing the Relationship between the Different Amounts

The relationship between Amount A and the other two Amounts (B and C) should be very small. The reason for this is that in theory they are not supposed to intersect at all. Amount A is income which is deemed to arise from certain transactions (remote sales) in circumstances where there is no (in the case of automated digital services) or limited (in the

---

[751] OECD Unified Approach, above n 715 at [30].

case of consumer-facing businesses) conventional taxable presence (but still insufficient to constitute a taxable entity or PE) in the source jurisdiction. In contrast, Amounts B and C arise only in circumstances where there is a conventional taxable presence. Amount A creates new taxing rights where there were previously none. If that is right, then, as postulated just above, there should be no double tax between Amount A and the other two amounts.

In contrast, Amounts B and C are strongly interrelated in the sense that they are seeking to achieve the same outcome (an arm's-length profit) but using a different methodology. If the formula in Amount B does not fully reflect all the assets, functions and risks undertaken by the taxable entity then Amount C comes into play to ensure the correct amount of tax at an arm's-length level. Alternatively, if Amount B reflects over-taxation, given the limited assets, functions and risks undertaken by the taxable entity, then one would assume that Amount C could be a negative adjustment ensuring that the arm's-length profit is a reduction from the formula proposed by Amount B.

These relationships are important from the perspective of eliminating double taxation between the various amounts or categories of income. A separate double tax issue arises between states-where income allocated to the market or source state under Amount A also falls to be subject to tax in the resident state under the existing arm's-length principle calculations. In respect of Amount A, this is discussed in Section 7.1.

7.4 Issues with Implementing Key Elements of Pillar Two

The proposals in Pillar Two are far-reaching.[752] They effectively propose coordinated rules which will make it very difficult for multinational enterprises to structure their affairs to pay less than a minimum amount of corporate tax. This requires a high degree of coordination as the implementation involves introducing consistent rules in different countries and organising ordering rules to ensure (or at least reduce) double taxation. As recognised by the OECD Secretariat's Proposal, it is anticipated that both public international law (treaties) and domestic law will be affected:[753]

---

[752] They are described in Section 5.7 "Pillar Two: Global Anti-Base Erosion Proposal".
[753] OECD Global Anti-Base Erosion Proposal ("GloBE") – Pillar Two Public Consultation Document (OECD, 8 November 2019) at [6] ("OECD GloBE").

These rules would be implemented by way of changes to domestic law and tax treaties and would incorporate a co-ordination or ordering rule to avoid the risk of double taxation that might otherwise arise where more than one jurisdiction sought to apply these rules to the same structure or arrangement.

7.4.1 The Income Inclusion Rule

In simple terms, the income inclusion rule requires a shareholder in a corporation to pay "top-up" taxes to a minimum rate in respect of their proportionate share of the income of the corporation if the corporation is not subject to tax at a minimum rate. This is the tax policy of controlled foreign company (CFC) legislation. Attributing profits to shareholders is a common technique used to prevent the aggregation of untaxed (or low-taxed) profits when these profits are held in a corporate entity controlled by the shareholder. The rules apply when a shareholder has a significant direct or indirect ownership interest in the company (the OECD has suggested that significant may mean 25 per cent or more).[754]

It is, however, intended that these rules would "supplement rather than replace a jurisdiction's CFC rules".[755] This will mean there will need to be some careful coordination not only with the existing CFC rules under each jurisdiction's domestic law but also a careful examination of the relationship between the domestic rules and each country's double tax treaties. The income inclusion rule will primarily be a domestic piece of legislation, presumably coordinated so that it is consistent between jurisdictions.

7.4.2 The Relationship between the Income Inclusion Rule and Tax Treaties

The new income inclusion rule will face similar issues to those that confront CFC rules and double tax treaties. Sometimes the treaty rules conflict with the CFC legislation providing that the residence state (through the obligations imposed on the parent company) has the right to tax the profits of the subsidiary located in another jurisdiction (in the presence of a double tax agreement). The problem arises because

---

[754] OECD *Addressing the Tax Challenges of the Digitalisation of the Economy Public Consultation Document* (OECD Publishing, February 2019) at [96].
[755] Ibid at [96].

Article 7(1) of the relevant DTA provides that: "Profits of an enterprise of a Contracting State shall be taxable only in that State unless the enterprise carries on business in that other Contracting State through a permanent establishment situated therein."[756] Applying Article 7(1), the argument is that the subsidiary's profit ought to be exclusively taxed in the state of *its* residence and not the other state (the state of the parent company's residence which is seeking to tax the subsidiary's profits through its CFC regime). Since the subsidiary company does not have a permanent establishment in the residence state, the taxing rights are not allocated to the residence state. Cases around the world have met with mixed results, with some striking down the application of the CFC rules and others leaving the rules unaffected.[757] The design of the CFC regime appears to be particularly important in this regard.[758] If the subsidiary is taxed by the residence jurisdiction (and the liability passed to the parent company as an agent) the result under Article 7 might be more problematic than if the liability accrues to income attributed to the parent company as a shareholder in its own right.

Leaving aside the technical question of whether the CFC rules result in taxing "new" income derived by the shareholder or the subsidiary's profits there is a larger question, which is whether domestic anti-avoidance rules (such as the CFC rules) can apply notwithstanding the treaty obligations. The Commentary to the 2017 Model Convention[759] suggests that the CFC rules will always prevail and that "there is nothing to see here, move along please". This is because Article 1(3) provides that there is no conflict in the treaty where a residence state imposes tax on its

---

[756] OECD *Model Tax Convention on Income and on Capital Condensed Version* (OECD, 21 November 2017).

[757] UK decision *Bricom Holdings Limited v Inland Revenue Commissioners* [1997] BTC 471 (CA) (CFC rules applicable despite Article 11 of the UK/Netherlands treaty); the French decision *Re Societe Schneider Electric* [2002] 4 ITLR 1077 (French CFC rules not compatible with the French/Swiss treaty so the treaty prevailed preventing the CFC rules from applying); the Finnish decision *A Oyi Abp* [2002] 4 ITLR 1009 (CFC rules would apply to a Belgian subsidiary); the Canadian decision *Canwest Mediaworks Inc (successor by amalgamation to Canvideo Television Sales (1983) Ltd) v Canada* [2006] 9 ITLR 189 (TCC) (Canadian CFC rules effective with the Canada/Barbados treaty); or in the Japanese (Supreme Court) decision *Glaxo Kabushiki Kaisha v Director of Kojimachi Tax Office* [2006] 12 ITLR 644 (Japanese CFC rules effective in the Japan/Singapore treaty); and in the Brazilian decision *Companhia Vale do Rio Doce v National Treasury* [2014] 17 ITLR 643 (Brazilian CFC rules violated the various treaties).

[758] James Halse "The Conflict between CFC Legislation and Double Tax Treaties: A New Zealand Perspective" (2008) 14(2) NZ J T L & Policy 262 at 262.

[759] OECD Model, above n 721, Commentary on Article 1 at [81].

residents.[760] Some treaties may not have this savings clause, but the OECD Commentary suggests that this is not a material omission as:[761]

> The same conclusion must be reached in the case of conventions that do not include a provision similar to paragraph 3 of Article 1; for the reasons explained in paragraph 14 of the Commentary on Article 7 and 37 of the Commentary on Article 10, the interpretation according to which these Articles would prevent the application of the controlled foreign company provisions does not accord with the text of paragraph 1 of Article 7 and paragraph 5 of Article 10. It also does not hold when these paragraphs are read in their context. Thus, whilst some countries have felt it useful to expressly clarify, in their conventions, that controlled foreign company legislation did not conflict with the Convention, such clarification is not necessary. It is recognised that controlled foreign company legislation structured in this way is not contrary to the provisions of the Convention.

Paragraph 14 of the OECD Commentary on Article 7 discusses the purpose of Article 7(1) and the relationship with domestic taxation. It records that:[762]

> The purposes of paragraph 1 are to limit the right of one Contracting State to tax the business profits of enterprises of the other Contracting State. As confirmed by paragraph 3 of Article 1, the paragraph does not limit the right of a Contracting State to tax its own residents under controlled foreign company provisions found in its domestic law even though such tax imposed on these residents may be computed by reference to the part of the profits of an enterprise that is resident of the other Contracting State that is attributable to these residents' participation in that enterprise.

This Commentary reflects the view of the OECD and, more importantly, records the purpose and policy behind Article 7(1), so it is likely to be influential in the interpretation of the relationship between domestic legislation and treaties. The rationale and policy behind the Income Inclusion rule and CFC legislation are virtually indistinguishable. Most courts would purposively interpret the domestic law to reflect that countries have retained their ability to tax their residents. Experience concerning controlled foreign companies would suggest that some

---

[760] Ibid at [81], see the OECD Model Convention itself, at Article 1(3), which reads: "This Convention shall not affect the taxation, by a Contracting State, of its residents except with respect to the benefits granted under paragraph 3 of Article 7, paragraph 2 of Article 9, and Articles 19, 20, 23[A] [B], 24, 25 and 28."
[761] OECD Model, above n 721, Commentary on Article 1 at [81].
[762] Ibid, Commentary on Article 7 at [14].

countries might take a more textual interpretation and not necessarily read the Commentary in the manner required by the Vienna Convention on the Law of Treaties.[763]

Whilst it is an oversimplification, the dualist view of an international legal system sees international and domestic law as separate systems of law. On one plane, international law regulates the relationship between sovereign states. On another plane, domestic law regulates legal matters relevant to that state. Under dualism, the application of international law occurs only when it is expressly incorporated into domestic law. A country may be described as dualistic if it requires some legislative or formal adoption of a treaty into its domestic law for the treaty to attain the force of law. A consequence of having a dualist legal system is that subsequent domestic law, such as the new Income Inclusion rule, can be enacted which can be effective in overriding treaty obligations even though this is a breach of those international treaty obligations. In the case of anti-avoidance legislation, such as CFC legislation and the similarly purposed Income Inclusion rule, it can be argued that such an override is acceptable for a variety of different reasons such as the purpose of treaties and the understanding that anti-avoidance rules generally override treaty obligations (according to the Commentary on Article 1).[764]

The monist view sees both international and domestic law as intrinsically part of the same legal system. A country may be described as monistic if it accepts international law automatically as part of its domestic legal system. In practical terms, this means that a double tax treaty which is validly executed in the international legal sense automatically takes full legal effect within domestic law. This makes it more difficult for a monist jurisdiction to assert deliberate override in its domestic enactment of the Income Inclusion rule since the international treaties the monist country has entered into normally have a superior legal status.

For this reason, it might be desirable for the domestic legislation in dualist countries to record that the Income Inclusion rule will override the double tax agreement, and in monist countries it would be highly desirable for there to be included in the multilateral instrument a

---

[763] For a good example of this see the lamentable approach of the New Zealand Court of Appeal in *Commissioner of Inland Revenue v Lin* [2018] NZCA 38; in Craig Elliffe "Interpreting International Tax Agreements: Alsatia in New Zealand" (2018) 28(1) NZULR 1.

[764] Craig Elliffe "The Lesser of Two Evils: Double Tax Treaty Override or Treaty Abuse?" (2016) 1 BTR 62.

7.4 ISSUES WITH IMPLEMENTING KEY ELEMENTS   259

recognition in the MLI that anything in the succeeding covered tax treaties will not override the application of the Income Inclusion rule.

Overall, for these domestic rules to be effective, it would be important and useful, from a tax administration perspective, to reduce the likelihood of arguments that the treaties rendered the Income Inclusion rules toothless. The best way to do this would be to include an express statement in the MLI implementing other Pillar One and Pillar Two changes that nothing in the succeeding covered tax treaties will prevent the application of these types of coordinated domestic law changes such as the Income Inclusion rule.

7.4.3   The Switch-Over Rule

This is another change that will be necessarily affected by the MLI as well as changes to domestic law. Essentially, under the Switch-over rule, profits which are undertaxed by the source jurisdiction (i.e. profits not subject to a minimum rate of tax, similar to how a subsidiary's profits are taxed under the Income Inclusion rule) in an exempt branch become subject to tax in the residence state. The domestic law will need to impose tax on the branch whilst the tax treaty implications arise from the need to "switch over" from an exemption method to a credit method for double tax relief. Such switch-over clauses are found in many countries' treaty networks.

7.4.4   The Undertaxed Payments Rule and the Subject to Tax Rule

The Undertaxed Payments rule denies a deduction (or impose a withholding tax at source) in respect of payments made to a related party unless the recipient is taxed at a minimum rate of tax. The disallowance of an expense or the imposition of withholding tax are primarily domestic law amendments. There may be tax treaty implications if the recipient is a resident of a Contracting State. This is where the subject to tax rule comes into play. If the undertaxed payments would be eligible for relief under a double tax treaty, the subject to tax rule would apply to deny the tax treaty benefits.

The OECD Model Convention would need to be varied by the MLI in the following areas:[765]

- The limitation on the taxation of business profits of a non-resident, unless those profits are attributable to a permanent establishment (Article 7 of the OECD Model Convention).

---

[765] OECD GloBE, above n 753 at [27] on 34.

- The requirement to make a corresponding adjustment where a transfer pricing adjustment is made by the other Contracting State (Article 9 of the OECD Model Convention).
- The limitation on taxation of dividends in the source state (Article 10 of the OECD Model Convention).
- The limitations on taxation of interest, royalties and capital gains in the source state (Articles 11–13 of the OECD Model Convention).
- The allocation of exclusive taxing rights of other income to the state of residence (Article 21 of the OECD Model Convention).

The implementation of the proposals in Pillar Two will, therefore, require careful domestic law coordination and treaty changes.

7.4.5 The Order of the Rules

Another key issue is the coordination or ordering of the various rules.[766] The problem is that two or more of the rules could apply simultaneously, creating a double tax situation. For instance, a parent company jurisdiction might impose an Income Inclusion requirement on a subsidiary based in a tax haven, whilst another subsidiary jurisdiction in the multinational group denies a deduction for a payment made to the same tax haven subsidiary based on the Undertaxed Payments rule. Unfortunately, this has the potential to get quite complicated very quickly as the implications for the ordering of the rules will have an impact on both domestic law and the relevant treaties.

7.5 Common Pillar One and Two Implementation Issues

7.5.1 Implementation by Way of a Multilateral Instrument?

As indicated, quite significant treaty changes are required to implement some of these amendments. This is particularly true in the case of the new taxing rights. It would seem a logical move to make these changes by way of the same type of instrument as that which introduced the BEPS measures.[767] One of the reasons for this is timing as there is an imperative for the changes to occur all at the same time. This is recognised by the OECD Secretariat as follows: "More fundamentally, however, the re-

---

[766] Ibid, Appendix B at [30] on 35.
[767] Multilateral Convention to Implement Tax Treaty Related Measures to Prevent Base Erosion and Profit Shifting (entered into force 1 July 2018).

7.5 PILLAR ONE AND TWO IMPLEMENTATION ISSUES 261

allocation of taxing rights raises important political considerations. A crucial one is that these changes would need to be implemented simultaneously by all jurisdictions, to ensure a level playing field."[768] Unless the changes are simultaneous, there will be winners and losers amongst states. Some problems will arise with double taxation unless the residence state either exempts or gives credit for the amount of income deemed to arise in the market jurisdiction.

Simultaneous implementation is no easy matter, but of course it may be possible for a significant number of the larger and more developed countries to enter into the arrangement with a reasonably firm timeline and therefore for a reasonable proportion of world trade to be brought within the new rules. The experience of the BEPS multilateral instrument (MLI) is an illustrative case that timing the implementation may be difficult. There are currently ninety-three countries that are signatories to the MLI. As at December 2019, only thirty-eight of them had deposited the instrument of ratification, acceptance or approval. The vast majority of countries signed the MLI in June 2017 but after two and a half years only 40 per cent of countries have formally ratified the agreement. This is telling us that for political or constitutional reasons the ratification or approval of the MLI takes time in many countries.

In addition to the question of timing, there is also an advantage in having great consistency in the changes. Using a multilateral instrument (whether it is the same one as introduced the BEPS changes or a new instrument) seems to be a very efficient way to make changes to treaty networks. Presumably, the changes would be more like minimum standards adopted by the MLI so that there was a uniform adoption of the changes by the signatories. Some of the optionality offered by the BEPS MLI, for example the decisions whether to adopt the changes to the definitions of PEs or the changes to hybrid mismatches, were, for a variety of reasons, not adopted by the signatories in their arrangements with the MLI.

7.5.2 Dispute Resolution

It is desirable that amongst the changes implemented if the proposals are accepted, there be a clear process for dispute resolution. The OECD Secretariat's Proposal had suggested, regarding adjustments to Amount

---

[768] OECD Unified Approach, above n 715 at [40] on 11.

C, that: "Any dispute between the market jurisdiction and the taxpayer over any element of the proposal should be subject to legally binding and effective dispute prevention and resolution mechanisms."[769] This was discussed in the public consultation conference on Pillar One in Paris in November 2019 but there was certainly no consensus on the nature of the dispute resolution mechanism. Some speakers were opposed to binding mandatory arbitration.[770]

It is anticipated that a new dispute prevention and resolution framework is necessary. The work being performed on this important issue is discussed in Section 5.6.[771]

---

[769] Ibid at [30].
[770] For instance, see the comments by Thulani Shongwe of the African Tax Administration Forum, during the OECD Public Conference, on the morning of 21 November 2019.
[771] See Section 5.6 "Dispute Prevention and Resolution".

8

The Influence of Alternative Policy Strategies on the 2020s Compromise

8.1 Where Do the Strategies of the 2020s Compromise Originate?

8.1.1 Introduction

The OECD Secretariat's proposed two Pillars of the Unified Approach and the Global Anti-Base Erosion Proposal ("GloBE")[772] are a mixture of bold strategy and pragmatism. As discussed in Chapter 5, especially Section 5.3.9, they depart from key elements of the 1920s compromise.[773] What is obvious, though, is that the two Pillars are an attempted compromise designed to make "modest but significant" changes to the international tax framework.[774] The 2020s compromise, when examining the allocation of taxing rights and nexus, considered three proposals described in some detail in the Inclusive Framework's Public Consultation Document, Addressing the Tax Challenges of the Digitalisation of the Economy.[775] While the design of the concepts around Amount A owes much to the proposal on marketing intangibles, other elements of the other proposals were adopted. Seen as a coordinated package, however, the proposals seem to address many of the challenges of the digital economy.[776] This is a positive thing.

There is, however, a bigger picture of reform here, not exclusively based on the specific proposals considered by the OECD and discussed in

---

[772] These are discussed in Chapters 5, 6 and 7.
[773] Establishing a new taxing right with a nexus based on remote sales and not physical presence, non-adherence to the arm's-length principle and the use of formulas and thresholds. See Chapters 5 and 6.
[774] D Bradbury (Head of the Tax Policy and Statistics Division, Centre for Tax Policy and Administration) when speaking at the International Fiscal Association Conference in Melbourne (June 2019).
[775] OECD *Base Erosion and Profit Shifting Project, Public Consultation Document, Addressing the Tax Challenges of the Digitalisation of the Economy* (February 2019) at 9–17.
[776] This is analysed in Chapter 6.

some detail in Chapter 5.[777] The route to the development of Pillar One and Pillar Two owes much to the other alternative policy choices which are the subject of analysis in this chapter. These are more radical international tax regimes incorporating techniques and regimes such as formulary apportionment and destination-based taxation. Many of these significant policy changes have some features of their design which had been adopted and incorporated into the OECD Secretariat's proposals. No single proposal has been fully adopted although there are significant parts of the residual profit allocation methodology employed in Amount A of Pillar One. It has to be remembered that the 2020s compromise requires a proposal which is pragmatic, effective and explicable. Policies that require too much change become vastly more difficult to implement and obtain consensus across a large number of nations. The problem of the quantum and speed of acceptable change may not be insurmountable over time.

This chapter looks at the major alternative policy choices open to the Inclusive Framework. It seeks to, first, describe the key characteristics of each of these major alternative policy choices and how they work. The intention behind this description is to highlight, briefly, how these alternatives operate but not to fully describe the regimes. Others have done so in greater detail and much better.[778] Secondly, the chapter seeks to reflect upon the advantages and disadvantages of these major policy alternatives in turn, and thirdly to analyse their distinctive features in the light of the 2020s compromise proposal to see where these features have been adopted. Lastly, the chapter considers under each reform policy the possibility of likely further change in the future direction of the 2020s compromise given these various alternative policy choices.

The chapter is divided into four sections. The first three of these policy reforms, destination-based cash flow taxation, residual profit allocation by income and formulary apportionment by sales, have one clear feature in common: a focus upon the destination basis of taxation (the place where goods and services are delivered and consumed) rather than a basis of origin (the place where capital is employed to produce or manufacture the goods or services). Even the fourth section, expanding the concept of a permanent establishment, requires a focus upon the allocation of income towards the place of destination to meet some of the

---

[777] See Section 5.2 "Pillar One: Allocation of Taxing Rights and Nexus".
[778] Readers will be referred to relevant reference material for that more detailed analysis in the course this chapter.

objectives which are necessary to overcome the challenges of the digital economy to the international tax framework. In other words, a key conclusion from this chapter is that the contribution to the reform process by many of these alternative reform options is simply: the proposal for reform must facilitate, most efficiently and pragmatically, the allocation of taxing rights on a destination basis.

8.2 Destination-Based Cash Flow Taxation

Some of the best minds in international tax have long been asserting the problems with the current international tax system. They have discussed concerns about the fragility of both residence-based and source-based taxation.[779] In many cases, they have proposed alternatives sometimes reflecting on one of the key features of consumption taxes, the stability of the tax base.[780] The common feature of consumption taxes is that they

---

[779] Articles and books dealing with the problems of the international tax regime include: H Ault *"Some Reflections on the OECD and the Sources of International Tax Principles"* (Tax Notes International, 17 June 2013); Reuven Avi-Yonah *International Tax as International Law* (Cambridge University Press, 2007); M Devereux and J Vella *Are We Heading towards a Corporate Tax System Fit for the 21st Century?* (Fiscal Studies, Oxford Legal Studies Research Paper No 88/2014); D Elkins "The Myth of Corporate Tax Residence" (2017) 9 Columbia Journal of Tax Law 5 at 12; M Graetz "Taxing International Capital Income: Inadequate Principles, Outdated Concepts, and Unsatisfactory Policies" (2001) 54 Tax L Rev 261 at 271; H Grubert and R Altshuler "Fixing the System: An Analysis of Alternative Proposals for the Reform of International Tax" (2013) 66 Nat'l Tax J 671; E Kleinbard "Stateless Income" (2011) 11 Fla Tax Rev 699; L Lokken "What Is This Thing Called Source?" (2011) 37 Int'l Tax J 21; D Pinto *E-Commerce and Source-Based Income Taxation* (IBFD Publications BV, 2003); W Schön "Persons and Territories: On the International Allocation of Taxing Rights" (2010) 6 BTR 554 at 554; W Schön "10 Questions about Why and How to Tax the Digitalised Economy" (2018) 72(4/5) BFIT 278; R Vann "Taxing International Business Income: Hard-Boiled Wonderland and the End of the World" (2010) 2(3) WTJ 291; K Vogel "Worldwide vs Source Taxation of Income: A Review and Re-evaluation of Arguments (in Three Parts) (1988) 8–9 Intertax 216.

[780] The work of the Oxford University Centre for Business Taxation is particularly notable in this regard, chaired by Professor Michael Devereux, and including many of the authors in this list. Articles focusing more on more on the destination based income taxes include: A Auerbach *A Modern Corporate Tax* (The Center for American Progress/The Hamilton Project, December 2010); A Auerbach, M Devereux, M Keen and J Vella *Destination-Based Cash Flow Taxation* (Oxford University Centre for Business Taxation, WP 17/01, January 2017); A Auerbach, M Devereux and H Simpson "Taxing Corporate Income" in J Mirrlees and others (eds) *Dimensions of Tax Design: The Mirrlees Review* (Oxford University Press, 2010) 837; Alan Auerbach and Michael Devereux *Cash Flows Taxes in an International Setting* (Oxford University Centre for Business Taxation,

are normally levied where the consumer is located, which is the importing country (described as the place of destination).

8.2.1 What Is Destination-Based Cash-Flow Taxation?

As its name would suggest, destination-based cash-flow taxation (DBCFT) has two elements.[781] These are to utilise a tax base, like a consumption tax, based on the destination of goods and services. This is coupled with taxation based upon cash flow.

The second component, cash flow, is dealt with first because it is a more widely known concept and slightly easier to explain.[782] Cash flow taxation operates, exactly as it says,[783] counting all receipts as income whilst deducting all expenditures when "paid".[784] Different from traditional financial accounting (and almost all income tax accounting), cash flow taxation allows an immediate deduction for all expenditure

---

2015); R Avi-Yonah and K Clausing "Problems with Destination-Based Corporate Taxes and the Ryan Blueprint" (2017) 8(2) Colum J Tax Law 229; M Devereux and J Vella "Value Creation as the Fundamental Principle of the International Corporate Tax System" (Oxford University Centre for Business Taxation, European Tax Policy Forum Policy Paper, 31 July 2018); M Devereux and J Vella *Implications of Digitalisation for International Corporate Tax Reform* (Oxford University Centre for Business Taxation, WP 17/07, July 2017); M Devereux and J Vella "Taxing the Digitalised Economy: Targeted or System-Wide Reform?" (2018) 4 BTR 387; M Devereux *Defining and Implementing a Destination-Based Corporate Tax* (Oxford University Centre for Business Taxation, Working Paper 14/07, 2014); Mirrlees Committee *Reforming the Tax System for the 21st Century: The Mirrlees Review* (Oxford University Press, 2011); W Schön "Destination-Based Income Taxation and WTO Law: A Note" in H Jochum et al (eds) *Practical Problems in European and International Tax Law: Essays in Honour of Manfred Mössner* (IBFD, 2016) 429.

[781] A much better description can be found in Auerbach et al Destination-Based Cash Flow Taxation, above n 780, which will soon be published by Oxford University Press.

[782] Cash flow taxation can occur in the context of a wholly domestic tax system analysis or an international tax system which involves cross-border transactions.

[783] Actually not exactly on a cash receipts/cash expenditure basis but on an accrual basis, so that a receipt becomes income when the payer has an obligation to make payment to the payee rather than when actual cash payment occurs. Likewise, the expenditure is deductible not upon actual cash payment, but when the expenditure is committed to definitively by the payer.

[784] Two major options qualify "all receipts" and "all expenditures". The two variants include those items purchased and sold as part of the ordinary conduct of business (the real base) or the real base together with financial transactions. In the first case of the real base, transactions involving borrowing, interest earned and paid, and repayments are ignored so that only purchases of non-financial assets (such as plant and machinery, trading stock are included). In the second case where financial transactions are included, the principal amount of a loan is included as income, whilst the repayment is an expense.

including those items regarded as capital. As a result, expenditure on capital assets, such as plant and machinery or indeed buildings, become immediately deductible.

It seems counterintuitive to allow a full deduction for the cost of a capital asset which will be used over a long period, but this intuitive thinking comes from matching concepts in accounting and the desire to quarantine profitability to a short period such as an annual profit. If you can briefly suspend the matching concept from your thinking, then the logic behind methods based on cash flow is that rational actors invest money to obtain a return over time. Rational and sophisticated actors will seek a return which represents the highest net present value (NPV) of the sum of all discounted cash flows associated with the investment. In other words, one would invest $100 in an investment to receive greater than $110 after one year if the discount rate was 10 per cent. This means the NPV takes into account the required return on the investment after the discount rate (the NPV of a cash receipt of $110 in one year is $100). The NPV, therefore, represents the economic rent or post-discount return.

Any investment is only worthwhile if the NPV is greater than zero.[785] Investors invest in forestry, which might have a twenty-five-year rotation cycle, because they expect the NPV of their investment to be greater than zero, meaning that the discounted cash flows associated with the receipts in twenty-five years are greater than the costs incurred (purchase of seedlings, tending and pruning etc.) in the intervening period. Over time, taxation is only on the overall economic rent earned by taxpayers in the economy and the government acts as a partner to the business providing refunds (for losses) as well as taxing NPV gains.[786]

The second concept, destination-based taxation, has an international relevance as it concerns the tax base when looked at from a jurisdictional perspective. A DBCFT brings within the tax base those sales and revenues derived from within the jurisdiction but excludes revenues from exports. Expenses incurred within the country are deductible against these revenues. Revenues derived from the import of goods and services to final consumers are included in the calculation, less relevant

---

[785] For a cogent explanation of this see Auerbach et al Destination-Based Cash Flow Taxation, above n 780.

[786] This can lead to unpredictable cash flow issues for a government under conventional income tax/corporation tax provisions, with most systems providing loss carry-forward regimes rather than cash tax refunds.

expenditure.[787] This tax base is focused on the destination of the goods and services. If the consumer is local then the revenue is included within the base. If the consumer is in an overseas export market, then the corporate income taxation takes place in that market. The similarity of the tax base to consumption taxes is obvious, and for those seeking to understand DBCFT it is very helpful to think about the types of adjustments made in indirect tax systems on exported and imported goods. Most Value Added Tax (VAT) and Goods and Services Tax (GST) systems operate so that exports are "zero-rated" or not taxed and imports are subject to tax at the border. So with the DBCFT, exports are excluded from tax and imported goods and services are subject to income tax at the border when the sale is made to a final consumer. While the mechanism of tax involves border adjustments, if businesses incur DBCFT on the importation of goods, it will either be charged and recovered (or excluded), meaning that it is only the location of the final consumer that is relevant for the ultimate incidence (and burden) of the tax.[788]

Expenses (including labour costs) under the DBCFT are deductible in the jurisdiction in which they are incurred. This is at odds with indirect taxation regimes, which impose a tax on value-added rather than net profit and so include labour costs.[789]

8.2.2 Advantages and Disadvantages

There are numerous advantages to a DBCFT. The first, most obviously, is that a destination-based tax utilises a relatively immobile base; the residence jurisdiction of the final consumer. As this is the same base as that used for consumption taxes, it is already established as being relatively robustly tax-planning proof (when compared to corporate income taxes). The BEPS Action plans largely concerned shoring up the corporate income tax base with only a small component of Action 1 dealing with the indirect consequences of cross-border supplies of services and intangibles. This robustness against tax planning extends to encompass transactions that use transfer pricing (in particular, the under-pricing of goods and services from the country of origin) to pay tax at lower rates

---

[787] Where a business imports goods and services the imported revenues could be regarded as assessable income, with a deduction available subsequently, or simply excluded altogether.
[788] Again the similarity with VAT and GST systems will be obvious.
[789] See Auerbach et al Destination-Based Cash Flow Taxation, above n 780 at 14.

8.2 DESTINATION-BASED CASH FLOW TAXATION

on goods and services on their way through to the final country of destination. A DBCFT simply charges tax in the final destination country. This feature of a DBCFT also assists in eliminating the undesirable aspects of locating investment in tax-preferred jurisdictions. In other words, tax competition through tax preferences would be hugely reduced. Together with intragroup financing and transfer pricing, both referred to in Chapter 3, another major area of tax avoidance, the use of profit shifting through royalties paid for the use of hard to value but highly valuable intangibles, would also be eliminated. The purchase of the right to use the intangible (categorised as an imported service or possibly goods) would give rise to income for the owner of the intangible in the importing (highly taxed) jurisdiction (or it could be exempt from tax if purchased by a business), but in either case, the net effect of transferring profits from a high-tax jurisdiction to a low-tax jurisdiction, which is the current system, would not occur under a DBCFT.

Other advantages include its ability to substitute as a consumption tax, allowing those jurisdictions that have not, or cannot because of the political environment, implemente) such a tax to access this destination-based tax base. Using cash flow taxation also reduces the current preference that corporate income tax provides to debt financing (interest being deductible) against equity financing (dividends being non-deductible). A preference towards debt financing leads to both over-indebtedness[790] and considerable opportunities for using cross-border financing to shift profits.[791] There are other significant advantages, such as administrative convenience, fairness and economic efficiency.[792]

The disadvantages do exist but they would not be insurmountable if there was sufficient consensus for change. One of the major problems is the potential breach of international trade laws.

For a time in 2016, it appeared the United States was seriously considering introducing a version of a DBCFT.[793] Concerns were raised as to whether the adjustments taking place at the border would be in breach of WTO trade obligations.[794] The view of some commentators

---

[790] Ibid at 12.
[791] OECD Base Erosion and Profit Shifting "Action 4 Limitation on Interest Deductions" <www.oecd.org/tax/beps/beps-actions/action4/>.
[792] See chapter 2 (Evaluating the DBCFT) in Auerbach et al Destination-Based Cash Flow Taxation, above n 780 at 22.
[793] For a description of a version of the DBCFT see House Committee on Ways and Means *A Better Way for Tax Reform* (United States House of Representatives, June 2016).
[794] J Gravelle *The "Better Way" House Tax Plan: An Economic Analysis* (United States Congressional Research Service, CRS Report, 7-5700, 3 August 2017).

suggests this could be a major issue: "Many market countries, of course, would like to extract some of the rents earned on highly profitable products developed elsewhere. In the context of imports, this is the equivalent of the tariff even though it is denominated is an income tax."[795]

The draft American version of destination-based tax was said to be problematic from both a WTO and tax treaty perspective.[796] For various reasons, the draft legislation was expressly drafted on the basis that it was not in any way a value-added tax or sales tax, leading Avi Yonah and Clausing to say:[797]

> the business part of the proposal can be seen as a modified subtraction method VAT. If it were a VAT, it would not have problems with tax treaties or with the WTO rules. But since it declares itself not to be a VAT, and has at least one crucial feature that differs from a VAT, it may have problems with both.

More generally (that is, not specifically commenting on the US proposals), Wolfgang Schön analysed the border adjustments proposed under the DBCFT and concluded there were problems with the compatibility of these border adjustments and the WTO legislation in the context of exported goods.[798] On the other hand, Alice Pirlot considers that the problems of the DBCFT and the WTO rules are overstated.[799]

As long as the DBCFT is meant to be a direct tax on the corporate profit, the full deductibility of value transfers to other countries has to be regarded as an "exemption" which is not justified by the overall scheme of the income tax. It is, therefore, to be regarded as an "export subsidy" prohibited under Article 16 of the GATT and the ASCM.

---

[795] H Grubert "Destination-Based Income Taxes: A Mismatch Made in Heaven" (2015) 69 Tax L Rev 43 at 48. See also P Oosterhuis and A Parsons "Destination-Based Income Taxation: Neither Principled nor Practical?" (2018) 71 Tax L Rev 515 at 518, which suggests a similar view.

[796] R Avi-Yonah and K Clausing "Problems with Destination-Based Corporate Taxes and the Ryan Blueprint" (2017) 8(2) Colum J Tax Law 229.

[797] Ibid at 331.

[798] W Schön *Destination-Based Income Taxation and WTO Law: A Note* (Max Planck Institute for Tax Law and Public Finance Working Paper, 3 January 2016).

[799] A Pirlot "Don't Blame It on WTO Law: An Analysis of the Alleged WTO Law Incompatibility of Destination-Based Taxes" (University of Oxford Centre for Business Taxation, WP 19/16, November 2019) <https://ssrn.com/abstract=3551877> or <http://dx.doi.org/10.2139/ssrn.3551877>.

In addition to these WTO issues, there is also a problem with cash flow taxes if rates change over time and this can constrain the possibility of change for a country, resulting in political difficulties. For example, if corporate income tax rates decline then there is an even greater incentive to "frontload" expenditure. In contrast to traditional accounting, there can be more significant differences with rate changes if capital items are expensed into the tax base.

A theoretical issue exists in that countries providing purely the residence of consumers (previously referred to as the source country) obtain the benefit of the tax. In other words, the country of production, innovation and capital does not receive compensation for the provision of the infrastructure of creation. This is quite a fundamental change when you consider that the existing rules permit remote sales with all the tax going to the residence country and none to the country of source.

The concept of the benefit theory was previously discussed in Chapter 1, to justify the right of the source country to taxation in circumstances where there is significant usage of the market country's infrastructure.[800] In this context, the benefit theory can also be extrapolated to justify taxation for the country of origin (as well as destination) in respect of export sales. A sharing of taxing rights would seem the more logical allocation, rather than a "winner takes all" outcome.

Overall, it is hard to know exactly why the DBCFT system of international taxation has not received more traction and international acceptance. Countries are perhaps conservative with their revenue sources and somewhat suspicious of new ideas. It may be that there is too much change in the proposal and the possibility of political consensus is simply too remote.

8.2.3 Features Adopted by the 2020s Compromise

There are few elements from the DBCFT adopted into the OECD Secretariat's proposals. The most important one is the element of destination-based taxation in respect of remote sales, which is the principle adopted for Amount A in the allocation of income and the new nexus rules. Although this aspect of international taxation is better articulated in other methods we will evaluate (such as the residual profit allocation of income method), it was still an important contribution to the debate.

---

[800] See Section 1.4 "Justifying Source and Residence Taxation".

8.2.4 The Possibility of Continuing Reform in This Area

Although this is a somewhat radical and fundamental reform to the international tax system, significant benefits are arising from the focus on the destination-based tax base, together with the difficulty of tax planning against it, in sharp distinction to the well-documented problems of the current international tax regime. In the event of a failure of consensus in respect of the 2020s compromise, some, or all, of the elements of the DBCFT may yet emerge.

8.3 Residual Profit Allocation by Income

The second major alternative reform examined is that of residual profit allocation by income (RPAI). This method shares one of the characteristics of the DBCFT in that it also allocates taxable income to the place of destination. Like the DBCFT, RPAI has also been considered by the team chaired by Michael Devereux at the Oxford University Centre for Business Taxation.[801]

There are also similarities between this reform proposal and an earlier residual profit formulary apportionment proposal offered in 2009 by Avi-Yonah, Clausing and Durst.[802] Both the RPAI and the residual profit method proposed by Avi-Yonah and colleagues employ some similar concepts which it might be helpful to explain.

8.3.1 The Use of Outsourcing Methodology

Transfer pricing is the art of trying to determine an arm's-length standard (the true taxable income of a taxpayer dealing at arm's length with an uncontrolled taxpayer). Most transfer pricing analyses are constructed and do not rely on specific third-party transactions. Rather, they are based on publicly available data of the revenues, costs and profitability of companies that perform similar activities and functions to those performed by one party to a controlled transaction being analysed. Typically, the analysis begins by (i) finding many public companies performing similar activities and functions to the one being examined,

---

[801] M Devereux et al *Residual Profit Allocation by Income* (Oxford International Tax Group, WP 19/01, March 2019).

[802] R Avi-Yonah, K Clausing and M Durst "Allocating Business Profits for Tax Purposes: A Proposal to Adopt a Formulary Profit Split" (2009) 9 Fla Tax Rev 497.

(ii) determining the ratio of relevant operating costs or revenues to operating profits (after making appropriate adjustments), and (iii) the controlled transaction (the one being examined) is priced to yield a profit within a range of outcomes deemed appropriate in the circumstances.[803] Oosterhuis and Parsons[804] explain that this approach is applied most frequently in the United States using the comparable profits method.[805] In the OECD Transfer Pricing Guidelines, it is applied using the transactional net margin method (together these two methods are described as "the profit methods").[806]

The profit methods are transfer-pricing mechanisms which employ an "outsourcing" methodology.[807] Such outsourcing methodologies seek to determine an appropriate value or profit for activities and functions based on what a third party engaged in the same business but contracting with the multinational enterprise might be expected to earn.[808] A key aspect of this is that, because they are contracting with third parties, the outsourcing arrangements would reflect a level of risk that reflects the ongoing nature of the outsourced business but, importantly, that outsourcing business alone. In other words, they need to keep fully occupied in their own business, but the returns that they generate do not need to compensate them for the risk of the success (or failure) of the multinational's products and services. As a consequence, any intangibles held by these third-party outsource contractors would be likely to be minimal. Oosterhuis and Parsons explain the usefulness of this approach as follows:[809]

> It provides a useful benchmark for the value of specific types of functions and activities. It permits jurisdictions in which marketing, distribution, contract manufacturing, and even contract research activities take place to expect a reasonable and relatively stable level of income based on activities and functions independent of whether the overall business of the multinational group is prospering or struggling.

---

[803] For an excellent discussion on this see Oosterhuis and Parsons, above n 795 at 529.
[804] Ibid at 530.
[805] Under Regulation 1.482-5 of the United States Regulations.
[806] OECD *Transfer Pricing Guidelines for Multinational Enterprises and Tax Administration* (OECD Publishing, 2017) at 117.
[807] Ibid at 530.
[808] According to Oosterhuis and Parsons (above n 795), this outsourcing methodology is consistent with the comparable profits method frequently applied in the United States under Regulation 1.482-5 (b) (1) and also reflects the OECD, Transfer Pricing Methods 6 (2010).
[809] See Oosterhuis and Parsons, above n 803 at 530.

The problem is that multinational groups have used these transfer pricing techniques to allocate routine profits to the jurisdictions where many of the activities and functions have taken place and have separated out the residual profits (which, as described below, represent the total profits less these routine profits) to low or favourably taxed jurisdictions.[810] These transfer pricing techniques have resulted in the significant shifting of profits to low-tax jurisdictions, particularly where the multinational enterprise has hard to value intangibles.

The question is whether, using this outsourcing methodology, the residual profits can be allocated in ways which are less capable of manipulation or, using pejorative language, could result in a fairer sharing of the tax revenue?

8.3.2 The Original Residual Profit Formulary Apportionment Method

The residual profit formulary apportionment proposal, proposed by Avi-Yonah and colleagues, allocates global profits to entities undertaking functions and activities, based on actual costs plus a 7.5 per cent additional mark-up. The purpose of this pragmatic and fixed mark-up is to approximate routine returns to the entities operating in different jurisdictions. Consistent with the transfer pricing outsourcing methodology, the use of the fixed mark-up "is intended to minimise disputes while providing a modest allocation of profit based on locally incurred costs".[811]

Having identified the routine profits and allocated them (using this fixed mark-up) to each jurisdiction where costs have been incurred by entities which are undertaking functions and activities, there will be a resultant and residual global profit. The next stage of the method apportions these residual global profits to each jurisdiction based on their proportion of sales made to third-party customers.[812]

We now turn to the RPAI proposal, which shares many of the same features as the residual profit formulary apportionment proposal. In addition to the work done by the Oxford University group in developing the RPAI, other scholars have been working in this area.[813]

---

[810] Ibid.
[811] Ibid at 541, citing Avi-Yonah et al, above n 802.
[812] Avi-Yonah et al, above n 802 at 508–9.
[813] This is not a comprehensive list and is included only for further reference. In addition to the Avi-Yonah et al (n 802) and Oosterhuis and Parsons (n 795) papers referred to above, other valuable papers include J Andrus and P Oosterhuis "Transfer Pricing after BEPS: Where Are We and Where Should We Be Going" Tax Magazine (2017) 95(3) at

8.3.3 What Is the RPAI?

The RPAI method draws on the same principles as many other forms of residual profit allocation schemes. It also utilises standard transfer pricing techniques. The common basic methodology of residual profit allocation methods is to split routine profits from the non-routine (or residual) profits of the whole of the multinational entity. Routine profits are those assigned to the activities and functions performed by the elements of the multinational business in each jurisdiction. The routine profits are those allocated on an arm's-length basis for "non-unique contributions in relation to the controlled transactions in which it is engaged".[814] Accordingly, routine profit is "the return for the functions and activities undertaken by the business in a particular period, taking into account only the risks that would be faced by an independent contractor".[815] This is consistent with the outsourcing methodology discussed above (Section 8.3.1).[816] It is a return that could be said to be "quarantined" to the particular activities of the outsourced service provider. The OECD Transfer Pricing Guidelines provide an example of the application of the Residual Profit Split Method and describe the

---

89; R Avi-Yonah "The Rise and Fall of Arm's Length: A Study in the Evolution of U.S. International Taxation" (1995) 15 Va Tax Rev 89; R Avi-Yonah "Between Formulary Apportionment and the OECD Guide-lines: A Proposal for Reconciliation" (2010) 2 WTJ 3; R Avi-Yonah and I Benshalom "Formulary Apportionment – Myth and Prospects" (2011) 3 WTJ 317; R Couzin "Policy Forum: The End of Transfer Pricing?" (2013) 61 Can Tax J 159; M Devereux and J Vella "Taxing the Digitalised Economy: Targeted or System-Wide Reform" (2018) 4 BTR 301; D Elkens "The Case against Income Taxation of Multinational Enterprises" (2017) 36 Va Tax Rev 143; M Kane "Transfer Pricing, Integration and Synergy Intangibles: A Consensus Approach to the Arm's Length Standard" (2014) 6 WTJ 282; S Morse "Revisiting Global Formulary Apportionment" (2010) 29 Va Tax Rev 593; D Rosenbloom "Angels on a Pin: Arm's Length in the World" (2005) Tax Notes International 523; W Schön "International Tax Coordination for a Second-Best World" (2010) 2 WTJ 227; Wolfgang Schön "International Taxation of Risk" (2014) 68 BFIT 280; LE Schoueri "Arm's Length: Beyond the Guidelines of the OECD" (2015) 69 BFIT 690; R Vann "Reflections on Business Profits and the Arm's-Length Principle" (2003) in B Arnold, J Sasseville and E Zolt (eds) *The Taxation of Business Profits under Tax Treaties* (Canadian Tax Foundation, 2013) 133.

[814] For discussion on the issue of a residual analysis see OECD, above n 806 at 317.
[815] Devereux et al Residual Profit Allocation by Income, above n 801 at 22.
[816] Routine profits are therefore those which an independent third party would earn if their activities were outsourced to the multinational entity and it would include a return for the capital employed, risks incurred and any return for specialist activities and functions performed. It does not include any return for the overall risk (success and failure of the products or services) of the multinational business.

ascertaining of routine profits to identify the residual profit.[817] With the RPAI method, the identification of the quantum and identity of the recipient of routine profits are determined using existing transfer pricing rules and would not be based on the type of fixed mark-up proposed in the Avi-Yonah method discussed above (Section 8.3.2).

8.3.4 Routine and Residual Profits

By using existing transfer pricing methodology to determine the amount of routine profits, and who has derived them, the RPAI uses the existing rules in the area in which it is generally acknowledged that there are comparatively few problems.[818] The problem area, as discussed, is where the residual profits have been allocated.[819] The traditional transfer pricing methodologies allocate residual profit returns based on contractual arrangements within the group, enabling multinationals to allocate profits to low-tax jurisdictions where they have "organised" their contracts, activities and functions.

Here is the departure from orthodoxy, as the RPAI proposal allocates the residual profits to the jurisdiction based broadly on sales to the ultimate third-party customer. Oosterhuis and Parsons comment as follows:[820]

> Thus, the local market affiliate earns any residual returns from the products sold in its market. The system is essentially the same as that used by many multinationals today, except the entity earning any residual profit is mandated to be the local market affiliate, rather than a tax-favoured affiliate designated by the multinational group through contractual arrangements.

---

[817] OECD, above n 806 at 317 (Annex II to Chapter II).
[818] Devereux et al Residual Profit Allocation by Income, above n 801 at 4–5: "The RPA-I thus adheres to existing transfer pricing rules where they are generally deemed to work reasonably well (to calculate routine profit) and departs from these rules in the context of residual profit, where these rules are generally deemed to struggle." Having said that, the OECD Secretariat's Proposal describes the use of Amount B to determine a formula or fixed mark-up for administrative convenience and to lessen the possibility of disputes. Accordingly, any sense that the rules for calculating routine profit are not able to be improved upon should be examined in light of the criticism and rationale for the policy changes associated with Amount B – see Chapter 5 at Section 5.4.2 " Policy Rationale in Respect of Amount B".
[819] See the discussion on the allocation of residual profits by multinationals to low-tax jurisdictions in Section 8.3.1 "The Use of Outsourcing Methodology".
[820] Oosterhuis and Parsons, above n 795 at 543.

The residual profits could be allocated using one of two methods but both employ the concept of allocating the residual profit to the location of the gross residual income. A bottom-up approach allocates the income based on sales less the cost of goods sold, including any expenses incurred in the jurisdiction concerned. If expenses cannot be specifically allocated to sales then they are allocated based on the proportion that any country's gross residual income bears to the total gross residual income. A top-down approach takes the total residual profits of the whole multinational group (the total profits less routine profits) and allocates profit to each jurisdiction based on the residual gross income in each country.[821]

Very significantly, the RPAI proposal allocates these residual profits to the market destination jurisdictions, irrespective of whether they have a formal entity there or not. As the Oxford paper states: "The RPA-I would apply irrespective of the nature of the presence of the MNE in the destination country. Residual profit is allocated to destination countries whether there is a subsidiary, branch, or simply a remote sale there."[822] Under the RPAI, all the residual profits are allocated to the market country. The Oxford paper notes that revenue sharing with the country of origin can be achieved through the reallocation of revenue to the origin countries.[823]

8.3.5 Advantages and Disadvantages

The RPAI method deals with some of the current problems in the international tax system. By using a destination basis for the residual profits, it simultaneously deals with, first, some of the problems in transfer pricing relating to profit allocation and manipulation, and other profit-shifting devices. These include how multinationals have selected low-tax jurisdictions to be the contractual recipients of residual profits and the difficulty of correctly quantifying and allocating arm's-length profits in dealing with residual profits. That is, how much residual profit should be received, and by whom. This feature, it can be argued, results in less distortion of economic decisions for tax reasons.[824]

---

[821] Devereux et al Residual Profit Allocation by Income, above n 801 at 4.
[822] Ibid at 4.
[823] Ibid at 59.
[824] Ibid at 7.

Secondly, particularly in the case of individual consumers, it allocates income to a relatively immobile tax base (making the system much less susceptible to tax avoidance). By ignoring intercompany interest expenses and royalties, and by only allowing third-party interest expenses based on income or assets, the ability to shift profits is greatly reduced.[825]

Thirdly, it uses much of the existing transfer pricing outsourcing methodology to determine routine profits, which makes it explicable and understandable to practitioners. It is, therefore, less of a challenge to introduce.

Lastly, and this is not so much a technical reason as it is a potential perception held by many people, it results in the allocation of income to the market jurisdiction which may accord with common views of fairness. This is more likely to be true in the area of highly digitalised businesses and their ability to interact directly with the customers in the market jurisdiction. This feature enables the market jurisdiction to tax remote sales provided they have the requisite domestic and international taxing rights.

The disadvantages are that it is new, and it does challenge traditional concepts long held in the international tax framework. For example, allocating profits to the destination jurisdictions without changing the concept of permanent establishment is meaningless. Therefore, the method envisages substantial change to the framework, effectively abandoning the concept of a permanent establishment in certain circumstances.

Allocating all the income to the market (or destination) jurisdiction is also likely to be controversial to the point of being unacceptable from a political perspective. It is noted, however, that it is not essential that this is the outcome and that other mechanisms can be deployed to ensure an allocation of part of the income to the market jurisdiction and part to the jurisdiction of origin.

Lastly, there will be some degree of complexity both in the calculation of income (or losses) and in the possibility of double taxation.

8.3.6 *Features Adopted by the 2020s Compromise*

It will be readily apparent that the concepts put forward by the RPAI and other residual profit methods make a significant contribution to the

---

[825] Ibid at 64.

OECD Secretariat's Pillar One proposal. The starting point is that Amount A is based on the allocation of part of the residual profit to the market jurisdiction, using existing transfer pricing outsourcing methodology to calculate routine profits. There are some differences in that the OECD Secretariat's proposal uses the profit arising from consolidated accounts to calculate the residual profit and that only *part* of this profit is allocated to the market jurisdiction, whereas there is a rather more complete allocation of *all* the residual profits to the destination or market jurisdictions under the RPAI. At the time of writing, there are still some unresolved issues, such as exactly how to exclude residual profits allocated to the market jurisdictions from the current countries of origin and thus prevent double taxation. It is also a little unclear as to the exact scope of "consumer-facing" businesses which will be caught in the Amount A deemed income calculations. The RPAI proposal does not rely on a marketing intangible or user participation policy rationale (and more controversially, the concept of value creation which the OECD presents as the underlying concept justifying taxation) and it therefore applies to *all* businesses with a much simpler policy rationale, namely that the immobile consumer base is a tax base that can be readily identified and taxed.[826]

The move towards destination taxation inherent in the OECD Secretariat's Pillar One proposal as it relates to Amount A, and the creation of a new nexus rule, means that remote sales can be taxed under the OECD proposal but this is not the only contribution to tax policy by the residual profit methods proposed. A further feature to note is that the use of a standard mark-up in the residual profit formulary apportionment method proposed by Avi-Yonah and colleagues has similarities to the formulaic approach proposed in the concept of Amount B, representing a range of arm's-length profitability in the calculation of profits attributable to baseline marketing and distribution functions.

8.3.7 *The Possibility of Continuing Reform in This Area*

Even if the OECD Secretariat's Pillar One proposal cannot obtain the requisite consensus amongst a sufficient number of nations, it is suggested that there are several breakthrough features of residual profit

---

[826] M Devereux "The OECD Pillar One Proposal" (22 October 2019) Oxford University Centre for Business Taxation Blog <http://business-taxation.sbsblogs.co.uk/2019/10/22/the-oecd-pillar-one-proposal/>.

methodology which can, and will, be adopted in future international tax reform. The first is the movement towards destination taxation facilitated by the allocation of residual profits to the market or destination jurisdictions. The second is the use of outsourcing methodology to separate the routine and residual profits. This has been a common enough transfer pricing technique and a powerful tool which has been in the hands of multinational tax planners. When the possibility to allocate profits to a relatively immobile tax base arises, governments will see the strategically long-term implications for international tax policy and it will be difficult to slow or stop this reform even if that were desirable, which it is not. What needs to be considered, however, is that there is a requisite return to the country encouraging the development of capital and entrepreneurial risk and not just the presence of consumers. This would suggest the need for a sharing of tax rights, rather than just the allocation exclusively to the country of destination.

8.4 Formulary Apportionment

The possibility of designing the international tax system based on formulary apportionment has been considered for quite some time.[827] It is probably fair to say that it is a controversial proposal, with many commentators considering it as capable of manipulation as the separate entity/arm's-length international tax system we currently have.[828] Formulary apportionment is at the heart of the European Commission's 2011 proposal for a Common Consolidated Company Tax Base (CCCTB). Relaunched in 2016, the CCCTB remains an important reform to facilitate the harmonisation of the calculation of profits, reduction of compliance costs, and the restriction of tax planning opportunities.[829] Both the United States and Canada employ different variations of formulary apportionment in their tax systems at the state

---

[827] For example, see R Avi-Yonah and K Clausing *Reforming Corporate Taxation in a Global Economy: A Proposal to Adopt Formulary Apportionment* (The Brookings Institute, Discussion Paper 2007-08, 1 June 2007).

[828] Grubert and Altshuler, above n 779 at 704-6; J Clifton Fleming Jr, R Peroni and S Shay "Formulary Apportionment in the US International Income Tax System: Putting Lipstick on a Pig?" (2014) 36 Mich J Int'l L 1.

[829] See the European Commission's website: Common Consolidated Corporate Tax Base (CCCTB) <https://ec.europa.eu/taxation_customs/business/company-tax/common-con solidated-corporate-tax-base-ccctb_en>.

level.[830] Like the previous two methods of international income allocation (DBCFT and RPAI), formulary apportionment can be viewed through the lens of a destination-based tax depending on whether the allocation key used in the formula is exclusively sales based. This concept is explained by how formulary apportionment works.

8.4.1 How Does Formulary Apportionment Work?

Formulary apportionment is essentially the allocation of the total net profit of the multinational to each of the states where the profits have been created. The multinational is regarded as a single (or is often described as a "unitary") business. A unitary business is defined as the consolidated multinational entities where the parent corporation exercises legal and economic control over its subsidiaries.[831]

The unitary business is regarded as a single taxpayer, notwithstanding that it might operate through many different entities in many different jurisdictions. As a result of the status as a single taxpayer, its income is calculated by aggregating all worldwide revenue and worldwide expenses to determine an overall net profit. As the determination of profits by separate entities in different jurisdictions does therefore not take place, there is just a single worldwide net profit or income. This worldwide net income is apportioned to the different jurisdictions in which the multinational has done business according to various allocation keys, such as sales, or capital employed, or the number of employees (or their remuneration). Each jurisdiction then applies its tax rate to the income apportioned to it by the formula, determined using these allocation keys, and then collects the amount of resulting tax.[832]

Many states in the United States used an allocation key, which is known as the Massachusetts formula and which represents a calculation which takes equal consideration of the assets, payroll costs and sales undertaken in any one state, and divides them by the total assets, payroll costs and sales made by the multinational in aggregate.

---

[830] W Hellerstein "Formulary Apportionment in the EU and the US: A Comparative Perspective on the Sharing Mechanism of the Proposed Common Consolidated Corporate Tax Base" in A Dourado (ed) *Movement of Persons and Tax Mobility in the EU: Changing Winds* (International Bureau of Fiscal Documentation, 2013) 413.
[831] Avi-Yonah and Clausing, above n 827 at 12.
[832] Ibid at 12.

The trend for US states is to increasingly use an allocation key exclusively based on sales.[833] Avi-Yonah and Clausing proposed sales-only allocation in their proposal in 2007.[834] This proposal rejected the other elements of the allocation keys used in the Massachusetts formula because:[835]

> Observers have noted that an FA system creates an implicit tax on the factors used in the formula, thus discouraging assets and employment in high-tax locations. This formula also leaves unresolved issues concerning the treatment of intangible property, hard to value property, and so on.

8.4.2 Advantages and Disadvantages

As noted, the Massachusetts formula has two components of origin (assets and employee numbers or compensation) and one component based on destination (sales). The following discussion concerns a formulary apportionment based only on sales, which was the suggestion made by Avi Yonah and Clausing.

The problems with an apportionment based on assets and employment are myriad and well canvassed.[836] As Grubert and Altshuler noted, when the components of the formula are based on the factors of origin (capital/assets and employee numbers or compensation), then it is very easy for multinationals to manipulate these factors to achieve tax planning results very similar to the existing international tax system.[837] They assert from their modelling that multinationals will locate capital intensive investment to low tax jurisdictions and that, furthermore, the basis of payroll is even more capable of manipulation as an additional worker hired in a tax haven whose "wage just equals the marginal product contributes a bonus to the company" because the excess returns will be allocated to the low tax jurisdictions and "the company has an incentive to hire relatively unproductive workers in the low tax country".[838] This leads them to conclude more generally:[839]

---

[833] Grubert and Altshuler, above n 779 at 705.
[834] Avi-Yonah and Clausing, above n 827.
[835] Ibid at 12.
[836] See the discussion in Oosterhuis and Parsons, above n 795 at 516; Grubert and Altshuler, above n 779 at 705; J Roin "Can the Income Tax Be Saved? The Promise and Pitfalls of Adopting Worldwide Formulary Apportionment" (2008) 61 Tax Law Rev 169.
[837] H Grubert and R Altshuler "Formula Apportionment: Is It Better than the Current System and Are There Better Alternatives?" (2010) 63(4) Natn'l Tax J 1145.
[838] Grubert and Altshuler, above n 779 at 705
[839] Grubert and Altshuler, above n 837 at 1148.

8.4 FORMULARY APPORTIONMENT

one of the general problems with formula apportionment, the potential asymmetry between the determinants of taxable income and the items that enter the formula. Intangible assets that increase taxable income but are impossible to measure are one example. If payrolls are in the formula, this becomes a source of another asymmetry because wage costs are deductible from taxable income. Companies can exploit the asymmetry by adding labor intensive activities in the low tax country. They would go beyond the normal equality of the marginal productivity of labor with wage costs because of the benefits of the lower tax rate.

Overcoming the problem of the country of origin allocation keys by omitting them, Avi-Yonah and Clausing point to the advantages of using a destination basis in selecting sales as the sole allocation element in the formula, namely that customers are fundamentally an immobile tax base, and that multinationals are always incentivised to make sales.[840] This immobility of the tax base is the same positive feature discussed in the first two fundamental reform options.

Using a destination-based allocation key is an advantage to reduce the opportunities for tax planning, but even then concerns are raised by some commentators that using sales alone does not eliminate these opportunities. Grubert and Altshuler suggest that even a sales-only formulation can result in the diversion of income to low-tax jurisdictions. The company could do its marketing and distribution in low-tax jurisdictions while selling to third-party distributors in high-tax jurisdictions. The wholesale prices are included in the formula for high-tax jurisdictions sales while retail prices are included in the low-tax jurisdiction sales.[841] This will have the effect of redistributing taxable profit under the formula to the low-tax jurisdiction.

One of the most fundamental disadvantages is that the allocation of profits based on sales distributes all the multinational profits to the country of destination. This is quite a radical outcome in terms of income sharing between the factors of production and the market jurisdiction. This would make international consensus hard to achieve because there is no reward for risk or entrepreneurialism. As Devereux and his Oxford

---

[840] They also note that if some countries adopt a destination-based sales-only formula, then other countries will be incentivised to do the same, otherwise they will lose payroll or assets (capital) to those countries that do not include these allocation keys in their formula.

[841] Grubert and Altshuler, above n 779 at 705.

University Centre state: "This means that formulary apportionment is undeniably a simpler approach, which should reduce compliance and administrative costs. But it also risks what some might see as a disproportionate allocation of revenue away from jurisdictions in which activities take place."[842]

Last, but not least, the question of whether a destination-based tax can be regarded as a tariff remains unresolved. In Grubert's analysis, he was concerned that market countries imposing a tax on highly profitable products developed elsewhere would have a problem with trade laws, suggesting "in the context of imports, this is the equivalent of a tariff even though it is denominated as an income tax".[843]

8.4.3 Features Adopted by the 2020s Compromise

There are two features adopted by the 2020s compromise that are consistent with formulary apportionment based on sales. These are that the starting point for the allocation of profits to the market or source country is a computation based on worldwide profitability. The second is the allocation of profits to the market or destination jurisdiction.

As indicated above (Section 8.4.1), it is not just the residual profits, but all profits are allocated to the market jurisdiction under formulary apportionment based on sales. Accordingly, the residual profit allocation based on income is a much closer analogy to the OECD Secretariat's formulation of Amount A.

8.4.4 The Possibility of Continuing Reform in This Area

It is possible to regard the three destination-based methods as parts of an evolutionary process. Viewed in that light, they are all contributors to the potential reform of the international tax system by allocating taxation rights and tax to the market jurisdiction. The relative simplicity of formulary apportionment is a strength, but it would seem problematic that all profits are allocated to the market jurisdiction. Reform in this area might need to be linked to the allocation of taxing rights to the jurisdiction of entrepreneurial activity and capital investment to achieve international consensus.

---

[842] Devereux et al Residual Profit Allocation by Income, above n 801 at 56.
[843] Grubert, above n 795 at 48.

8.5 Expanding the Concept of Permanent Establishment

In many respects, reform to the concept of "permanent establishment" (in some form) was the most likely change in the international tax framework to meet the challenges of the digital economy. This is because much of the existing framework could be retained, although some key concepts needed changing. There is a portmanteau nature to the idea of reform to the permanent establishment concept. It varies from a systematic change to the definition of permanent establishment and the allocation of taxing rights, which is discussed first, then, secondly, to addressing the problem in other ways, such as individual countries issuing declarations or proclamations about how they will interpret the concept of a permanent establishment, or, lastly, introducing domestic anti-avoidance legislation such as diverted profit taxes and other multinational avoidance legislation. All three of these approaches have been very much a part of the international tax scene over the last few years and in many respects, they reflect an increasing frustration on behalf of governments and tax administrations to the challenges of digital businesses.

8.5.1 A New PE Nexus

As discussed in Chapter 5,[844] the third proposal of the Inclusive Framework's Public Consultation Document, Addressing the Tax Challenges of the Digitalisation of the Economy[845] looked at changing the definition of permanent establishment. The idea of a significant economic presence constituting a permanent establishment had already been discussed in some detail and it was part of the *Action 1 Final Report, Addressing the Tax Challenges of the Digital Economy*.[846]

This proposal focuses on "expanding" the concept of what constitutes a taxable presence in a jurisdiction away from the traditional permanent establishment to incorporate features unique to the digital economy. The current PE definition focuses on physical factors as discussed in Chapter 3, especially Sections 3.2.2–3.2.4 (although it does include

---

[844] See Section 5.2.4 "The 'Significant Economic Presence' Proposal".
[845] OECD *Addressing the Tax Challenges of the Digitalisation of the Economy* (OECD Base Erosion and Profit Shifting Project, Public Consultation Document, 13 February 2019) at 9–17.
[846] OECD *Addressing the Tax Challenges of the Digital Economy, Action 1-2015 Final Report* (OECD/G20 Base Erosion and Profit Shifting Project, 2015) at 107 [7.6.1].

deemed PEs arising from contractual relationships such as dependent agents). Instead, this proposal focuses on "factors that evidence a purposeful and sustained interaction with the jurisdiction via digital technology and other automated means" which could constitute a "significant economic presence" when combined with revenue generated on a sustained basis. All of this leads the OECD to consider whether there should be the new concept of a PE involving factors from the digital economy.[847]

In early 2015, Peter Hongler and Pasquale Pistone published a blueprint for a revised concept of permanent establishment suggesting some of these digital factors.[848] Examining their proposal is a good way to demonstrate this concept because it is illustrative of the type of suggested reform in this area, albeit that the Hongler and Pistone proposal is a very good example, being well constructed from both a theoretical and practical perspective.

8.5.2 How Does the Revised PE Concept Work?

When dealing with the taxation of business profits and the concept of a PE, it is necessary to address two major issues. The first issue is the question of nexus: what is the requisite nexus to establish the threshold of a taxable presence or PE. The second issue relates to allocating income to this taxable presence and establishing the taxing rights to facilitate taxation.

Hongler and Pistone suggested that this new digital PE nexus should consist of four main elements or requirements: (i) digital services; (ii) user threshold; (iii) a certain time threshold; and (iv) a *de minimis* revenue threshold. When these requirements were met the new PE threshold was reached, justified by the idea of a "digital presence".

From a theoretical perspective, this new nexus finds its inspiration in a "revised theoretical framework for the traditional sourcing theory, reflects the benefit theory, and reduces the existing bias in the tax treatment of cross-border digital and physical business activities with a view to achieving a broader consistency between the two categories".[849]

Their envisaged amendments to the current PE definition, by expanding the new PE definition through the incorporation of the four

---
[847] OECD, above n 845, [51] at 16.
[848] P Hongler and P Pistone *Blueprints for a New PE Nexus to Tax Business Income in the Era of the Digital Economy* (IBFD, Working Paper 20, January 2015).
[849] Ibid at 2–3.

elements discussed above (i.e. digital services etc.), makes it clear that only certain e-commerce enterprises which are part of the digital economy would be affected by the changes. As a result, non-digital businesses would be dealt with under the existing rules, creating quite a lot of pressure on the definition of "what is digital?".

While the proposals would establish a new, expanded definition of PE, as indicated, another key issue that would have to be addressed is the allocation of income. Large multinationals which do not have a physical presence in the jurisdiction in which they are undertaking remote sales do not have to allocate income to the market jurisdiction under the current transfer pricing guidelines of the OECD.[850] As there are no traditional risks and functions of the enterprise associated with the digital PE, no profit can be allocated to the foreign PE without a further amendment.

After considering various options, Hongler and Pistone suggest the potential application of a modified profit-split method with an upfront income allocation of a partial profit to the market jurisdiction to determine the taxable income to be allocated to the PE jurisdiction. Their discussion considers that the state of origin creates value, and therefore "a certain income should be taxed" together with the market jurisdiction because "the demand side is also value creating".[851]

They refer to the work of de Wilde to suggest that the output side (i.e. the demand side of the economic equation) should also be considered as a part of the value creation proposition.[852] From Chapter 1,[853] it will be remembered that the conclusions reached on a theoretical basis in this book are similar to the suggestions from Hongler and Pistone. When looking at value creation (and recognising that many academics regard this as a vexed question),[854] Maartin de Wilde, in an article after his PhD thesis, asks the question: "If the demand side is relevant for creating income, why then does international tax law currently take no account of this when apportioning companies' international profits? The answer would seem to be that this is simply how things have evolved as "a 'product of history'".[855]

---

[850] Ibid at 32.
[851] Ibid at 33.
[852] M de Wilde "Sharing the Pie: Taxing Multinationals in a Global Market" (PhD thesis, Erasmus University Rotterdam, 2015) at 303.
[853] See also the discussion in Section 1.5.5 "The Relationship between Value Creation and the Existing International Tax Framework".
[854] See Section 1.5 "The Benefit Theory and Its Relationship to Value Creation".
[855] M de Wilde "Tax Jurisdiction in a Digitalizing Economy: Why 'Online Profits' Are so Hard to Pin Down" (2015) 43(12) Intertax 796 at 798.

As a consequence of this, Hongler and Pistone argue "that the market jurisdiction should have the right to tax at least parts of the income of an enterprise and the cross-border income allocation should partly rely on a destination-based key".[856]

They then go on to suggest that income should be allocated with one-third of the total profit going to the market jurisdictions (being a division of the global profits allocated based on sales amongst all of the jurisdictions that qualify under the requirements for the new digital deemed PE) and two-thirds being allocated under existing transfer pricing concepts (to the country(ies) of origin). They concede that this is a matter of negotiation and that further economic studies could produce different outcomes.[857]

The Hongler and Pistone suggestion is not completely new, Georg von Schanz suggested something similar in the nineteenth century when he developed the concept of "economic allegiance" and suggested that the state of source had the right to tax three-quarters of the income on international trade, leaving the state of residence the residual one-quarter.[858]

8.5.3 Advantages and Disadvantages of the Expanded PE Method

One of the advantages of the expanded PE method is that it does go some way in addressing the concerns about vanishing business profits earned by remote sales made by digital businesses. This is one of the major challenges posed by the digital economy. Expanding the PE definition directly addresses this challenge. In the same way as it is necessary for Amount A, it is not just a case of establishing a new nexus threshold; taxing rights must be changed as well so that the destination or market jurisdiction can tax income in respect of the (remote) digital transactions. The significant economic presence expansion of the PE definition, accompanied by a reallocation of taxing rights, is therefore certainly one way to address the vanishing profits challenge.

There is also an attraction in using the amended PE definition to establish the nexus because it is an extension of a familiar concept, namely the century-old taxation of business profits when the PE

---

[856] Hongler and Pistone, above n 848 at 33.
[857] Ibid at 34.
[858] See the discussion in Section 1.4.4 "The Renaissance of the Benefit Theory".

threshold is established. The change could be seen as more incremental, but still a direct response to the digital challenge.

Some of the disadvantages include the major problem that the solution is very focused on the digital economy alone. The OECD has already suggested that the solution to the challenges to the digital economy could not be limited to the digital economy. The reason given for this is summed up by the International Monetary Fund in its report, which records that the only consensus in the initial OECD/G20 Report[859] on digitalisation and taxation "was that attempts to isolate for special treatment a 'digital economy' (or 'digital activities') are misplaced, given how pervasive these technologies are, and so unpredictable is their future development".[860]

Another issue (which may not necessarily be a disadvantage) is that it is the *whole* of the multinational profits which are split so that one-third is allocated to the destination market. This is similar, at least conceptually, to the formulary apportionment by sales method. In other words, under the Hongler and Pistone method *all* of the profits are split (and one-third allocated to the market jurisdiction), which has similarities to the formulary apportionment by sales outcomes (except all of the profits are allocated to the market jurisdiction).

There is also a significant difference between this profit split methodology and the residual income profit split by income developed by the Oxford University International Tax Group. Under the RPAI method, all of the *residual* profits are split. In other words, the RPAI method separates out the routine profits before doing the profit-split allocations.

8.5.4 Features Adopted by the 2020s Compromise

The features of the expanded PE concept adopted in the OECD Secretariat's Proposal relate to taxation on a destination basis to the extent that part of the worldwide profits on transactions made by digital businesses are taxed in the destination state. At a fundamental level, the concepts are quite similar.

The OECD Secretariat's Proposal (as amended in January 2020) does differ in some respects, the nexus is established by the presence of "in-scope" revenue derived over some time and commensurate with the size

---

[859] OECD, above n 846.
[860] IMF *Policy Paper: Corporate Taxation in the Global Economy* (International Monetary Fund, Washington DC, 10 March 2019) [20] at 14.

of the market. The revenue threshold is the only test for certain digitally focused and automated businesses, whereas with consumer-facing businesses additional factors are required.

The OECD Secretariat's Proposal also focuses on the residual profits (and not the total profits) being allocated to market jurisdictions.

8.5.5 The Possibility of Continuing Reform in This Area

The so-called Unified Approach does bring together many aspects of residual profit allocation, formulary apportionment and significant economic presence. If the OECD methodology under the Unified Approach does not achieve consensus then many of the component parts may survive to modify and reallocate taxing rights.

8.5.6 Establishing the PE Nexus by "Interpretation and Declaration"

Another approach which has been taken by some states is to define their approach to the taxation of the digital economy and to issue interpretation statements or "official circulars" on their view of what income is attributable to a permanent establishment in their jurisdiction. The best examples of these might be the approach taken in countries such as Israel and India. This approach suggests that the existing rules are sufficiently broad to enable taxation of the digital economy without amendment to the existing framework. In other words, these jurisdictions refuse to accept that the current international framework does not permit them to tax remote sales made by certain types of highly digitalised businesses.

In examining this type of approach, we focus first on the Israeli approach to this problem as it is illustrative of the type of response involving primarily interpretation. The Indian approach also involves interpretation but the situation is a little more complicated with the introduction of domestic legislation, and a history of a different approach to the apportionment of taxable income related to business transactions and the recognition that the demand side of a transaction should lead to profits for the jurisdiction of destination.

The Israeli Tax Authorities (ITA) originally issued a draft circular in April 2015 but this was followed up by an official circular ("Circular") issued in the same month of the following year.[861] The background to the

---

[861] The Israeli Tax Authority "Circular No. 4/2016" (11 April 2016).

Israeli approach arose from the work done by the OECD but the ITA uses the concept of a significant economic presence "even though this concept was dropped from the final BEPS recommendations".[862]

8.5.7 How Does This Work?

(a) Israel

The ITA took what some might describe as an aggressive stance on the question of what constitutes a PE for the taxation of foreign corporations that provide services (mostly through the Internet) to Israeli resident customers. The head of the ITA at the time, Moshe Asher, explained it was a case of obtaining information and then using the professional, legal and international parts of the authority to raise assessments.[863] The expectation is that such disputes would be litigated, through the Tel Aviv District Court and with the potential of an appeal to the Supreme Court. The possibility of settlement always exists with litigation.

For treaty countries (countries with which Israel has a double tax treaty), the Circular provides that if a company has a significant digital presence in Israel and conducts activity on the ground, then that may constitute a PE in Israel (even if the activity is of a preparatory or auxiliary character only, such that it would normally be excluded under the OECD Article 5 (4)). The ITA may determine that a foreign supplier has a significant digital presence in Israel based on the following:[864]

- The foreign supplier has a significant number of contracts for online (internet-based) services with Israeli customers;
- The foreign supplier's online services are highly used by Israeli customers;
- The foreign supplier's website has been adapted for use by Israeli customers in terms of language, currency, etc.;
- A high volume of web traffic between Israel and the foreign supplier's website/services;
- Other factors, such as representatives of the foreign supplier performing activities in Israel (such as sourcing customers or collecting

---

[862] Ernst & Young "Israeli Tax Authorities Publish Official Circular on Internet Activities of Foreign Companies in Israel" (15 April 2016) at 1.
[863] The author was grateful to meet with Moshe Asher in Tel Aviv in April 2019 and to discuss the ITA's thinking at that time.
[864] The author is grateful to use this information provided by Ernst & Young, above n 862 at 1. The circular is of course in Hebrew.

information, engaging in and maintaining ongoing contact with the Israeli customers, providing substantial marketing and support services); and
- An individual is formally employed by an Israeli resident company, but is managed by the foreign supplier and/or the foreign supplier is involved in the recruitment and setting of employment terms.

For non-treaty countries, the activities of a foreign company of a similar kind may give rise to a taxable presence in Israel under domestic law. That is, the ITA will take the view that there is a taxable presence in Israel under domestic law and the income is generated from the business activity conducted in Israel. As a clear statement, the Circular pronounces that a foreign company might have a taxable activity in Israel even without any physical presence there.

The determination as to whether a significant digital presence exists will be made on a case-by-case basis and will involve consultation with the ITA. For this purpose, the ITA is authorised to demand information from foreign digital suppliers and related companies in Israel.

Where a PE is deemed to exist, the ITA will allocate profits following the OECD Report on the attribution of profits to permanent establishments. This seems to have occurred. In early 2019 the *Times of Israel* reported that the ITA had presented technology multinationals with substantial tax assessments.[865] A spokesperson told the *Times* that "tax assessments have been issued during this year to several multinational firms and others will be issued shortly". The newspaper noted that Google, Facebook and Apple all have operations in Israel with Google's income estimated to be NIS 560 million per year (US$151 million).

(b) India

In some respects, India seems to be pursuing a somewhat similar approach, albeit with subtle variation. The government of India (or more accurately the Committee of the Central Board of Direct Taxation – "the Committee") in 2019 released a draft proposal which looks at both the nexus issue and, equally importantly, the question of attribution of profits.[866] India is not a member of the OECD and is not bound by

---

[865] "Multinational Tech Giants Get Slapped with Israeli Tax Bills" *Times of Israel* (online ed, Jerusalem, 6 January 2019).

[866] Committee to Examine the Issues Related to Profit Attribution to Permanent Establishment in India and Amendment of Rule 10 of Income Tax Rules, 1962 *Proposal for Amendment of Rules for Profit Attribution to Permanent Establishment*

8.5 CONCEPT OF PERMANENT ESTABLISHMENT

OECD conventions and commentary.[867] Under the Finance Act of 2018, India legislated for a taxable nexus based on significant economic presence. This Act established that if a foreign entity breached a turnover threshold for revenue in India and a threshold level of the number of Indian users, it would be sufficient for it to have a significant economic presence and therefore prima facie a domestic business income tax obligation.

The PE provisions in India's DTAs are broadly similar to the UN model and the Committee observed that under these provisions, profits are to be attributed to a PE as if it were a "distinct and separate entity",[868] using either: (i) a direct accounting method based on the separate accounts of the PE or (ii) an indirect apportionment method under Indian domestic legislation (Rule 10), where detailed and accurate accounts are not available. One of the main implications of the 2010 Authorised OECD Approach (AOA) changes is that in cases where business profits cannot readily be determined based on accounts, income now has to be determined by undertaking a functions, assets and risks (FAR) analysis, ignoring the demand-side factors. The Committee notes that India has consistently objected to the FAR-based AOA approach:[869]

> The Committee also observes that India has documented its disagreement with the revised Article 7 by not only reserving its right not to include it in its tax treaties, but also documented the rejection of the approach inherent in it. Further, India has consistently communicated and shared its view that since business profits are dependent on sale revenue and costs, and since sale revenue depends on both demand and supply, it is not appropriate to attribute profits exclusively on the basis of function, assets and risks (FAR) alone. Lastly, since the revised Article 7 recommended by OECD since 2010 onwards has not been incorporated in any of the Indian tax treaties, the question of applying AOA for attribution of profits does not arise.

Instead of the AOA approach, the Committee favours a "fractional apportionment approach" based on the apportionment of profits derived from India and which recognises the importance of the demand-side contribution to profit. In the Committee's opinion, profits calculated under the fractional apportionment approach can be assessed under

(Central Board of Direct Taxes, Department of Revenue, Ministry of Finance, Government of India, 2019).
[867] See Deloitte and tax@hand "CBDT Committee Releases Draft Report on Attribution of Income to PEs" (3 May 2019).
[868] Proposal for Amendment of Rules, above n 866 at [169] on 73.
[869] Ibid at [110], on 54.

Article 7(4) of India's DTAs and Rule 10. The Committee proposes a profit-apportionment method based on three factors, each given equal weight: sales (representing demand) and employee costs and assets (representing supply). The method would be applied in three steps:

1. Determine the profits derived from the Indian operations, defined as revenue derived from India multiplied by the global operating profit (EBITDA) margin. Where the enterprise incurs global losses or its global operating profit margin is less than 2 per cent, the profits derived from India will be deemed to be 2 per cent of the revenue derived from India.
2. Apportion the profits from Indian operations of the enterprise to the SEP based on the three factors of sales (33 per cent weighting), employee costs and assets (67 per cent aggregate weighting).
3. Deduct from the resulting profits any profits that already have been taxed in India.

The Committee observes that because the significant economic presence (SEP) or nexus provisions introduced by the Finance Act, 2018 trigger tax implications when a prescribed user/revenue threshold is breached, it is important to clarify the principles of profit attribution to SEP for digitalised businesses. For emerging business models, where users significantly contribute to an enterprise's profits, the Committee proposes to include users as a fourth apportionment factor, in addition to sales, employee costs and assets. The Committee proposes a 10 per cent weighting for users where the business model involves low or medium user intensity and 20 per cent for models with high user intensity.

The incorporation of a fractional apportionment method in Rule 10 as recommended by the report would enable the tax position of an Indian SEP of a non-resident entity to be determined where there is no tax treaty between India and the non-resident's jurisdiction, but where a DTA applies the position is less clear.

Most of India's DTAs provide for the attribution of income to a PE on the basis that the PE is a "single, distinct and separate" enterprise, while also stating that the treaty does not preclude attribution to a PE based on a country's "customary approach". Deloitte notes that: "In India, whether the customary approach is the apportionment-based Rule 10 or the arm's length principle requirement of transfer pricing legislation introduced in 2001 and extended by CBDT circulars 14/2001 and 5/2004 is a matter for debate."[870]

---

[870] See Deloitte and tax@hand, above n 870.

Deloitte suggests that the proposed inclusion of market factors in the concept of income attribution to a PE would require international agreement and changes to India's DTAs.[871] If treaty partners do not accept the approach, this may result in double taxation and a whole lot of other consequences arising from international disputes.

8.5.8 Advantages and Disadvantages

In the case of both Israel and India, the respective governments and tax administrations are taking an approach to the interpretation of their tax laws and treaties to expand the ambit of the traditional concepts of permanent establishment and to seek to impose tax on digital transactions and profits. Both countries, in their different ways, are refusing to accept the traditional view that the existing international framework and the concept of the permanent establishment are not sufficiently broad to tax highly digitalised businesses, and in particular multi-sided platforms. Both Israel and India have widely publicised their stances and given their reasons for the approach that they have taken. In the case of India, it represents a view which they have articulated for some time.

Taking an aggressive approach to the taxation of highly digitalised businesses is controversial. This is not to say that such an approach is wrong but it must be conceded that it is unilateral in the sense that other states which are parties to their double tax conventions would be unlikely to agree with the approach. If there is a difference in view there will be significant consequences in terms of double taxation when the jurisdictions in which the multinational is a resident do not take the same approach. There are several major concerns. The first is uncertainty. The position of an expanded PE for digital transactions in both Israel and India is made clear by the revenue authorities but it is unclear at this stage whether it will receive approval by the courts. Until these matters have been litigated, with all the expense and uncertainty associated with that, it is hard to know what the correct legal position for tax purposes is. This makes investment decisions hard for businesses and it also is difficult for the revenue authorities in terms of decisions of assessment/ penalties and collection of tax. The second concern, as already highlighted, is double taxation. Will any tax paid in Israel or India be available

---

[871] Ibid.

as a foreign tax credit (or the income exempt) under the rules of the jurisdiction in which the multinational is resident?

In conclusion, like digital services taxes which are discussed in Chapter 9, unilateral approaches to taxation by countries run the risk of causing significant problems to international trade by causing costly disputes, exposing businesses to the risk of double taxation which is not able to be relieved, and generally are seen as undesirable.

8.5.9 Using Domestic Legislation to Both Buttress and Expand the PE Concept

Another form of unilateral action pursued by other countries is the use of specific and targeted domestic legislation designed to address arrangements intended to avoid the PE concept. Examples of this can be found in the United Kingdom, with its "diverted profits tax" (DPT), Australia with its version of the DPT and New Zealand with its amendments of a new PE anti-avoidance rule and new source rules.

This approach differs from that used by countries which are discussed in Section 8.4.2. Rather than sticking to the interpretation of the law as Israel and India have done, this approach involves passing domestic law with the express intention of expanding the taxing rights beyond the conventional definitions of PE and possibly nexus.

These new domestic laws have some common features, such as an overall anti-avoidance focus and, in the case of both Australia and the United Kingdom, a diverted profits tax. The UK and Australian types of diverted profits taxes have two elements or limbs which are both designed to counter profit shifting. One limb counters arrangements that exploit tax mismatches between related parties which lack economic substance.[872] The second aspect, discussed here, is the limb or part of the legislation aimed at arrangements that circumvent the PE rules. In other words, it is domestic legislation designed to overcome structures which have avoided establishing a PE.

---

[872] An example of this is when "profits are taken out of a UK subsidiary by way of a large tax deductible payment to an associated entity in a tax haven", see the website description of the DBT offered by Pinsent Masons at <www.pinsentmasons.com/out-law/guides/diverted-profits-tax-regime>.

It is beyond the scope of this enquiry to look at the "effective tax mismatch outcomes" and the "insufficient economic substance condition" contained in the diverted profits charge in section 80 of the Finance Act 2015 (UK), or the somewhat similar Australian "sufficient economic substance test" contained in the Australian DPT.

One of the earliest (and therefore most controversial) examples of this approach was that taken by the United Kingdom. When a DPT was announced in December 2014 this preceded the issuance of the Final Reports produced through the BEPS project. This was described as both "a surprise to the business community" and "a unilateral move that seem to jump the gun on BEPS work in order to protect the UK tax base".[873]

8.5.10 How Does This Work?

(a) United Kingdom's DPT Limb Concerning PEs

The DPT aims to "deter and counteract the diversion of profits from the UK by large groups that ... seek to avoid creating a UK permanent establishment that would bring a foreign company into the charge to UK Corporation Tax".[874] The UK legislation[875] does not expand the concept of a PE but imposes a tax in circumstances where a person (namely the "avoided" PE) carries on their activities in the United Kingdom. Briefly, the tax applies where a non-UK resident company supplies goods or services to customers resident in the United Kingdom without a PE (the avoided PE) and it is reasonable to assume that the activity of the avoided PE (or the non-UK resident company) is designed to avoid the creation of the UK PE. This can occur even if the avoided PE is designed to secure commercial or other objectives, but various exemptions and thresholds can prevent the application of the DPT.[876]

According to Avi-Yonah, the DPT was aimed at structures such as Google's Double Irish Dutch Sandwich and to support this he points to the similarity between that structure and Example 3 of the guidance published by HMRC.[877] In this example, HMRC has a European company (say Irish) which books all the sales contracts to UK customers. A subsidiary company located in the United Kingdom provides sales and

---

[873] S Wasimi, J Nario and K Bertram "Diverted Profits Tax: UK, Australian and New Zealand Approaches" (24 July 2017) Tax Notes Int'l 349 at 349.
[874] Her Majesty's Revenue and Customs *Diverted Profits Tax: Guidance* (December 2018).
[875] Finance Act 2015 (UK), s 86.
[876] Wasimi et al, above n 873 at 353. For example, section 86 does not apply if the total UK sales revenue of the foreign company does not exceed £10 million or if the value of UK-related expenses does not exceed £1 million. Also, agents of independent status are exempted from the avoided PE limb of the DPT.
[877] R Avi-Yonah "Three Steps Forward, One Step Back? Reflections on "Google Taxes' and the Destination-Based Corporate Tax" (2016) 2 Nordic Tax Journal 69 at 70. See Example 3 at page 40 in Her Majesty's Revenue and Customs, above n 874.

services to support those UK customers of the Irish company. Profits allocated to the subsidiary company are minimal, being based on a mark-up percentage over the costs incurred (cost plus profits for the services provided).[878] This arrangement set out in Example 3 enables the European company to avoid a UK PE. Thus, the UK PPT applies because (i) the European company is carrying on a trade, (ii) the UK resident subsidiary is carrying on activities in the United Kingdom in connection with the supply of goods or services by the European company, and (iii) it is reasonable to assume that the activity of both the UK subsidiary and the European company was designed to avoid the European company being subject to UK Corporation tax. There are also threshold requirements eliminating small and medium-sized enterprises from the net.[879]

In analysing whether an assumption is "reasonable", HMRC advises:[880]

> For it to be reasonable to assume that activity is designed to ensure that the foreign company is not carrying on a trade through a UK PE there will be some degree of contrivance in the arrangements present in the accounting period, irrespective of the accounting period in which that contrivance was designed. They will differ in some material way to the arrangements that we would expect to have been made if there had been no considerations around the PE threshold.

The effective tax rate for the DPT is 25 per cent and it is for the taxpayer to advise HMRC that they are potentially within the scope of the rules. Failure to notify could result in penalties.

(b) Australia and Its Multinational Anti-Avoidance Law (MAAL)

Shortly after the United Kingdom announced its DPT, the Australian government announced the MAAL, which was designed to "to counter the erosion of the Australian tax base by multinational entities using artificial or contrived arrangements to avoid the attribution of business

---

[878] Although it is irrelevant for the PE component of the structure, profits in the Irish company are shifted to a Dutch company through the payment of a royalty without withholding tax (because of the Ireland–Netherlands double tax agreement) and then further moved by royalty to another Irish company which is regarded as being neither subject to Irish tax (as it is a resident of a tax haven) nor subject to withholding tax (because the Netherlands does not tax outbound royalties).

[879] Taxation (International and Other Provisions) Act 2010 (UK), s 172.

[880] Her Majesty's Revenue and Customs, above n 874.

8.5 CONCEPT OF PERMANENT ESTABLISHMENT

profits to Australia through a taxable presence in Australia".[881] This was not a new tax but an amendment to the Australian general anti-avoidance legislation (GAAR).[882] The MAAL was effective from the beginning of the 2016 calendar year, while a second limb focusing on diverted profits (like the United Kingdom's version of the DPT) applied from 1 July 2017 (the beginning of that income tax year in Australia).[883]

The threshold for the application of the MAAL is significantly higher than that in the United Kingdom, with the Australian MAAL and DPT applying to significant global entities (where the global parent or a consolidated group has an annual global income of at least AU$1 billion). Like the United Kingdom, however, the MAAL is aimed at structures like the "Double Irish Dutch Sandwich". This is made clear by an example (example 3.9) given in the Explanatory Memorandum, which describes effectively the original Google structure, and concludes that it would be subject to the anti-avoidance legislation.[884] This anti-avoidance rule will apply in the following circumstances: (i) a significant global entity, has (ii) entered into or carried out a scheme (or part thereof) for a principal purpose of enabling a taxpayer to obtain a tax benefit (i.e. "the purpose test"), or to obtain both the tax benefit and reduce at least one of its foreign tax liabilities, and (iii), under the scheme, a foreign entity makes supplies for, and derives income from, Australian customers, where activities are undertaken by an Australian entity (or a PE) in Australia directly or in connection with the supplies, and that Australian entity is an associate of or commercially dependent on the foreign entity, and (iv) some or all of the income is not attributable to an Australian PE of the foreign entity.

In example 3.9 of the Explanatory Memorandum, the "purpose test" will be met if obtaining the tax benefits constitutes a principal purpose for the foreign entity structuring its affairs because of the following key factors:

- in practice, and contrary to its services agreement, most of the activities that are undertaken to bring about the contracts for supply are undertaken by the Australian subsidiary;

---

[881] *Tax Laws Amendment (Combating Multinational Tax Avoidance) Bill 2015: Explanatory Memorandum* (The Parliament of the Commonwealth of Australia, House of Representatives) at 7.
[882] Contained in Part IVA of the Income Tax Assessment Act 1936 (Aust).
[883] The multinational tax avoidance rules are contained in the Income Tax Assessment Act 1936 (ITAA 1936), s 177DA.
[884] See Example 3.9 in Tax Laws Amendment, above n 881 at 43.

- the parent company, a significant global entity, does little to contribute to the solicitation of customers, the identification of customer needs to the supply, negotiating the details of the supply to be provided and the contractual terms under which the supply will be provided, optimising the sales provided to customers in Australia and finalising the contracts;
- the parent company employs only a small number of staff and they do not have the necessary capability or knowledge to undertake any of the functions necessary for bringing about contracts with customers in Australia, nor do they undertake such functions with customers in Australia;
- the division of activities between the parent company and the Australian subsidiary appears contrived to avoid creating a permanent Australian establishment;
- income from the supply to Australian customers is being returned to a no-tax jurisdiction in which little real economic activity occurs; and
- royalty income paid by the parent company to a related company based in a tax haven in connection with the scheme is not subject to royalty withholding tax in Australia because the parent company does not have an Australian permanent establishment.

As a result of the scheme, the foreign entity avoids income from the supply of software to Australian customers being attributed to a permanent establishment in Australia. The related tax haven entity also avoids a royalty withholding tax liability.

The corporate tax rate for the year ended 30 June 2020 is 30 per cent and the avoided PE rate through the application of the MAAL is imposed at the same level.[885]

(c) New Zealand's PE Anti-Avoidance Rules

In contrast to the UK and Australian reforms, New Zealand took a somewhat low-key approach to legislate on the perceived tax gaps that multinational enterprises were exploiting.[886] Nonetheless, a raft of international changes were implemented in a major piece of international tax

---

[885] It seems unlikely that the lesser rate imposed on small companies would be relevant given the AU$1 billion threshold for the significant global entity requirement.

[886] Commentators on these changes speculated that the New Zealand political environment was less highly charged than those in the United Kingdom and Australia and that the relatively strong economy in New Zealand meant that the government was not under the same fiscal pressures. See Wasimi, above n 873 at 350.

8.5 CONCEPT OF PERMANENT ESTABLISHMENT

reform, effective 1 July 2018.[887] The particular change, relevant to this discussion, was the introduction of a new PE anti-avoidance rule designed to address similar problems that the United Kingdom and Australia had legislated for in their DPT and MAAL respectively.[888]

The background to this legislation was that New Zealand is a signatory (effective 6 July 2017) to the Inclusive Framework of the OECD BEPS Action Plan and the Multilateral Convention (also known as the MLI). One of the substantive changes to existing treaties brought about through the adoption of the MLI is a change to the dependent agent's test in Article 5(5) of the OECD Model. Where countries have adopted Article 12 of the MLI they have expanded the dependent agent test so that if a person habitually plays the principal role leading to the conclusion of contracts, without material modification, then a PE will exist.

For a variety of distinct and different reasons, only approximately one-third of New Zealand's DTA treaty partners mutually signed up to a variation to their treaties in adopting Article 12 via the MLI. The New Zealand policy, however, is consistent with that of the OECD's BEPS Plan and would encompass the expansion of the PE definition to include an "in substance" dependent agent concept. New Zealand also wishes to tax multinational entities when they do not have a DTA with New Zealand at all or have a DTA that has not been modified by the MLI through the adoption of Article 12. Thus the new anti-avoidance rule expressly does not apply if the relevant New Zealand DTA incorporates Article 12(1) of the MLI.[889]

The New Zealand anti-avoidance legislation targets a non-resident carrying on significant sales-related activity assisted by someone "on the ground" in circumstances where the sales-related activity does not give rise to a PE. If all of the following criteria exist, then the anti-avoidance rule deems the non-resident entity to have a PE in New Zealand:[890]

- the non-resident is part of a large multinational enterprise with a consolidated global turnover of at least €750 million; and
- the non-resident entity supplies goods or services to New Zealand customers; and

---

[887] Through the passing of the Taxation (Neutralising Base Erosion and Profit Shifting) Act 2018 (NZ). This made changes to the Income Tax Act 2007 (NZ).
[888] Contained in the Income Tax Act 2007 (NZ), s GB 54.
[889] Income Tax Act 2007 (NZ), s GB 54(1)(e)(i).
[890] Ibid.

- a person (called a "facilitator") carries out activities in New Zealand making it possible for the supply to occur, which are more than preparatory or auxiliary; and
- the facilitator is associated with or commercially dependent (derives 80 per cent or more of its income from services provided to the non-resident) on the non-resident entity; and
- the income provided to the non-resident is subject to a double tax agreement which does not include the OECD's new PE article implemented in the OECD; and
- the arrangement has a more than merely incidental purpose or effect of avoiding New Zealand tax or both New Zealand and foreign tax.

If the anti-avoidance rules apply, then a deemed PE will exist. Profits can be attributed using the normal attribution rules and would be subject to tax at the New Zealand corporate tax rate of 28 per cent.[891] The activities of the facilitator with the supplies are attributed to the PE to determine the profit attributable to it.[892] In this respect, note that New Zealand applies the PE profit attribution rules under the earlier version of Article 7 as New Zealand does not agree with the "authorised OECD approach", or AOA. None of New Zealand's DTAs incorporates the latest version of Article 7 concerning business profits of the OECD Model Treaty and New Zealand has an explicit reservation against the AOA approach.

As discussed above, the anti-avoidance rules can deem a PE to exist in circumstances where there is no treaty at all with New Zealand. It does so by defining a PE in a schedule to the Income Tax Act 2007. If income is determined to be attributable to this deemed PE, then the New Zealand Tax Act automatically deems the income to have a New Zealand source.[893]

8.5.11 Advantages and Disadvantages

It is a common feature of each of the above regimes in the United Kingdom, Australia and New Zealand that they use domestic anti-

---

[891] See Wasimi et al, above n 873 at 354, where they point out that the taxpayer can also be liable for 100 per cent penalty for taking an abusive tax position (i.e. the tax burden would increase to 56 per cent).
[892] See Income Tax Act 2007 (NZ), s GB 54(2)(b).
[893] Income Tax Act 2007 (NZ), s YD 4 (17C).

avoidance provisions to expand the scope and definition of existing PE provisions.

The introduction of such specific domestic anti-avoidance rule raises the question of treaty override, namely whether domestic law is being introduced expressly to override international treaty obligations. The problem is that such override is a breach of the treaty itself and contrary to international law. Deliberately overriding an international treaty, therefore, carries significant political and economic risk.

It is asserted in the United Kingdom that the DPT is not a treaty override because it is a new tax which is not within the scope of the existing UK tax treaty network. But even if it is not a new tax, one view is that common law countries like the United Kingdom, Australia and New Zealand can override their treaty obligations generally, but particularly in circumstances where the treaty is being abused.[894] The treaty only becomes part of domestic law through the approval of the legislature and the legislature can pass subsequent legislation to override any law including the treaty. Case law in such jurisdictions generally supports domestic override although the courts require a clear situation of override to exist.[895] That is, the override must be authorised by parliament through clearly expressed intent, or implication, in the overriding legislation. Reuven Avi-Yonah suggests that the UK taxpayer cannot challenge the DPT as being inconsistent with our UK tax treaty "because UK

---

[894] See C Elliffe "The Lesser of Two Evils: Double Tax Treaty Override or Treaty Abuse?" (2016) 1 BTR 62.

[895] In the UK see the Court of Appeal decision *Padmore v IRC* (Padmore) [1989] STC 493, and *Padmore v IRC* (No 2) [2001] STC 280 (Ch), where the Special Commissioners and the High Court had to consider specific domestic legislation which was designed to overturn the reduction in tax offered under a double tax treaty between the United Kingdom and Jersey. The Court of Appeal, affirming the High Court's decision, found that the taxpayer was exempt from tax on his foreign income from a Jersey partnership. The UK/Jersey double tax treaty exempted Jersey resident enterprise from UK tax unless the Jersey enterprise carried on business through a permanent establishment in the United Kingdom. The taxpayer argued that the double tax arrangement took effect "notwithstanding anything in any enactment" – the wording in the Income and Corporation Taxes Act 1988 (UK), s 788(3). This was unsuccessful in this instance of express or clear legislative override. Philip Baker suggests in his book *Double Taxation Conventions* (Sweet and Maxwell, 2014), F.07, that the non obstante clause in the UK legislation ("notwithstanding anything in any enactment") means that a treaty will prevail over subsequent legislation unless that legislation expressly or by clear implication overrides section 788 of the ICTA. In the United States, see *Whitney v Robertson* 124 US 190 (1888) and *Cook v United States* 288 US 102, 120 (1933).

treaties are not 'self-executing' and have not been applied to the DPT by legislation".[896]

Reinforcing the general principle that Parliament can pass legislation to override a treaty is the legislative relationship between general anti-avoidance rules and tax treaties in different jurisdictions. The three countries concerned (the United Kingdom,[897] Australia[898] and New Zealand[899]) have all passed legislation making it clear that their respective domestic anti-avoidance rules apply irrespective of their tax treaty obligations.

Beyond these three countries, it should also be noted that treaties concluded after 2003 have been negotiated with the understanding that more generally domestic anti-avoidance rules can override treaty obligations.[900] This is consistent with the Commentary on Article 1 of the OECD Model that it is a main purpose of any tax treaty negotiated with the OECD Model to prevent tax avoidance and evasion.

All of this should be seen as a determined and somewhat desperate approach by governments to respond to political and media-driven commentary which suggests that multinational enterprises have not been paying their "fair share" of tax – whatever that is. All of the three legislative regimes rely on anti-avoidance tests which include requirements such as having a "principal purpose", or a "more than merely incidental purpose or effect", of tax avoidance. These tests will necessarily create uncertainty for business and the potential for double taxation.

---

[896] Avi-Yonah, above n 877 at 71.

[897] The general anti-abuse rule (GAAR) introduced in the United Kingdom by the Finance Act 2013, Pt 5 and Sch 41, is intended to override treaties and Taxation (International and Other Provisions) Act (TIOPA) 2010, s 6(1). Section 209(1) of the Finance Act 2013 provides that all priority rules, as defined in s 209(2), are to have effect subject to the GAAR.

[898] The general anti-avoidance rules contained in Part IVA of the Income Tax Assessment Act 1936 (ITAA 1936) are not restricted by the application of Australia's tax treaties (see subsection 177B(1) of the ITAA 1936 and subsection 4(2) of the Agreements Act 1953) and therefore the GAAR prevails regardless of whether the resultant tax is contrary to the provisions of a treaty.

[899] Although tax treaties (pursuant to section BH 1 (4)) generally have overriding effect in terms of other provisions of the Income Tax Act 2007, this is expressly subject to sections BG 1 (the New Zealand anti-avoidance rules) and GB 54 (the deemed PE rules).

[900] C Elliffe "Cross Border Tax Avoidance: Applying the 2003 OECD Commentary to Pre-2003 Treaties" (2012) 3 BTR at 307.

9

Interim Solutions and Long-Term Reforms

9.1 Crossroads: Responding in a Unilateral or a Unified Way?

The extraordinary consequences of the COVID-19 crisis mean that the world arrives at the crossroads of international tax reform with a greater sense of urgency.[901] Most countries around the world will have largely emptied their coffers, and borrowed heavily, to fund strategies to support their businesses and workers. The International Monetary Fund (IMF) forecast that the cumulative loss to global GDP over 2020 and 2021 from the pandemic crisis could be around US$9 trillion, greater than the economies of Japan and Germany combined.[902] This suggests that governments will need revenue from every source and multinationals are likely to be part of a logical tax base, particularly when cross-border trade recovers, as undoubtedly it will.

In many respects the crisis confirms the dominance of many highly digitalised businesses in certain key areas highlighted by the effect of the pandemic. This is because many countries, to slow the rapid contraction of the virus, have imposed rules requiring self-isolation or small group isolation. Most people in such situations have become even more reliant on social media, remote and online shopping, streamed entertainment, online education and many other forms of technology-enabled connection.

This suggests that the key challenges which are the focus of this book, namely how to respond to the tax implications of a highly digitalised

---

[901] Gita Gopinath "The Great Lockdown: Worst Economic Downturn Since the Great Depression" (14 April 2020) International Monetary Fund <https://blogs.imf.org/2020/04/14/the-great-lockdown-worst-economic-downturn-since-the-great-depression>; see where the International Monetary Fund projects that global growth in 2020 to fall to −3 per cent. This is a downgrade of 6.3 percentage points from January 2020, a major revision over a very short period. This makes the Great Lockdown the worst recession since the Great Depression, and far worse than the Global Financial Crisis.

[902] See Gopinath, above n 901.

economy, do not become something that can be unduly deferred. The world needs to either come to a consensus-driven multilateral solution, or we will see the introduction of interim, or unilateral, domestic taxes. These domestic taxes vary in their design and scope, but the most common form is a group most usually known as digital services taxes (DSTs).

This chapter examines the implications of adopting a unilateral approach of DSTs by looking at some key generic design issues they have in common. Highlighting the issues associated with unilateral taxes necessarily results in comparison to the multilateral solution proposed by the Inclusive Framework. Standing back, there are clear advantages to implementing a multilateral consensus-driven international framework. This has been the view of most countries for several years.[903] The fact that there is a clear desire to obtain a consensus does not necessarily make it easy to identify exactly what that is, or reach an agreement between all the relevant parties.

Focus then turns to the multilateral solution proposed by the Inclusive Framework, to analyse the likely direction of long-term change in the international tax framework of the twenty-first century. Even if a consensus cannot be achieved with the existing proposals it seems more than possible that some of the fundamental aspects of the 2020s compromise will become central tenets of the new international tax framework.

9.2 Key Generic Design Issues with DSTs

9.2.1 Problems with Scope

One of the difficulties identified with DSTs is that they are usually narrowly targeted at certain highly digitalised business models. This causes problems in accurately and fairly identifying the targeted businesses, particularly because of the inherent difficulty of separating the digital economy from the rest of the economy.[904] Key decisions must, therefore, be made as to exactly what is in and what is out of "in-scope" activities.[905] This is not necessarily just a problem with the DSTs; indeed,

---

[903] OECD *Tax Challenges Arising from Digitalisation – Interim Report 2018: Inclusive Framework on BEPS* (OECD Publishing, 2018) 407 at [178].

[904] See the discussion in Section 2.1.1(b) "The Difficulty of Separating the Digital Economy from the Rest of the Economy".

[905] Other key decisions include the threshold for the size of business and, saliently, the relationship between the turnover of an entity and the extent to which it operates as a

9.2 KEY GENERIC DESIGN ISSUES WITH DSTS

the same difficult decisions are required in the determination of "automated digital services" in formulating how Amount A applies to such businesses.[906]

It means, however, that the DSTs are targeted towards a particular type of business and so, necessarily, do not address the detailed challenges of the digital economy in respect of all the other aspects considered as part of the problems with the existing international tax framework. In other words, of the seven challenges to the tax system discussed in Chapter 3, DSTs deal with only a few of the challenges posed. Arguably, just two of the challenges are addressed by DSTs: first, the vanishing ability to tax business profits, but only to the extent of automated digital services and not consumer-facing businesses, and secondly, the use of data and the contribution of users.

Other problems with scope depend on design. For example, the Italian DST seeks to capture transactions where a user, residing in a third country (say New Zealand), opens an application in Italy to book accommodation in France on a multi-sided platform based in the United States of America. Italy seeks to impose DST on this transaction because the application was used (opened) in Italy, even though it is a non-resident booking for services which take place outside of Italy.[907] Complex territorial rules apply to determine the place of the transaction and to identify the user of the taxable service. It is anticipated that these types of rules will be difficult to administer in practice.[908]

The biggest concern with scope is that to meet some of the legal concerns which are discussed in Section 9.2.3, the tax must be imposed as an excise tax. Accordingly, two major adverse consequences flow from

---

highly digitalised business. Many large businesses with high turnover in areas such as retail or commodities (supermarkets and petrol companies) may have a relatively small percentage of their business in the highly digitalised business model.

[906] See the discussion in Section 5.3.2(b) "What Are the Types of Businesses Included within the Scope of Amount A?"

[907] Article 1, [35–50] of Law 145 of 30 December 2018, Italy. The Italian DST is in force from 1 January 2020 and it provides, inter alia, that (paraphrasing an unofficial translation): For digital intermediation services, the DST would be due if the service involves a multi-sided digital interface that facilitates the provision of underlying supplies of goods or services directly between users, when the users utilizes a device in Italy. Reference is made to the number of users having concluded underlying transactions on the digital interface in Italy in that tax period.

[908] The author wishes to thank Carlo Romano and his team at PricewaterhouseCoopers Rome, who, together with other distinguished commentators, were most helpful in discussing the putative Italian DST with him in April 2019.

this requirement. First, the tax must be imposed on gross income rather than net income leading to the possibility of over-taxation in circumstances where the highly digitalised business is in loss or low profitability. Conceivably, a low rate on gross income could also lead to under-taxation if the highly digitalised business delivered extraordinary residual profits or had a very low or zero marginal cost of operating in a given jurisdiction. Secondly, it will not be creditable against other direct income taxes. This means that there is likely to be double taxation. As discussed in Chapter 4, such attributes make DSTs comparatively "ugly" taxes.[909]

9.2.2 Economic Concerns

Commentators frequently regard DSTs as unprincipled, in the sense of them being deliberately designed to be outside of existing treaty and trade obligations. For example, Ruth Mason and Leopold Parada described the European Union's version of the DST as follows:[910]

> The EU's DST has been roundly and justly criticized. Commentators claim that digital taxes would inefficiently discriminate against particular sectors and countries, operate as a tariff, result in double taxation, be passed on to consumers, and invite retaliation. The DST was designed as an unapologetic stopgap, a less-than ideal proposal that would apply until the EU can work out a better solution to the challenges of taxing an increasingly digitized economy. Such a stopgap could inhibit lasting reform.

This statement recognises that there is a mixture of legal objections (discrimination and tariffs) and economic problems (inefficiency, double taxation, the incidence of tax passed on to consumers and trade wars) in introducing a DST. The economic concerns are justified. The imposition of a DST, and it not being available as a credit against other direct income taxes, is likely to increase the cost of capital, thereby reducing the return for the company. Such outcomes would act as a disincentive to innovation and growth. Alternatively, the entity will pass the true cost of the DST on to the consumer in circumstances where the price is inelastic because of inadequate substitutes and competition. In either event, there is concern that more resources are used to achieve the same level of

---

[909] See the discussion in Section 4.3 "Interim Measures".
[910] Ruth Mason and Leopold Parada "Digital Battlefront in the Tax Wars" (2018) 92 Tax Notes Int'l 1183 at 1184.

9.2 KEY GENERIC DESIGN ISSUES WITH DSTS

production, resulting in a deadweight cost and a negative impact on the overall welfare of the economy.

There are, of course, alternative views. Wei Cui, for example, defends the economic rationale for DSTs. He bases this claim on the assertion that digital platforms earn significant forms of location-specific rent, much of which arises "from personalisation, or from data, which should be attributed to the jurisdiction of users when the technology is non-rival".[911] He argues that the highly digitalised platforms earn supra-normal profits and they do so because of the location-specific rent attributable to the technology-enabled capture of personal data. He also notes that the indirect network effect in two-sided business models creates a misalignment between value creation and the source of the payment. This means that location-specific rent can be "plausibly attributed" to the subsidised side of the platform in circumstances where the platform offers monetised monopoly access to the other side.[912] This means that the subsidised social media platform made up of users resident in one jurisdiction are generating the economic rents in that jurisdiction when the platform derives advertising revenue from advertisers located on the other side of its platform. He suggests it is both efficient and fair to tax the rent earned from a location where technology is deployed to that location. Professor Cui's arguments have some force and in a world where consensus breaks down for a multilateral solution may well serve as a justification for the introduction of DSTs.

As indicated in the Mason and Parada article, at the pragmatic level there is also the possibility of retaliatory action and trade wars.[913] The consequence of the introduction of the French DST was an investigation by the USA Trade Representative which concluded that "France's Digital Services Tax (DST) discriminates against U.S. companies, is inconsistent with prevailing principles of international tax policy, and is unusually burdensome for affected U.S. companies".[914] The US Trade Representative Office found that the French DST is inconsistent with prevailing tax principles on account of its retroactivity, its application to revenue rather than income, its extraterritorial application and its

---

[911] Wei Cui "The Digital Services Tax: A Conceptual Defense" (22 April 2019) Social Science Research Network <https://papers.ssrn.com/sol3/papers.cfm?abstract_id=3273641> at 30.
[912] Ibid at 30.
[913] Mason and Parada, above n 910.
[914] Office of the United States Trade Representative "Conclusion of USTR's Investigation under Section 301 into France's Digital Services Tax" (press release, 2 December 2019).

purpose of penalising particular US technology companies for their commercial success. The United States warned it may levy 100 per cent trade tariffs on up to US$2.4 billion of French goods, including cheese and champagne. In late January 2020, President Emmanuel Macron agreed to suspend the French DST on American technology giants in exchange for a postponement of threatened retaliatory tariffs on French goods by the Trump administration.[915]

9.2.3 Legal Concerns

There are also significant legal concerns associated with the introduction of a DST. Chapter 4 discussed the range of legal questions associated with the relationship between generic DSTs and generic double tax agreements.[916] There is a significant possibility that there will be litigation on whether the DTAs prevent the successful application of the DSTs on the basis that the DST is a "tax" under Article 2 of the OECD Model. A detailed examination of the interpretation of Article 2, relevant case law, guidance from the OECD, the stated reasoning of governments proposing or implementing DSTs and academic commentary suggests that the characteristics of many DSTs will fall outside the scope of Article 2. Furthermore, it seems highly unlikely that the non-discrimination article would apply.[917]

Another area of significant legal uncertainty and concern for DSTs is the constraints imposed by membership of the World Trade Organization (WTO). These rules apply to some 160 countries (with more waiting for acceptance), so the possibility of a challenge arguing that interim DSTs are in breach of WTO obligations is high. After examining the three articles most relevant to the General Agreement on Trade in Services (GATS), the conclusion reached in Section 4.6 is that there is a reasonable case to suggest that neither the Most-Favoured-Nation (MFN) obligations in Article II, nor the National Treatment (NT) obligations in Article XVII, nor the consultation and dispute settlement provisions in Article XXII should apply. Such a conclusion can be

---

[915] Liz Alderman, Jim Tankersley and Ana Swanson "France and U.S. Move toward Temporary Truce in Trade War" (21 January 2020) The New York Times <www.nytimes.com/2020/01/21/business/france-US-digital-tax.html>.
[916] See Section 4.4 "Constraints Imposed by the Scope of Double Tax Agreements (DTAs)".
[917] See Section 4.4.6 "Restrictions within the DTA: Application of the Non-Discrimination Article in the DTA".

9.2 KEY GENERIC DESIGN ISSUES WITH DSTS 311

justified on the broad policy grounds that the WTO rules ought not to apply to normative taxation.[918]

These conclusions, namely that neither DTAs nor the WTO trade obligations apply to DSTs, are based on key features of the DST which include:

- It must not be an income tax (or creditable against an income tax) but rather an excise tax imposed on gross revenues. This feature is a critical part of the argument that it is not a tax under Article 2 of the OECD Model Tax Treaty.
- It must apply to residents and non-residents alike. This feature is required under WTO International Treaty obligations, rather than Article 24 of the OECD Model Tax Treaty.[919] That is, it must not discriminate between residents of different countries (MFN obligations) nor between non-residents and residents (NT obligations).

These two significant features place real constraints on the compatibility and coherency of DSTs with the international framework in particular because of the near certainty of double taxation. From the perspective of tax policy design, however, this incoherence must be tolerated because when these two features are incorporated into the DST then they appear to greatly reduce the risk of legal challenge under existing legal obligations in tax law and trade law.

Further development in this area was the recent decisions of the Grand Chamber of the Court of Justice of the European Union (CJEU) in the *Tesco-Global*[920] and *Vodafone*[921] cases concerning the compatibility of Hungarian turnover taxes and fundamental freedoms under European Union law. These Hungarian cases involved challenges to a tax on net turnover from retail and digital advertising. The cases are seen as preparing the ground for potential challenges under EU law for DSTs.[922] The CJEU held that the Hungarian turnover tax was not discriminatory. A tax

---

[918] See Section 4.6 "Constraints Imposed by the Membership of the WTO".
[919] Although of course it assists in the argument that Article 24 of the OECD Model Treaty does not apply.
[920] Case C 323/18 *Tesco-Global Áruházak Zrt v Nemzeti Adó- és Vámhivatal Fellebbviteli Igazgatósága* ECLI:EU:C:2020:140.
[921] Case C-75/18 *Vodafone Magyarország Mobil Távközlési Zrt. v Nemzeti Adó- és Vámhivatal Fellebbviteli Igazgatósága* ECLI:EU:C:2020:139.
[922] Ruth Mason "What the CJEU's Hungarian Cases Mean for Digital Taxes" (8 March 2020) Social Science Research Network <https://papers.ssrn.com/sol3/papers.cfm?abstract_id=3550757>.

that was progressive in its targeting of turnover – it applied to high-turnover foreign-owned subsidiaries but not to low-turnover domestic Hungarian-owned companies – was not offensive to the fundamental freedoms doctrine. A commentator, Ruth Mason, views this as the CJEU "laying the groundwork for rejecting fundamental freedoms challenges to digital taxes".[923]

9.2.4 Revenue and Other Tax Administration Concerns

As discussed in Chapter 4, while there was a common view that many attributes of the DSTs were undesirable, a consensus was absent that the downsides of implementing DSTs outweighed the need to address the digital tax challenges.[924] Accordingly, the OECD Interim Report did not advocate against a DST but rather set out guidance on the design of DSTs.[925]

The qualified approbation of the OECD could be viewed as an attempt to minimise the damage to the international tax system by standardising the response and mitigating some of the adverse consequences referred to. The suggestion from the OECD was that any DST would be:

1 interim (in the sense it would be immediately replaced if, and when, a multilateral consensus was reached;
2 targeted exclusively at highly digitalised business models (i.e. it should not apply to the ordinary sale of goods and services over the Internet);
3 should minimise over-taxation by imposing a low rate;
4 should minimise its impact on, and ensure that it did not impose unreasonable compliance costs upon start-ups, unprofitable entities, and small and medium-sized businesses (which can be achieved by ensuring that the DST is applied only to entities which are very large using appropriate thresholds for the size of the entity and the jurisdiction concerned).[926]

The consequence of having a highly targeted, low-rate and (potentially) temporary tax suggests that in the short term it will run the risk of being inefficient in the sense that the costs upon taxpayers and tax administrators will be high relative to the amount of revenue collected.

---

[923] Ibid at 16.
[924] See Section 4.2.2 "More than BEPS".
[925] OECD, above n 903 at [178].
[926] Ibid at [178–80].

9.2.5 Compared to the OECD Consensus-Driven Multilateral Solution?

The key concerns about DSTs listed above, such as problems in scope, economic efficiencies, legal constraints and revenue and administrative inadequacies, suggest that these types of taxes are the least preferred option in comparison to the Organisation for Economic Co-operation and Development (OECD) and the Inclusive Framework proposals. In comparing the multilateral solution to DSTs, the points of differentiation are a threefold list of "big picture" benefits in taking the multilateral approach:

- The opportunity to reform the international tax framework coherently to address the particular problem. In other words, to change the system to address the challenges posed by highly digitalised businesses and other businesses that make use of marketing intangibles in the market jurisdiction. It would be much more desirable for this problem to be addressed within the whole international tax system rather than "bolting on" a largely incompatible additional tax. If this can be done in a way where there is a long-term agreement to the changes then they will be durable and coordinated.
- To ensure that the tax paid under the 2020s compromise is fully creditable[927] against any tax arising under the existing framework settings. In particular, to focus on making sure tax payable under the new taxing rights for market jurisdictions established by Amount A is creditable against income which might otherwise be earned under the separate entity approach in the residence jurisdiction.
- To have a unified tax system where the same approach is taken by all jurisdictions, leading to reduced double taxation, lower compliance and administration costs, fewer and less expensive disputes, and fewer opportunities for tax avoidance and profit shifting.

These major advantages suggest that an obvious conclusion is that it would be highly preferable to adopt a consensus-driven multilateral solution.

9.3 Significant Areas of Change in the 2020s Compromise

9.3.1 A Move to Destination Taxation

This final section of the book reflects on five major changes that are proposed in the 2020s compromise. They represent the most noteworthy

---

[927] Alternatively, double taxation could be relieved by the relevant income receiving exemption from tax.

areas of current and future change and could, therefore, be referred to as trends or a direction of travel. The proposed reforms are broader than a tax response demanded exclusively by the challenges of highly digitalised businesses but it is clear that digital business models are the catalyst for the reform of the twenty-first-century tax system.

The first change of consequence is a move towards destination taxation in the international tax system. When focusing on the problems and issues in the existing system it is sometimes easy to lose sight of the overarching taxation principles involved. As discussed throughout this book our existing international tax system was a compromise.[928] In essence, the 1920s compromise involved the allocation of taxing rights for different categories of income between residence and source jurisdictions. In the case of business profits, of course, after the report of the Committee of Technical Experts in 1927[929] and the draft bilateral convention in the report of Government Experts of 1928,[930] an enterprise resident in one jurisdiction would be taxed in its residence jurisdiction. It would only be taxed in another jurisdiction when the enterprise concerned was doing business in that other jurisdictions and possessed a permanent establishment there.

In Chapter 3, seven challenges to the international tax system were identified that are posed by the digitalisation of businesses. Not all of the seven challenges are addressed by changes involving a partial move towards destination taxation,[931] but four of them are.

First, highly digitalised business models do not need a permanent establishment to be significantly involved, and do business successfully, in another jurisdiction.[932] As discussed in Chapter 6, dealing with the vanishing ability to tax business profits is a compound challenge as not only is it necessary to address the nexus (PE issue), it is also necessary to address the allocation of profits to that PE.[933]

---

[928] See in particular Section 1.3 "The History of International Double Taxation: The '1920s Compromise'".

[929] League of Nations (Technical Experts from Argentina, Belgium, Czechoslovakia, France, Germany, Great Britain, Italy, Japan, Netherlands, Poland, Switzerland, USA, Venezuela) *Double Taxation and Tax Evasion Report Presented by the Committee of Technical Experts on Double Taxation and Tax Evasion* (League of Nations, Geneva, April 2017).

[930] League of Nations (General Meeting of Government Experts) *Double Taxation and Tax Evasion* (League of Nations, Geneva, October 1928).

[931] As detailed in Chapter 4, other components of the OECD's multilateral solution, such as those proposed in Pillar Two, are relevant to the other challenges.

[932] See Section 3.2 "The Vanishing Ability to Tax Business Profits".

[933] See Section 6.2 "Dealing with the Vanishing Ability to Tax Business Profits".

9.3 SIGNIFICANT AREAS OF CHANGE

At the heart of the current international tax system is that taxation is fundamentally imposed based on origin, that is, where the goods were produced (i.e. where capital was employed to manufacture the goods or produce the services). A taxing right exists for the importing country/consumer market but only where a PE exists and, more importantly, only to the extent profits are attributable to the activities carried out by that PE. Conventional transfer pricing rules can be utilised so that a local affiliate (or PE) can have no ownership in intangible assets, does not perform DEMPE functions,[934] and does not assume any risks related to assets.[935]

This means that the current system of taxation, which utilises the principle of the place of origin, offers two significant and legal opportunities for tax planning multinationals. First, avoid having a PE in your marketplace jurisdiction, and secondly, if the first is not possible, ensure that the functions and risks attributable to any entity operating in the marketplace are modest. This will result in a commensurately small allocation of profits.

The multilateral solution described in Chapter 5, and particularly concerning Amount A, is designed to address the above two opportunities as they relate to the vanishing ability to tax business profits. It does so by changing the nexus rules by abolishing the PE threshold. This means that "in-scope" automated digital services[936] are included within Amount A provided that the relevant thresholds are met.[937] In contrast, for consumer-facing businesses, some additional requirements will be necessary to establish a taxable nexus. These further factors are those which could indicate a significant economic presence and the generation of revenue on a sustained basis, and are likely to include the existence of a physical presence of the multinational in the market jurisdiction, and/or targeted advertising directed at the market jurisdiction.

---

[934] OECD *Transfer Pricing Guidelines for Multinational Enterprises and Tax Administrations* (OECD, 2017); see for determining whether an entity has economic ownership of an intangible asset, the OECD Guidelines prescribe that it should be delineated whether an entity performs the so-called DEMPE functions. DEMPE stands for development, enhancement, maintenance, protection and exploitation. To determine the DEMPE function, therefore, you need to determine: who has control, who is funding, and who is incurring the risks related to the function.

[935] See Section 6.2.5 "The Challenge: Allocation of Profits".

[936] See Section 5.3.7 "Nexus Rules".

[937] See Section 5.3.6 "Relevant Thresholds, the Included Company Threshold and the Included Jurisdiction Threshold".

It is not just the challenge posed by the vanishing ability to tax business profits that is addressed, in part, by the multilateral solution of moving to taxation on a destination basis, but also the challenge posed by the use of data and the contribution of users.[938] The multilateral solution – that is, using the destination basis – allocates taxing rights to the jurisdiction where users reside.

The third challenge involves one of the most important practice areas and is the failure of transfer pricing to adequately address certain multinational enterprises and their transactions.[939] This is discussed in greater detail below in Section 9.3.3 as one of the significant areas of change in its own right. In the context of taxation on a destination basis, it is important to note that the "new" profit allocation rules provide that a part of the non-routine residual profits are allocated to the market where the product or services are consumed (i.e. taxation in the country of destination).

Fourthly, the partial move to destination taxation can be seen through the lens of tax competition. The existing rules, in favouring highly digitalised and developed jurisdictions through taxation based on origin, are amended to allocate taxing rights to the market, which generally means that there is greater sharing of revenues between jurisdictions. Destination taxation does not support the relocation of activity (or the more cynical relocation of intellectual property or other assets) into tax-preferred jurisdictions since taxation takes place in the marketplace of the end-consumer.

In conclusion, the most significant change in the whole of the 2020s compromise is this movement towards taxation on a destination basis in respect of Amount A. As indicated in Chapter 5,[940] the potential amounts of revenue may be more modest but the moving away from taxation based on the country of origin to the country of destination is a profound transformation. There are numerous advantages to destination taxation, including robustness against tax planning (particularly encompassing transactions that use transfer pricing), the elimination of some undesirable aspects of locating investments in tax-preferred jurisdictions (tax competition) and other profit-shifting techniques which are discussed in Chapter 8.[941]

---

[938] See Section 3.3 "The Use of Data, the Contribution of Users, and the Measurement of Their Value".
[939] See Section 3.6 "The Failure of Transfer Pricing with Certain Multinational Enterprises and Their Transactions".
[940] See Section 5.8 "Conclusion".
[941] Discussed in the various advantages and disadvantages sections of the various alternative policy choices. For example see Section 8.2 "Destination-Based Cash Flow Taxation".

9.3.2 Changing the Nexus of Taxation

The concept of permanent establishment has been under threat for some significant time. In 1999, the Committee on Fiscal Affairs set up a Technical Advisory Group (TAG) on Monitoring the Application of Existing Treaty Norms for Taxing Business Profits with the general mandate to examine how the current treaty rules for the taxation of business profits apply in the context of electronic commerce and examine proposals for alternative rules.[942] The final report of the TAG considered the emerging new digital business models and included some suggestions for clarification of the definition of permanent establishment. Concerns continue to be raised on a variety of topics throughout the next decade, including important issues such as the meaning of "at the disposal of", "to conclude contracts in the name of the enterprise", the "fragmentation of activities" and "preparatory or auxiliary activities".[943] By 2015 the OECD, through the Base Erosion and Profit Shifting Project and the activities undertaken as part of Action 7, had elevated their work to carry out "changes to the definition of permanent establishment in the OECD Model Tax Convention that will address strategies used to avoid having a taxable presence in a country under tax treaties".[944] Action 7 proposed changes to ensure that where the activities that an intermediary undertakes in a country were intended to result in the regular conclusion of contracts to be performed by a foreign enterprise, that enterprise would be considered to have a taxable presence in that country unless the intermediary is performing these activities in the course of an independent business.[945] Other changes restricted the application of several exceptions to the definition of permanent establishment to activities that are preparatory or auxiliary in nature, and ensured that it is no longer possible to take advantage of these exceptions by the fragmentation of a cohesive operating business into several small operations. Likewise, they also addressed situations where the exception applicable to

---

[942] OECD Centre for Tax Policy and Administration "Are the Current Treaty Rules for Taxing Business Profits Appropriate for E-Commerce?" (June 2004) OECD <www.oecd.org/tax/treaties/35869032.pdf>.

[943] OECD Centre for Tax Policy and Administration *Interpretation and Application of Article 5 (Permanent Establishment) of the OECD Model Tax Convention* (12 October 2011) OECD <www.oecd.org/tax/treaties/48836726.pdf>.

[944] OECD *Preventing the Artificial Avoidance of Permanent Establishment Status, Action 7 – 2015 Final Report* (OECD Publishing, 2015).

[945] OECD *Model Tax Convention on Income and on Capital Condensed Version* (OECD, 21 November 2017) at Article 7.

construction sites is circumvented through the splitting up of contracts between closely related enterprises. Countries had, and indeed still have, the opportunity to implement these changes through the Multilateral Instrument.[946]

What seems clear now is that countries both were and are wedded to the PE concept because it is such a fundamental part of the 1920s compromise, and that an enormous amount of effort was undertaken to try to shore it up against the advancing technology and ability to make remote sales using digital business models.

Chapter 8 considered the reforms to the concept of PE which had been either proposed or, in the case of a few proactive countries, implemented. This included such actions as a revision to the PE concept by expansion to its conceptual basis,[947] domestic law interpretation or declaration,[948] or domestic law anti-avoidance legislation (such as diverted profit taxes).[949]

The 2020s compromise suggests the abolition of requiring a nexus of a PE in the case of automated digital businesses. In the case of consumer-facing businesses, a nexus of something less than a PE may still be required. There is no doubt that this is a significant change and one of the most important future trends.

9.3.3 Changing the Allocation of Profits in Transfer Pricing

The third noteworthy feature of the 2020s compromise is the use of one of the aspects of transfer pricing and the sharing of tax revenue. A key component of Amount A involves utilising a transfer pricing technique involving the separating out of residual profits and allocating a part of it to the market jurisdiction. It is worthwhile reflecting on the transfer pricing technique which is being used to perform this function.

As was previously explained in Chapter 8, certain profit methods[950] in transfer pricing employ an "outsourcing" methodology when a multi-

---

[946] Multilateral Convention to Implement Tax Treaty Related Measures to Prevent Base Erosion and Profit Shifting (entered into force 1 July 2018).
[947] See Section 8.5 "Expanding the Concept of Permanent Establishment".
[948] See Section 8.5.6 "Establishing the PE Nexus by 'Interpretation and Declaration'".
[949] See Section 8.5.9 "Using Domestic Legislation to Both Buttress and Expand the PE Concept".
[950] This approach is applied most frequently in the United States using the comparable profits method and in the OECD transfer pricing guidelines it is applied using the transactional net margin method.

9.3 SIGNIFICANT AREAS OF CHANGE

national is seeking to determine its separate entity profits in different jurisdictions.[951] Oosterhuis and Parsons describe these techniques as determining an appropriate arm's-length value or profit for activities and functions based on that which an independent party contracting with the multinational enterprise earns.[952] A multinational allocates its profits using these profit methods so that subsidiaries involved in, for example, marketing and distribution are allocated part of the overall multinational group's profit. The consequence of using this technique is that a routine return is ascribed to jurisdictions in which marketing, distribution, contract manufacturing and contract research activities have taken place.

This provides a reasonable and relatively stable level of income to those jurisdictions which receive the routine returns attributable to such outsourced activities. The consequence of the separation, however, means that the transfer pricing rules have separated the residual profits from the abovementioned routine profits.

The problem is that the separation of residual profits from routine profits has encouraged multinationals to shift part or all of the residual profits to ensure that they are earned in low or favourably taxed jurisdictions.

As indicated and discussed in Chapter 8, the residual profit formulary apportionment proposal formulated by Avi-Yonah and others, and the residual profit allocation by income (RPAI) proposal put by the team chaired by Michael Devereux at Oxford University Centre for Business Taxation, use these techniques to separate residual and routine profits.[953] So too does the Unified Approach in the calculation of Amount A.

While some of the more traditional elements of transfer pricing remain, the use of this outsourcing methodology to establish the residual profit utilises a different starting point from some of the traditional transaction-based transfer pricing methodologies of allocating profits to separate entities on an arm's-length basis. This is because it uses the concept of the whole of the multinational entity's profits to determine the residual profit. It therefore owes some of its conceptual origins to the areas of formulary apportionment and residual profit allocation.

---

[951] These are discussed in Section 8.3.1 "The Use of Outsourcing Methodology".
[952] Paul Oosterhuis and Amanda Parsons "Destination-Based Income Taxation: Neither Principled nor Practical?" (2018) 71 Tax L. Rev 515 at 530.
[953] See Section 8.3 "Residual Profit Allocation by Income".

9.3.4 Redefining Residence Taxation

The fourth feature of the 2020s compromise is the planned bolstering of residence-based taxation. As previously discussed,[954] many of the proposed changes concern source-based taxation (for example, allocation of profits to the source jurisdiction, changes to the nexus rules, attribution of residual profits to the source jurisdiction), but the Inclusive Framework in the OECD project identifies the inadequacy of residence-based taxation. This stems from two major problems:[955]

1. The ease of establishing corporate residence and, in particular, subsidiaries resident in favourable tax jurisdictions. It has been a long-time practice of international tax planning to carefully establish tax residence in such jurisdictions, allowing multinationals the opportunity to shelter global earnings.
2. The separation of taxation of the corporate income from the income (if any) derived by the shareholders.

Given the opportunity extended by (1) to reduce corporate tax, it has been possible under (2) for multinationals to defer shareholder, and hence overall, taxation.

The income inclusion rule proposed in Pillar Two was described in Chapter 6 as "a type of worldwide controlled foreign company regime".[956] By providing for a connection between the shareholders and the earning of the corporate income, at least to ensure that profits are subject to a minimum tax, some of the issues concerning residence-based taxation are addressed. This feature of the reform is not particularly attributable to the growth in highly digitalised businesses. It is, however, possible to speculate that the combination of little or no taxation in the source country, together with little or no taxation in the residence country (including little or no taxation of the shareholders of the residence country) led to tax authorities blowing the whistle and calling time on the game.

9.3.5 Addressing Tax Competition

The final noteworthy feature of the 2020s compromise could be the most controversial and ultimately may lead to some elements of the proposals

---

[954] See Chapters 3 and 6 generally, but in particular Section 3.7 "The Inadequacy of Residence-Based Taxation".
[955] See Section 3.7 "The Inadequacy of Residence-Based Taxation".
[956] See Section 6.7 "Tackling the Inadequacy of Residence-Based Taxation".

discussed in Chapter 5 being side-lined. The challenge of tax competition, that countries acting in their interests have an incentive to undermine the international consensus, is discussed in Chapter 3.[957] The Programme of Work response, addressing taxing rights in the source jurisdictions, bolstering the parent jurisdiction's residence-based taxation, and seeking to prevent profit and investment shifting through additional base erosion and profit-shifting measures, are discussed in Chapter 6.[958]

Perhaps the awful fiscal consequences of the COVID-19 pandemic might see a more coherent and consensus-driven approach being taken around the world. It is hoped this is better than the disjointed and varying approaches to the health-related crisis taken by individual countries.

The international tax framework needs the 2020s compromise, now more than ever.

---

[957] See Section 3.8 "Competition by States".
[958] See Section 6.8 "Competition by States".

# INDEX

1920s compromise, the, 9, 25, 34, 38, 40, 45–46, 56, 89, 117, 119, 149, 167, 177, 192, 216, 218, 228, 232, 263, 314, 318
1923 Report, the, *See* Bruins, Einaudi, Seligman and Stamp Report on Double Taxation (League of Nations Economic and Financial Commission, Document E.F.S.73. F.19, April 1923)
1925 Report, the, *See* League of Nations (Technical Experts from Belgium, Czechoslovakia, France, Great Britain, Italy, Netherlands and Switzerland) Double Taxation and Tax Evasion (F 212, Geneva, February 1925)
1927 Report, the, *See* League of Nations (Technical Experts from Argentina, Belgium, Czechoslovakia, France, Germany, Great Britain, Italy, Japan, Netherlands, Poland, Switzerland, USA, Venezuela) Double Taxation and Tax Evasion (C. 216. M. 85, Geneva, April 1927)
1928 Report, the, *See* League of Nations (General Meeting of Government Experts) Double Taxation and Tax Evasion (C. 562. M. 178. Geneva, October 1928)

2011 Proposal for a Common Consolidated Company Tax Base (CCCTB), 280

2020s compromise, 5, 41, 167, 176, 200, 213, 223, 228, 237, 242, 263, 272, 284, 306, 313, 316, 318, 320
2020s compromise proposal, the, 264

Ability to pay theory, the, 14, 16, 18–20, 22–23
"Ability to pay", 249
Accounting standards
  Generally Accepted Accounting Principles (GAAP), 188
  International Financial Reporting Standards (IFRS), 188
Adams, Thomas, 15
"Interstate and International Double Taxation" in Roswell Magill (ed) Lectures on Taxation (1932), 15
Alderman, Liz, Tankersley, Jim and Swanson, Ana
"France and U.S. Move Toward Temporary Truce in Trade War" (21 January 2020), 310
Allocation key, 217, 221, 281, 283
Allocation method, 12
Allocation of income, 54, 143, 216, 226, 250, 264, 271, 278, 287
Amount A
  "Earn-out" approach to the recognition of losses, 246
  "In scope" automated digital services, 315
  Claw-back or "earn out" mechanism, 245
  Deemed income, 180, 191, 193, 196, 200, 217, 225, 228, 239, 244–46, 248, 250, 279

INDEX

Non-routine profits, 217
Routine profits, 217
Amount B
   Formulaic profits, 253
Andrus, Joe and Oosterhuis, Paul
   "Transfer Pricing after BEPS: Where Are We and Where Should We Be Going" (2017) 95(3), Tax Magazine, 274
Aquinas, Thomas, 17
Arnold, Brian, 89
   "Threshold Requirements for Taxing Business Profits under Tax Treaties" (2003), 89
Association for Supply Chain Management (ASCM), the, 270
Ault, Hugh, 54
   "Some Reflections on the OECD and the Sources of International Tax Principles" (2013), 54, 303
Australia, 35
   Australian Treasury Discussion Paper "The Digital Economy and Australia's Corporate Tax System" (October 2018), 35
   Bywater Investments Ltd v Commissioner of Taxation and *Hua Wang Bank Berhad v Commissioner of Taxation* [2016] HCA 45, 42
   De Romero v Read (1932) 48 CLR 649 (HCA), 130
   Federal Commissioner of Taxation v Mitchum (1965) 113 CLR 401 (HCA), 49
   Harding v Commissioner of Taxation [2018] FCA 837, 42
   Income Tax Assessment Act 1936 (Cth), 299
   Nathan v Federal Commissioner of Taxation (1918) 25 CLR 183 (HCA), 50
   Tax Laws Amendment (Combating Multinational Tax Avoidance) Bill 2015: Explanatory Memorandum (The Parliament of the Commonwealth of Australia, House of Representatives), 299
   Thiel v Commissioner of Taxation (1990) 171 CLR 338, 139
Automated digitalised businesses, 187, 238–39
Automated digital and consumer-facing and marketing intangible-rich businesses, 239
Avery Jones, John
   "2008 OECD Model Place of Effective Management – What One Can Learn from the History" (2009), 42
Avi-Yonah, Reuven, 22
   "The International Implications of Wayfair" (2018), 29
   "Three Steps Forward, One Step Back? Reflections on 'Google Taxes' and the Destination-Based Corporate Tax" (2016), 297
   "Treating Tax Issues Through Trade Regimes" (2001), 150
   "Between Formulary Apportionment and the OECD Guidelines: A Proposal for Reconciliation" (2010), 275
   "The Rise and Fall of Arm's Length: A Study in the Evolution of U.S. International Taxation" (1995), 275
   Double Irish Dutch Sandwich, 297, 299
   International Tax as International Law (Cambridge University Press, 2007), 22, 43, 46, 53, 246, 265
Avi-Yonah, Reuven and Benshalom, Ilan
   "Formulary Apportionment – Myth and Prospects" (2011), 275
Avi-Yonah, Reuven and Clausing, Kimberly
   "Problems with Destination-Based Corporate Taxes and the Ryan Blueprint" (2017), 266, 270

Avi-Yonah, Reuven, Clausing, Kimberly and Durst, Michael "Allocating Business Profits for Tax Purposes: A Proposal to Adopt a Formulary Profit Split" (2009), 272
Formulary apportionment proposal, 272
Residual profit method, 272

Backstop tax, 43
Baez, Andres and Brauner, Yariv Withholding Taxes in the Service of BEPS Action 1: Address the Tax Challenges of the Digital Economy (International Bureau of Fiscal Documentation, No. 2015 – 14, 2 February 2015), 250
Baker, Philip Double Taxation Conventions (3rd ed, Sweet and Maxwell, 2019), 303
Baseline marketing and distribution functions, 193, 202, 222, 230, 279
Assumed baseline activity, 198, 253
Baseline distribution activities, 195
Baseline distribution and marketing activities, 251
Profits attributable to, 279
Routine marketing and distribution activities, 202
Becker, Johannes and Englisch, Joachim "Taxing Where Value Is Created: What's 'User Involvement' Got to Do With It?" (2019), 97, 224
Border adjustments, 268, 270
Bradbury, David Head of the Tax Policy and Statistics Division, Centre for Tax Policy and Administration, "Keynote Presentation – Tax and the Digital Global Economy – Issues for the Region and Globally" (International Fiscal Association Conference, Melbourne, June 2019), 211

Bradford, David, 21
US Treasury Tax Policy Staff Blueprints for Basic Tax Reform (2nd ed, 1984), 21
Brauner, Yariv, 53
"An International Tax Regime in Crystallisation" (2003), 54, 246
Brazil
Brazil–Canada DTA, the, 141
Brazil–Germany DTA, the, 141
Companhia Vale do Rio Doce v National Treasury [2014] 17 ITLR 643, 256
National Treasury v COPESUL— Companhia Petroquímica do Sul, 15 ITLR 18, 141
Business models in digital markets, types of, 67
input suppliers, 76
multi-sided platforms, 68
resellers, 76
vertically integrated firms, 76
Byrnes, William
"Comments and Recommendations OECD Public Consultation Document Secretariat Proposal for a 'Unified Approach' under Pillar One" (12 November 2019), 249

Canada
Canwest Mediaworks Inc (successor by amalgamation to Canvideo Television Sales (1983) Ltd) v Canada [2006] 9 ITLR 189 (TCC), 256
Kempe v The Queen [2001] 1 CTC 2060 (TCC), 130
Minister of National Revenue v Tara Exploration & Development Co [1972] CTC 328 (SCC), 139
Schedule of Specific Commitments; Canada –Trade in Services S/DCS/W/CAN, 24 January 2003 (Draft Consolidated Schedule of Specific Commitments), 158
Specific Commitment, 157
Capital and entrepreneurial risk, 280
capital export neutrality (CEN), 8

INDEX   325

capital import neutrality (CIN), 7
Characterisation of transactions and
    income, the, 215
Characterisation of transactions for tax
    purposes
  "Infrastructure as a Service" (IaaS),
    105
  "Platform as a Service" (PaaS), 105
  "X as a service" (XaaS), 105
  Technical service fee, 105
Characterisation of transactions for tax
    purposes, the
  International taxation of services,
    104
China
  VAT on Integrated Circuits (ICs),
    160
Cloud computing
  Infrastructure as a Service ("IaaS"),
    62
  Platform as a Service ("PaaS"), 62
  Software as a Service ("SaaS"), 62
Compliance costs, 108, 186, 193, 195,
    197, 208–9, 280, 312
Consumer preferences and private
    information, the capturing of,
    80
Consumer-facing business, 180–83,
    186–87, 219–20, 225, 238–39,
    254, 279, 290, 307, 315, 318
  Consumer and user-facing business
    transactions, 239
  Consumer-facing rationale, 185
  Intermediaries, 182
  Third-party resellers, 182
Contractual recipients of residual
    profits, 277
Controlled foreign company (CFC)
    rules, the, 207–8, 255–56
  Controlled foreign company (CFC)
    legislation, 255
  Significant direct or indirect
    ownership interest, a, 255
  Underlying foreign corporation's
    profits, 207
  Worldwide controlled foreign
    company regime, 233, 320
Corporate financing
  Cross-border financing, 269

Debt financing, 269
Equity financing, 269
Country of origin, the, 271, 277, 283,
    316
  Basis of origin, 264
  Factors of origin, 282
Country of production, innovation and
    capital, the, 271
Country-by-country (CbC) reporting
  See Amount A
Couzin, Robert
  "Policy Forum: The End of Transfer
    Pricing?" (2013), 275
COVID-19 crisis, the, 305
Credit method, the, 12, 259
Critical mass, 65, 70, 98, 169
Cross-border supplies of services and
    intangibles, 268
Cui, Wei
  "The Digital Services Tax:
    A Conceptual Defense" (22
    April 2019), 309

Dagan, Tsilly
  "The Tax Treaties Myth" 2000, 150
Daly, Michael
  The WTO and Direct Taxation (WTO
    Publications, Discussion Paper
    Number 9, June 2005), 148
  Traditional economic approach to
    trade agreements, 148
Dannon, R J and Chand, V
  Letter from RJ Danon and V Chand
    (on behalf of the Tax Policy
    Center of the University of
    Lausanne (Switzerland)) to
    David Radbury (Tax Policy and
    Statistics Division Centre for Tax
    Policy and Administration
    Organisation for Economic
    Co-operation and Development)
    regarding comments to public
    consultation document:
    Secretariat Proposal for a
    "Unified Approach" Under Pillar
    One (12 November 2019), 178
Data
  Data collection and exploitation, 183,
    225

Data (cont.)
  Generating business value, 88
  Use, creation and valuation of data, 225
Data management platforms, 75
De minimis amount, 246, *See* Amount A
De minimis exemptions. *See* Amount B
de Wilde, Maartin
  "Sharing the Pie: Taxing Multinationals in a Global Market" (PhD thesis, Erasmus University Rotterdam, 2015), 287
  "Tax Jurisdiction in a Digitalizing Economy; Why 'Online Profits' are so Hard to Pin Down" (2015), 39, 287
Deduction rules, the, 237
Defining characteristics of digital markets, the, 64
Definition of a "permanent establishment"
  Contractual or relationship "deemed" test, 92
  Physical "situs" tests, 92
  Temporal or physical presence test, 92
Degrees of digitalisation, 190
Deloitte and tax@hand
  CBDT committee releases draft report on attribution of income to PEs (3 May 2019), 293
Dependent agent, 92–93, 95–96, 238, 301
Destination-based cash flow taxation (DBCFT), 264, 266, 316
Destination-based taxation, 214, 264, 267, 271
  Destination-based methods, the, 284
  Destination-based tax base, 269, 272
  Final country of destination, the, 269
Development, enhancement, maintenance, protection and exploitation of intangibles (DEMPE) functions, 115, 174, 220, 315
Devereux, Michael and Vella, John, 17

"Taxing the Digitalised Economy: Targeted or System-Wide Reform?" (2018), 275
Are We Heading Towards a Corporate Tax System Fit for the 21st Century? (2014), 17, 265
Value Creation as the Fundamental Principle of the International Corporate Tax System (Oxford University Centre for Business Taxation, WP 17/07, 31 July 2017), 85
Digital business models, types of, 66
  free model, 66
  freemium pricing, 66
  on-demand model, 66
  subscription model, 66
Digital PE nexus, elements of the, 286
  De minimis revenue threshold, 286
  Digital services, 286
  Time threshold, 286
  User threshold, 286
Digital Services Tax, 98
  Digital interfaces, 98
  Direct interaction between users, 98
  Intermediary digital interfaces, 98
Digital-centric businesses *See* OECD Public Consultation Document: Secretariat Proposal for a "Unified Approach" under Pillar One (OECD Publishing, October 2019)
Digitalised businesses, features of
  Data and user participation, 116
  Development, enhancement, maintenance, protection and exploitation of intangibles (DEMPE) functions, 115
  Reliance upon intangible assets, 116
  Scale without mass, 116
Discrimination
  Covert or indirect discrimination *See* Double tax agreement
  De facto discrimination, 161
  De jure position, 161
Disintermediation *See* Amount A
Disintermediation of entities, 216

INDEX

Dispute resolution
  Binding dispute resolution, 200–1
  Dispute prevention and resolution framework, 200, 262
  Enhanced dispute resolution process, development of an, 200
  Mandatory arbitration, 200, 262
Distributive rules, 241
Diversion of income, the, 283
Diverted profit tax, 285, 318
Double non-taxation, 169
Double tax agreement
  Bilateral flows of income, 149
  Developed and developing countries, 91
  Economic behaviour of foreign investors, the, 149–50
  Lex specialis principle of interpretation, the, 122
  Mutual agreement procedures, 201, 204
  Non-discrimination article, the, 122, 142–43, 156, 310
  Public international law arena, the, 237
  Relieving jurisdiction, the, 201
  Unilateral credit system, 149
Double taxation
  Double jurisdictional taxation, 203
  Double same jurisdiction taxation, 203
  Ordering rules, 254, 260
Dualism
  Dualist legal system, 258
  Dualist view of an international legal system, the, 258
  Dualistic countries, 258
Dubut, T
  "Article 2 from an Historical Perspective: How Old Materials Can Cast New Light on Taxes Covered by Double Tax Conventions" in T Ecker and G Ressler (eds) History of Tax Treaties-The Relevance of the OECD Documents for the Interpretation of Tax Treaties (Linde, 2011), 128

Earnings stripping regime, 210
Economic decisions, 277
Economic rent, 28, 267
Elkins, D, 21
  "The Myth of Corporate Tax Residence" (2017), 21, 265
  "The Case against Income Taxation of Multinational Enterprises" (2017), 275
Elliffe, Craig
  "Cross Border Tax Avoidance: Applying the 2003 OECD Commentary to Pre-2003 Treaties" (2012), 304
  "Interpreting International Tax Agreements: Alsatia in New Zealand" (2018), 258
  International and Cross-Border Taxation in New Zealand (2nd ed, Thomson Reuters Ltd, 2018), 139
  "The Lesser of Two Evils: Double Tax Treaty Override or Treaty Abuse?" (2016), 246, 303
Emerging tax policies and principles, 214
Equalisation levy, 138
Ericsson, 63
  "Internet of Things forecast", 63
European Commission, the
  Communication from the Commission to the European Parliament and the Council (COM, Brussels, 21 March 2018), 34
  Expert Group on Taxation of the Digital Economy Working Paper: Digital Economy – Facts and Figures (European Commission, March 2014), 58
  Proposal for a Council Directive laying down rules relating to the corporate taxation of a significant digital presence (European Commission, COM (2018) 147 final 2018/0072 (CNS), March 2018), 87

European Commission, the (cont.)
Proposal for a Council Directive on the common system of a digital services tax on revenues resulting from the provision of certain digital services (European Commission, COM (2018) 148 final 2018/0073 (CNS), March 2018), 134
Time to establish a modern, fair and efficient taxation standard for the digital economy (European Commission, COM(2018), 98
European Parliament Special Committee on Tax Rulings, the
Directorate General for Internal Policies Tax Challenges in the Digital Economy (European Parliament, IP/A/TAXE2/2016-04 PE 579.002, June 2016), 110
European Union Court of Justice, the
Case C 323/18 *Tesco-Global Áruházak Zrt v Nemzeti Adó- és Vámhivatal Fellebbviteli Igazgatósága* ECLI:EU: C:2020:140, 311
Case C-75/18 *Vodafone Magyarország Mobil Távközlési Zrt. v Nemzeti Adó- és Vámhivatal Fellebbviteli Igazgatósága* ECLI:EU: C:2020:139, 311
European Union, the, 29
Council of the European Union Opinion of the Legal Service (European Parliament, SJ-0601/18, November 2018), 135
Exchange theory, the, 14
Benefit theory, the, 14, 16, 18, 20, 23, 26, 28, 31, 34, 37, 40, 46, 56, 91, 271, 286, 288
Cost theory, the, 14
Exemption method, the, 12, 259
Extractive industries, 181, 184, 219, 225, 239
Extractive and commodity businesses, 184

Faculty theory, the *See* Ability to pay theory, the
Finland
A Oyi Abp [2002] 4 ITLR 1009, 256
Fixed tax rate *See* Controlled foreign company (CFC) rules
Fleming, C, Peroni, R and Shay, S, 22
"Fairness in International Taxation: The Ability-to-Pay Case for Taxing Worldwide Income" (2001), 22
"Formulary Apportionment in the US International Income Tax System: Putting Lipstick on a Pig?" (2014), 280
Foreign tax credit, 11–12, 14, 16, 47, 130, 193, 209, 296
Formulary apportionment
Formulary apportionment by sales, 264
Four Modes of Supply
Commercial presence, 157
Consumption abroad, 157
Cross-border supply, 157
Presence of natural persons, 157
France
Code General des Impots, 248
Re Societe Schneider Electric [2002] 4 ITLR 1077, 256
Frontloading expenditure, 271
Functions, assets, and risks (FAR) analysis *See* Authorised OECD Approach (AOA)

General Agreement on Tariffs and Trade (GATT), the, 152, 159–60, 270
General Agreement on Trade in Services (GATS), the, 152, 310
Annex on Article II Exemptions, the, 153
Consultation and dispute settlement provisions, the, 152, 310
Council for Trade in Services, the, 164
Market access obligations, 157
Most-Favoured-Nation (MFN) obligations, the, 152, 310

National Treatment (NT) obligation, the, 152
General exemptions *See* Most-Favoured Nation (MFN) obligations, the
Globally operating marketplaces, 73
Graetz, Michael, 8
"Taxing International Capital Income: Inadequate Principles, Outdated Concepts, and Unsatisfactory Policies" (2001), 265
Graetz, Michael and O'Hear, Michael
"The 'Original Intent' of US International Taxation" (1997), 9
Grant Thornton
"Say Goodbye to the Arm's Length Principle" (24 July 2019), 107
Green, Robert
Antilegalistic Approaches to Resolving Disputes Between Governments: A Comparison of the International Tax and Trade Regimes" (1995), 159
Gross revenue thresholds *See* Amount A
Grubert, H
"Destination-Based Income Taxes: A Mismatch Made in Heaven" (2015), 270
Grubert, H and Altshuler, R
"Formula Apportionment: Is it Better than the Current System and are there Better Alternatives?" (2010), 282
"Fixing the System: An Analysis of Alternative Proposals for the Reform of International Tax" (2013), 265

Hagiu, Andrei and Wright, Julian, 71
Multi-Sided Platforms (Harvard Business School, 16 March 16 2015), 67
Haig, Robert *See* Simons, Henry
Harding, Arthur, 25
Double Taxation of Property and Income, a Study in the Judicial Delimitation of the Conflicting Claims of Taxing Jurisdiction Advanced by the American States (Harvard University Press, 1933), 25
Harmonisation of the calculation of profits, the, 280
Hattingh, Johann, 10
"On the Origins of Model Tax Conventions: 19th-Century German Tax treaties and Laws Concerned with the Avoidance of Double Tax" in John Tiley (ed) Studies in the History of Tax Law (Volume 6, Hart Publishing, 2013); 10
Helminem-Kossila, H M
"The Notion of Tax and the Elimination of Double Taxation or Double Non-Taxation: General Report" (2016), 123
Hey, Professor Johanna, 35
"'Taxation Where Value is Created' and the OECD/G20 Base Erosion and Profit Shifting Initiative" (2018) 35
Hohenwarter, D, Kofler, Mayr and Sinnig
"Qualification of the Digital Services Tax Under Tax Treaties" (2019), 131
Hongler, Peter and Pistone, Pasquale
Blueprints for a New PE Nexus to Tax Business Income in the Era of the Digital Economy (International Bureau of Fiscal Documentation, No. 2015 – 15, 20 January 2015), 249, 286
Modified profit split method, 287
Upfront income allocation, 287
Hufbauer, G C and Lu, Z
"Computer-Related Services" and "Advertising", 162
The European Unions Proposed Digital Services Tax: A De Facto Tariff (online ed, Peterson Institute for International Economics), 161

Hybrid mismatches, 261
hybrid systems, 6, 56

Import tariff
  De facto tariff, 161
  Unilateral tariffs, 148
Imposition of tax, the
  Ultimate incidence, 268
Income generation for online platforms
  display advertisements, 75
  Search advertisements, 75
Income inclusion rule, the, 205, 207–9, 227–28, 231, 233, 237, 255, 257–58, 320
  Income inclusion requirement, 260
  Switch-over rule, 209
  Top-up tax, 208
Independent entity, 239
  Deemed independent agency, 240
  Separate entities, 241, 281, 319
  Separate entity profits, 242, 319
  Single entity profits determined on an arm's length basis, 241
India
  Committee of the Central Board of Direct Taxation, the, 292
  Committee to Examine the Issues Related to Profit Attribution to Permanent Establishment in India and Amendment of Rule 10 of Income Tax Rules, 1962 Proposal for Amendment of Rules for Profit Attribution to Permanent Establishment (Central Board of Direct Taxes, Department of Revenue, Ministry of Finance, Government of India, 2019), 293
  Finance Act, 293–94
  Importance of the demand side contribution to profit, the, 293
Indirect network externality, 70
Information and communication technology (ICT), 94
Infrastructure of creation, the, 271
In-scope business turnover *See* Amount A

In-scope foreign income, 186
Intangibles, types of
  Marketing intangibles, 169, 173–74, 176, 178–79, 184–85, 191–92, 194, 217–19, 263, 313
  Trade intangibles, 172, 191
Intellectual property
  Mobility of location for intellectual property, 103
Interest allocation regime, 210
Interim tax
  Austria, 135
  Czech Republic, 135
  France, 225
  Italy, 135
  Poland, 135
  Spain, 135
International Chamber of Commerce, 10–11
  1920 Brussels Conference, 10
International Fiscal Association
  General Report
    Lee, Chang Hee and Yoon, Ji-Hyon Withholding Tax in the Era of BEPS, CIVs and the Digital Economy (Volume 103(B), IFA Cahiers de Droit Fiscal International, Seoul, 2018), 141
International law
  Customary international legal norm, 247
  Historical international customary legal, 247
International Monetary Fund, the, 59
  Gita Gopinath "The Great Lockdown: Worst Economic Downturn Since the Great Depression" (14 April 2020), 305
  IMF Policy Paper: Corporate Taxation in the Global Economy (IMF Publications, Policy Paper No 19/007, March 2019), 221
  Measuring the Digital Economy (International Monetary Fund, April 2018), 58

International obligations
  European Economic Area, the, 121, 146
  World Trade Organization, the, 121, 160, 310, 313
international tax dilemma, 7, 9
International tax framework, the, 34, 38, 42, 45, 47, 84, 87, 110, 113, 168, 170, 172, 177–78, 192, 207, 211, 213, 220, 229, 232, 234–36, 239, 242, 245, 251, 263, 265, 278, 285, 287, 306–7, 313, 321
International framework norm, 238
Internet of Things ("IoT"), 62
Israel
  "Multinational Tech Giants get Slapped with Israeli Tax Bills" Times of Israel (online ed, 6 January 2019), 292
  Ernst & Young Israeli Tax Authorities Publish Official Circular on Internet Activities of Foreign Companies in Israel (15 April 2016), 291
  Moshe Asher, Head of the Israeli Tax Authorities, 291
  The Israeli Tax Authority Circular No. 4/2016 (11 April 2016), 290
Italy, 10
  Professor Einaudi, 10

Japan
  Glaxo Kabushiki Kaisha v Director of Kojimachi Tax Office [2006] 12 ITLR 644, 256
Jimenez, Adolfo Martin
  BEPS, the Digital(ized) Economy and the Taxation of Services and Royalties (UCA Tax Working Papers 2018/1, August 2018), 137
  SEDP PE Directive, 138
Johnson & Johnson
  Letter from K Amos and L Weingrod (on behalf of Johnson & Johnson) to Tax Policy and Statistics Division, Centre for Tax Policy and Administration, Regarding Public Comments on the Secretariat Proposal for a "Unified Approach" Under Pillar One (11 November 2019), 195
  Submissions at the OECD "Public Conference on the Possible Solutions to the Tax Challenges of Digitalisation" (OECD Public Consultation, March 2019), 194–95
Jones, John Avery
  "2008 OECD Model: Place of Effective Management What One Can Learn from the History" (2008), 109
Jurisdiction of entrepreneurial activity and capital investment, the, 284

Kaka, Porus, 50
  "Source Taxation: Do We Really Know What We Mean?" (2017), 49, 247
  Australia, 248
  France, 248
  Japan, 248
  New Zealand, 248
Kane, Mitchell
  "Transfer Pricing, Integration and Synergy Intangibles: A Consensus Approach to the Arm's Length Standard" (2014), 275
Kaplow, L, 7
  "Taxation" in M Polinsky and S Shavell (eds) Handbook of Law and Economics (Volume 1, Elsevier, 2007), 7
Kingdom of Prussia and Austro-Hungarian Empire double tax agreement, 10
Kleinbard, E
  "Stateless Income" (2011), 265

Lang, M
  "'Taxes Covered'-What is a 'Tax' according to Article 2 of the OECD Model?" (2005), 123

League of Nations, 10
  Bruins, Einaudi, Seligman and Stamp Report on Double Taxation (League of Nations Economic and Financial Commission, Document E.F.S.73. F.19, April 1923), 10
  Financial Committee of the League of Nations, 10
  League of Nations (General Meeting of Government Experts) Double Taxation and Tax Evasion (C. 562. M. 178. Geneva, October 1928), 11
  League of Nations (Technical Experts from Argentina, Belgium, Czechoslovakia, France, Germany, Great Britain, Italy, Japan, Netherlands, Poland, Switzerland, USA, Venezuela) Double Taxation and Tax Evasion (C. 216. M. 85, Geneva, April 1927), 11
  League of Nations (Technical Experts) Double Taxation and Tax Evasion (F 212, Geneva, February 1925), 11
Lee, Chang Hee and Yoon, Ji-Hyon
  "Withholding Tax in the Era of BEPS, CIVs and the Digital Economy" (2018), 104
Lennard, Michael, 31
  "Act of Creation: The OECD/G20 Test of 'Value Creation' as a Basis for Taxing Rights and its relevance to Developing Countries" (2018), 31
  "The GATT 1994 and Direct Taxes: Some National Treatment and Related Issues" (2005), 159
Limited risk distributor (LRD), 172–73, 198, 220, 230
  Fixed rate percentage return, 214
  Restructuring risk, the, 221–22
Lokken, L
  "What Is This Thing Called Source?" (2011), 265
Loss carry-forward rules, 209

Marketplace business models, types of, 72
Mason, Ruth
  "What the CJEU's Hungarian Cases Mean for Digital Taxes" (8 March 2020), 311
Mason, Ruth and Parada, Leopold
  "Digital Battlefront in the Tax Wars" (2018), 308
Matching concept, the, 267
Matchmaking services, 75
McDaniel, Paul
  "The David R Tillinghast Lecture: Trade Agreements and Income Taxation: Interactions, Conflicts, and Resolutions" (2004), 150
  Free trade principles, 151
  Normative income tax structure, 151
McKinsey & Co, 58
  Bhatia, Tushar, Imtiaz, Mohsin, Kutcher, Eric and Wagle, Dilip "How Tech Giants Deliver Outsize Returns – and What It Means for the Rest of Us" (September 2017), 57
  McKinsey Global Institute Disruptive Technologies: Advances That Will Transform Life, Business, and the Global Economy (McKinsey & Company, May 2013), 62
McLure, Charles, 32
  "Source-Based Taxation and Alternatives to the Concept of Permanent Establishment" in Canadian Tax Foundation (ed) 2000 World Tax Conference Report (2000), 32
MFN principle, the *See* Most-Favoured-Nation (MFN) obligations, the
Mill, John Stuart, 19
  Principles of Political Economy (WJ Ashley ed, Longmans, 1921), 19
mobility of capital, 7
Monism
  Monist view of an international legal system, the, 258
  Monistic countries, 258

INDEX

Morse, Susan
  "Value Creation: A Standard in Search of a Process" (2018), 35
  "Revisiting Global Formulary Apportionment" (2010), 275
Multilateral instrument, the, 237, 258, 260–61, 301, 318
Multinational entity
  Legal and economic control, the exercise of, 281
  Notional cumulative loss, 246
  Special-purpose subsidiary, 235
  Unitary business, 281
  Value chain structures, the employment of, 229
Musgrave, Richard, 17
  The Theory of Public Finance: A Study in Public Economy (McGraw-Hill, 1959), 18

Netherlands, 10
  Professor Bruins, 10
Network effects
  Direct network effects, 64
  Indirect network effects, 64
  Network effects and globalisation, 78
New Zealand, 35
  Commissioner of Inland Revenue v Lin [2018] NZCA 38, 258
  Commissioner of Inland Revenue v N V Philips' Gloeilampenfabrieken [1955] NZLR 868 (CA), 52
  Commissioner of Inland Revenue v United Dominions Trust Ltd [1973] 2 NZLR 555 (CA), 145
  Income Tax Act 2007, 301
  Inland Revenue Policy and Strategy Options for Taxing the Digital Economy – a Government Discussion Document (June 2019), 35, 137
  New Zealand–United Kingdom DTA (1966), 145
  Taxation (Neutralising Base Erosion and Profit Shifting) Act 2018, 301
  Van Uden v Commissioner of Inland Revenue [2018] NZCA 487, 42

Nexus Rules
  Included company threshold, 186, 188, 315
  Included jurisdiction threshold, 187–88, 315
  In-scope digital or consumer-facing activities, 186
Non-neutral pricing strategy, 69
Non-routine or residual profit split approach, 170
Non-routine profits
  Non-routine residual income, 244
Normative taxation, 164

OECD, 5
  "Update on Economic Analysis and Impact Assessment" (webcast, 13 February 2020), 212
  Authorised OECD Approach (AOA), 293
  Inclusive Framework on BEPS, Progress Report July 2018–May 2019 (9 June 2019), 35
  OECD Addressing the Tax Challenges of the Digital Economy, Action 1-2015 Final Report (OECD Publishing, 2015), 5
  OECD Aligning Transfer Pricing Outcomes with Value Creation, Actions 8-10 Reports (OECD/G20 Base Erosion and Profit Shifting Project, 2015), 35
  OECD Centre for Tax Policy and Administration "Are the Current Treaty Rules for Taxing Business Profits Appropriate for E-Commerce?" (June 2004), 317
  OECD Centre for Tax Policy and Administration Interpretation and Application of Article 5 (Permanent Establishment) of the OECD Model Tax Convention (12 October 2011), 317
  OECD Committee on Fiscal Affairs Application and Interpretation

INDEX

of Article 24 (Non-Discrimination): Public Discussion Draft (OECD Publications, June 2008), 146

OECD Explanatory Statement: 2015 Final Reports (OECD/G20 Base Erosion and Profit Shifting Project, 2015), 34

OECD Model Tax Convention on Income and on Capital: Condensed Version 2017 (OECD Publishing, November 2017), 5

OECD Secretary-General Report to G20 Finance Ministers and Central Bank Governors, (OECD Publishing, June 2019), 168

OECD Technical Advisory Group on Monitoring the Application of Existing Treaty Norms for Taxing Business Profits Are the Current Treaty Rules for Taxing Business Profits Appropriate for E-Commerce? Final Report (Centre for Tax Policy and Administration, 2003), 31

OECD/G 0 Inclusive Framework on BEPS Programme of Work to Develop a Consensus Solution to the Tax Challenges Arising from the Digitalisation of the Economy (2019), 35, 41

OECD/G20 Base Erosion and Profit Shifting Project: Addressing the Tax Challenges of the Digital Economy, Action 1 – 2015 Final Report (OECD Publishing, October 2015), 113

OECD/G20 Base Erosion and Profit Shifting Project: Addressing the Tax Challenges of the Digitalisation of the Economy, (OECD Publishing, February 2019), 238

OECD/G20 Base Erosion and Profit Shifting Project: Addressing the Tax Challenges of the Digitalisation of the Economy – Policy Note (OECD Publishing, January 2019), 116

OECD/G20 Inclusive Framework on BEPS: Progress Report July 2017 – June 2018 (OECD Publishing, July 2018), 168

Preventing the Artificial Avoidance of Permanent Establishment Status, Action 7 – 2015 Final Report (OECD Publishing, Paris, 2015), 317

Public Consultation Document: Global Anti-Base Erosion Proposal ("GloBE")- Pillar Two (OECD Publishing, November 2019), 176

Public Consultation Document: Secretariat Proposal for a "Unified Approach" under Pillar One (OECD Publishing, October 2019), 168

Safe harbours for certain categories of taxpayers, 197

Statement by the OECD/G20 Inclusive Framework on BEPS on the Two-Pillar Approach to Address the Tax Challenges Arising from the Digitalisation of the Economy (OECD, January 2020), 213, 238, 251

Tax Challenges Arising from Digitalisation – Interim Report 2018: Inclusive Framework on BEPS (OECD Publishing, 2018), 57

Taxing Profits in a Global Economy-Domestic and International Issues (OECD, 1991), 28

Technical Advisory Group (TAG) on Monitoring the Application of Existing Treaty Norms for Taxing Business Profits, the, 317

Transfer Pricing Guidelines for Multinational Enterprises and Tax Administrations (OECD Publishing, 2017), 106

Working Party number 30 of the
    OECD Fiscal Committee
    (Austria-Switzerland), received
    on 12 June 1969, FC/WP 30
    (69), 126
Oosterhuis, Paul and Parsons, Amanda,
    270
  "Destination-Based Income
    Taxation: Neither Principled
    nor Practical?" (2018), 106, 249
  Affiliated group of taxpayers, 250
  International reform alternatives,
    249
  Unrelated "captive" service
    providers, 250
Organisation for European Economic
    Co-operation (OEEC), the, 128
Outsourcing methodology, 273
Over-indebtedness *See* Corporate
    financing
Oxford International Tax Group, the
  Michael Devereux and others
    Residual Profit Allocation by
    Income, A paper of the Oxford
    International Tax Group
    chaired by Michael Devereux
    (Oxford International Tax
    Group, WP 19/01, March
    2019), 106

Parent jurisdiction, 207, 209, 217,
    233–34, 251, 321
Peace of Westphalia, 4
Permanent establishment
  Permanent establishment rule, the,
    242
  Significant economic presence, 96,
    169, 174–76, 217–18, 240, 285,
    288, 290–91, 293–94, 315
Permanent establishment principle *See*
    Permanent establishments:
    A domestic taxation, bilateral
    tax treaty and OECD
    perspective (4th ed, Wolters
    Kluwer Law & Business, 2015)
Pillar One, 41, 96, 108, 116–17, 167–68,
    176, 178, 193, 195–96, 199–200,
    205–6, 214–15, 219, 225–26,
    228, 230, 232, 234, 239, 244,
    259–60, 262, 264, 279
  Amount A, 176–77, 180–81, 183–86,
    188, 190–91, 193, 195–96,
    200–1, 203, 206, 217, 219–22,
    225, 228, 230, 237–38, 242–44,
    246–47, 249–51, 253–54, 263,
    279, 284, 288, 307, 313, 315,
    318–19
  Amount B, 177, 193–94, 196, 198,
    200, 202, 204, 214, 222, 230,
    251, 253, 276, 279
  Amount C, 177, 196, 198, 200,
    202–3, 230, 252–53, 262
Pillar Two, 117, 167, 177, 204–7,
    211–12, 215, 226, 228–29,
    231–32, 234, 237, 244, 254,
    259–60, 264, 314, 320
Pinto, Professor Dale, 32
  E-Commerce and Source-Based
    Income Taxation (IBFD
    Publications BV, 2003), 32, 265
Pirlot, Alice
  "The WTO as Tax Scarecrow?"
    (2019), 151
Primary taxing rights, 205
Prisoners' Dilemma, the, 148
Procter & Gamble
  Letter from TM McDonald (on
    behalf of the Proctor & Gamble
    Company) to Tax Policy and
    Statistics Division, Centre for
    Tax Policy and Administration,
    Organisation for Economic Co-
    operation and Development
    regarding public comments on
    the Secretariat Proposal for a
    "Unified Approach" Under
    Pillar One (11 November 2019),
    195
Multiple taxation, 212
Profit allocation
  "In scope" B2C businesses/
    transactions, 184
  "Winner takes all" outcome,
    271
  Allocation keys, 176, 281–83
  Cost-based methods, 174

Profit allocation (cont.)
  Formulary apportionment, 178, 229, 264, 272, 274, 279–82, 284, 289, 319
  Fractional apportionment, 175, 221–22, 293–94
  Methods of international income allocation (DBCFT and RPAI), 281
  Modified residual profit split (MRPS) method, 178, 221, 229
  New profit allocation rules, the, 176, 243
  Profit adjustment, 174
  Profit allocation and manipulation, 277
  Profit allocation principles, 174
  Profit allocation rules, the, 39, 41, 111, 116, 170, 178, 221, 229, 245, 316
  Residual profit split analysis, 174
  Residual Profit Split Method, 275
  Separate entity accounting system, 192
  Separate entity approach, 229, 239, 313
  Single-entity concept, 178, 229
  Taxable nexus, 187, 232, 235, 238–39, 293, 315
Profit allocation and nexus rules, the, 111–12, 115, 117, 169, 173, 176
  New nexus rules, the, 176, 239–40, 271
  Nexus or taxing rights, 216
Profit distortion *See* Amount A
Profit shifting
  Capital structuring, 205, 226
  Intragroup financing, 205, 226, 269
  Payments made for the use of intellectual property, 206
  Tax-free deductible payments, 210

Quarantine profitability, 267

Rau, Schmoller, Schaffle, Vocke and Wagner *See* Vogel, Klaus
Rawlsian principles, 22

Reimer, Ekkehart, Schmidt, Stefan and Orell, Marianne
  Permanent Establishments: A Domestic Taxation, Bilateral Tax Treaty and OECD Perspective (4th ed, Wolters Kluwer Law & Business, 2015), 91
Remote sales, non-taxation of trading in rather than trading with a country, 84
Residual profit allocation by income (RPAI), 264, 272, 275–77, 289, 319
Retention of the arm's length principle, the *See* Amount C
Revenue estimation *See* Byrnes, William
Rhodesia, 51
  The liquidator, Rhodesia Metals Limited (in liquidation) v Commissioner of Taxes 1940 AD 432 (PC), 51
Rosenbloom, David
  "Angels on a Pin: Arm's Length in the World" (2005), 275
Rotation cycle, 267
Routine profits
  Non-routine residual global profits, 242

Schon, Wolfgang, 44
  "10 Questions about Why and How to Tax the Digitalised Economy" (2018), 46, 93, 216, 265, 276
  "Persons and Territories: On the International Allocation of Taxing Rights" (2010), 5
  "Destination-Based Income Taxation and WTO Law: A Note" in H Jochum, P Essers, M Lang, N Winkeljohann and B Wiman (eds) Practical Problems in European and International Tax Law – Essays in Honour of Manfred Mössner (IBFD, 2016), 266

"International Tax Coordination for a Second-Best World" (2010), 275
"International Taxation of Risk" (2014), 275
Schoueri, Luis
  "Arm's Length: Beyond the Guidelines of the OECD" (2015), 275 See Amount A" See Degrees of digitalisation" See Hongler, Peter and Pistone, Pasqualees See Marketing intangibles"
Seligman, Edwin, 17
  Progressive Taxation in Theory and Practice (2nd ed, American Economic Association, Princeton University Press, 1908), 17
Separate entity/arm's-length international tax system, 280
Sharing economy, the, 33, 58, 66
Shongwe, Thulani
  From the African Tax Administration Forum, during the OECD Public Conference, on the morning of 21 November 2019, 262
Silk Roads, 4
  Chang'an–Tianshan corridor, 5
Simons, Henry, 24
  Personal Income Taxation: The Definition of Income as a Problem of Fiscal Policy (6th ed, University of Chicago Press, 1938), 24
Skaar, Arvid, 32
  Permanent Establishment: Erosion of a Tax Treaty Principle (Kluwer Law and Taxation Publishers, 1991), 32
Smith, Adam, 20
  The Wealth of Nations (E Cannan ed, Volume 2, GP Putnam's Sons, 1904), 20
Social contract theory, the See Benefit theory, the

Source of income, the, 45, 49–50, 53–54, 74, 89, 246–47
South Africa, 51
  Commissioner for Inland Revenue v Lever Bros and Another (1946) AD 441, 51
Specific Member exemptions, See Most-Favoured-Nation (MFN) obligations, the
Stability of the tax base, 265
Suarez, Francisco, 17
Subject to tax rule, 208, 233, 259
Sustained interaction, 175, 187, 218, 238, 286
Sustained and significant involvement, 239
Switch-over rule, the, 227, 255
Switch-over clauses, 259

Targeted tax rules, 168
Task Force on the Digital Economy (TFDE) See OECD
Tauscher, Karl and Laudien, Sven
  "Understanding Platform Business Models: A Mixed Methods Study of Marketplaces" (2016), 72
Tax avoidance
  Multinational avoidance legislation, 285
Tax base correction, 193
Tax competition, 36, 55, 85, 110, 112, 206, 233–34, 269, 316, 320–21
Tax on base eroding payments, 205, 210
Tax risk management See Byrnes, William
Tax sovereignty, 205
Taxable nexus
  Separate taxing nexus, 242
Taxable presence, 42, 108, 173, 188, 216, 239, 242, 250, 252, 285–86, 292, 299, 317, See Significant economic presence proposal, the
  Conventional taxable presence, 254
Taxation of remote sales of goods and services, the, 192

Terms of trade
    "Market access" issues, 149
    Terms of trade externality, 148
Theory of economic allegiance, the, 16
Thick capitalisation, 207
Thin capitalisation, 145, 210
Three Proposals, the, 169
    "User participation" proposal, the, 171–73, 179, 224–25
    "Marketing intangibles" proposal, the, 169, 219
    "Significant economic presence" proposal, the, 169, 174, 240, 306
Timing rules, 209
Traditional financial accounting, 266
Traditional services, 214
Transfer pricing
    "Outsourcing" methodology, 273, 318
    Comparable profits method, the, 273, 318
    Hard to value intangibles, 274
    Outsourcing methodology, 274–75, 280, 319
    Profit methods, 272
    Traditional transaction-based transfer pricing methodologies, 319
    Traditional transfer pricing models, 170
    Transactional net margin method, the, 273, 318
    Transfer pricing outsourcing methodology, 274, 278–79

Undertaxation of multinationals in the market jurisdiction, 199
Under-pricing of goods and services from the country of origin, 268
Undertaxed payments rule, the, 208, 227–28, 235, 259–60
    Undertaxed payments, 208, 227–28, 231, 235, 259
United Kingdom, 10
    Bricom Holdings Limited v Inland Revenue Commissioners [1997] BTC 471 (CA), 256

Development Securities (No 9) Ltd & others v HMRC [2017] UKFTT 0565, 42
Finance Act 2015, 305
Her Majesty's Revenue and Customs Diverted Profits Tax: Guidance (December 2018), 297
HM Treasury Corporate Tax and the Digital Economy: Position Paper (November 2017), 35
HM Treasury Corporate Tax and the Digital Economy: Position Paper Update (HM Treasury, March 2018), 224
HM Treasury Digital Services Tax Consultation (November 2018), 135
HMRC v Smallwood and Another [2010] STC 2045, 42
Padmore v IRC (No 2) [2001] STC 280 (Ch), 303
Padmore v IRC (Padmore) [1989] STC 493, 303
Sao Paulo (Brazilian) Railway Co Ltd v Carter [1896] AC 31, 51
Stamp, Sir Josiah, 10
Yates (HMIT) v GCA International Ltd (formerly Gaffney Cline & Associates Ltd) [1991] BTC 107 (Ch), 129
United Nations
    United Nations Model Double Taxation Convention between Developed and Developing Countries (United Nations, 2017), 91
United Nations, the, and World Bank, the
    Options for Low Income Countries' Effective and Efficient Use of Tax Incentives for Investment (International Monetary Fund, October 2015), 206
United States, 11
    Department of the Treasury Office of Tax Policy Selected Tax Policy Implications of Global Electronic Commerce (November 1996), 23

House Committee on Ways and Means A Better Way for Tax Reform (United States House of Representatives, June 2016), 269
Internal Revenue Code, the, 154
Massachusetts Formula, the, 281–82
National Bellas Hess, Inc v Cap department of Revenue of Ill, 386 U.S. 753, 28
Office of Tax Policy, United States Department of the Treasury Approaches to Improve the Competitiveness of the US Business Tax System for the 21st century (December 2007), 23
Office of the United States Trade Representative "Conclusion of USTR's Investigation Under Section 301 into France's Digital Services Tax" (press release, 2 December 2019), 309
Professor Seligman, 11
Quill Corp. v Cap North Dakota, 504 U.S. 298, 28
South Dakota Act, 29
South Dakota v Wayfair Inc, et al, Certiorari to the Supreme Court of South Dakota (Argued 17 April 2018, decided 21 June 2018), 26, 28–29
Tax Cuts and Jobs Act, 151
US-specific exclusion, 155
Uruguay Round, the, 153, 159
User participation intensity, 82
  Low level of user effort, 81
  Medium level of participation, 82
User participation policy rationale, 279
User participation, key aspects of
  Contribution to the brand, 100
  Depth of engagement, 99, 224
  Network effect, 99
  User utility, 99
  User-generated content, 61, 99
Utilitarian doctrine, the, 21
  Bentham, Jeremy, 21
  Mill, John Stuart, 21

Van, Professor Richard
  "Taxing International Business Income Hard-Boiled Wonderland and the End of the World" (2010), 265
VanderWolk, Jefferson
  "The Arm's Length Standard Enters Its Second Century" (2019), 107
Vanishing ability to tax business profits, the, 215, 217, 220, 307, 314, 316
  Compound challenge, a, 216, 314
  Vanishing ability of the source state to tax business income generated in their jurisdiction, 234
Vann, Professor Richard, 44
  "Taxing International Business Income: Hard-Boiled Wonderland and the End of the World" (2010), 44
  "Reflections on Business Profits and the Arm's-Length Principle" in B Arnold, J Sasseville and E Zolt (eds) The Taxation of Business Profits Under Tax Treaties (Canadian Tax Foundation, 2013), 275
Vienna Convention on the Law of Treaties, the, 258
Vocke, 20
  Die Abgaben, Auflagen und die Stuer vom Standpunkt der Geschichte und der Sittlichkeit (1887), 20
Vogel, Klaus, 17, 265
  "The Justification for Taxation: A Forgotten Question" (1988), 17
  "Worldwide vs Source Taxation of Income: A Review and Re-evaluation of Arguments (in Three Parts) (1988), 19
  Worldwide vs Source Taxation of Income: A Review and Re-evaluation of Arguments (Part I)" (1988), 19
Volume-based selling, 80
von Schanz, Georg, 24

von Schanz, Georg (cont.)
  "Zur Frage der Steuerpflicht" (1982), 24
  Concept of "economic allegiance", the, 288
von Stein, Lorenz, 24
  Lehrbuch der Finanzwissenschaft (5th ed, Erster Theil and Zweiter Theil, Erste Abtheilung, 1885), 24

Wasimi, S, Nario, J and Bertram, K
  "Diverted Profits Tax: UK, Australian and New Zealand Approaches" (24 July 2017), 297

Withholding tax
  "One-stop-shop" regime, 251
  Enforcement mechanisms, 250
  Final liability, 251
World Trade Organization, the
  "Marrakesh Agreement Establishing the World Trade Organization" (15 April 1994), 147
  Agreement on Subsidies and Countervailing Measures, 160
  Dispute Settlement Body of the WTO (DSB), the, 161
  Tax scarecrow, 151

CPSIA information can be obtained
at www.ICGtesting.com
Printed in the USA
LVHW011048030821
694401LV00005B/347